BEST
LAID
PLANS

Also by David Martin

Wilderness of Mirrors

BEST LAID PLANS

The Inside Story of America's War Against Terrorism

David C. Martin & John Walcott

1817

HARPER & ROW, PUBLISHERS, NEW YORK
Cambridge, Philadelphia, San Francisco, Washington
London, Mexico City, São Paulo, Singapore, Sydney

FIRST EDITION

Designed by Helene Berinsky

Library of Congress Cataloging-in-Publication Data
Martin, David C.
  Best laid plans.
  1. Terrorism—Near East. 2. Terrorism—Government policy—United States. 3. Hostages—Near East. 4. Hostages—United States. 5. United States—Foreign relations—Near East. 6. Near East—Foreign relations—United States. I. Walcott, John. II. Title.
HV6433.M5M37 1988   363.3'2'0973   87-45646
ISBN 0-06-015877-8

88 89 90 91 92 CC/RRD 10 9 8 7 6 5 4 3 2 1

For Allison, Cate, Jennifer, Rachel and Zach,
and especially for Nancy and E. D.

CONTENTS

Illustrations follow page 234

"The best laid schemes o' mice an' men
Gang aft a-gley . . ."
—ROBERT BURNS

PREFACE

This book begins and ends with an account of failure, with precious few victories in between. Such is the history of America's war against terrorism. Between the beginning of 1980 and the end of 1987—the period covered by this book—363 Americans died in terrorist incidents, most of them in one blinding flash when a suicide bomber crashed his truck into the headquarters of the Marine Battalion Landing Team at Beirut International Airport. We covered that and most of the other events described in this book as reporters, first working together at *Newsweek,* then going our separate ways to *CBS News* and *The Wall Street Journal.* Tracking back over these events has been an exercise in humility, a revelation of how much we missed or got wrong the first time around. We tried to keep that lesson in mind when it came to judging the protagonists in these events—those who played the game while we looked on from the safety and comfort of the sidelines. They, too, were experiencing these events for the first time, usually while bent under the weight of workloads that would crush most of us.

Best Laid Plans is not just a tale of unrelieved failure, it is also a story of courage and conviction, of brave men doing what they believed was right. In researching a lengthy series of military operations involving hundreds of soldiers, sailors, and airmen, we came across one instance of what might be called cowardice, although some would call it good sense. A Navy pilot chosen to fly a helicopter in pitch dark into the middle of the Iranian desert broke down and wept in the arms of his commanding officer, sobbing that he couldn't go through with it. The pilot was removed from the mission and given a career-ending fitness report. The pilots who flew into Iran were, if anything, too brave, pressing on through a sandstorm that was grounds for aborting the mission. The failures recounted here are not failures of nerve.

Our technique in reconstructing the war against terrorism is the standard journalistic one of starting with the public record and seeking to expand on it in interviews of our own. As anyone who has been a journalist knows, there is always one more person to interview, and the list of people we didn't talk to is disconcertingly long. In some cases, geography was the deciding factor. Military, foreign service, and intelligence officers move around the world even faster than journalists, and we never caught up with some of them. Lt. Col. Oliver North originally agreed to be interviewed but later declined at the insistence of his attorney. Rear Adm. John Poindexter also remained silent on the advice of his lawyer. Other people just didn't want to talk to us. Col. Timothy Geraghty, the commander of the Marines in Beirut, was one of those. We were obnoxiously persistent, and he was unfailingly polite, but the answer was always no.

Overall, however, a surprising number of people were willing to talk to us openly and on the record; so many, in fact, that we were able to throw away the journalistic crutch of the anonymous quote. Throughout this book, the reader will know exactly who is speaking. That is not to say we didn't have any anonymous sources; we did, and some of them made very important contributions. But, as the Chapter Notes reveal, the unnamed officials are relatively few and far between. Our hope is that since so much of this book can be readily verified, the reader will not doubt us when he comes to those pieces of information for which no source is identified.

A word about quotations. There are many reconstructed conversations in this book, all of them based on the recollections, and in some cases the notes, of participants. We recognize that such recollections are not verbatim but rather an attempt to capture the gist of the exchanges. We have relied on punctuation to help the reader distinguish between these reconstructed conversations and verbatim statements made directly to us or preserved on video or audio tape or in documents, memoirs, and transcripts. Verbatim statements are identified by quotation marks, which have been omitted from reconstructed conversations.

Best Laid Plans covers a period of almost eight years, and many of the characters held more than one title or rank during the events described. Robert McFarlane, for instance, first appears as the State Department counselor, reappears as the President's deputy national security adviser, takes on the job of special Middle East envoy, is promoted to national security adviser, then leaves government service. In an attempt not to overburden the reader with all of these job changes, we have simply identified each character by the position he held at the time of the action described. Nine characters are identified only by first names, nicknames or pseudonyms. That is because we were convinced that to identify them accurately would expose them to danger. We have used asterisks in the body of the text to remind the reader of this fact. All the other identifying features of these characters—physical description, background, and so on—are accurate.

We are responsible for everything that appears between these covers, but there is a lot here that was done for us. We owe a special debt to our researcher, Nancy Ganahl, who during the preparation of this book was the librarian in the Washington bureau of the *New York Times.* When we couldn't find something, we asked Nancy, and invariably she came up with the elusive fact before the day was out. She also checked the manuscript for accuracy, and if any errors of fact slipped through, it's our fault. Finally, Nancy compiled the chronology, which we hope will help the reader pick his way through sometimes overlapping events and scc thcm in context.

At the Pentagon, a number of public affairs officers helped us track down servicemen who had moved on to other duty posts or who had retired. Jimmie Finkelstein, Kendall Pease and Rob Donovan in the Navy and Mike McRaney and Rick O'born in the Air Force were particularly helpful in finding people for us. Jay Coupe in the office of the chairman of the Joint Chiefs of Staff provided more than one valuable introduction. John Barbee at the Third Armored Division in Frankfurt helped arrange an interview that otherwise would not have happened. The Air Force's Current News division allowed us free run of their one-of-a-kind dip files. At the State Department, Joe Reap, in the Office for Combatting Terrorism, tracked down several obscure references, always with a smile.

Although the research closely paralleled our daily work as reporters for CBS and *The Wall Street Journal,* we spent more than a little time working on this book when we should have been doing our jobs. We are indebted to Jack Smith and Joe Peyronnin at CBS and Al Hunt at the *Journal* for looking the other way. As if that weren't enough, we were forever asking favors of colleagues like Susan Zirinsky, Roxanne Russell, and Deirdre Hester at CBS, and David Rogers, Ken Bacon, Ed Pound, and Andy Pasztor at the *Journal*—not to mention competitors like Fred Francis at NBC and Elaine Shannon at *Time* magazine. Walt Mossberg of the *Journal* served as our computer consultant, enabling an Apple and an IBM to coexist peacefully.

This book was begun at the urging of a former Army general named Sam Wilson, who is worth a book himself. It didn't turn out the way he thought it would, but it wouldn't have been possible without him. You can travel a long way on an introduction from "General Sam."

The contract for this book was originally signed in 1982, and it required the skill of our agent Theron Raines and the patience of our editor Buz Wyeth to keep it alive for so long. When at long last we actually delivered the manuscript, it was skillfully copy-edited by Ann Adelman, carefully vetted for legal problems by Debbie Orenstein, and ruthlessly scrutinized by Dot Gannon and Daril Bentley. A number of people—wives, parents, in-laws, friends, sources—took time to read the manuscript and point out trouble spots, but no one devoted more time and talent to our work than Irving and Marion Wechsler, whose only responsibility was that of friendship but who spent hours laboring over the manuscript. Their skills are responsible for more than one inflated reputation in this town.

No one, however generous, was required to make the sacrifices our families made. They had to live with this project as much as we did—the endless litter of work in progress, nighttime and weekend disappearances, vacant stares at dinner, the social life of a single-cell animal, the chores left undone, the errands not run. It's an open and shut case of neglect, of which the only nice thing you can say is that anyone willing to put up with it must really love you.

CHRONOLOGY: 1979-1987

1979

Nov. 4—Militant Iranian students take over the American Embassy in Tehran, kidnapping sixty-six Americans. Fifty-two hostages will be held a total of 444 days.

Dec. 27—The Soviet Union invades Afghanistan.

1980

April 24—A mission to rescue the hostages held in Tehran is forced to abort in the middle of the Iranian desert.

April 30—Iranian extremists seize the Iranian Embassy in London, taking twenty hostages. Five days later, after a hostage is killed, British commandos storm the embassy, killing five of the six gunmen.

Oct. 14—Faisal Zagallai, a Libyan student at Colorado State University and a vocal foe of the Qaddafi regime, is shot twice in the head by Eugene Tafoya, but survives the attack.

Nov. 4—Ronald Reagan is elected President.

1981

Jan. 20—Ronald Reagan takes the oath of office.

—The fifty-two American hostages are released and leave Iran minutes after Reagan is sworn in.

Jan. 27—In a speech to the returning hostages on the South Lawn of the White House, Reagan vows "swift and effective retribution" against terrorists.

March 28—A hijacked Indonesian airliner is flown to Bangkok, where three days later Indonesian commandos storm the plane. All passengers are freed and four of the five hijackers are killed.

March 30—President Reagan is shot in the chest outside a Washington, D.C., hotel.

May 6—The State Department orders the closing of the Libyan People's Bureau in Washington.

May 13—Pope John Paul II is shot in St. Peter's Square by Turkish gunman Mehmet Ali Agca.

August 17—Bashir Gemayel, head of the Christian militia in Lebanon, secretly visits the United States.

Aug. 19—In a two-minute dogfight over the Gulf of Sidra, Libyan pilots fire on two Navy fighter jets, only to be shot down themselves.

Oct. 6—President Anwar el-Sadat of Egypt is assassinated while watching a parade in Cairo.

Dec. 2—The White House confirms news reports that Libyan hit squads have entered the United States.

Dec. 13—Martial law is declared in Poland.

Dec. 17—Brig. Gen. James Dozier is kidnapped in Verona, Italy, by the Red Brigades.

1982

Jan. 18—Lt. Col. Charles Robert Ray, a military attaché at the American Embassy in Paris, is shot and killed by Lebanese terrorists.

Jan. 28—General Dozier is rescued.

March 10—The United States imposes a ban on imports of Libyan oil.

April 2—The Falkland Islands War begins with the landing of Argentine troops on the two islands in the South Atlantic.

June 3—Israel's Ambassador to Great Britain, Shlomo Argov, is shot and gravely wounded outside a London hotel.

June 6—The Israeli Army crosses into Lebanon.

June 14—The Israeli Army and Bashir Gemayel's militia meet on the outskirts of Beirut, trapping the PLO leadership inside the city.

June 25—Alexander Haig resigns as Secretary of State. George Shultz replaces him.

July 19—David Dodge, acting president of the American University in Beirut, is abducted as he leaves his office.

July 23—Two American, two British, and two Australian tourists are kidnapped and later killed by rebel forces in Zimbabwe.

Aug. 11—A bomb explodes under the seat cushion of a Pan Am jet during the approach into Honolulu Airport. One Japanese teenager is killed.

Aug. 25—A bomb is found on a Pan Am jet after the plane arrives in Rio de Janeiro. The bomb does not go off.

Aug. 25—Eight hundred U.S. Marines go ashore in Lebanon, along with Italian and French forces, to help evacuate the PLO from Beirut.

Sept. 10—The Marines withdraw from Lebanon and return to their ships in the Mediterranean.

Sept. 14—Bashir Gemayel, president-elect of Lebanon, is assassinated in Beirut, nine days before he is to take office.

Sept. 16 and 17—Phalangist troops, loyal to the dead Bashir Gemayel, enter two Palestinian refugee camps, Sabra and Shatila, and slaughter between 700 and 2,000 unarmed Palestinian men, women, and children.

Sept. 29—The Marines return to Beirut along with Italian and French troops.

Nov. 10—Leonid Brezhnev, leader of the Soviet Union for the last eighteen years, dies.

1983

April 18—A delivery van packed with explosives blows up in front of the American Embassy in Beirut, killing sixty-three people, seventeen of them Americans.

May 25—Navy Lt. Cdr. Albert Schaufelberger, the deputy commander of the U.S. military group in El Salvador, is assassinated.

July 27—In Portugal, five Armenian terrorists seize the residence of the Turkish Ambassador. The terrorists blow up the building, killing themselves and two other people.

Sept. 1—A Soviet fighter pilot shoots down Korean Air Lines Flight 007, killing all 269 aboard.

Sept. 4—Israel's forces withdraw from the mountains east of Beirut to more defensible positions in southern Lebanon.

Oct. 23—The headquarters of the Marine Battalion Landing Team at Beirut airport is blown apart by a truck filled with explosives: 241 men are killed. A second bomb goes off at the French headquarters, killing fifty-nine.

Oct. 25—The United States invades Grenada.

Nov. 17—The French bomb the Sheik Abdullah Barracks in Lebanon's Bekaa Valley in retaliation for the bombing of their peacekeeping force three weeks earlier.

Nov. 23—The first Pershing II nuclear missiles are delivered to Europe, prompting the Soviets to walk out of arms negotiations.

Dec. 3—An F-14 reconnaissance plane from aircraft carrier *Kennedy* is shot at by heat-seeking SA-7 antiaircraft missiles over Lebanon.

Dec. 4—The United States attempts an air raid against Syrian antiaircraft missiles sites. One American airman is killed and another is captured by the Syrians.

Dec. 12—Suicide bombers attack six targets in Kuwait, including the American and French embassies. Five people are killed and eighty-six injured. Within weeks the Kuwaitis announce the arrest of 14 Iraqis and three Lebanese.

1984

Jan. 18—Malcolm Kerr, president of the American University of Beirut, is murdered near his office.

Feb. 10—Frank Regier, an electrical engineer at the American University of Beirut, is kidnapped.

Feb. 26—The last American Marines withdraw from Lebanon.

March 7—Jeremy Levin, the Beirut bureau chief for Cable News Network, is kidnapped.

March 16—William Buckley, the CIA station chief in Beirut, is kidnapped.

April 3—President Reagan signs National Security Decision Directive 138 outlining U.S. policy toward terrorism.

April 6—*The Wall Street Journal* reports commandos laying mines in the Nicaraguan harbors were trained by the CIA.

April 15—Frank Regier is freed by Shitte militiamen loyal to Nabih Berri.

April 17—Anti-Qaddafi demonstrators protesting in London are fired on from the Libyan People's Bureau. A police constable is killed, prompting England to break diplomatic relations with Libya.

May 8—The Rev. Benjamin Weir, a Presbyterian minister, is kidnapped in Beirut.

July 31—Venezuelan commandos storm a hijacked Venezuelan airliner in Curaçao, killing the two hijackers and leaving the seventy-nine aboard unharmed.

July–August—Mines are found in the Red Sea. Evidence later establishes that Libya planted them.

Sept. 20—A van bearing diplomatic plates explodes in front of the U.S. Embassy annex in Christian East Beirut, killing two American military officers.

Oct. 12—A bomb explodes in the Grand Hotel in Brighton, England, where Prime Minister Margaret Thatcher and most of her cabinet are staying. The Provisional Irish Republican Army claims responsibility.

Oct. 31—Indira Gandhi is assassinated as she walks from her home to her office in New Delhi.

Nov. 6—Ronald Reagan is overwhelmingly elected to a second term.

Dec. 3—Peter Kilburn, librarian at the American University of Beirut, is kidnapped.

Dec. 3—A Kuwaiti airliner on its way from Dubai to Karachi is hijacked by Shiite terrorists and flown to Tehran, where two Americans are murdered.

1985

Jan. 8—The Rev. Lawrence Martin Jenco is kidnapped in Lebanon.

Feb. 14—Jeremy Levin escapes from captivity.

March 8—A car bomb explodes in a Beirut suburb, killing 80 people and wounding 200. The bombing is an attempt to assassinate Sheikh Mohammed Hussei Fadlallah, spiritual leader of Hezbollah.

March 12—Arms talks between the United States and the Soviet Union resume in Geneva after a sixteen-month delay.

March 16—Terry Anderson, Associated Press bureau chief, is abducted in Beirut.

May 28—David Jacobsen, administrator of the American University Hospital in Beirut, is kidnapped.

June 3—William Buckley, the kidnapped CIA station chief, dies in captivity.

June 9—Thomas Sutherland, dean of American University's School of Agriculture, is kidnapped in Beirut.

June 11—A Royal Jordanian Airlines jet is hijacked in Beirut by Shiite Muslims. The hostages are released and the plane is blown up.

June 14—TWA Flight 847 is hijacked on its way from Athens to Rome with 153 people on board.

June 19—Thirteen people, including four U.S. Marines and two American businessmen are gunned down at an outdoor café in San Salvador.

June 23—An Air India jetliner explodes in mid-air near the coast of Ireland killing all 329 passengers and crew aboard.

June 30—The 39 remaining hostages from TWA Flight 847 are released in Beirut.

July 13—President Reagan has surgery for the removal of a cancerous polyp in his lower intestine.

Aug. 20—Israel sends ninety-six TOW antitank missiles to Iran.

Sept. 14—Israel sends 408 more TOW missiles to Iran. Rev. Benjamin Weir is released the same day.

Oct. 1—Israel raids the headquarters of the PLO in Tunisia, retaliating for the murder three days earlier of three Israelis on a yacht in Cyprus.

Oct. 4—Islamic Holy War announces the execution of William Buckley.

Oct. 7—Four armed men hijack an Italian cruise liner, the *Achille Lauro,* off the coast of Egypt. One American is killed.

Oct. 9—U.S. Navy jets intercept an Egyptian airliner carrying the hijackers of the *Achille Lauro.*

Nov. 19–21—President Reagan and Mikhail Gorbachev meet for the first time, in Geneva.

Nov. 23—An EgyptAir jet is hijacked to Malta by three members of the Abu Nidal organization. Sixty passengers are killed, making it the bloodiest skyjacking on record.

Nov. 24–25—Eighteen Hawk antiaircraft missiles are shipped from Israel to Iran aboard a plane belonging to a CIA-owned company.

Dec. 27—Simultaneous attacks are carried out at the El Al ticket counters in the Rome and Vienna airports by Palestinian terrorists; nineteen people, including five Americans, are killed.

1986

Jan. 7—The United States severs all economic ties with Libya and orders all Americans to leave immediately, in retaliation for the attacks at the Rome and Vienna airports.

Jan. 17—Reagan signs an intelligence "finding" authorizing U.S. arms sales to Iran.

Feb. 7—Both Ferdinand Marcos and Corazon Aquino claim victory in a bitterly contested election in the Philippines.

—President-for-life Jean-Claude Duvalier flees Haiti after rioting leaves the country in a state of emergency.

Feb. 17—The United States sends 500 TOW missiles to Israel for shipment to Iran.

Feb. 25—Ferdinand Marcos and his wife Imelda flee the Philippines.

Feb. 27—Another 500 TOW missiles are sent to Iran.

March 24—During a naval exercise held in the Gulf of Sidra, U.S. aircraft are fired on by Libyan SA-5 missiles. The United States fires back.

March 25—Qaddafi sends a message to his People's Bureaus in East Berlin, Paris, Rome, Madrid, and other European capitals to plan terrorist attacks against American targets.

April 2—A bomb under a seat on TWA Flight 840 en route from Rome to Athens explodes, sucking four Americans, one a nine-month-old baby, out the gaping hole.

April 5—The La Belle disco is bombed in West Berlin. One American is killed instantly; another is mortally wounded.

April 14—American warplanes bomb Tripoli and Benghazi in retaliation for the disco bombing.

April 15—William Calkins, a communication expert at the U.S. Embassy in Khartoum, is shot in the head from a passing car. On the same day Libyan forces launch two missiles at the U.S. Coast Guard station on the Italian island of Lampedusa.

April 17—Peter Kilburn, one of the hostages in Lebanon, is found shot to death. His killing is in retaliation for the bombing of Libya three days earlier.

April 17—El Al security men at Heathrow Airport in London find a bomb hidden in the bottom of a suitcase belonging to a young Irishwoman.

May 23–24—508 more TOW missiles and 240 spare parts for Hawk missiles are sent from the United States to Israel for Iran.

May 27–29—Former national security adviser Robert McFarlane makes secret trip to Tehran.

July 26—Reverend Jenco is released from captivity.

Sept. 9—American Frank Reed is kidnapped in Lebanon.

Sep. 5—A Pan Am 747 is hijacked in Karachi, Pakistan; 21 people die when Pakistani commandos storm the plane.

Sep. 6—Palestinian terrorists launch a suicide attack against a synogue in Istanbul, killing 22.

Sept. 12—Another American, Joseph Cicippio, is kidnapped in Lebanon.

Oct. 5—A cargo plane carrying supplies and arms for the contras is shot down over Nicaragua. The only survivor, Eugene Hasenfus, is taken captive.

Oct. 10–11—President Reagan and Mikhail Gorbachev meet in Reykjavik, Iceland, for two days of talks.

Oct. 21—Edward Tracy is kidnapped in Beirut.

Oct. 28—The last 500 TOW missiles are sent from Israel to Iran.

Nov. 2—David Jacobsen is freed from captivity.

Nov. 3—A Lebanese magazine, *Al-Shiraa,* discloses that Robert McFarlane has visited Tehran secretly and that the United States has been selling arms to Iran.

Nov. 25—Attorney General Edwin Meese announces that money from the sale of arms to the Iranians had been diverted to the Nicaraguan contras. National security adviser John Poindexter resigns and Lt. Col. Oliver North is fired.

1987

Jan. 15—Mohammed Ali Hamad, a suspect in the hijacking of TWA 847, is arrested in Frankfurt.

Jan. 20—Terry Waite, the Anglican Church envoy, disappears in Beirut.

Jan. 24—Three Americans and one U.S. resident are kidnapped in Beirut after kidnapped in Beirut.

Jan. 31—Gerald Seib, a correspondent for *The Wall Street Journal,* is detained in Tehran after entering the country at the invitation of the Iranian government. Seib is released four days later.

Feb. 26—The Tower commission releases its report on the Iran-Contra affair.

March 7—The United States formally offers to protect eleven Kuwaiti oil tankers in the Persian Gulf.

May 5—Congressional hearings on the Iran-contra affair begin.

June 17—Charles Glass, an ABC reporter on leave, is kidnapped in Lebanon.

Aug. 7—The leaders of Costa Rica, Guatemala, Honduras, El Salvador, and Nicaragua sign a peace agreement that calls for a cease-fire in the five Central American countries.

Aug. 18—Charles Glass regains his freedom.

Sept. 13—FBI agents arrest suspected Palestinian terrorist Fawaz Younis aboard a yacht in the Mediterranean.

Nov. 18—The congressional committees investigating the Iran-contra affair release their final report, stating that "ultimate responsibility" for the affair belongs with the President.

Nov. 27—Two French hostages held in Lebanon are released. Two days later the French allow a suspected Iranian terrorist to leave the country.

Dec. 8—Gorbachev and Reagan meet in Washington for their third summit and sign an arms treaty removing all intermediate and short-range missiles in Europe and Asia.

1988

Feb. 17—Marine Lt. Col. William Higgins, a former aide to the Secretary of the Defense, is kidnapped in southern Lebanon.

March 16—A federal grand jury indicts Oliver North, John Poindexter, Richard Secord, and Albert Hakim on charges of "deceitfully exploiting for their own purposes" the secret arms sales to Iran.

PROLOGUE

A one-legged man landed a small, twin-engined plane in pitch darkness just north of the lone road running through Iran's Dasht-E-Kavir Desert. A U.S. Air Force major named John Carney jumped down from the plane and felt the reassuring crunch of hard-packed sand beneath his feet. It had been a long flight, taking off from the Sultanate of Oman more than six hours before and flying a low-level, roundabout route through the gaps in Iranian radar. There had been one nasty moment when the pilot picked up a radar signal, but he had simply driven the plane lower and continued. Once on the ground, Carney walked ahead, searching for gullies and sinkholes as the plane taxied 100 yards away from the road, far enough so no passersby would spot it. The one-legged man, a pilot for the CIA, shut down the engines of the Twin Otter. Carney unloaded a Honda dirt bike from the rear of the plane and drove into the night, crossing over to the south side of the road. Navigating by compass, he staked out a primitive landing strip and implanted four remote-controlled lights in a 500-foot square on the desert floor to mark the touchdown point. A fifth light 3,000 feet away marked the end of the runway. Every time a vehicle passed by, Carney flattened himself against the desert floor. There was no place else to hide.

It was April Fool's Day, 1980. John Carney was the vanguard of the first mission in America's war against terrorism. In three weeks, this moonscape which Carney called Desert One would be transformed into a forward base for Operation Rice Bowl, a daring, desperate attempt to rescue fifty-two Americans held hostage in Tehran. Rice Bowl was a tacit

1

admission that everything else had failed, that five months of negotiations between the Carter administration and the revolutionary regime of the Ayatollah Khomeini had brought the American hostages no closer to freedom than they were on the day a mob of Iranian "students" had scaled the walls and seized the U.S. Embassy. It would be a hellishly complicated operation, involving scores of aircraft and hundreds of men. The rescue force had to travel undetected more than 900 miles, from the Gulf of Oman to the middle of Tehran, stopping at Desert One long enough to refuel its helicopters. The plan had been painstakingly developed through endless nighttime rehearsals in out-of-the-way places like Holtville, California, and Indian Springs, Nevada, but right now it all came down to a simple question: Could the Iranian desert support the weight of the transport planes that would bring in the fuel for the helicopters?

Carney collected core samples of the desert floor, but he already knew what they would tell him. Beneath the loose surface, the desert had the consistency of concrete, so hard that he had trouble digging the holes for the landing lights. Except for the road and its occasional traffic, this was an ideal landing strip. Carney climbed back aboard the Twin Otter. The plane made a short run through the sand, bounced aloft, and headed south toward the Gulf of Oman. If all went according to plan, the next plane to land at Desert One would be carrying combat troops.

It took Carney about thirty-six hours to get back to the Pentagon, flying the last leg of the journey aboard the supersonic Concorde from London. While the core samples were sent to the laboratory for analysis, Carney briefed Gen. David Jones, the chairman of the Joint Chiefs of Staff, and Maj. Gen. James Vaught, the commander of the rescue force, on what he had found at Desert One. Immediately afterward, he left to catch another plane, this one to Edwards Air Force Base in California to set up a final rehearsal of the desert refueling plan on a dry lakebed.

On the night of April 16, Jones, Vaught, and Col. Charlie Beckwith, the burly, charismatic commander of the Army's elite Delta counterterrorist force, changed into civilian clothes and went to the White House to give the President and a handful of his top advisers a final briefing. They were an odd trio, thrown together by the moment. Jones, dark-haired and handsome, had spent the past six years inside the Pentagon, a master military bureaucrat climbing to the highest rank the nation had to offer. Vaught, who had fought in both Korea and Vietnam, was a paratrooper who had nothing but disdain for "parlor Pershings." His body slightly stooped from a broken back he had suffered in Vietnam's Ashau Valley, he spoke so slowly and deliberately that he frequently made a poor impression on those who did not know that there were few officers in the U.S. Army who knew more about war than Vaught. "Chargin' " Charlie Beckwith was as impetuous as Vaught was stolid. He offended with his intemperate outbursts, and he had been known to beat up those who defied him, but he inspired fierce loyalty among his troops. Many of the men who had volunteered for Delta had done so because he was the commander. "Chargin' " Charlie always seemed to be where the action was, and he had the scars to prove it. He had almost bled to death when a round from a Viet Cong machine gun tore into his belly. As it was, he had lost his gall bladder and 2 feet of small intestine. Beckwith and Vaught both knew a good soldier when they saw one, but they detested each other.

According to the plan presented to Jimmy Carter, eight Sea Stallion helicopters would take off from the aircraft carrier *Nimitz* in the Gulf of Oman and fly under cover of darkness through the Iranian backcountry to Desert One, 270 miles southeast of Tehran. At the same time, six propeller-driven C-130 cargo planes carrying 18,000 gallons of fuel and 120 members of the Delta force would launch from the island of Masirah off the coast of Oman and fly a similar backcountry route to meet the helicopters at Desert One. While a team of Army Rangers sealed off the area, the helicopters would refuel from the C-130s and the Delta commandos would transfer to the helicopters for the next leg of the journey. The C-130s would return to Masirah, while the Sea Stallions flew Delta to a daytime hideout 50 miles east of Tehran. The following night, agents already infiltrated into Tehran would pick up Delta in trucks and drive the force to the American Embassy. Seventy-five men would scale the 12-foot wall on padded aluminum ladders and move through the 27-acre compound, collecting the hostages and sending them to a soccer stadium across the street to be picked up by the helicopters. The Sea Stallions would fly from their hiding place into Tehran to pick up the hostages and their rescuers, then fly 50 miles southwest to an unused airfield at Manzireyah. Protected by a force of 200 Rangers flown in from Egypt, the hostages would be transferred to giant C-141 jet transport planes, self-destruct charges would be set in the helicopters, and the entire force would fly out of Iran.

General Jones, the chairman of the Joint Chiefs of Staff, already had explained to the President that if Delta could get to the embassy wall without being detected and if all the hostages were inside, the chances for success were high. Delta should have no trouble overpowering the students holding the hostages. It was the overall complexity of the mission that troubled Jones. Each part—the long flight in, the assault on the

embassy, the nerve-racking ride out—had to be strung together flaw-
lessly over a two-day period.

Speaking in a gravelly Georgia rumble that struck an immediate reso-
nance with Carter, Colonel Beckwith, the Delta force commander, told
the President he expected to encounter between 70 and 125 Iranians
inside the embassy compound. Only twenty to twenty-five would be
guarding the hostages in the middle of the night; the rest would be
sleeping in a barracks that would be covered by a machine gun. How
many casualties do you see here? the President asked. Major General
Vaught, the mission commander, jumped in with an estimate of six or
seven members of Delta and two or three hostages. Beckwith explained
to Carter that the primary threat to the hostages would come not from
their captors but their rescuers. If in the melee of the rescue, a hostage
were to overpower a guard and seize his weapon, well, Delta's shooters
were trained to kill anyone carrying a weapon. This is going to happen,
Beckwith warned the President. I hope it doesn't, but we gotta count on
it happening.

Deputy Secretary of State Warren Christopher asked what would
happen to the "students" who were guarding the hostages. Beckwith said
Delta would "take out" the guards. Christopher, a lawyer by training,
immediately spotted a loophole and asked what Beckwith meant by
"take out." Would they shoot them in the shoulder? No, sir, Beckwith
replied. We're going to shoot each of them twice, right between the eyes.

Beckwith didn't say exactly how many Iranians he planned to shoot
between the eyes, but personally he didn't expect a single Iranian to
survive. As he later put it, "When the shooting started, the students
would run like fuck, and when they did, they would be hosed." No one
in Delta had any doubts that most or all of the Iranians in the embassy
would be killed. "We were not there to arrest anybody," said Maj. Logan
Fitch, who would lead the assault on the embassy. "We were there to
kill them. We were going to kill a lot of people." Like Beckwith, Fitch,
a small-town Texas boy, had been there before—three tours in Vietnam,
two Purple Hearts. For all his combat experience, Fitch would never go
very far in a peacetime Army which prized management skills more than
fighting ability. But right now he was exactly where he wanted to be—the
first man to hit the embassy.

As Beckwith recorded it, the President concluded the meeting in the
White House Situation Room by saying, "I do not want to undertake this
operation, but we have no other recourse. The only way I will call it off
now is if the International Red Cross hands back our Americans. There's
not going to be just pre-positioning forward. We're going to do this
operation." As a practical matter, the mission could not be postponed.

Summer was coming and with each day that passed the nights grew shorter.

The United States had crossed a Rubicon. For Jimmy Carter, who boasted that not one American had died in combat on his watch, it was a particularly momentous decision. The plan had been carefully laid, but no one who listened to Charlie Beckwith could mistake the fact that the President was sending men to their deaths. Who and how many would depend on the fog and friction of war. If there were no illusions in the situation room that night, neither was there the slightest hint of what was to come. Nor was there the slightest understanding that whatever happened, success or failure, Operation Rice Bowl was only the first skirmish in America's war against terrorism.

★ 1 ★

DESERT ONE

Dick Meadows had been on missions behind enemy lines before, but never one like this. Ten years before, in November of 1970, his helicopter had crash-landed in the middle of the Son Tay prisoner-of-war camp, 23 miles from Hanoi. Meadows had been the leader of an assault team that was to rescue American POWs from Son Tay. He had searched each cell and, finding them empty, he had reported "negative items, negative items" in a voice so matter of fact it had been difficult to believe that he was in the middle of the most daring, high-risk operation of the Vietnam War, that six months of planning and training had just gone down the drain because intelligence somehow had failed to detect that the prisoners had been moved. His mission aborted, Meadows had dashed across a field toward a waiting helicopter. Running in the dark, he had pitched headlong into a drainage ditch. With the wind knocked out of him and every chance of being left behind in North Vietnam, he had lain there, fighting panic, telling himself it couldn't end like this. Finally he regained his breath and ran to the helicopter, the last man to board.

Ten years later, in April of 1980, unarmed, wearing a business suit, and carrying an Irish passport in the name of Brian McCarthy, Dick Meadows stepped off the Sunday night Lufthansa flight from Frankfurt to Tehran, waving at a nonexistent face in the crowd as if someone was there to greet him. Meadows had come to lay the groundwork for the most audacious American military mission since the end of the Vietnam

6

War. It wasn't a shooting war, not yet anyway, but in 1980 Tehran was enemy territory just as surely as Hanoi had been in 1970.

Meadows was gifted in the art of war—meticulous in training, fearless in combat. He had led twenty-five missions into North Vietnam and Laos, searching for downed pilots and scouting the Ho Chi Minh Trail, and he had never lost a man. Unknown to the public, he was a legend within the Army. When he had retired in 1977 after thirty years as both officer and enlisted man, he immediately had been brought back as a civilian adviser to the Army's elite new Delta force. America was committing its best soldiers to the war against terrorism, but they were woefully unprepared for battle.

The passport Meadows carried was a last-minute forgery by the CIA; his Irish brogue was a farce. Meadows had spent months building a different cover story. His original cover was that he had been born of British parents in Portugal, but just days before he was to leave for Tehran, Portugal had announced an economic boycott of Iran. Meadows's false identity as a dual British-Portuguese citizen suddenly looked more like a lightning rod than a cover story.

The CIA had never been keen on the idea of sending Meadows to Iran. As he traveled around Europe absorbing the minutiae of his cover—his "birthplace," the graveyard where his "parents" were buried—Meadows was periodically assessed by the CIA. "The agency came back several times and said he's not catching on fast enough," Wade Ishimoto, the Delta force's intelligence officer, recalled. Meadows had little patience for the CIA's tradecraft, arguing that the only real requirement was self-confidence. I'm going in as Richard Meadows if I have to, he had threatened when the CIA balked at giving him a new identity to take the place of his useless Portuguese cover. The CIA had no choice. Meadows was the linchpin of the entire operation.

Meadows was by no means the only American agent in Tehran, but he was the only one Delta trusted. "Delta's experience with the CIA had been less than fully satisfactory," explained Logan Fitch, the officer who was to lead Delta over the embassy wall. The CIA had no "stay behind" capability in Tehran, no means of conducting espionage operations other than through the CIA officers assigned to the embassy, all of whom now were held hostage. Constructing a "stay behind" network was one of the most basic of all intelligence tasks, a standard precaution against a break in diplomatic relations. "If the U.S. ever gets caught like that with its pants down again, somebody's ass ought to burn," Beckwith growled.

When the CIA finally activated its first agent in Tehran, it had not been through its own initiative. A wealthy Iranian named Franco* had taken it upon himself to contact the CIA. Franco had worked for the agency before the revolution, gathering intelligence about the Soviet presence in Iran. Shortly after the embassy was seized, Franco left Iran at his own expense and called his former CIA case officer at home. With no other agents in sight, Franco had been made part of the rescue mission, although letting an Iranian in on the operation had upset several members of Delta who feared he was an agent sent by the Ayatollah to sniff out just such a plan. Even those who trusted Franco realized he did not possess the necessary military skills—the ability to read a contour map, for instance. The CIA had to come up with another agent, one with a military background, who could work with Franco in Tehran and, not incidentally, keep an eye on him to make sure he was on the right side.

The CIA had not had many candidates for the job. Virtually all its paramilitary operatives had been let go in the aftermath of Vietnam. Finally, the CIA's computer found a retired agent named Bob Plan living in Trieste, Italy. Plan spent much of his time sailing the Adriatic, but his background included World War II service behind the lines with Tito in Yugoslavia. Plan, who struck everyone as a dead ringer for Anthony Quinn, could read a map and speak several languages, but not Farsi. He went into Iran posing as a German businessman, a deep cover case officer to run Franco as his agent and travel in and out of Iran to meet with his CIA controllers. Both Plan and Franco were "deniable." If either was picked up for questioning, he could not be traced to the United States.

Still, Delta's Logan Fitch said, "Neither Beckwith nor I would send our soldiers into action without one of our own men first confirming that all arrangements for their support had been completed." With Meadows in Tehran, the Delta commandos could be sure that everything would be ready when they got there, never mind that his cover story was shallow with no backup. To help Meadows unravel the mysteries of a foreign city, Delta sent along a young Air Force sergeant named Fred, who had been born in Iran and still had relatives there. His job was to help Meadows read the street signs, figure out the money, and cope with all the other things businessmen in foreign countries are supposed to know but Meadows didn't.

On Monday morning, April 21, Meadows checked into the Tehran Sheraton and Fred registered at the Hilton, joining other American agents scattered around the city. In addition to Plan and Franco, now

*Several of the agents infiltrated into Tehran are identified only by a first name or nicknames in order to conceal their true identities. All other names are real.

in their fourth month in Tehran, there were Clem and Scotty, two Green
Beret sergeants from West Berlin who were to be the reception committee for a thirteen-man Special Forces team that would rescue the three
Americans being held at the Foreign Ministry, apart from the rest of the
hostages. Scotty, who was indeed of Scottish descent, had a full head of
white hair, wore horn-rimmed glasses, and looked more like a college
professor than an Army sergeant. Clem, who spoke fluent German, had
hair down over his ears and a striking handlebar mustache.

Using Franco's house as their base, the agents fanned out to make the
final preparations. Meadows drove into the foothills east of the city to
reconnoiter the hideout where the Delta force would spend the daylight
hours. He decided he didn't like it and chose a place where there was
less chance of being discovered by workers on the Iranian state railway
line that ran through the area. He visited the warehouse where Franco
had stored six British Ford trucks and two Mazda vans. He installed
false partitions in the backs of the vehicles and checked the oil, gas,
water, and tires. He drove the route to the embassy, walked around the
compound, sat in a coffeehouse across the street and watched the guards
lolling behind their sandbags. He went to the soccer stadium, searching
for obstacles which might make it impossible to land helicopters there
to retrieve the hostages and their rescuers. He worried that the stadium's
light poles could be a hazard to the helicopters but decided 3-pound
charges would be enough to bring them down. He bought knives, com-
passes, canteens, blankets,—supplies for the night in the foothills when
he would be waiting for the helicopters to bring in Delta. He sent a telex
to "Jonas," his backstop in England, inserting the phrase "piece of cake."

But it wasn't. Some Iranian workmen had dug a trench in front of the
warehouse, blocking the trucks from reaching the street. Were the Iranians onto the plan? Six brand-new trucks and two vans had been sitting
idle in the warehouse since January, and as General Vaught, the mission
commander, put it, "No Iranian in his right mind would tie up assets like
that without using them." Meadows sent Fred to ask the attendant at
a gas station next to the warehouse about the ditch. The attendant said
it could not be filled in without the local revolutionary committee's
approval.

Doubts about the mission's security turned to paranoia when Franco
announced he was leaving the country. Fred had never trusted Franco.
All those gold chains he wore made him seem too much of a wheeler-
dealer. Now it smelled as if he might be setting them up. Franco left for
the airport at six-thirty on the morning of the 23rd, one day before the
mission. The ditch in front of the warehouse still had not been filled. Fred

took some fruit and soft drinks out to the warehouse to see if he could con the workmen into doing him a favor. At midday, he returned with the news that the ditch had been filled in just enough for the trucks to reach the street. That afternoon, Meadows picked up some satellite communications gear that had been smuggled into the country and left at a dead drop. He put the gear in the trunk of a new Mercedes which Franco had purchased for $50,000.

On Thursday morning, April 24, Clem, Scotty, and Meadows set off in the Mercedes to drive the route from the hide site to the embassy one more time. Clem, who was at the wheel, mistakenly entered an express lane reserved for buses and taxis. A policeman stopped the car, and Clem began apologizing for his error. Concentrating on the policeman at his window, Clem somehow let the car creep forward until the bumper nudged a second policeman. Angered by what he thought was a deliberate affront, the second policeman slammed his fist down on the hood and pulled his pistol. As if that were a signal, police cars pulled in front of and behind the Mercedes.

The three Americans inside were trapped. The police demanded to see Clem's driver's license. Clem said it was in his briefcase in the trunk. So was the communications gear. As Clem got out of the car and walked back to open the trunk, Meadows muttered to Scotty, This is it. Clem opened the trunk, snatched his briefcase out, and slammed the lid shut as fast as he could. The policeman did not notice the other equipment there, possibly because he couldn't take his eyes off Clem's handlebar mustache. With his briefcase now on top of the trunk, Clem produced his yellow international driver's license. No longer apologetic, he acted indignant at being detained for so long over such a minor traffic violation.

★   ★   ★

While Clem was talking his way past the police, the elite troops of the Delta force were standing at attention, singing "God Bless America" inside a Soviet-built aircraft hangar in Egypt. Two weeks ago the old, abandoned MiG base called Wadi Keena had been littered with human feces and swarming with flies. An Air Force contingent from Europe had cleaned the place up and brought in an air-conditioned hospital tent and two trailers—one to serve as General Vaught's command post, the other as a weather station. Nineteen planes—C-130 and C-141 transports and KC-135 aerial tankers—were parked on the runway. They were only part of the fleet of aircraft needed to support the mission. For the past eleven days, airplanes had been flying in and out of Wadi Keena, bringing in everything from ammunition to cots, all within full view of Soviet spy satellites. A special unit within the Joint Chiefs of Staff had spent the past five months moving planes through Wadi Keena, establishing a pattern of activity that would make this heavy traffic appear normal.

The Delta commandos had something to sing about. They had just received an intelligence windfall that was almost too good to be true. The embassy's Pakistani cook finally had been allowed to leave the country with his wife. By sheer coincidence, the couple had left Tehran on April 23 on the same flight as Franco. By still greater coincidence, the two men had sat next to each other and struck up a conversation. At the plane's first stop, Franco arranged for the cook to be debriefed by the CIA. The cook confirmed that all the hostages—except the three being held separately at the Foreign Ministry—were indeed inside the embassy compound and that they all were being held in the chancellery building. Instead of having to search all fourteen buildings in the compound, Delta could concentrate on just one.

Awakened from his last sleep before the mission, Beckwith convened a meeting of his principal commanders to revise the assault plan in light of the new intelligence. "We had this mockup of the embassy compound, had it sitting in a hangar," Delta's Logan Fitch said. "I remember going with Beckwith to the mockup. . . . We reorganized our assault plan. . . . We oriented the majority of the forces to the chancellery." Eight four-man teams would now hit the chancellery. One team would force a door on the east end of the building, race down the corridor, let the rest of the force in through the front door, and begin a systematic search of the building's ninety rooms.

The timing of this intelligence windfall, coming on the night before the mission, struck everyone as suspicious. "I said, 'Someone's either sucking us in or [the CIA has] known it all along and we're the suckers,' " Fitch recalled. "I didn't necessarily believe [the cook's information] that much," Vaught, the mission commander, said, "He was an untested source, a last-minute flash in the pan." Vaught now considered finding "all the hostages in the chancellery building the most likely situation we would encounter," but as far as he was concerned the intelligence was not reliable enough to justify radical revisions in the assault plan. "It doesn't mean you pare down your force," Vaught said, even though cutting back the number of shooters would have eased the load each of the helicopters had to carry.

At 9:00 A.M. on Thursday, April 24, the 132 members of the rescue mission's ground force began trooping aboard C-141 transports for the first leg of the journey to Tehran. With his equipment, each man weighed about 295 pounds, an uneasy compromise between what he needed and what the helicopters could lift. Maj. Lewis "Bucky" Burruss, Delta's deputy commander, took only one quart of water to last him two nights and a day. Each man wore a Navy watch cap, Levi's, flak vest, and a field jacket dyed black with an American flag sewn on the sleeve. For the moment, the flag was covered by a piece of tape; it would come off when the rescue force reached the embassy. The C-141s took off for Masirah Island off the coast of Oman, where the commandos transferred to the slower C-130s for the low-level flight to Desert One.

★   ★   ★

Back in Tehran, Meadows bought oranges and filled canteens for the night ahead. Late in the afternoon, he went to the warehouse to get the pickup truck his reception party would drive to the hideout that night. There was still another hitch: Fred had left the papers for the pickup back at the hotel. They would need those papers if they were stopped by the police again, so Fred drove back to the hotel to retrieve them. When Meadows, Clem, and Fred finally left the warehouse for the hideout, they discovered the headlights on the pickup were out. They stopped at two garages, trying unsuccessfully to get them fixed, then gave up and pressed on. They could delay no longer.

★   ★   ★

At three minutes past seven, a NOAA 6 weather satellite made one of its two daily passes over Iran. In one of the trailers parked at Wadi Keena, a printer instantaneously spat out what the satellite's sensors had recorded. The mission's weather officer turned to Vaught and reported that the conditions along the desert route were exactly as forecast. There were thunderstorms in the Zagros Mountains 50 miles to the west of the route, but it was clear in the desert valley. There was a 10,000-foot ceiling and the wind was blowing from the northwest at 10 miles per hour. The weather officer's only concern was about the following night. A frontal system was moving in, and that could cause thunderstorms over Tehran.

★   ★   ★

At five minutes past seven, Lt. Col. Ed Seiffert, the commander of the eight Sea Stallion helicopters, lifted his Dash One off the deck of the aircraft carrier *Nimitz*, 60 miles south of the Iranian coast. Ordinarily, the Navy used the giant, twin-engined Sea Stallion to sweep mines, but it had been pressed into service for Operation Rice Bowl because it was one of the few helicopters with the range to reach Desert One and the only one with a plausible excuse for being on an aircraft carrier.

Seiffert, a thin, no-nonsense officer, should have just completed a year's tour of duty on the Japanese island of Okinawa. But in December he had been whisked away to the Yuma Proving Grounds in Arizona and placed in command of the pilots selected to fly the mission. Like most of the others, he had started from scratch, learning to fly at night without any external aids to navigation other than the terrain features he could make out through his night-vision goggles, battery-powered devices that amplified the available light from the moon and stars. Seen through night goggles, the world was green and gauzy. It was the equivalent of 20/70 eyesight with no depth perception and less than half the normal field of view. The lenses had to be constantly refocused unless, like Seiffert, the wearer had mastered the trick of using one eye for looking at nearby objects inside the cockpit and the other for distant objects outside. The cumbersome devices invariably produced a splitting headache. Nevertheless, Seiffert said, "it's better than having no eyes at all."

The other seven helicopters, all painted with Iranian markings, joined up with Seiffert at an altitude of 400 feet and headed north at 120 knots in a loose diamond formation, spread out to dissipate the noise. It was thirty minutes before sunset, but there was so much moisture in the air that visibility was reduced to three miles. The Soviet intelligence trawler which usually trailed the *Nimitz* was 200 miles to the south eavesdropping on the carrier *Coral Sea,* which had been sent off on a high-speed run as a diversion.

To be on the safe side, the *Nimitz* had stayed farther from the coast than originally planned, so the helicopters were twelve minutes behind schedule by the time they crossed the beach at a point midway between two Iranian radar stations at Jask and Chah Bahar. They crossed the coastline 100 feet above the ground, traveling in complete radio silence.

Below them, the pilots could make out campfires and trails in the fading light. According to Maj. James Schaefer, who was flying Dash Three, "we were probably three quarters of a mile west of where we were supposed to be." The helicopters climbed to clear a 4,600-foot pass, then settled back to 200 feet. "Once we crossed that first mountain, it was amazing how familiar everything became," Schaefer said. "All the checkpoints kept coming up. It was very reassuring."

Schaefer was the most experienced night flyer among the helicopter pilots, and he had been in tight spots before in Vietnam, but that had not spared him a case of pre-mission nerves. He had slept only fitfully the past few days and had gone to the trouble of making out a last will and testament. Now airborne and immersed in the task of flying, Schaefer could relax enough to feel like eating something for the first time that day. The mission was a go. Just before crossing the beach, he had looked up and seen the lead C-130 inbound to the rendezvous at Desert One.

★   ★   ★

The lead C-130 was carrying the Delta commander, Charlie Beckwith, Logan Fitch and his squadron, a road watch team, a combat control team to direct traffic at Desert One, drivers for the trucks that would take Delta to the embassy, and Air Force Col. James Kyle, the mission's air boss—eighty-eight passengers and crew in all, plus a small arsenal of antitank and antiaircraft weapons, two motorcycles, and a jeep. The plane was so heavily loaded that "had we lost one engine during the first hour of the flight, it was kiss-off time," the pilot, Lt. Col. Bob Brenci, said. Both men and machines were operating at the outer limits of their capabilities. Brenci traversed the Gulf of Oman in the fading light, then descended to 400 feet and crossed the coast of Iran right on schedule. Wade Ishimoto, Delta's intelligence officer, felt a rush of hot air up his back and said to himself, God damn, we're really going. Once past the coastal radar, Brenci climbed to 3,000 feet so his engines wouldn't be heard by anyone on the ground. Even at that altitude, it was a bumpy ride which made several passengers airsick.

One hour after the first C-130 crossed the coast, five more C-130s carrying the remainder of the rescue force and all the fuel for the Sea Stallion helicopters took off from Masirah. Just before takeoff, there was a near disaster when two of the heavily laden planes almost collided while taxiing in the cramped confines of a single runway.

Back at Wadi Keena, a team from the National Security Agency (NSA) that was eavesdropping on Iranian police radios heard a gendarmerie post report seeing two C-130s flying toward Chah Bahar with lights out. They couldn't be the American C-130s; those were still a good half hour away from the coast. Vaught concluded that the Iranians had spotted two of their own planes. There was another scare when the NSA picked up the signals of two F-4 fighters scrambling aloft from Mehrabad Airport in Tehran, but the Iranian jets headed in the direction of the Iraqi border. The rescue force still had not been detected.

After four hours, the lead C-130 with Charlie Beckwith aboard was 20 miles from Desert One. Standing in the cockpit, John Carney switched on the remote-control lights that he had installed three weeks before, and the primitive desert landing strip lit up. The pilot, Bob Brenci, lowered an infrared camera in the nose of the plane and began a pass over Desert One, searching for obstructions or intruders. The camera spotted a truck on the road, and Brenci broke away to give it time to clear the area. He circled once and began his approach. "It just didn't look right to me," Brenci recalled. He had studied satellite photographs of Desert One, but coming in low and at an angle, it didn't look the same. He missed his first approach and came around again. The C-130 came down hard—hard enough to knock out the satellite radio that linked air boss Jim Kyle with the command post at Wadi Keena. "That's got to be the worst landing of my life," Brenci recalled. "I just kind of fished for the spot and just crashed in." The moment he came to a complete stop, Brenci yelled Go into his microphone, and the C-130's loadmasters began lowering the rear ramp. Kyle used a backup radio to signal Vaught that he had landed: Hammer, this is Woodpecker. Q Tip. It was 10:40 P.M. The mission was ten minutes behind schedule because of the extra passes Brenci had been forced to make.

As soon as the C-130's ramp was lowered, Wade Ishimoto ran straight into the desert for 100 yards and waited for the rest of his road watch team. Ishimoto's job was to make sure no stray travelers or Iranian troops interrupted the rendezvous at Desert One. Sgt. Robert Rubio rode up on his dirt bike, and Ishimoto jumped on the back. They had to go nearly a mile to reach the point where they were to set up their road-block. "Next thing I see is these damn lights coming down the road," Ishimoto recalled, an eerie sight when seen through the maelstrom of dust kicked up by the C-130's propellors. "Next thing I hear was 'Ka-room.'" Sgt. David Littlejohn had fired his grenade launcher at the oncoming lights. The round went long, but it was a signal for the rest of the road watchers to open fire on the unidentified vehicle, which, for all they knew, could be carrying Iranian troops. The vehicle, whatever it was, ground to a halt, its engine riddled with bullets.

Logan Fitch came off the C-130 at a more leisurely pace than Ishimoto. At this point in the mission, Fitch and the rest of Delta were just straphangers changing aircraft. "We were maybe just a little too relaxed," Fitch said. "We were in Iran and all that business, but I wasn't very excited about it." Smothered and blinded by the dust, he recalled, "I put my head down to breathe and led with my arm, almost feeling my way toward the road, which was about fifty yards north. Then I looked over my arm and through the sand cloud and saw . . . a large, ultramodern bus with its interior lights on."

A Ranger sergeant was standing at the head of the aisle, covering forty-three petrified Iranians with his weapon. "He was trying to get them off the bus," Fitch recalled. "He wanted to know if he should fire his weapon over their heads." Fitch ordered his men to search each of the passengers at gunpoint, then lead them one by one off the bus. He walked around to the other side of the bus where he found the driver huddled beside the front wheel. Using what little Farsi he knew, Fitch ordered the man to join the passengers outside. When the man did not move, Fitch fired a round into the dirt next to him. The driver began to move, but not quickly enough. Fitch hit him with the butt of his rifle.

On its way to rescue fifty-two American hostages, Delta now had forty-four Iranian hostages of its own. While the bus passengers were being searched, Wade Ishimoto and Sergeant Rubio were nearing a bend in the road that they had picked from satellite photos as the best spot to lay an ambush. As they approached the bend, Ishimoto saw another set of headlights coming toward them. Ishimoto got off the motorcycle and stood in the middle of the road to flag down the vehicle while Rubio covered him with a small rocket called a Light Anti-tank Weapon (LAW).

The headlights kept coming. When they were about fifty yards away, Ishimoto opened up with his automatic carbine, aiming at the engine. He knocked out one headlight, but the vehicle still kept coming.

Rubio, cock your LAW, Ishimoto shouted.

Yes, sir, Rubio replied.

You ready?

Yes, sir.

Fire.

"We hear the 'whoom,' which was the rocket being fired," Ishimoto recalled. "The next thing I see is flame shooting straight up. The next words out of my mouth were, 'Holy shit, a fuel truck!'" Rubio's rocket had gone under the truck and ricocheted upward directly into several hundred gallons of fuel being smuggled across the Iranian desert. "This time," said Ishimoto, "the vehicle stops."

With the one headlight still shining on him, Ishimoto left the road for the cover of darkness. He circled around to approach the truck from the side, yelling the Farsi phrases for "Hands up" and "Come here." He could hear voices, but as he drew closer he realized they were coming from a radio. The occupants of the truck were nowhere in sight. Then, Ishimoto saw another pair of headlights coming down the road. Feeling outnumbered, he ran back to Rubio's position. Rubio told him he had seen a man jump out of the burning fuel truck and run back toward the approaching vehicle. Ishimoto told Rubio to go after the vehicle with his one remaining LAW. "Rubio gets on the motorcycle and the damn thing took five kicks before it started," Ishimoto said. The motorcycle finally started, but Rubio sat there fiddling with his night-vision goggles which suddenly had failed him. In frustration, Rubio dropped the goggles and took off after the vehicle, but by now it had too much of a head start.

Ishimoto was confident the smugglers had seen nothing that would compromise the mission. They had seen no one in uniform, had not heard any English spoken, and were too far away to have seen or heard the C-130. Besides, smugglers were not about to go running to the local police. There was the slight matter of the burning fuel truck, which continued to send flames shooting 100 feet into the air, but the only people likely to see it were nomads with no allegiance to the government in Tehran. The fuel truck would eventually burn itself out, but the blackened hulk would remain behind as evidence that something untoward had happened in the middle of nowhere. Ishimoto set his road watch team to picking up spent cartridges. With no expended brass lying around, perhaps passers-by would think the truck had had an accident.

The truck was still burning when the second C-130 arrived overhead. At first, the cockpit crew thought the lead plane must have crashed. By now John Carney's combat control team had laid out an extensive runway lighting system, but the blinding glare of the burning truck made landing difficult. Some of the follow-on C-130s needed as many as three tries to get down. Beckwith's deputy, "Bucky" Burruss, came down the ramp of his C-130 and looked around at the bullet-riddled bus and the flaming fuel truck. Welcome to World War III, Beckwith said.

★   ★   ★

Two hundred miles to the north, Meadows, Clem, and Fred left their pickup truck, shouldered the rucksacks containing their food and communications gear, and set off across the desert on foot. A half moon in a clear sky lit up the landscape, and they covered the two miles to the landing zone quickly. From time to time, they could hear a train in the distance. They surveyed the terrain and decided to move the landing zone several hundred yards to slightly smoother ground.

Meadows would bring the helicopters in using one of his radios and an infrared beacon which the pilots could see through their night-vision goggles. He zeroed his other radios on the communications satellite overhead and discovered that one of them had a dead battery. He tuned in the BBC and sat down to wait for the transmission that would tell him the mission was still on. When a woman began reading the agreed-upon numerical code, Meadows allowed himself to think the mission was really going to happen. Ten minutes later, he established contact via satellite with Desert One and heard the familiar voice of Delta's communications officer. Meadows spoke in double talk, reporting from support base Romeo: The groceries are on the shelf. When can Romeo expect spare parts? he asked. Unknown at this time because trucks have not arrived, came the answer. Meadows, Clem, and Fred shared a can of cold beans and tried to catch a little sleep before the "trucks" arrived.

★ ★ ★

Dash Six was the first of the "trucks" to drop out. About two hours into the mission a cockpit indicator warned that one of the rotor blades was losing pressure. The pilot, Maj. Bill Hoff, landed Dash Six on a dry lakebed. Dash Eight followed him down. On the ground, Hoff shut down his engines, took a flashlight, and climbed on top of his helicopter to verify the reading he was getting in the cockpit. The indicator attached to the rotor blade also showed a loss of pressure, which meant that somewhere in the blade there was a hairline crack that was allowing the pressurized gas inside to escape. Hoff had an impending blade failure on his hands. Along with his co-pilot and three crew members, Hoff collected all their classified materials, boarded Dash Eight, and resumed the trip to Desert One.

As the remaining seven helicopters approached a major east-west road, they spread out in a line four miles wide. They were more than halfway to Desert One and about to pass over the most populated area on the backcountry route. A number of little towns were strung out along the road and a policeman in any one of them might phone in a report of an unidentified aircraft overhead. With the helicopters spread out, each person below would hear only one set of rotors. If they started checking with each other, they would all think they had heard the same aircraft. One helicopter was not as likely to set off an alarm as seven.

About fifteen minutes after they crossed the road, the seven Sea Stallions began to tighten their formation. "As we did so, I noticed what looked like fog in front of us," said Maj. James Schaefer, the pilot of Dash Three. A fog bank like that would usually be rising off a lake, but Schaefer didn't remember any lake at this point in the journey. He asked his co-pilot, Major Leslie Petty, to check the map. Petty said there was no lakebed on the map. "I said, 'I wonder if that's one of those dust storms,'" Schaefer recalled. There had been a one-line mention in the weather annex to the operations plan that thunderstorms in the Zagros Mountains sometimes kicked up dust storms, known in that part of the world as "haboobs."

The lights of Dash One and Dash Two disappeared into the cloud. Schaefer slowed his air speed from 130 to 90 knots and turned right 15 degrees to open up some distance with the other helicopters. He was flying at 300 feet and could still see the ground below, but he no longer could see anything in front. "Off we went," Schaefer said, "anticipating the thing to be over any second." But this wasn't like any dust storm he had ever seen. There was no wind, no turbulence, just a fine talcum-like powder that sifted into the cockpit, caking the pilots' lips. The temperature, already a sticky 88 degrees, rose about 5 degrees, and the pilots started calling to their crews for water.

The dust cloud was grounds for aborting the mission, since the operation plan called for a minimum of five miles visibility. Lt. Col. Ed Seiffert in Dash One and his wingman B. J. McGuire in Dash Two immediately reversed course, got out of the dust cloud, and landed. Using his satellite radio, Seiffert called the command post in Egypt to report the dust cloud to General Vaught. Vaught asked if it was possible to continue. Seiffert asked what the weather was at Desert One. Vaught said it was clear. Seiffert said he thought it was possible to continue, so Vaught ordered him forward. After twenty minutes on the ground, Seiffert and McGuire took off again.

Schaefer in Dash Three had not seen Seiffert and McGuire land, so he continued on, not knowing he was now in the lead. After about thirty minutes in the cloud, Schaefer no longer could see the ground, so he climbed to 1,000 feet to give himself a greater margin for error. The map showed they were approaching the first major vertical obstacle, a 6,000-foot mountain range, so he kept climbing. Schaefer had just climbed through 5,900 feet when suddenly he broke out of the cloud. Sure enough, the mountain was off to his left, exactly where it should be. Despite the cloud, he was still on course. "The confidence factor went way up," Schaefer said. But then he was back in the cloud, this time having to worry about a 9,000-foot mountain ahead, the last obstacle before Desert One. Schaefer climbed to 9,000 feet and broke out of the cloud just before he reached the mountain. Once again able to see, he descended to 300 feet and went around the mountain. He had spent a total of two hours and forty-five minutes in the dust cloud; he was already overdue and still thirty-five minutes from Desert One.

That was a lot better than Lt. Rod Davis was doing in Dash Five. Davis's gyroscope had overheated and failed. Unable to see any landmarks or to use the artificial horizon provided by the gyroscope, Davis became disoriented in the swirling dust, which one of the pilots likened to being inside a bottle of milk. At one point, the helicopter slipped into a 40-degree bank and nearly crashed. Davis descended to 75 feet but still could not see anything on the ground to help him regain his bearings. He still had 110 miles to go to Desert One and a 9,000-foot mountain ahead. He couldn't climb over it without the risk of exposing himself to Iranian radar. He couldn't go around it because his electronic navigation aids weren't working.

Opting for the devil he knew, Davis reversed course and headed back through the cloud toward the *Nimitz*. It was an act of desperation. When he turned back, Davis did not have enough fuel to make it to the carrier, so he broke radio silence to tell Seiffert in Dash One that he was heading for the *Nimitz*. If Seiffert relayed the message on his satellite radio, the carrier could steam closer to the coast, cutting the distance Davis had to travel. Seiffert did not acknowledge receiving Davis's message. As Dash Five began the long journey back, Davis did not know whether Seiffert had heard him, much less relayed his message to the *Nimitz*.

★   ★   ★

Dash Three was the first helicopter to reach Desert One—fifty minutes behind schedule. When Schaefer saw the flame of the burning fuel truck, his first thought was that one of the C-130s had crashed. Instead of coming straight in, he made a loop around the field, counting the C-130s. They were all there, so he decided to land. Not only was Schaefer late, but he appeared to members of the ground force to be coming in from the wrong direction.

After landing, Schaefer taxied to his refueling station behind a C-130 "fuelbird." He told one of the Air Force crewmen how much fuel he needed, then turned to face a very perturbed Charlie Beckwith. "He came in the helicopter and asked me what the hell was going on and why were we late," Schaefer recalled. "I said, 'They'll be here. They're either coming or they're up against the side of a hill.' . . . I probably was a little short in temper." Schaefer had to relieve himself, and Beckwith followed him into the desert. "He was upset," Schaefer said. "He was burning off all the adrenaline he'd saved up." According to Beckwith, Schaefer spoke "words to the effect that if we had any sense we would move the helos out into the desert and load everyone on the C-130s and go home." Schaefer was regarded as perhaps the best of the helicopter pilots, but he was exhausted by the ordeal of navigating through the dust cloud.

Dash Four was next to land, followed ten minutes later by Capt. Larry Walt in Dash Seven. Walt got out of his helicopter and, according to Beckwith, said, "some very careful consideration ought to be given to calling off this operation. You have no idea what I've been through. The damnedest sandstorm I've ever seen hit us . . . I'm really not sure we can make it." Logan Fitch heard Walt but had no idea what he was talking about. The weather at Desert One was clear.

It took thirty-five minutes for the rest of the helicopters to straggle in.

Seiffert in Dash One was the last to land, one hour and twenty-five minutes behind schedule. "When I came in, I said to myself, 'We've got four helos on the ground and two with me,' " Seiffert recalled. " 'We're still go.' " The operation plan specified that a minimum of six helicopters had to make it to where Meadows, Clem, and Fred were waiting in order to carry out the rescue the following night.

For the plan to work, the rescue force had to reach the hideout where it would spend the daylight hours before the sun came up. There were nine hours and sixteen minutes of darkness to cover the 900 miles from the *Nimitz* to the hiding place. With no delays, the flight would take eight hours. The last helicopter was nearly an hour and a half late and still had to refuel, which probably would take another hour. What Beckwith called his "drop dead time"—the time by which he no longer could make it to the hiding place outside Tehran by first light—had come and gone. He already had decided he would take the chance of arriving at the hideout after sunup.

On the ground, it was safe to break radio silence, so Seiffert was talking with the other pilots for the first time since they'd left the *Nimitz*. Beckwith jumped aboard Dash One and requested permission to begin loading his men and equipment. Seiffert ignored him, concentrating instead on a report that Dash Two had fluctuating hydraulic pressure. "I was getting very anxious, not to say pissed," Beckwith related. "To get his attention, I rapped his helmet with my palm." Finally, Seiffert gave permission to load. Amidst the din and dust of Sea Stallion rotors and C-130 propellors, Delta began to board, dragging the camouflage nets that would hide the helicopters the next day.

Delta had nearly finished loading when B. J. McGuire in Dash Two confirmed what his cockpit gauge had been telling him for the last two hours—one of his two hydraulic systems had failed. The hydraulic pump was burned out. A leak in the line had bled the system dry of hydraulic fluid, which also lubricated the pump. The pump would have to be replaced, but there was no spare. Dash Two could still fly using its backup hydraulic system, but if that system failed, the helicopter would probably crash and certainly would be of no further use.

Logan Fitch said later that "I spoke to the pilot of that helicopter who said he had a problem with the hydraulic system, and he told me he was quite confident he could continue." But it was not the pilot's decision to make. "I'm the guy that made the decision not to fly the aircraft with the hydraulic failure," Ed Seiffert, the helicopters' commander, said. "My decision is to leave [Dash] Two right where it is. So we're down to five. I tell Jim Kyle we are down to five aircraft."

Kyle then radioed General Vaught at Wadi Keena that they were below the required number of six helicopters. Vaught asked Kyle to consider going ahead with five. As Beckwith recounted it, Kyle turned to him and asked, " 'Would you consider taking five and going ahead? And think about it before you answer me,' he said. 'Really, you're the guy who's got to shoulder this, Charlie.' I said, 'I know that. Give me a couple of seconds to think it over.' "

Pressing on with less than six helicopters meant leaving behind one of two things—troops or fuel. The helicopters were already 6,000 pounds overweight. Adding more weight by dividing Dash Two's load among the remaining five helicopters was simply not possible. Beckwith and Fitch already had discussed who they would leave behind if they had to go forward with less than six helicopters. "Beckwith says to me, 'What do you think?' " Fitch recalled. "I say, 'We've been through this. We've got to have six helos or we can't go. Who the hell are we going to leave behind?' The cold hard facts were there was no room for argument or discussion. You don't have six, you can't go."

The only way all of Delta could go aboard five helicopters was by jettisoning fuel which might be needed the next night in Tehran. "Then what are your options in the city?" Seiffert asked. "They diminish to zero. You don't have enough gas reserve to go into a hold pattern waiting for Delta to call you into the compound. You can only make a straight shot from the hide site to the city. That's assuming all five airplanes are ready to go. . . . Can the helos continue and get the hostages out of the compound with the presumption that nothing else fails? The answer is yes. Can you do the mission with the assuredness of success as originally anticipated at the inception of the mission? The answer is no. . . . To change the plan at that time is tantamount to disaster. . . . It's not a close call for me."

Beckwith said to Kyle, "Ain't no way, Jim. No way." Vaught, at his command post in Egypt, agreed. "At Desert One, there was this set of facts," he recalled. "The helicopters had flown just less than five hours. They started out with eight helos and at that point three had failed. . . . If you were commander and started off with eight, and you're only three fifths of the way through the mission flying hours and only five are left . . . you'd have about one helo left when you got to Manzireyah. You've got two choices—take the record of achievement thus far and predict what your chances are, or just gut it out [and continue]. If they had done that, we very likely could have had Delta scattered over half of Iran."

Back at the Pentagon, Marine Commandant Gen. Robert Barrow and Army Chief of Staff Gen. Edward "Shy" Meyer had joined Joint Chiefs

Chairman David Jones in a small room off the National Military Command Center where they could talk to Vaught and listen to the communications with Desert One. Neither Barrow nor Meyer said anything, but both agreed with the decision to abort. "I didn't think they should go on," Barrow said. "I didn't. . . . We'd have been absolute fools to continue." Meyer said, "I would have fallen on my sword on that issue. We'd decided at the table if there were not enough helos the mission would be scrubbed. There was never any question. It was go-no go."

The only person for whom it was a close call was the President's national security adviser, Zbigniew Brzezinski. At 4:45 P.M. Washington time, Defense Secretary Harold Brown called Brzezinski on a secure telephone line from the Pentagon with the news that they were in an "abort situation." "I was stunned and quizzed Brown sharply on whether the abort was necessary," Brzezinski recounted. "Why couldn't we go ahead, given the emergency, with five?" Brown insisted that planning indicated that six was the minimum. Brzezinski told him to consult with Jones and Beckwith. Brzezinski rushed into the Oval Office to tell the President. "I stood in front of his desk with my mind racing: should I press the President to go ahead with only five helicopters? Here I was, alone with the President. Perhaps I could convince him to abandon military prudence, to go in a daring single stroke for the big prize, to take the historic chance." Brzezinski knelt in front of the President's desk to take notes while Carter spoke with Brown. "The President asked Brown for the field commander's assessment, and then I heard the President say, 'Let's go with his recommendation.' He hung up, looked at me, confirmed that the mission was aborted, and then put his head down on top of his desk, cradling it in his arms for approximately five seconds."

★ ★ ★

Meadows, Clem, and Fred were still waiting at the hiding place outside Tehran. At 2:40 A.M. Tehran time, Meadows received a radio message from Desert One: Spare parts will not arrive due to broken truck. Test canceled. Meadows asked for clarification. Vaught came on the circuit in no uncertain terms: Close test base Romeo. Meadows, Clem, and Fred spent thirty minutes hiding the radio gear in case the mission could be revived. Then they hiked back to their pickup truck. Still not knowing what had gone wrong, Meadows dropped the truck at the warehouse, returned to Tehran, checked back into his hotel, and fell asleep.

★ ★ ★

"The abort situation neither relieves me nor takes anything off my mind," Ed Seiffert said. "It's a change of goddamn plans. We know we're going to take as much out of Desert One as we possibly could. I decided on flying five [helicopters] back to the ocean," leaving Dash Two with its burned-out hydraulic pump behind. Fuel was now a major problem. All the aircraft had been on the ground, their engines running, for much longer than planned. If the C-130 piloted by Capt. Hal Lewis didn't leave Desert One within five minutes, it would not have enough gas to make it out of Iran. Before Lewis could take off, Dash Three would have to move. If Lewis brought his engines up to the power required to turn his aircraft around in the sand, the resulting sandstorm would choke Dash Three's engines and another helicopter would be stranded. But Schaefer in Dash Three could not taxi out of the way because on landing he had blown a tire when he ran across a rut left by one of the C-130s. So Schaefer prepared to lift Dash Three into a hover to get clear of Hal Lewis's C-130.

Until now, Schaefer had relied on the refueling hoses—black snakes against the white desert floor—to tell him where he was in the maelstrom of dust that was Desert One. But now the hoses were stored aboard the C-130s, and the only thing Schaefer could see was the black-clad figure of a sergeant from the Air Force control team who was standing between Dash Three and Lewis's C-130. Schaefer lifted off and turned 10 degrees to the left, keeping his eyes fixed on the sergeant. But the sergeant backed away from the 100-mile-per-hour blast of Schaefer's rotors. What Schaefer thought was a stationary object was now moving: Schaefer believed he was drifting left when in fact the sergeant was moving right. Reacting to the optical illusion, Schaefer banked back to the right and flew into Hal Lewis's C-130, his rotor blade slicing into the left wing and setting off an explosion of flaming gasoline.

Seiffert in Dash One witnessed the accident from less than 100 feet away. "It was instantaneous," he said. "Flame had engulfed the whole area by the time the rotor blade stopped turning. I said to myself, 'Nobody's getting the hell out of that thing.'"

In the cockpit of Dash Three, Schaefer heard the noise and felt the shock but didn't realize what he had hit. He looked over to his co-pilot, Major Leslie Petty, but Petty was no longer there. He had climbed through the window on the left side, landing in a puddle of aviation gas from the ruptured fuel tanks. He ran away from the helicopter, but the flames caught up with him. Still in the cockpit, Schaefer heard the screams of his crew chief, Sgt. Dewey Johnson, coming from the rear of the helicopter. Two 300-gallon internal fuel tanks had ruptured, and the back was awash in burning aviation gas. Schaefer reached back, trying to pull Johnson forward into the cockpit, but the heat was too intense, burning his fingertips through his flameproof gloves. The screaming stopped.

Schaefer removed his shoulder holster, afraid the bullets in his revolver would overheat and explode. He started throwing switches, automatically going through the procedure for shutting down his aircraft, until he realized that didn't make much sense. He sat for a moment with his arms folded, not knowing what to do next. He held his breath in order not to inhale the flames licking at the cockpit. Then he punched out his emergency window and started to climb through it, only to realize he was still strapped to his seat. Releasing his shoulder harness, he climbed through the window and dove—literally dove—to the ground, cracking two vertebrae in his neck. He got up and tried to run, but the pain in his left side was so intense he could only take two or three steps before collapsing. He looked up, saw a C-130 moving away from him, and thought he was about to be left in Iran. Then a figure came running toward him, picked him up, and carried him to the C-130. As he was being lifted aboard, Schaefer turned and saw for the first time the burning skeleton of the C-130 he had hit.

★   ★   ★

Logan Fitch was inside Hal Lewis's C-130, sitting next to the troop door in the left rear. "I felt a shudder and felt two thunks." At first he thought the plane had hit a pothole. Then he saw sparks and flames. "I jump up, thinking we've been attacked. I want to get off the airplane." Fitch and one of the plane's Air Force crew members threw open the troop door, but the only thing outside was a wall of flame. Everybody would have to get out through the door on the right side. Flames were racing from the cockpit toward the rear, fed by the residual gas in the fuel bladder which had been used to refuel the helicopters. "My men shouted, staggered, stumbled onto the hot bladder. They fell over and clawed one another in the urge to escape. I'm standing at the back of the airplane. I have it in my mind I'll get everybody off, then get myself off. I see the flames advancing. I decide we're not going to make it. So I enter the stream of troops going out the door." Knocked down, Fitch scrambled up, only to be knocked down again. At last, he got out the door, was knocked down again by the man coming out behind him, then got up and ran 100 yards away from the plane before stopping to look back. "I stood there and watched until no one came off," Fitch said.

The last man off was Air Force Sergeant Joseph Beyers, who was blown out the door by an explosion. He had been one of seven men in the C-130's cockpit. Five had been incinerated. A member of Delta had grabbed him by the collar and dragged him toward the rear of the aircraft. Unable to stand the heat, the Delta man had dropped him to save his own life. But when the explosion blew Beyers out the door, the commando crawled back to the aircraft to drag him to safety.

Seiffert in Dash One ordered his pilots to abandon their helicopters. "We took a piece of shrapnel through number one internal fuel tank," he said. "We now have loose fuel sitting in a turned-up aircraft with exhaust temperatures of seven hundred degrees Centigrade. All we need is a spark. . . . To sit there and wait for something else to happen with a blazing inferno seventy-five feet in front of me did not make much sense." Three of the helicopters were within 150 feet of the fire, close enough to be in danger.

Two of the helicopters were out of danger on the other side of the road. Before boarding the C-130s, the crews of those two helicopters sanitized their cockpits, scooping up all the classified material along with thousands of dollars in Iranian currency that was to be used if the rescue force had to bribe its way out. The crews of the three helicopters closest to the fire did not retrieve their classified material. "There's nothing that important to go back and make an issue out of sanitizing the aircraft," Seiffert said. The alternative to going back aboard the cooking helicopters was destroying them with thermite grenades. "I did not recommend to Kyle to destroy the aircraft," Seiffert added. "He doesn't need any more fire than what he's got."

The C-130s were taxiing to get away from the fire and explosions. Logan Fitch ran to the closest one and pounded on the door until someone opened it. Then Fitch and the other survivors from Lewis's C-130 piled aboard, one man sobbing and saying over and over, Thanks a fucking lot, thanks a fucking lot. Leslie Petty, Schaefer's co-pilot from Dash Three, mumbled over and over, I told him to pull up. You're too low.

With all the helicopter crews and Delta force aboard, the C-130s were dangerously heavy. To lighten the load, the jeep and motorcycles used by the road watch team were jettisoned, along with a live Claymore anti-personnel mine someone suddenly remembered.

Twenty-three minutes after the crash occurred, the last C-130 took off, bumping across the road with such force that Logan Fitch thought for a moment it had crashed. Vents were opened to relieve the toxic stench of aviation gas. The soldiers stared listlessly up at the stars, wondering if they would get back to the safety of Masirah Island before an Iranian fighter plane shot them out of the sky.

★ ★ ★

Dash Five, which had turned around 110 miles short of Desert One, was still making its way back to the *Nimitz,* a non-stop round trip of nearly 1,000 miles. As Rod Davis approached the coast, the crew rooted about for life jackets, certain that they would run out of fuel before they reached the carrier. They made it, but just barely. The number two engine quit just as Davis was starting to shut the helicopter down, eight hours almost to the minute after its journey had begun.

★ ★ ★

Dick Meadows awoke in his hotel room at one o'clock in the afternoon and heard the news about the crash in the desert on the BBC. The BBC didn't report it, but among the classified materials left at the scene of the crash were maps pinpointing the location of the warehouse where the trucks had been stored. It was only a matter of time before the Iranian authorities showed up at the warehouse and started asking for descriptions of any strangers who had been hanging around there.

Knowing there was no chance of a second rescue attempt, Meadows began looking for a way out. Some of the agents, like Bob Plan, already had reservations on commercial flights out of Tehran. But those like Meadows, Clem, and Scotty who were going to take part in the actual rescue did not have seats booked because they had expected to fly out of Iran with the hostages. Meadows went to the Lufthansa office to purchase a ticket, but the office was still closed for the Iranian weekend. He would have to sweat it out for a while, forcing himself out of his hotel room and into the city, trying to look as if he was going about business as usual, even though that meant taking taxis past large crowds of demonstrators who no doubt would have lynched him had they known who he was.

On Saturday evening Meadows took the elevator down to the hotel lobby. When the elevator doors opened, he found himself face to face with three armed men. There was nothing for him to do but brush past them, without the slightest idea what would happen next. He walked into the hotel gift shop to buy time while he thought about his next move. The three guards were still standing in front of the elevator when he emerged from the gift shop. Meadows crossed the lobby, walked directly in front of the armed men, went up to the hotel cashier to exchange some money, and asked what was going on. The cashier explained that one of Iran's leading political figures was attending a meeting in the hotel and the men by the elevator were his bodyguards.

When the Lufthansa office opened after dusk on Saturday, Meadows bought a ticket on a Sunday-morning flight to Frankfurt. He checked out of the Sheraton at four-thirty Sunday morning and hailed a cab to the airport. On the way, he talked about coming back in two weeks with his fiancée and asked the driver if he would be available to take them to the Caspian Sea. The airport was chaos, the disorder of a society in revolution compounded by the hunt for American spies. Speaking in Farsi, the driver talked his way past several checkpoints while Meadows sat helplessly in the backseat, not knowing what was being said. When the driver finally reached the terminal, a grateful Meadows tipped him handsomely, explaining that part of the money was a retainer for when he returned with his fiancée.

Once inside the terminal, Meadows was on his own, facing a gauntlet of ticket takers, baggage inspectors, and passport stampers. His progress through the line was tedious but smooth until he reached the final station. Just beyond was the waiting room for passengers cleared to board Lufthansa Flight 601. Clem and Scotty were already there. They saw Meadows present his passport at the final station, and for a while it looked as if that was the last they would ever see of him.

Suddenly, the functionary at this final station began gesturing angrily and shouting in pidgin English which Meadows could only vaguely comprehend. It seemed he had skipped an earlier station which he thought, mistakenly, was only for Iranians. As a result, he had failed to get a required stamp on his passport. Someone grabbed him by the arm and whirled him around. A tall, blue-eyed Iranian customs agent marched him back to the station he had skipped. There an Iranian Air Force officer pulled out a folded newspaper and spent what seemed like five minutes alternately looking up at Meadows and down at the paper. Meadows could only guess that the paper contained descriptions of the Westerners who had been seen hanging around the warehouse and that this Iranian officer was trying to decide whether any of those descriptions matched the Westerner standing in front of him. The officer asked Meadows how much money he was carrying and in what currencies. When Meadows told the truth, the officer wanted to know why he had so much. Meadows explained that he was going to use the money to buy chickens for Iran. That seemed to satisfy the officer, who put the required stamp in Meadows's passport and sent him back to the final station. This time he passed muster.

As Meadows entered the boarding area, Clem glanced up over the magazine he was reading and breathed a silent "Whew!" Meadows walked over to a tea counter. Only when his tea cup rattled against the saucer did he realize his hands were shaking.

★   ★   ★

The nation's humiliation was total. Eight Americans had died, their charred corpses left behind to be desecrated by Iranian mullahs. Fifty-two Americans remained hostage, their prospects for release now worse than ever. No one felt the failure more keenly than Charlie Beckwith. When President Carter flew to the CIA base at Camp Peary, Virginia, where Delta was being debriefed in isolation, he found an entirely different man from the self-assured colonel who had briefed him in the White House Situation Room just two weeks before. "When I stepped off the helicopter, Colonel Beckwith was waiting," Carter related. "His chin was quivering and tears were running down his cheeks. I opened my arms and we embraced and wept together. He said, 'Mr. President, I'm sorry we let you down.' " Beckwith seemed a broken man. He lashed out blindly, looking for someone to blame. At the Pentagon, he burst into Army Chief of Staff "Shy" Meyer's office, calling the helicopter pilots cowards, saying he'd been ready to pull his sidearm on one of them in the desert. "I just told him, 'Forget it, Charlie. Those guys were doing the best they could,' " Meyer said.

Within two days of the disaster at Desert One, Carter ordered the Pentagon to begin preparing a second mission. The President was clearly smarting from charges that the first mission had failed because of an insufficiency of force. He directed his Secretary of Defense to make sure the mission planners had every resource they needed, and he told Vaught, who would command this second attempt as well: The only person who won't give you what you need will be me.

Vaught began immediately by commandeering virtually all the long-range helicopters the Pentagon owned and sending them to Norton Air Force Base in California to be fitted for new fuel tanks to extend their range. Within a matter of weeks, Blackhawk helicopters were flying up to 1,200 miles unrefueled—400 miles farther than the RH-53 Sea Stallions left at Desert One. Every helicopter, every airplane, was modified to carry a satellite communications set. This time there would be no confusion caused by the inability to talk with one another.

An Air Force major general named Richard Secord became Vaught's deputy to develop the plan for inserting the helicopters into Iran to pick up the hostages, now scattered in different locations. The plan, code-named "Honey Badger," was more an invasion than a rescue mission. It called for sending in two battalions of Rangers to seize Tehran's main airfield, then flying in the helicopters aboard C-141 transports. The helicopters would be rolled off the transports and launched to the locations where the hostages were being held. At the same time, Delta operatives who had slipped into the country aboard commercial airliners and trucks would be freeing the hostages from their captors. In all, Honey Badger involved more than two thousand men. Despite all the rumors of an "October surprise" designed to salvage Carter's bid for reelection, the rescue force managed to conduct two dress rehearsals at Reese Air Force Base in Texas and cover up a fatal helicopter accident without attracting attention to themselves. "During one exercise," Vaught boasted, "we moved sixty helos and thirty to forty airplanes coast to coast over a four-day period without being detected."

But all the planning and training meant nothing without accurate intelligence on the whereabouts of the hostages. Secord constantly harassed the CIA for better information. He had served in Iran and thought it was an easy intelligence target, with businessmen from every corner of the globe streaming into the country to get in on the ground floor with the new, but still oil-rich, theocracy. Finally, in October, the CIA announced that it had located the hostages: most of them were still in the embassy and the Foreign Ministry where they had been all along, but about two dozen had been moved into two large houses in a posh neighborhood in northern Tehran. The CIA's briefing came complete with photographs of the two houses taken by an agent on the ground. Secord called it "the Eureka briefing."

The trouble was that there were too many clues from other intelligence sources—satellite photographs and communications intercepts—pointing in other directions. The CIA's intelligence was never hard enough to bet a second rescue mission on. In fact, the CIA's intelligence turned out to be, in Secord's words, "incorrect . . . absolutely incorrect."

★　★　★

Hundreds of billions of dollars were invested each year so military forces and the intelligence to guide them would be there when all else failed. In Iran, all else had failed, and then the Pentagon and CIA had failed, too. Had Carter, who came into office vowing to cut the Pentagon budget and corral the rogue CIA, given the military and the intelligence community less than they needed to do the job? Had the military, still bearing the scars of Vietnam, lost its nerve? Or was it just plain incompetent? A commission of active duty and retired military officers headed by the former Chief of Naval Operations, Adm. James Holloway, was appointed to investigate the disaster at Desert One.

The immediate cause of failure was there for all to see: the rescue force had not had enough helicopters. The Holloway Commission concluded that "an unconstrained planner would more than likely have initially required at least ten helicopters . . . and up to twelve using peacetime historical data." The planners were not, of course, unconstrained. More helicopters needed more fuel, and the more fuel that had to be flown into Desert One the more difficult it would be to get out before daybreak. The planners' statistical analyses had indicated that starting with eight helicopters would give them a 97 percent chance of having enough to carry out the mission. Given the hazards of increasing the number of helicopters, a 97 percent chance seemed a chance worth taking.

In fact, neither the planners' nor the commission's statistics meant much because they were all based on the Sea Stallion's performance under normal operating conditions, conditions totally unlike the mission they were being asked to perform. For the RH-53, normal operating conditions amounted to flying at sea level, towing a minesweeping sled behind. Its record under those conditions told little about how it would perform operating 6,000 pounds overweight and in much thinner air 4,000 feet above sea level. Eight helicopters to do the job was at best an educated guess, but then so was twelve.

The number of helicopters was driven by the number of passengers— the rescue force plus fifty-two hostages. Beckwith originally had planned on a force of eighty men, for which eight helicopters would have been more than enough, even by the Holloway Commission's "unconstrained" calculations. But the more Beckwith pondered the details of the operation, the more men he added to his force. The add-ons smacked of overkill, of the American penchant for excess, but the intelligence about what Beckwith would find at the embassy was so deficient that he had no choice but to configure his force for the worst.

Eight helicopters would have been enough if Rod Davis in Dash Five had known the weather was clear at Desert One. Davis told the Holloway Commission he would have pressed on instead of turning back to the *Nimitz* had he known there was an end to the dust cloud which engulfed him. He never knew because the helicopter pilots had been ordered to keep strict radio silence. The Holloway Commission concluded that "the great emphasis on opsec [operational security], although vital to mission success, severely limited the communications necessary to coordinate the operation."

Operational security—the need to maintain secrecy—crippled the mission from the start. At the first hint Delta was coming, the Iranians had only to disperse the hostages and the mission would fail. The Holloway Commission concluded that the concern for secrecy had been excessive and criticized the mission planners for "a seemingly nondiscriminate overemphasis on opsec." But what would the commission have said if the operation had leaked?

The best way to preserve secrecy was to limit the number of people who knew enough about the mission to compromise it. Walling off as many people as possible would reduce the likelihood of leaks; but as the Holloway Commission pointed out, it also had one unintended effect— "plans review was performed largely by those involved in the planning process." In other words, there was no independent critique of the plan, no hard-eyed analyst who did not share pride of authorship in what he was reviewing.

The closest thing to an outside review panel was the Joint Chiefs of Staff, by law the President's principal military advisers. But the chiefs were extremely busy men charged with all the responsibilities of running their respective services. As a result, both Army Chief of Staff "Shy" Meyer and Marine Commandant Robert Barrow, the two service chiefs with the most experience in operations of this kind, said afterwards that they had not asked all the hard questions they should have.

The chiefs approved the plan in the mistaken belief that the mission had been thoroughly rehearsed from start to finish. "Somehow we had it in our heads that this thing had had what one would call a full dress rehearsal," Barrow said. In fact, a test of the Desert One refueling plan, conducted just two days before the chiefs gave their final approval, included only two C-130s and four helicopters. The Holloway Commission found that "the plan for the desert rendezvous was soft," but the chiefs had not dug very hard for soft spots. Like everyone else, they were swept up in the determination to bring the hostage crisis to an end.

Early on, at one of the first Pentagon meetings in which the possibility of a rescue mission was discussed, Marine Commandant Barrow had told Defense Secretary Brown that, Any thought of having any kind of rescue was simply impossible, if not crazy.

That was early on. "A year later, with the pressures . . . that were everywhere, you tended to be more willing to take a risk," Barrow said. "National emotions tended to displace earlier caution."

Vaught, the mission commander, didn't have much use for all this after the fact analysis. As far as he was concerned, the mission had failed for one reason and one reason only: "the Navy's failure to adequately maintain those helicopters." When the Sea Stallions were first dispatched to the Indian Ocean at the start of the hostage crisis, they had just returned from a joint exercise with the Canadians in Nova Scotia where they had been flown long and hard, some of them beyond their recommended maintenance intervals. They were badly in need of upkeep, and an aircraft carrier in the middle of the Indian Ocean was the last place to get it. An aircraft carrier does not ordinarily carry spare parts for the RH-53 Sea Stallion, since it is not part of the ship's normal complement of aircraft. Without spare parts, the helicopters could not even maintain their recommended monthly flying hours—the time in the air needed to keep them in peak operating condition—much less prepare for a mission that would tax them to their limits and beyond. Gradually, an inventory of spare parts had been built up as the Navy diverted its RH-53 supply system to the Indian Ocean, but in the meantime the helicopters had to be grounded. During their first two months in the Indian Ocean, each helicopter was flown only about five hours. Optimum flying time was about thirty hours a month. "We were not happy with what was happening," said Ed Seiffert, who flew Dash One. Beginning in February, though, the helicopters began flying between twenty-five and thirty hours a month, and James Schaefer, the pilot of the doomed Dash Three, said that when he visited the *Nimitz* in March, "I had no worries about maintenance when I left the ship."

Still, the helicopter pilots who arrived aboard the *Nimitz* four days before the mission were hand-carrying parts needed to fix two of the eight aircraft. "The supply system was not being as responsive as required," in delivering spare parts to the ship, Seiffert said. One helicopter—Dash Eight—had not flown in one hundred days. Dash Eight—the hangar queen—had seemed jinxed. Once while being lowered below decks, its tail had been struck by the ship's elevator. On the morning of the mission, a crewman accidentally activated the hangar's fire-fighting system, dousing Dash Eight and four other helicopters with a corrosive mixture of foam and salt water. When an inspection showed that all the doors, hatches, and maintenance bays on Dash Eight and the other helicopters had been securely fastened, the panic receded. The one remaining fear had been that in the process of washing down the helicopters with fresh water, the crew might scrub off the brown paint which had just been applied to make them look like Iranian aircraft.

It was impossible to connect any of these mishaps with anything that went wrong on the night of the mission. Dash Eight, for instance, made it to Desert One and was prepared to continue if the mission had not been aborted. Still, it was hard to resist the conclusion that what the Holloway Commission called the "unexpected helicopter failure rate" was somehow related to the quality of the maintenance performed aboard the *Nimitz.* Dash Five had lost its gyroscope and its electronic aids to navigation; Dash Two had sprung a leak in its primary hydraulic system. But it was the loss of Dash Six, the helicopter which had showed a loss of pressure in one of its main rotor blades, that told the real story of why the mission failed—and it had nothing to do with shoddy maintenance.

The loss of a rotor blade was a show stopper. "There is no way you can fly the aircraft if you lose a blade at the gross weights and air speeds we were flying at," said Dash One's Seiffert. For the pilot, the first warning of an impending blade failure occurred when a small cockpit indicator showed a drop in the pressure of the nitrogen gas sealed inside the rotor blade. The pilot was supposed to land at once, climb on top of his helicopter, and verify the cockpit reading by checking a second indicator attached to the rotor. If that, too, registered a loss of pressure, the pilot was not to fly the helicopter any further, and the blade was to be sent back to the manufacturer to be examined for microscopic cracks. Seiffert himself had experienced a loss of blade pressure while training for the mission in California's Death Valley.

What Seiffert had not known was that there had never been a confirmed blade crack in an RH-53. He did not know that because he was a Marine used to flying CH-53s. The CH version had a titanium blade; the Navy's RH model had an aluminum one. The titanium blades had experienced a total of thirty-one cracks, three of which had resulted in crashes. But after nearly 40,000 flying hours with the RH-53, not one crack had been found in an aluminum blade. "I'm not going to stand here and tell you had I known that I would have changed the abort criteria," Seiffert said. "I will tell you that had I known I *may* have changed the abort criteria, or I would have recommended to my superiors that *they* change the abort criteria." General Vaught, the mission commander, concluded flatly, "We should have said . . . we will not terminate without other indications [of blade failure] such as vibrations."

A helicopter that was almost certainly still in operating condition had dropped out of the mission because one tiny detail had been overlooked. If only Seiffert had known! But he was a Marine officer commanding a squadron of Navy helicopters. That, in microcosm, was why the mission failed. The Joint Chiefs of Staff had found it necessary to artificially join together disparate elements from the services in order to carry out a complex, unconventional mission. Under pressure, the shotgun marriage had fallen apart.

Helicopters and their pilots were absolutely crucial to the mission, yet no unit existed that was remotely qualified for the job. Helicopters were scrounged from one unit, pilots from another, and they were thrown together on a crash basis. The pilots called themselves the "poof squadron" for the way they had disappeared from their regular assignments.

"God, it was a nightmare," Logan Fitch said. "It was a zoo. You've got people who are milk-run aviators, and all of a sudden you throw them into damn night flying . . . I've been in some pretty hairy places, and I've never been more scared than I was riding around in the back of those helicopters." Seiffert had no illusions about his pilots' skills. "We had the best trained people in the world for the mission at hand," he said. "I didn't say we had the best pilots in the world . . . I knew this group of pilots was not the very best of stick and rudder men we had." But Seiffert was operating under orders which said he had to be ready to go on ten days' notice, and under those conditions, he observed, "you do not have the option of taking all those people off to gain access to better qualified aviators." At some point they had to stop looking for better people.

The helicopter pilots were asked to do in ten days what it had taken Delta two years to do—develop special skills and mold themselves into a cohesive fighting unit. "Delta is a very well structured, disciplined, regimented force," Seiffert said. "Our group was an ad hoc organization formed within a matter of days and told to get ready to do the job."

★   ★   ★

Delta had been created in 1977 not so much by the Army as in spite of the Army. There was by then overwhelming evidence that a military response to terrorism was both necessary and possible. The whole world had watched the massacre of Israeli athletes at the 1972 Munich Olympics, a massacre that might have been averted had German police not botched a plan to pick off the Black September terrorists as they marched their hostages across the airport tarmac to their get-away plane. Then, on July 4, 1976, an Israeli C-130 carrying eighty-six paratroopers had touched down at Entebbe Airport in Uganda. In the span of just three minutes, the paratroopers had burst into the terminal building, gunned down four terrorists, and rescued ninety-five passengers of an Air France plane which had been hijacked eight days earlier. Two hostages were killed in the crossfire and one soldier, the paratroop commander, died, but the raid on Entebbe had been a worldwide sensation—a clearcut victory against terrorism.

For "Shy" Meyer, the need to fight back against terrorism had begun to register during the 1973 Arab-Israeli War. Meyer, who was then the Deputy Chief of Staff for Operations for the U.S. Army in Europe, had directed the emergency shipment of American war materiel to Israel. At Munich, Black September already had demonstrated the ability to launch a major terrorist operation in Europe, and Meyer had begun to fret that the emergency shipments to Israel might be targeted. Once the seed was planted, Meyer had realized that local terrorist groups like the

Baader-Meinhof gang could sabotage the phone lines and radio antennas which were a vital part of the Army's command and control network.

At his next assignment in Washington, Meyer had become part of a small cabal lobbying within the ranks for developing a military response to terrorism. His fellow conspirators included Charlie Beckwith, who had been pushing for the creation of an elite counterterrorist unit since 1962 when he spent a year training with Britain's Special Air Service (SAS), and Maj. Gen. Robert Kingston, another veteran of British training who had become the commander of the Army's Special Forces, the Green Berets. There had been one other conspirator, Robert Kupperman, the chief scientist for the Arms Control and Disarmament Agency, a civilian who, by default, was running the federal government's studies on terrorism. "It was very, very hard to find anybody else in the Department of Defense—or for that matter the U.S. government—who was at all interested in [what to do about] a sizable hostage situation abroad," Kupperman remembered.

If any evidence was needed to show that the Pentagon was unprepared to deal with a hostage situation, it had been vividly presented in May of 1975 when forty-one Marines were killed trying to rescue the thirty-nine crewmen of the American merchant ship *Mayaguez* which had been seized by the Cambodian government. "Nobody wanted to think about it," Kupperman said. Nobody except Kupperman, Meyer, Kingston, and Beckwith, who had passed ideas and papers back and forth, an informal counterterrorist network lost in the complacency of the federal bureaucracy. Beckwith already had a name for the unit they hoped to create—Special Forces Operational Detachment Delta—but it had taken several more shocks before Delta became a reality.

★   ★   ★

Creating a new military unit is a major bureaucratic feat, even for a unit as small and secret as Delta was meant to be. To begin with, it requires innovation within an organization that reveres tradition. "Any military organization tends to be conservative," "Shy" Meyer said. "Putting new ideas into it is very difficult." The belief that old and established ways are best is indispensable in an organization with a turnover as high as the American military's. Young men and women—boys and girls, really—enlist for a few years, then leave to be replaced by new recruits. Even veterans change units every two years. Like Henry Ford's assembly line, the system is designed to run on interchangeable parts. Tradition is the common denominator. It keeps the ranks straight, but it also stifles original thinking. The court-martial of Billy Mitchell, who tried in the

1920s to convince the Army that the airplane was the weapon of the future, is only the most melodramatic example of what happens to innovative thinkers who challenge accepted doctrine. And thinking is the easy part. Translating the idea into reality is the hard part. New ideas, said Meyer, are "forced through the meat grinder of conservatism which then spits out hash."

When it came to Delta, tradition weighed double. Delta was to be an unconventional force used against an unconventional enemy. There has never been a fondness or even an understanding of unconventional warfare in the United States military, even though the nation owed its independence to a motley assortment of backwoodsmen and farmers who often fought like Indians but defeated the greatest conventional military power of their day. During World War II, the armed services delegated guerrilla warfare to the Office of Strategic Services. In Korea, Ranger battalions—lightly armed units trained for quick raids behind the lines— were sent to the front as conventional units and decimated on suicidal missions. In Vietnam, Green Berets frequently found themselves assigned the mission they were least equipped to perform—holding ground against attacks by North Vietnamese regulars.

Senior officers who made the decisions about where and how to commit unconventional forces rarely had experience in unconventional warfare. "The largest segment of the military hierarchy has had little or no experience in special operations," Meyer said. "There are people in positions of authority who have no understanding or appreciation of special operations." Most Army generals did not even approve of the berets special operations units were authorized to wear—they were an insult to uniformity. And Delta was even worse, since the concept envisioned soldiers with long hair and shaggy beards who could pass as civilians. Worse still, Delta was modeled after a foreign unit, the British SAS. It was, to use Meyer's phrase, "unconventional unconventional."

On another level, a proposal to create a new unit represents an acknowledgment that there is a mission the present array of forces cannot perform—an admission of failure, in other words. Billy Mitchell at least could argue that a new technology, the airplane, was changing the nature of warfare. The case for Delta was just the opposite. It rested on the fact that all the new technology in which the Army was investing so heavily—tanks, helicopters, air defense guns, armored personnel carriers, and all the other machinery of the modern-day battlefield—was useless against terrorists.

Even when the void was recognized and the need for an unconventional force grudgingly accepted, the Army still looked upon Delta not as the answer to a problem but as an additional drain on limited resources. The money and manpower for Delta would have to come out of someone else's hide. The money, at least, was a relatively small amount—hundreds of millions in a budget of tens of billions—but Delta was supposed to be manned only by the best soldiers, and no commander likes to give up his best soldiers.

★   ★   ★

Another shock occurred in March of 1977, when a small religious sect called the Hanafi Muslims seized three buildings in downtown Washington. The Hanafis held a total of 139 hostages and were threatening to kill them all if their demands for revenge against a rival Muslim sect were not met. While negotiations dragged on, FBI and police teams surrounded the three buildings, looking for a way to end the standoff by force if it came to that. The FBI called General Kingston, the commander of the Army's Special Forces, in the middle of the night at Fort Bragg to ask if he could put Bureau SWAT teams on the rooftops in helicopters. Kingston said he could, but that was as far as the matter went.

The Hanafis surrendered peacefully, providing what President Carter called "vivid proof that a slow and careful approach was the effective way." In fact, it had been the only way, since the capability to end the standoff with force simply had not existed. The Hanafi Muslim siege had exposed just how poorly prepared the government was to use force against terrorism. If the United States government did not have the option of force in the nation's capital where it had total control of the surroundings, how would it ever come to the aid of Americans held hostage overseas? That would be the job of the armed services, but the military's only contribution to ending the Hanafi Muslim siege had been the shots it didn't fire—a twenty-one-gun salute for a visiting head of state which was called off at the last minute for fear of spooking the Hanafis.

Kingston summoned Charlie Beckwith and told him to draw up a budget and table of organization for a new counterterrorist unit. "We grossly underestimated the budget," Beckwith later confessed, "because at the time I was afraid that if Delta carried too big a price tag, we'd scare the Army off." On June 2, 1977, five years after Munich, two years after *Mayaguez,* one year after Entebbe, the concept of a counterterrorist team was presented for the first time to Army Chief of Staff Gen. Bernard Rogers. Rogers gave the project his blessing, but it took still another terrorist incident to breathe life into Delta.

On October 19, 1977, a squad of West German commandos known as

GSG 9 stormed a hijacked Lufthansa 737 sitting on the tarmac in Mogadishu, Somalia, rescued all eighty-six passengers, killed three terrorists, and captured a fourth. Even more than Entebbe, Mogadishu offered stunning proof that it was possible to use military force against terrorists in a way that could save the lives of hostages. Israel was a nation perpetually at war and prepared to run risks that a country at peace would not. At Mogadishu, the West Germans had shown it was possible for a nation at peace to wage war successfully against terrorists.

Beckwith was in the Pentagon the day GSG 9 stormed the Lufthansa jet. A frantic officer rushed up to him, asking if he knew what a "flash bang" was, and if he did would he please see the chief of staff immediately. Beckwith explained to General Rogers that a "flash bang" was a stun grenade whose concussive force and blinding flash incapacitated its victims without killing them. GSG 9 had used them in Mogadishu. As Beckwith later recounted it, "General Rogers told me of a note from the President. It had surfaced in the tank [the room where the Joint Chiefs of Staff meet] earlier in the day." The handwritten note was addressed "To Harold and Zbig" and directed his Secretary of Defense and national security adviser to find out how West Germany and Israel had developed such effective counterterrorist forces. "Ask Schmidt (or perhaps Begin) for a thorough briefing on handling terrorists. Develop similar U.S. capabilities." One month later, on November 19, 1977, Delta was officially activated, with Charlie Beckwith as its commander. The American military had finally been embarrassed into joining the war against terrorism.

Beckwith said he would need two years to build the Delta force. To begin with, he needed about thirty-five men who could be trained to serve as instructors for the rest of the force. He sent 150 volunteers to the Uwharrie National Forest in North Carolina for a selection course lifted straight out of the SAS manual. Cecil "Bud" Morgan, an Army sergeant who had served in both Rangers and Special Forces, was one of the first to go through the Uwharrie selection—in the dead of winter, living in open tents. "Everything was done on an individual basis. There was no teamwork whatsoever. No one would wake you up. They would just tell you what time to be at a certain point out front. You were put on a truck, taken to a dropoff point, given a set of coordinates [for the next rendezvous point]. You had to make it there as fast as possible. Mountainous terrain. No trails or roads. Your rucksack started out at forty-five pounds and went up to seventy-five pounds. You don't know how many rendezvous points there would be. When you get to the first, you would be given another point. Each leg was five, six, seven klicks [kilometers]. This continued all day. You'd say to yourself, 'This has got to be the last one.' You get there, and they give you another. Every day for five, six, seven, eight days. They would just wear you down, see who would quit. Each night you'd come in and there would be ten spaces in the tent empty. The next day ten to fifteen more would be gone. A lot of people didn't drop out voluntarily. Some got messed up in land navigation. Also, in the physical condition you're in, accidents happen, like you step in a rotted stump hole. We had a ninety percent failure rate."

The survivors were then given a battery of psychological tests. "It's easy to find studs," said Logan Fitch, one of Delta's original officers and a member of its selection board. "I was looking for a combination of physical capability, mental dedication, and native intelligence. Is he something more than the typical Ranger—you know, a fifty-inch chest and a two-inch head—so one of the things you do is ask the basic question that has no good answer and see how the guy handles it."

"We looked for loners," Beckwith wrote. "Guys who could operate independently and in the absence of orders, men who had just half an ounce of paranoia." They were, according to Fitch, the elite of the elite. "When you get a Special Forces team or a Ranger squad, you have one or two leaders who stand head and shoulders above all the rest. In Delta, we had taken those people. Everyone in there was a leader . . . a group of really superb soldiers and over-achievers. I mean, I thought *I* was really what's happening, but when I got in Delta, I felt inferior."

Although the men selected for Delta had all the military skills anyone could want, those skills were not particularly useful in fighting terrorism. None of their prior military training had taught them how to take down an airplane: what to do if the target was a 737 instead of a 727, how much fuel had to be in the tanks before it was safe to crawl along the wings without rocking the plane. Even the most elite soldiers did not know how to dive through a window into a darkened room and come up firing a "double tap"—two shots to the groin with a .45-caliber revolver. For that and much, much more, survivors of the selection phase had to complete a six-month Operator Training Course.

Delta prepared for several different hostage scenarios—in buildings, on airplanes, and out in the open—but they all had one thing in common. They occurred in foreign countries where the host government had invited Delta to end the standoff. The model for this so-called "permissive environment" was GSG 9's Mogadishu operation. Delta never trained for the "nonpermissive environment" the Israelis had encountered at Entebbe, where the host government was in league with the terrorists.

Events would expose this predilection for the Mogadishu model to be a fundamental error. It is always easy to pinpoint mistakes in retrospect, but this basic flaw had been exposed early on—and simply ignored. In the summer of 1978, two CIA officers, Howard Bane, head of the CIA's office on terrorism, and Burr Smith, the agency's liaison with Delta, toured Europe and the Middle East, briefing the local CIA station chiefs on Delta and, in much more guarded terms, sounding out the various governments about their willingness to let Delta step in if American lives were threatened by terrorists. The reactions, which Bane and Smith recorded in a memo, were uniformly, sometimes vehemently, negative. No sovereign country was about to permit a foreign military force to operate on its territory. Mogadishu was not the model for future operations but the exception.

There was one other loose underpinning to the Delta concept—intelligence about the nature of the terrorist threat. The CIA and the Defense Intelligence Agency [DIA] had over the years become expert at amassing detailed data on the numbers and capabilities of Soviet weapons. But terrorism was an altogether different intelligence target, one with no weapons of any consequence to count and no technical specifications to calibrate. "We were casting about desperately trying to put together a terrorist data base," said Wade Ishimoto, who headed Delta's small intelligence staff.

The two years Beckwith had been given to build Delta expired in November of 1979. Delta's final exam was held at Hunter Army Air Field at Fort Stewart, Georgia, ending in the early morning hours of Sunday, November 4. Delta was now officially certified as America's counterterrorist unit. As Delta members and exercise observers rehashed the test over drinks in their motel rooms, a mob was scaling the walls of the American Embassy in Tehran.

★   ★   ★

The United States had the Delta force, but it did not have a strategy for combatting terrorism. The Pentagon had an unparalleled group of shooters but that was all it had. Delta had none of the support mechanisms—intelligence, logistics—it needed to become an effective combat unit. Confronted with the task of developing a plan for rescuing the hostages in Tehran, the Joint Chiefs of Staff had, in the words of the Holloway Commission, "to start literally from the beginning to . . . create an organization, provide a staff, develop a plan, select the units, and train the force before the first mission capability could be obtained."

It had taken half a year to assemble and train the rescue force. The failure of the mission had been the fault not of the men who conducted it but of the men who had thrown them together. It was perhaps understandable, given the short rations and low esteem accorded the military and the intelligence community in the years following Vietnam, but it was a failure nevertheless. "We should have had the capability already," "Shy" Meyer said. "We were derelict in not having the capability."

★   ★   ★

In the end, the combined military and intelligence capabilities of the world's most powerful nation contributed little to the resolution of the hostage crisis. In the end, events over which the Carter administration had absolutely no control forced the Iranians to negotiate. On September 22, 1980, Iraq invaded Iran and started what would become the bloodiest conflict since World War II. With its national survival at stake, Iran needed money and weapons more than it needed hostages. Specifically, Iran needed the billions of dollars which sat in American banks, frozen by order of the Carter administration and the billions of dollars worth of U.S. military equipment the Shah had bought but which was now locked up in American warehouses.

As the American presidential election approached, the Iranians apparently decided that they would get a better deal before the election than after, that a President fighting for his political life was more likely to compromise than one assured of four years in office. In their first official approach to the United States, the Iranians specified that an agreement to terminate the crisis be worked out by November 4, 1980.

Once events presented Carter with an opening, he capitalized on it in admirable fashion, stubbornly refusing to compromise on any matters of principle, refusing, for instance, to lift the arms embargo against Iran. In their haste to settle, the Iranians accepted a bad deal—agreeing to the return of $8 billion of the $12 billion in assets that had been frozen.

But nothing in the fine print of the agreement could conceal the fact that for fourteen months American foreign policy had been paralyzed and a presidential campaign overshadowed by the hostages. Each day had added to the perception of American impotence and, after the failed rescue mission, incompetence. The United States could not afford to let that happen again, and Ronald Reagan set out to see that it wouldn't.

★ 2 ★

"SWIFT AND EFFECTIVE RETRIBUTION"

"Let terrorists beware that when the rules of international behavior are violated, our policy will be one of swift and effective retribution," declared the new President of the United States. It was January 27, 1981, and if ever there was a new beginning, it was this day. After 444 days of captivity, the hostages were home.

Hundreds of thousands lined the streets of the capital, surging forward in a delirious crush as the buses carrying the hostages and their families to the White House passed. Now the new President, inaugurated just seven days earlier, was standing on the White House lawn vowing to fight back against terrorism. "We hear it said that we live in an era of limits to our power," he intoned. "Well, let it also be understood there are limits to our patience." All the agony, humiliation, and frustration of the past fourteen months seemed to have vanished. There was Bruce Laingen, the senior American official among the hostages, giving thanks "for the way in which this crisis has strengthened the spirit and resilience and strength that is the mark of a truly free society." There was Charlie Beckwith, his old cocky, charismatic self, resplendent in his battle ribbons and his Green Beret, no longer the broken man who had limped home from Iran in shame.

★   ★   ★

America was out of Iran, but it was not free of Iran. At the same time Ronald Reagan was setting forth to reassert American power in the world, Iran was preparing to spread the Ayatollah Khomeini's Islamic revolution beyond its borders. For Khomeini and his disciples, Iran was the "redeemer nation," the only country to have established "the government of God." Now it was time, in Khomeini's words, "to establish divine justice in the world"; in other words "to overthrow all treacherous, corrupt, oppressive and criminal regimes," by which he meant any government that did not live by the dictates of the Koran as interpreted by the mullahs. "Islam is a sacred trust from God to ourselves and the Iranian nation must grow in power and resolution until it has vouchsafed Islam to the entire world," Khomeini preached.

No one in the United States knew it at the time, but one of the leaders of the students who had seized the American Embassy had just been rewarded for his role in humbling the Great Satan with a sensitive new job in the Foreign Ministry. His name was Hosein Sheikholislam.

Born on November 29, 1952, Sheikholislam had grown up in Isfahan, Iran's second largest city and the home during the Shah's reign to some 11,000 American military advisers and dependents. He had been plucked from a middle-class family in 1971 and sent to school in the United States at his government's expense; he was part of the Shah's feverish effort to westernize Iran. He had entered the University of California at Davis and then transferred to the College of Engineering at Berkeley, but he had dropped out in 1975, three months short of graduation. While living in the Bay area, the young Iranian had witnessed first-hand how grabbing a hostage could capture America's attention. In 1974, he had lived just two and a half blocks from the apartment where a group of terrorists calling themselves the Symbionese Liberation Army had kidnapped newspaper heiress Patricia Hearst.

Sheikholislam's own politics had grown increasingly radical as he had been swept up in the campaign to topple the Shah. He had presided over anti-Shah meetings at Berkeley and had become a fervent supporter of the Ayatollah Khomeini. He was last seen in Berkeley in the spring of 1979, reemerging in early November at the U.S. Embassy in Tehran. Nicknamed "Gaptooth" by his captives because of a chipped front tooth, Sheikholislam spoke fluent, idiomatic English and appeared on American television reading CIA files seized in the takeover of the embassy. Just 28, Sheikholislam was to become one of the chief architects of the campaign to spread the Islamic revolution through subversion and terror.

Much of the work of spreading the revolution was done in a heavily guarded, four-story concrete building in downtown Tehran called the Taleghani Center. With Revolutionary Guards, the fanatical enforcers of the revolution, posted outside, the center served as headquarters for revolutionary movements from Iraq, Saudi Arabia, Kuwait, Bahrain, Lebanon, even the Philippines. Thousands of Shiite youths from throughout the Muslim world flocked to Iran to answer the call of the Taleghani Center. Met at Mehrabad Airport and dispersed to training camps run by the Revolutionary Guards, they were soon sent back to their homelands to set up revolutionary cells. Although the cells, which were often based on family ties, operated in all but impenetrable secrecy, their strategy was plain enough. "We have announced that we are for the export of the revolution," said Hashemi Rafsanjani, the speaker of the Iranian parliament. "We have launched an Islamic movement and Islam must prevail in the region."

The Iran crisis had not ended with the return of the hostages. Rather, it had entered a new and deadlier phase.

★   ★   ★

Later, Ronald Spiers, head of the State Department's Bureau of Intelligence and Research, remembered standing there on the White House lawn thinking Reagan would regret the day he had vowed "swift and effective retribution" against terrorism. In his post as the State Department's chief intelligence officer, he understood too well how little the United States knew about this new enemy. Frank Perez, the deputy director of the State Department's Office for Combatting Terrorism, had the same reaction. "My own personal feeling was that 'swift and effective retribution' against an enemy that you can't really identify is a very iffy proposition," Perez recalled. Even though he was the number two man in the Office for Combatting Terrorism, which was supposed to be in charge of the government's policy toward terrorism, Perez had not known the President was going to take this public vow.

The President's vow also had come as a surprise to the head of the Office for Combatting Terrorism, Anthony Quainton. Just the day before, on the first Monday of the Reagan administration, Quainton had briefed the country's new national security establishment—the President and Vice President, the Secretaries of State and Defense, the President's national security adviser, the heads of the CIA, the FBI, and the Secret Service, along with senior White House aides. They had all gathered in the Cabinet Room to confront the problem that, with the possible exceptions of arms control and aid to freedom fighters, would become the dominant foreign policy issue of the decade. They had listened politely for half an hour as Quainton stood behind a podium and outlined all that the federal government had done to combat terrorism—everything from Delta to the various interagency working groups that met to implement

U.S. policy on terrorism. Quainton later admitted to feeling a little defensive, knowing he was viewed by most of the men in the room as the symbol of the Carter administration's failure to take effective action against terrorism. Quainton felt quite a bit had been done, but then he held a much less alarmist view of what needed to be done. "My view was that it was a manageable threat," Quainton recalled.

There had been a sea change in terrorism over the last decade. In the past, terrorism usually had been the work of ethnic or separatist groups that confined themselves to small geographic areas and very selective targets—the Basque separatists in Spain, the Irish nationalists in Northern Ireland. Beginning in the late 1960s, however, terrorism went ideological with the founding of left-wing groups like the Red Brigades in Italy and the Red Army Faction in West Germany that began seeking out "imperialist" targets, particularly in the major cities of the Western democracies. In 1980, for the first time, U.S. diplomats outnumbered American businessmen as the most frequent victims of terrorist attacks, a rather startling fact since there were so many more businessmen than diplomats. Over the years, five U.S. ambassadors had been killed by terrorists, more than the number of American generals killed in Vietnam.

There also was the new phenomenon of state-supported terrorism—nations resorting to terrorist tactics to obtain concessions that they could never win through traditional diplomatic or military means. State-sponsored terrorism tended to be the deadliest form of terrorism, with nearly half of the incidents resulting in deaths or injuries. The only good news about state-sponsored terrorism was that Americans were rarely its targets. With the exception of the embassy seizure in Iran, such terrorism consisted of assassins from one Middle Eastern country killing diplomats from another Middle Eastern country, most of the time in Lebanon.

In 1980, international terrorism had caused more casualties than in any year since the CIA started compiling statistics in 1968. Americans were the primary targets. Nearly two out of every five incidents involved U.S. citizens or property. There had been a total of 278 terrorist incidents involving Americans in 1980; 10 U.S. citizens had been killed and 94 injured. Ten Americans killed was, of course, a very small number—fewer than had been killed by lightning that same year. It was, perhaps, worth asking what all the fuss was about. Was terrorism really a threat to national security; or was it just an attention-getting device? Would terrorism be a threat if it weren't for all the "America held hostage" publicity? As the conservative intellectual Walter Laqueur snidely put it, "our media resemble the Bedouin warriors described by Lawrence of Arabia, who were sturdy fighters except for their mistaken belief that weapons were dangerous in proportion to the noise they created."

No matter what the death toll, no one in the Cabinet Room that Monday had to be convinced that terrorism was a matter of vital significance. After all, the fact that this group of men was sitting around that table in the White House was due at least in part to a terrorist incident in which none of the hostages had died.

When Quainton finished his briefing, Edwin Meese, the President's Counsellor, wanted to know if the efforts to combat terrorism were in any way hampered by the restrictions that had been placed upon the CIA and other intelligence agencies by the Ford and Carter administrations. FBI director William Webster and deputy CIA director Bob Inman, the only bona fide intelligence professionals present, explained that restrictions were not the real problem. The lack of resources, the steady cutback of money and personnel which had begun with the end of the Vietnam War, was the real problem.

The intelligence community had lost a quarter of its people over the decade of the seventies. Less than half the CIA's intelligence analysts now spoke the language of the country they were assigned to cover, and an even smaller proportion had ever visited the country about which they were supposed to be expert. Furthermore, the CIA was about to suffer another major loss of talent since fully three fourths of its station chiefs overseas were eligible for retirement. The only new initiative in intelligence had been to develop the technical capabilities needed to verify arms control treaties with the Soviet Union. The low-tech, labor-intensive job of recruiting informants, conducting surveillance, and piecing it all together into a meaningful picture of the terrorist threat had been paid only lip service. Not even a massive infusion of funds could turn the situation around quickly. The pipeline was dry. The intelligence agencies did not even have enough people to do the recruiting, run the security clearances, and conduct the training needed to rebuild their strength.

Before the meeting broke up, the new administration had set itself three tasks: to relieve some of the restrictions that hampered the collection of intelligence; to come up with a five-year investment plan for revitalizing the nation's intelligence capabilities; and to take a fresh look at all existing intelligence on terrorism to see what really was known. In short order, the CIA directed its stations around the world to elevate terrorism on their lists of "Essential Elements of Intelligence." In some countries, it became the agency's number one priority. But as Quainton pointed out, a simple reordering of priorities would not necessarily improve the quality of the intelligence. "It's easy enough to say your collection priority is terrorism," Quainton later reflected. "But if you don't have the sources, you can't create the sources overnight." In view of the admitted lack of intelligence on the terrorist threat, the President's brave words the next day at the ceremonies welcoming the hostages home seemed like so much whistling in the dark.

"Swift and effective retribution" had come from Kenneth Adelman, a brash young member of the Reagan transition team who had traveled to West Germany with now ex-President Carter to greet the hostages on their way home from Iran. Returning to Washington ahead of the hostages, Adelman briefed the new President and his aides on their condition, reporting that their treatment had been much worse than anyone realized. According to Adelman, CIA doctors told him that some of the hostages had been beaten with rubber hoses. One hostage, a CIA officer, had been kept in solitary confinement the entire time. Adelman could see that the President was "very disturbed" by what he was telling him and wanted to ask a question. But each time the President started to speak, aides jumped in first with questions of their own. Finally, Reagan got his chance and asked, What about the ladies? Adelman assured him that there was no evidence the women had been sexually abused. That took the edge off the President's anger, but he was still receptive to Adelman's suggestion that now was the time to make a strong statement about terrorism. Adelman returned to his office in the State Department and drafted the phrase "swift and effective retribution," a statement he would later come to recognize as a mistake. At the time, Adelman said, "it just sounded good," and he had no doubt Reagan would make good on his threat.

Neither, apparently, did Alexander Haig. "International terrorism will take the place of human rights in our concern because it is the ultimate abuse of human rights," Haig told his first press conference as Secretary of State. Without knowing what it was talking about, the Reagan administration was giving the war against terrorism the same high profile that the Carter administration had given the campaign for human rights, which for many had symbolized Carter's naiveté in thinking he could impose his own morality on the rest of the world. On top of that, Haig accused the Soviet Union of "training, funding and equipping" international terrorists. The Soviets, Haig said, "today are involved in conscious policies, in programs, if you will, which foster, support and expand this activity, which is hemorrhaging in many respects throughout the world today."

According to Ronald Spiers, Haig privately expressed even harsher views about the Soviet role in terrorism. "Haig said some things in the staff meetings about how the Soviets were using international terrorism as a weapon against the West," Spiers recalled. "He believed that Moscow controlled the terrorist *apparat.* At first, I thought he was kidding."

Spiers sent Haig a short paper prepared by the Intelligence and Research staff during the Carter administration which concluded that while there was some evidence of collusion, terrorist groups essentially operated independently, both of Moscow and of each other. Haig sent the paper back to Spiers with a handwritten note in the margin: If you really believe this hogwash, you've been brainwashed.

Stints as White House chief of staff during the final days of the Nixon administration and as NATO commander had not satisfied Haig's burning ambition. He was determined to take control of the nation's foreign policy, and he was not about to let any soft-headed foreign service officers stand in his way. Most of them, he once declared, were Democrats, anyway. Haig surrounded himself with a coterie of yesmen, and when the bureaucracy had the temerity to disagree with him, as it did on the issue of terrorism, he turned to a battery of special assistants; to his counselor, Robert McFarlane; or to ambassador-at-large Vernon Walters, a former deputy director of the CIA, sometimes dispatching them on secret missions without telling anybody else. Within two months of taking office, Haig was feuding with Defense Secretary Caspar Weinberger and the Joint Chiefs of Staff, who did not share his enthusiasm for saber-rattling and gunboat diplomacy. Once, after Weinberger ordered the Sixth Fleet to steam away from a simmering Israeli-Syrian clash in Lebanon, a fuming Haig told his aides the Defense Secretary was a bozo.

Haig's distrust of the bureaucracy, his disdain for the Pentagon's habitual caution, and his penchant for running his own secret operations would finally reach full flower not in the State Department, but in the Reagan White House, which was ironic. The Secretary of State could never conceal his contempt for the President's men, whom he egotistically considered a bunch of amateurs ceaselessly plotting against him. Asked about his relations with the White House staff, Haig thrust out his chin, rolled his eyes, and demanded: "Have you ever met Ed Meese? My God!" Angered by Haig's tantrums, Meese and the other Californians around Reagan would eventually get even by unceremoniously dumping him after seventeen months in office.

Haig's strong feelings about terrorism were understandable. In 1978, five days before he was to retire as NATO commander, Haig had narrowly missed being blown up by a remote-control bomb which exploded almost directly under his limousine. The blast lifted the Mercedes into the air, gouged a 10-foot crater in the road, and demolished a pursuit car carrying his three bodyguards. No one was killed, but had the bomb detonated a fraction of a second earlier, Haig almost certainly would not have survived. Robert McFarlane, an old friend whom Haig had brought in as State Department Counselor, told Spiers the attempt on Haig's life was a "seminal" event.

If that brush with death had brought home the menace of terrorism in a way that only a victim could understand, it also demonstrated the elusive nature of the threat. Several groups claimed responsibility for the attack on Haig, but no one was ever apprehended. West German police said the attack was almost certainly the work of "left-wing circles" attempting to knock off one of the most visible symbols of American power in Europe. Privately, a low-level West German intelligence officer told Haig the attack had been directed by the Soviets, but his superiors said they had no evidence to support the charge. Scotland Yard thought the blast was the work of a radical cell of the Irish Republican Army which had mistaken Haig for a senior British officer. Against whom would a President order "swift and effective retribution" in this instance?

It was not surprising that the combined resources of Western intelligence and police agencies frequently were left fencing with shadows; that was precisely what the terrorists intended. Yet here was Haig, reaching behind the shadows to spotlight the Soviet Union as the hidden hand behind international terrorism. In fact, he was saying no more than a few European officials already had said. In 1979, for instance, Hans Josef Horchem, head of West Germany's Office for the Defense of the Constitution, stated flatly: "The KGB is engineering international terrorism. The facts can be proven, documented, and are well known to the international Western intelligence community."

By virtue of who he was, Haig's remarks carried more weight. In a few sentences, he brought to the fore an issue that had been smoldering in Europe for years. His words were given staying power by the publication of a book called *The Terror Network* by an American expatriate journalist, Claire Sterling. Her thesis was simple: "there is such a thing as an international terrorist circuit, or network, or fraternity . . . a multitude of disparate terrorist groups . . . helping one another out and getting help from not altogether disinterested outsiders." The "outsiders" were the Soviets and their satellites who helped the terrorists obtain the money, weapons, training, and international connections needed to be effective. "The Soviet Union had simply laid a loaded gun on the table, leaving others to get on with it," Sterling wrote. "It was never part of the Soviet design to create and watch over native terrorist movements, still less attempt to direct their day-to-day activities. . . . The whole point of the plan was to let the other fellow do it . . . terror by proxy."

The Terror Network was a prodigious piece of research, pulling together much that had been reported in the European press and testified to in European courts and making it accessible to the American public for the first time. But to those in the American intelligence community whose job it was to keep track of these matters, it was nothing new. As far back as 1976, the CIA had noted the "trend toward greater international contact and cooperation among terrorist groups." In an unclassified research paper, a CIA analyst pointed out, among other things, that members of the Baader-Meinhof gang had helped Black September prepare the attack on the Israeli athletes at the 1972 Olympic Games in Munich. As for the Soviet role, the same report said that Moscow's longstanding policy of indoctrinating and training Third World revolutionaries had produced a number of people who subsequently cropped up on the international terrorism scene—most notably the infamous "Carlos," leader of the 1975 kidnapping of oil ministers in Vienna. The CIA report went on to say that "there is also a considerable body of circumstantial evidence linking Moscow to various terrorist formations in Western Europe." Since then, the issue had dropped from sight. During the Carter administration, the CIA continued to publish annual research papers on international terrorism but made no mention of the Soviet role. As the State Department's Anthony Quainton put it, "although the facts were known, they were not being spoken about." Now Haig had spoken with all the authority and visibility of an American Secretary of State. As an afterthought, he asked the intelligence community to produce a National Intelligence Estimate (NIE) of the Soviet role in terrorism.

★   ★   ★

NIEs are both the best and worst the intelligence community has to offer—the best because they bring together all that is known about a given subject; the worst because they are the product of a committee. An NIE is an "all source" document based on intelligence collected from agents, defectors, reconnaissance satellites, communications intercepts, and any other sources available to the U.S. government. The facts contained in an NIE are rarely in dispute. The hard part is reconciling all the differing interpretations of the facts. The fewer the facts, the more diverse the interpretations as opinions rush in to fill the void.

Each intelligence agency—the Pentagon's Defense Intelligence Agency (DIA) and the State Department's Bureau of Intelligence and Research (INR), in particular—reflects the proclivities of its parent department. The DIA takes the most alarming view of the facts, a view which usually buttresses a Defense Department request for money to develop a weapons system that can counter the alarming development. INR usually arrives at a more benign interpretation of the facts, an interpretation which supports the State Department view that the matter can be handled through normal diplomatic exchanges without political or military confrontation. The CIA, which has no parent department, usually ends up somewhere in the middle, preferring to "let the facts speak for themselves" as the surest way to avoid the possibility of being proved wrong by events. Writing for an in-house CIA publication, one veteran NIE drafter described the state of the art: "The wise drafter will stop and point in both directions."

In theory, the creative tension of these competing analyses should produce a sharper document, one that incorporates the best of each. In practice, the competing analyses usually produce an intellectual stalemate—a Supreme Court ruling without a majority opinion. The semantic gymnastics the agencies go through trying to accommodate all points of view often make for impenetrable reading and neutered conclusions. The process is not dishonest, merely human, but the result is frequently a sterile NIE, a colossal waste of time for both producers and consumers. A presidential commission concluded in 1975 that NIEs "appear to have little impact on policy makers."

Over the years, the directors of Central Intelligence—the men who actually sign the NIEs—had attempted various bureaucratic solutions to the problem. The latest was a four-member Senior Review Group which went over each NIE in an effort to make it more relevant to policymakers. The members were of sufficient intellectual stature to deal with the brightest of analysts, of sufficient government experience to know what policymakers needed to know, and of sufficient age to be beyond ambition and the desire to please anyone but themselves. The four served as advisers to the National Intelligence Council, a panel made up of about a dozen National Intelligence Officers—senior analysts, many of them recruited from outside the Agency. Each had specific areas of responsibility—the Middle East, Latin America, Soviet strategic forces, international narcotics, technology transfer, etc.—and oversaw the production of NIEs in those areas. There was a menu of NIEs to be produced each year; some of them, like the estimate on Soviet strategic forces, ran to several volumes and took the entire year to write. The director of Central Intelligence could, of course, order up an estimate on a topic not on the menu. That would be a Special National Intelligence Estimate, or SNIE.

In 1981, no National Intelligence Officer was responsible for terrorism, so the task of producing a SNIE on the Soviet role in international terrorism fell to Jeremy Azrael, the officer responsible for the Soviet Union. He had no expertise in terrorism, but at least he was an acknowledged authority on the Soviet Union. He also knew a minefield when he saw one. With Haig having spoken first and asked for the estimate later, there was more than a hint of political pressure to make the intelligence conform to the policy. "Everybody considered this an important test case for the integrity of the intelligence process," Azrael said. "It was interesting to watch the CIA dig in its heels when it felt an attempt was being made to politicize it. It was just palpable inside the building. It was very impressive in a lot of ways, this determination to protect the integrity of the agency." Whatever evidence existed on Soviet support for terrorism would be sifted through the finest sieve possible.

What was terrorism, anyway? One research guide cited 109 different definitions of terrorism set forth between 1936 and 1981. As the original CIA research paper in 1976 had pointed out, "one man's terrorist is another man's freedom fighter." The first draft of the intelligence estimate defined terrorists by their intentions. Those groups whose intentions were to commit violence against innocent victims were considered terrorist groups. The definition meant that the estimate dealt only with "nihilistic" groups like the Baader-Meinhof gang in West Germany and the Red Brigades in Italy, groups that had no identifiable political program other than to lash out at symbols of the status quo. It ignored groups like the Irish Republican Army [IRA] and the Palestine Liberation Organization [PLO] which used violence as a means to achieve a political goal, to gain a homeland or some other type of political recognition. "It seemed to me it was much too narrowly drawn," said Lincoln Gordon, the member of the Senior Review Group who was asked to critique the first draft. "The effect of defining terrorism that narrowly was to rule out many cases where the Soviets might be actively involved," said Gordon, a former ambassador and university president. "The finding that the Soviets didn't have much to do with nihilistic terrorism was probably correct."

The first draft posed an artificially easy question and came up with an artificially reassuring answer. CIA director William Casey received a strongly worded memo from Lt. Gen. Eugene Tighe, head of DIA, stating that the estimate was grossly inadequate and grossly understated the Soviet contribution to international terrorism. Casey agreed, and so did his deputy, Bob Inman, who wrote on the initial draft: This reads like the prosecution's argument on why we decided not to prosecute. Casey invited the DIA to produce a draft which, according to Gordon, went to the other extreme. "It went whole hog, took every kind of national liberation movement, every left-wing movement that used violence, and called them terrorists."

The DIA draft was the work of Dr. Wynfred Joshua, a tiny spitfire who was known throughout the intelligence community for her virulently anti-Soviet views. Gordon wrote a memo complaining that under her definition George Washington, Robert E. Lee and Simon Bolivar would all be terrorists. At the State Department, Ronald Spiers wrote a memo urging Casey to call the effort off. The facts were agreed upon, but the analysts were so tangled up in the definition of terrorism that there was no prospect of shedding new light on the issue. Casey ignored Spiers's memo. This was his first special estimate, and he was determined to complete it, if nothing else just for the exercise.

Casey asked Gordon to take over the estimate. Richard Mansbach, a political scientist on a two-year leave from Rutgers University, was assigned to assist Gordon. Like Gordon, Mansbach was in, but not of, the CIA and had no career concerns to cloud his judgment. Unlike Gordon, Mansbach had some expertise in the field.

Mansbach agreed with Gordon that the definition used in the initial draft was "ridiculous." The two decided they would define terrorist groups by what they did, not what they wanted. That made terrorism a behavioral phenomenon—the use of violence against innocent victims and directed at an audience other than the victims. Motives—so elusive in any event—no longer mattered.

The issue of Soviet support for groups that practiced terrorism remained, however, a complicated one. The Libyan connection was a case in point. Weapons Libya had purchased from the Soviet Union showed up in the hands of groups engaged in terrorism. Was that what the Soviets intended? "There were reasonable and plausible arguments on both sides," Mansbach recalled. "It was perfectly clear that sales of weapons were a vital source of hard currency for the Soviet Union. On the other hand, you could argue sincerely that the Soviets must know what was going on. You could not judge conclusively. All you could state was that the Soviets were an indirect source of arms."

In fact, the estimate found that the Soviet Union was much more than an indirect source of arms. The Soviets were, to use Inman's term, "the grandparents" of modern-day terrorism. Moscow's involvement had begun in the wake of the 1967 Arab-Israeli War when a major shift in Palestinian strategy coincided with a Soviet determination to insert itself more firmly into the Middle East. The Israeli victory had exposed the powerlessness of conventional Arab armies. If Israel could not be defeated by conventional force of arms, the Palestinians would have to take up arms themselves, would have to mount a guerrilla war against Israel, as the Algerians had against France, or the Viet Cong against the United States. As in any guerrilla war, terror would be used to demonstrate

Palestinian power and to goad Israel into repressive countermeasures that would further alienate refugees, provoking more and more of them to join the war effort. The Soviet Union and its East European satellites helped transform the Palestinian rabble into an army, and taught some of these newly trained fighters to be terrorists.

Commando training took place at camps in Czechoslovakia run by Soviet, East German, and Czech instructors. "From '67 to '69 a very large number of PLO recruits went through the camps and then went on to create other training camps in Lebanon, Jordan, Syria, Iraq, Yemen, Algeria, and Libya," the CIA's Bob Inman said. Over time, the training expanded to include not just PLO fedayeen but also members of the so-called nihilist groups—Baader-Meinhof, Red Brigades, Japanese Red Army. In return, the nihilist groups would give the PLO political support in Europe. According to Inman, "there was no credible evidence of any Soviet direction of operations conducted by people who'd been trained in these camps." And, "after the '67–'69 time frame, there was very sparse Soviet involvement in the training camps." Still, "there is no question that the Soviets are the grandparents. They built the original training camps and gave the PLO the capability to train their own."

By the beginning of 1969, the Israelis were reporting that more than 1,200 incidents of sabotage and terrorism had taken place on their borders since the end of the Six Day War. The more radical factions of the PLO were not content to wage guerrilla war in Israel but sought to take the fight to "imperialist" forces everywhere. The Marxist Popular Front for the Liberation of Palestine, for instance, declared it would attack Jewish property anywhere in the world. To the extent that the guerrilla war against Israel was going poorly, various Palestinian factions resorted increasingly to indiscriminate terror elsewhere.

According to Gordon, the estimate concluded in essence that "there was a significant degree of Soviet support for a considerable number of these groups . . . but it was essentially opportunistic. There was not an orchestrated terrorism program in Moscow. It was not a major instrument of Soviet policy. . . . The group who wanted support would come to Soviet agents and see whether they could pick up support. The initiative was on the side of the terrorist groups, but the Soviets clearly did not have a policy of turning them down. The Soviets presumably saw in this some advancement of their geopolitical interests by creating trouble for their opponents . . . 'the enemy of my enemy' business."

An unclassified version of the estimate stated that "the Soviets are deeply engaged in support of revolutionary violence. . . . Such violence frequently entails acts of international terrorism." Specifically, "the Soviets sell large quantities of arms to Libya—knowing that Libya is a major supporter of terrorist groups—and they back a number of Palestinian groups that have conducted terrorist operations." At the very least, Mansbach said, the Soviets were "irresponsible."

The real message of the estimate was that international terrorism had attained critical mass, that thanks to the initial Soviet training of the late sixties terrorist groups now had the capability to sustain the offensive on their own. "One of the policy implications of the estimate was a negative one," Gordon said. "Just getting the Soviets to lay off wouldn't solve the problem." In other words, the issue of Soviet support for terrorism was largely irrelevant. Haig, who had started the whole debate with his first press conference, was not heard from again on the subject. "The net of this was certainly not to confirm Haig's original speech," Gordon said.

Nevertheless, evidence of a Soviet hand behind acts of international terrorism would not go away. After a Turkish gunman tried to shoot Pope John Paul II in St. Peter's Square in 1981, Italian investigators uncovered a wealth of evidence linking the Bulgarian intelligence service to the crime. The inescapable inference was that the Bulgarians, who were the KGB's most slavish surrogates, had acted at the Soviets' behest. For all its fulminating against the Soviets for their support of terrorism, the Reagan administration was loathe to finger Moscow for the attempt on the Pope's life. The plot against the Pope posed two problems, both of them endemic to the fight against terrorism. First, the evidence was not airtight. Second, even if the Soviets were guilty, what could the United States do about it? Terrorism simply was not a grave enough threat to the national security to risk a confrontation with the other nuclear superpower.

The issue of Soviet involvement in terrorism would continue to generate more heat than light, and the Reagan administration would continue to confuse terrorism and communism. The SNIE would remain as a reminder of the deep divisions within the U.S. government over the issue of terrorism. Any policy that started with such fundamental disagreements about how to define terrorism was bound to have tough going. The first hostage crisis of the Reagan administration would prove just how tough.

★ 3 ★

THE KNOCK ON THE DOOR

It was growing dark on December 17, 1981, as a Fiat sedan wound through the narrow streets of Verona, Italy, bearing Brig. Gen. James Dozier home from his office. The car and driver were among the fringe benefits that went with the job of deputy chief of staff for logistics and administration for Allied Land Forces in Southern Europe. It was far, far down the NATO chain of command, but it made Dozier the senior American officer at LANDSOUTH, as it was called, and entitled him to perquisites a brigadier general in the Pentagon could only dream of. It was the cushiest assignment Dozier had had in his thirty years in the Army.

Once back in their seventh-floor apartment overlooking the Adige River, Dozier sat down at the kitchen table with a drink to go over the day's mail, while his wife Judy fixed dinner. When the doorbell rang, Dozier said, "I just got up and walked to the door and asked who was there." Later, Judy Dozier recalled feeling vaguely uneasy because the building was supposed to be locked at the street entrance to keep out peddlers. Speaking Italian, the man on the other side of the door said he was a plumber trying to find the source of a leak in the apartment below. Dozier opened the door and found two young men dressed in blue uniforms. "They looked like plumbers, so I let them in," Dozier said. He led them to the utility room, where they pretended to look for a leak. One of the plumbers said something Dozier didn't understand, so he went to the kitchen to look up the word in his Italian-English dictionary.

"The next thing I knew I was spun around and looking down the barrels of two silenced pistols," Dozier recalled. There was a brief scuffle which ended when one of the plumbers struck Dozier in the face. "I saw a big blinding flash, and the next thing I knew I was looking up and they were handcuffing my hands behind me." His wife called out to him to do as they said. "One of them had a pistol pointed at my wife's head, and that was enough for me," Dozier said. They gagged and blindfolded him, taped his arms and ankles together, plugged his ears, and dumped him in a steamer trunk. "I was all scrunched up in there, and once they stood it up on end, I settled to the bottom," Dozier recalled. "I realized that I was going to have trouble breathing."

The kidnappers placed the trunk inside a refrigerator carton and carried their prize downstairs to a panel truck. They drove for what seemed to Dozier like ten minutes, pulled into what sounded like an underground garage, and transferred the trunk to a second vehicle. This time they drove for an hour and a half without stopping, opening the trunk occasionally to let air in and to check Dozier's pulse. When at last the truck stopped, he felt himself being picked up and loaded onto an elevator that went up and down several times until he could no longer tell where it stopped. They carried the trunk into an apartment, lifted Dozier out, and laid him face down on a steel cot inside a pup tent. They chained him by an arm and a leg to the cot, took the blindfold off, and told him he was a prisoner of the Red Brigades.

The Red Brigades had terrorized Italy for the better part of a decade, committing murders, kidnappings, and kneecappings of government officials, magistrates, and business executives in an effort to trigger a police crackdown that would reveal the true repressive nature of the state and arouse the proletariat to take up arms against their oppressors. The Red Brigades had been wildly successful, pulling off a series of terrorist spectaculars, including the 1978 kidnapping and murder of the country's most prominent politician, Aldo Moro. By 1981, however, the Red Brigades had become victims of their own success. As their numbers grew beyond the hard core of dedicated revolutionaries, their once impenetrable security had been breached by informers and thrill-seekers. Police had begun to raid their *covos*, or safehouses, finding treasure troves of documents—expense accounts, diaries, operations plans, target lists—that served as road maps for unraveling the rest of the network. Some of the captured leaders had offered full confessions, betraying their revolutionary comrades for a reduced sentence. It seemed only a matter of time and manpower before the Red Brigades were mopped up.

That did not mean they were no longer a threat. Some of the captured leaders had not turned states' evidence but had continued to direct operations from their cells, using their attorneys as messengers. In announcing their annual fall campaign, the Red Brigades had singled out members of NATO and Americans in particular as targets. To the north, in West Germany, the Red Army Faction, another terrorist gang thought to be in decline, had opened a vicious campaign against American installations and personnel. In September of 1981, they narrowly missed killing Gen. Frederick Kroesen, his wife, and an aide with a rocket-propelled grenade. Kroesen, the commander of the U.S. Army in Europe, was riding in an armored limousine, but the grenade penetrated the trunk and would have killed him had it not malfunctioned and failed to explode. Two weeks before that, a good friend of the Doziers' was one of several Americans injured when a terrorist bomb went off at Ramstein Air Force Base in West Germany. The Red Army's campaign seemed tied in part to U.S. plans to deploy nuclear-armed cruise and Pershing missiles in West Germany, and since cruise missiles were going into Italy as well, Americans there were likely targets. "We knew there was a danger to Americans," said Stanton Burnett, the public affairs officer at the U.S. Embassy in Rome. "I had sat next to Dozier a month earlier at a meeting of senior military officers to discuss security precautions. . . . We had a lot of warning to do things like vary our schedules."

Dozier would later claim he had received too many warnings, that they were so frequent and so vague as to be meaningless. "There was just an awful lot of information with varying degrees of credibility with regard to terrorist activities," he said. "It was a sort of cry wolf type of thing." He did nothing to vary his routine. "I was guilty of that," Dozier conceded. "I was very predictable. I would go out and run at the same time every morning. I like to show up for work right on time." Dozier later learned he and at least two other American military officers had been under surveillance for six weeks. His car had been trailed, and his kidnappers had cased his apartment building, masquerading as municipal employees. The Red Brigades' tactic was to stake out a half dozen potential victims and to select the one who by his habits looked like the easiest mark.

"A lot of us violated the warning to vary your schedule," Burnett agreed. "It's hard to vary your schedule, particularly at the beginning of the day." As a practical matter, security precautions consisted of little more than an ostentatious show of looking up and down the street before setting out for work in the morning, hoping that might be enough to divert the kidnappers to a more complacent target. Security precautions didn't have to be perfect, after all, just better than the next American's.

With a schedule as rigid as his crew cut, Dozier was an easy target, exactly the kind who could be duped into answering the door. The night before, someone had rung the bell at Air Force Brig. Gen. William Cooney's home in Vicenza, but he wasn't there and his wife had refused to answer the door. The incident took on meaning only after Dozier was kidnapped. The Reagan administration eventually would spend $17 million on a computer system called TRAP/TARGIT that matched the *modus operandi* of known terrorist groups with "pre-incident indicators" like the Cooneys' night visitors in an attempt to predict terrorist attacks, but the system soon became overloaded with extraneous reports of barking dogs. One of the many dilemmas of the war against terrorism is that the more sensitive the warning system, the more susceptible it is to false alarms.

The knock on Dozier's door was not a false alarm. Some of the kidnappers stayed on in the Dozier apartment for nearly two hours, keeping watch over Judy. When they finally left her trussed in chains on the washroom floor, she began banging on the washing machine with her knees. After an hour of banging, a neighbor finally came to her rescue, climbing down from the roof and in the bathroom window. It was shortly before nine o'clock on December 17, mid-afternoon Washington time, and the Reagan administration was abruptly plunged into its first hostage crisis—and quickly mired in jurisdictional disputes that revealed it was no better prepared than the Carter administration had been to deal with terrorist incidents.

As a result of the Holloway Commission's finding that the Iranian rescue attempt had been crippled by the lack of an organization to direct the mission, the Pentagon had created the Joint Special Operations Command (JSOC). Based at Fort Bragg, North Carolina, JSOC united the special operations forces of all the services—the Army's Delta, the Navy's SEALs, a new helicopter unit known as Task Force 160, and the Air Force's Special Operations Wing—under a single commander responsible for their day-to-day training and their deployment in time of crisis. JSOC already had trained extensively for one particular mission: the rescue of American diplomats in Managua in the event the Sandinistas took them hostage in retaliation for the Reagan administration's attempts to overthrow Nicaragua's revolutionary regime. Never again would forces have to be thrown together to jury rig a rescue mission—in theory, at least. In the Dozier case, however, "you could basically characterize the whole operation as bureaucratic fighting between various interest groups," said Col. Robert Kvederas, an officer on the staff of the Joint Chiefs of Staff. "There was a terrible problem with coordination between virtually everyone involved."

When word of Dozier's kidnapping reached the Pentagon, Defense Secretary Caspar Weinberger dispatched a six-man "survey team" of intelligence and communications specialists. The survey team would serve as the advance party for a rescue force if it ever came to that. The team belonged to JSOC, which reported to the Joint Chiefs of Staff, but it was being sent to the operating area of the European Command. While somewhere in Italy Dozier lay chained to his cot, wearing headphones that blasted out rock music so loudly he would suffer a permanent loss of hearing, the survey team sat in Stuttgart, West Germany, arguing with the European Command over who would be in charge. Fortunately for Dozier, the outcome of the debate would prove irrelevant, thanks largely to the American Ambassador in Rome.

Maxwell Rabb couldn't learn to speak Italian because, his staff said, he had never learned to speak English. He was inarticulate, cantankerous, old—and savvy as hell. Rabb understood that finding Dozier was a job for Italian police, not American commandos. Italy was, by treaty, responsible for the security of NATO forces stationed on its soil; kidnapping was a crime; and the Red Brigades were an Italian phenomenon. "The house rules were, don't piss the Italians off," said Noel Koch, the Deputy Assistant Secretary of Defense responsible for counterterrorism. "We had to make sure we didn't offend the Italians and cause them to throw up their hands and say, 'Okay, you guys are so smart. You do it.' " As a result, said Koch, "our contribution was to keep pressure on the Italians by offering to help, shoveling information and gadgets at them." And money—a half-million-dollar reward for information leading to Dozier's rescue. In most matters, America's strong suit is money, but in this case the U.S. government with its 780-billion-dollar budget could not come up with half a million dollars. Each department claimed it did not have the legislative authority to dispense reward money overseas, a bureaucratic gridlock broken by a gung-ho young Marine major named Oliver North, who was assigned to the staff of the National Security Council and would in the ensuing years become expert at getting over, under, through, and, increasingly, around the bureaucracy.

North had come to the White House staff in mid-1981 as an "easel-carrier," one of the faceless assistants who handled the visual aids for their superiors. His first job had been to help schedule congressional testimony on the administration's plan to sell AWACS surveillance planes to Saudi Arabia. After the administration narrowly won that battle, North helped draft top-secret plans for trying to govern the nation in the aftermath of a nuclear attack, and he supervised the creation of a high-tech "crisis management center," complete with fancy teleconferencing equipment, in Room 208 of the Old Executive Office Building next door to the White House. North thrived on crises. They provided an outlet for his boundless energy and they demanded two qualities he possessed in abundance, persistence and creativity.

North suggested turning to the Texas billionaire H. Ross Perot for help. During the Vietnam War, Perot had invested millions of dollars in efforts to free American prisoners of war, and he was still financing attempts to determine whether any of the missing in action were held captive in Indochina. He had mounted a private rescue mission to free two of his employees from a Tehran jail, and he had offered his services to the Carter administration in preparing for the doomed Iran rescue mission. Working with North and Lt. Gen. Philip Gast, the director of operations for the Joint Chiefs of Staff, Perot wired $500,000 to a bank in Italy, where the money was converted to lire and hand carried to the American Embassy. But the informant who was demanding the reward money turned out to be a fraud.

In the end, the reward money was never spent, the gadgets were never used, and the information was useless. The gadgets consisted of sophisticated electronic equipment which futilely searched the air waves for sounds of the Red Brigades conversing over walkie-talkies or CB radios. Much of the information came from an Air Force project called "Distant Viewing"—which contacted psychics who claimed to know where Dozier was being held. One said he was tied up in the bottom of a boat in Lake Como; another had him on a farm in Austria; another in "the place of the shepherds." All the leads were checked. None of them panned out. "It was just a big zero," Kvederas said. Finally, the Italians asked the Pentagon to stop helping so much.

The only American assistance that amounted to anything was Rabb's street smarts. He persuaded the Italian Minister of the Interior to herd all the imprisoned Red Brigade leaders into one location and hold them incommunicado from their lawyers—to seal them off from the outside world so they could not advise Dozier's kidnappers. Cut off from their leaders, the kidnappers lost the initiative as the largest manhunt in Italy's history—5,000 men—blanketed the country, picking up and questioning more than 400 suspected terrorists. Dozier sensed that his captors knew time was running out.

The first break came on Monday, January 25, 1982, the thirty-ninth day of the kidnapping, when a police sweep in Verona netted the brother of an imprisoned terrorist. He did not know where Dozier was being held, but he gave police the name of the driver who had carted Dozier from his apartment to his jail. In return for a promise that his prison term would be cut in half, the driver led police to a second-floor apartment above a grocery in Padua, little more than an hour's drive from where Dozier had been kidnapped. Police put the apartment under surveillance and by Wednesday were convinced he was there.

Just before noon on Thursday, ten members of the Italian counterterrorist unit known as "Leatherheads" stormed the apartment, using the roar of a nearby bulldozer to cover the sound of their movements. "I was lying on my bunk reading *1984*," Dozier recounted. "I looked up from the bunk, and the guard had a pistol. His attention was directed to something going on outside the tent. A figure burst through the flaps of the tent and knocked the guard down. The guy that knocked the guard down was dressed the same way [as the terrorists] and was wearing a ski mask. I thought I was caught up in a jurisdictional dispute between rival factions. I pushed him out. He asked me, 'Are you the General? We're the police.' I wouldn't answer him. I wouldn't tell him who I was. Then I felt his body armor and realized it really was the police." Five terrorists—three men and two women—were captured without a shot, along with a small arsenal of weapons. Later, the captured terrorists would lead police to the Rome apartment where they had held the former Italian prime minister, Aldo Moro, for fifty-two days before they killed him.

The Dozier case was a triumph for the Italians, who had delivered a body blow to the Red Brigades, and a miracle for Dozier, whom most Americans had given up for dead. Although the Reagan administration was able to bask in the glow, those officials who knew what really had happened saw the Dozier case for what it was. "We realized that we had a fucking mess," Koch said. Rabb had the good sense to let the Italians walk point, but that could not obscure the fact that the American performance was feckless at best, counterproductive at worst. The Joint Special Operations Command and the European Command had never worked out their jurisdictional dispute. The Pentagon had tied up Italian manpower running down dead-end leads provided by psychics. The CIA, with all its intelligence assets, had not even been brought in until the third week of the kidnapping. The State Department found it did not have a secure telephone system with which to talk to Rabb. Washington had to talk with the embassy either over an open phone line or through the time-consuming process of sending cables. The JSOC survey team had brought its own satellite communications package but had refused to let the State Department use it. "I raised hell," Koch said. "We've got to change the way we're structured."

Koch had long since learned the necessity of raising hell. In 1962, as a young Army sergeant assigned to the National Security Agency, he had learned just how hard it is to get the bureaucracy's attention. Stationed in Saigon as part of the vanguard of the American buildup, he had barraged headquarters at Fort Meade, Maryland, with suggestions for upgrading NSA operations in Vietnam. He had returned to Fort Meade certain that his cables had ignited a firestorm of reorganization. At headquarters, they had listened patiently to Koch—who pronounced his name Cook—then assigned him the task of reading a drawerful of cables some guy named Koch—pronounced Kotch—had sent in from Vietnam. No one had even bothered to read them. In the ensuing years, Koch had learned to play bureaucratic hard ball, first as the Washington representative for Philadelphia Mayor Frank Rizzo, then as a presidential speechwriter for Richard Nixon. Sardonic and curt, Koch didn't hesitate to offend. Frustrated at the obstinacy of senior military officers, he took to displaying a volume called *On the Psychology of Military Incompetence* on his desk at the Pentagon. When it came to fighting terrorism, there was much to be frustrated about.

The existing structure seemed to reflect institutional prerogatives more than the needs of a terrorist crisis. The Justice Department was in charge of dealing with terrorist incidents in the United States; the State Department in charge overseas; unless the incident occurred aboard an airplane in flight, in which case the Federal Aviation Administration was in charge; or unless military force was to be used, in which case the Defense Department was in charge. It made sense on paper but not in the real world where lines of authority had a nasty habit of getting tangled. Koch argued that only the White House could cut across those lines and that a small cell should be created within the National Security Council staff to manage terrorist incidents. The trouble was, said Koch, "the White House didn't want this over there. It was a loser. The chances of having somebody killed are greater than the chances of having somebody recovered." The State Department agreed with the White House. "I argued that you had to keep terrorism out of the White House," said Robert Sayre, the new director of the department's Office for Combatting Terrorism. "You have an obligation to protect the President. Don't stick him with this tar baby."

The debate sounded like another of Washington's petty bureaucratic turf wars—all ego and no substance—but it had real significance when it came to the use of military force. At one point, a Delta team was sent to Honduras to help the local military deal with a wave of terrorist incidents that included the kidnapping of a judge's granddaughter. When the Hondurans learned where the girl was being held, the American chargé d'affaires ordered the Delta team to rescue her—an order which, in theory, only the President as commander-in-chief had the authority to issue. The Delta team finessed the situation by stalling until the Hondurans could organize their own rescue, but to Koch the incident was evidence of the tangled chain of command which would persist unless the White House took control of terrorist incidents.

The White House issued National Security Decision Directive 30, which codified the existing structure. At Koch's recommendation, Defense Secretary Weinberger refused to endorse NSDD 30. Koch confronted John Poindexter, a Navy admiral assigned to the National Security Council staff: "I said, 'You're going to have to fix this thing, or you can count the Department of Defense out of terrorism because we're not going to play.' " One year after the President had vowed "swift and effective retribution" to terrorists, the Pentagon said it was not going to play. "To mollify me and Cap [Weinberger], they created an addendum [to NSDD 30]," Koch said. The addendum established a Terrorist Incident Working Group. Chaired by Poindexter, the group was composed of representatives from all the relevant agencies—including State, Defense, CIA, FAA, FBI—and could be convened by any member. Now at least Defense would not have to await State's pleasure. When it came to exercising this new organization, however, Koch found that very little had changed. Every time the working group convened in response to a mock terrorist incident, Poindexter would suddenly be called away on more pressing business, leaving the State Department in charge.

The organizational dispute was, in essence, a dispute over the nature of terrorism and how to fight it. "If you believe that in 90 percent of the cases terrorism is going to be dealt with by the local government, you have one organization," Sayre argued. "If you believe terrorism is going to be dealt with by military force, you have a different organization." To Sayre, the choice was self-evident. "Domestically, in the United States, terrorism is a police problem. They are always the first on the scene. In every other country in the world, they handle it the same way we do. So why should all of a sudden, if a U.S. citizen is involved in a terrorist incident overseas, why should all of a sudden the problem become a Defense Department problem?"

Koch felt the problem went beyond finding a way to streamline the government's response to a terrorist incident. "I was arguing that basically terrorism had changed," Koch said. No longer would there be what Koch called "incidents of duration" in which hostages were taken and held for days, weeks, or even months. "Incidents of duration are theater," Koch argued. "But we'd become good at it, and they were no longer a no-risk deal for the terrorists." The Italian Leatherheads had rescued Dozier, the German GSG 9 had captured the terrorists at Mogadishu, the Israelis had rescued their citizens from Entebbe. It was inevitable that the terrorists would shift tactics. Democracies were not the only ones who learned by their mistakes; terrorists did, too. Koch predicted a shift to what he called "conclusive incidents"—bombings and assassinations which were over before anybody could react. To deal with conclusive incidents, Koch argued, the West would have to take "proactive" or "preemptive" action—it would have to shoot first, in other words. There was nothing in NSDD 30 about that.

As Koch later told it, the concept of pre-emptive attacks against terrorists "proved to be a difficult matter even to discuss," much less implement. "I prepared a memo for then-Deputy Defense Secretary [Frank] Carlucci to discuss with William Casey . . . It suggested a number of actions for consideration, among them the elimination of identifiable terrorist leaders where helpful. Carlucci came to my office that morning to urge me never to put anything like that on paper. Any discussion of such matters could constitute a conspiracy to commit murder."

After more than a year in office, the Reagan administration was doing little more than waiting for bombs to go off. When it did act, the new administration relied on the traditional instruments of diplomatic and military power—conventional measures against an unconventional foe.

★ 4 ★

THE SHORES OF TRIPOLI

At six o'clock in the morning of August 19, 1981, Navy Commander Hank Kleeman taxied his F-14 into launch position on the deck of the *Nimitz.* He moved his stick forward, backward, left, and right, then pushed the rudder pedals down with his feet. As a memory aid for this last-minute check of the plane's flight controls, some pilots mumbled to themselves, "Father, Son, Holy Ghost, Amen," which was entirely fitting given the risks of what they were about to do. In the course of a twenty-year career, a carrier pilot stood a one in four chance of being killed. Kleeman himself had only four more years to live before he, too, would be killed flying a Navy jet.

Armed with six missiles, locked inside 30 tons of metal, electronics, and jet fuel, Kleeman saluted the deck crew through the plastic bubble of his canopy, then tensed his head forward. The steam catapult shot him off the deck, accelerating his plane from 0 to 150 knots in just two seconds, smashing him against his seat with nine times the force of gravity. After hundreds of launches, some pilots could actually wisecrack with the radar officer in the back seat as the jet shot down the deck, but Kleeman, who had been flying off carriers for sixteen years, didn't say anything to his radar officer, Lt. David Venlet. Kleeman had a reputation for being very quiet in the cockpit, so quiet that a lot of radar officers didn't like flying with him, didn't like returning to the ship and finding out there had been some minor emergency he never told them about.

It was still dark as Kleeman climbed through the overcast and began looking for an airborne tanker to top off his fuel load before heading south to his patrol station 60 miles off the coast of Libya. He was scheduled to arrive on station just as the sun was coming over the horizon. "I expected nothing to happen," Kleeman said later.

The carriers *Nimitz* and *Forrestal,* along with thirteen other ships of the Sixth Fleet, were in the second day of a two-day live-fire exercise that was both a routine naval maneuver and an open challenge to Col. Muamar Qaddafi, Libya's erratic dictator. Public notices had marked off a 3,200-square-mile exercise area, extending into the Gulf of Sidra, a 300-mile-wide bite taken out of the Libyan coast between the two main cities of Tripoli and Benghazi. Qaddafi claimed the Gulf of Sidra as his own, declaring as far back as 1973 that it "constitutes an integral part of the territory of the Libyan Arab Republic and is under its complete sovereignty." The State Department had quickly denounced the claim as an "unacceptable . . . violation of international law," and the Sixth Fleet had occasionally exercised inside the Gulf to prove that it did not recognize any claims beyond the traditional 12-mile territorial limit. Operations off Libya always entailed a certain amount of risk. In 1973 and again in 1980, Libyan fighter planes had harassed U.S. reconnaissance aircraft flying missions well outside Libyan air space. For the present exercise, the Joint Chiefs of Staff, the Defense Intelligence Agency, and the European Command had all performed "risk assessments" and concluded that the likelihood of a hostile reaction by Qaddafi's forces was "low." Still, the Reagan administration was taking no chances.

The administration had devised an elaborate "stairstep plan" of proportionate responses to every conceivable Libyan provocation. Leery of being accused of going off half-cocked, the Pentagon wanted specific orders from the President for every contingency. The task force commander, Rear Adm. James Service, had been recalled to Washington to go over the exercise plan in detail with the Joint Chiefs of Staff.

When the exercise began on August 18, the American fleet was cocked and loaded. Although Defense Secretary Weinberger would later claim that "we . . . had no reason to suppose that anybody would fire on any of our planes or ships," the crew of the *Forrestal* had broken out all the missiles and bombs needed for a strike against Libyan territory—just in case. Under the Rules of Engagement, the F-14s were to intercept any approaching aircraft and escort them away from the exercise area, firing only if fired upon. That was a change from the Carter administration which required pilots to request permission from the task force commander before returning fire. Under the Carter rules, if the enemy was disengaging and returning to his base, the American pilot had to hold his fire. Under the Reagan rules, there would be no free shots at Americans. What we should do is follow them back into the hangar, the President said when he approved the stairstep plan.

On the first day of the exercise, a total of seventy-two Libyan jets, mostly French-built Mirages and Soviet-built MiGs, flew toward the American fleet. The intercepts were all routine but exciting, since this was the first time most of these Navy pilots had ever seen a real Soviet warplane. Except for old-timers like Kleeman, most of them were too young to have fought in Vietnam.

The 19th promised to be a slow day for Kleeman in Fast Eagle 102 and his wingman, Lt. Larry Muczynski, flying Fast Eagle 107. They had been assigned a southern patrol area, and most of the Libyan planes had been coming out of Tripoli on the western side of the Gulf and Benina airfield on the east. As they cruised toward their station, Kleeman and Muczynski listened over the radio to the voices of other pilots already conducting intercepts to the west. "We were talking about how we could get off this station just as soon as possible," Muczynski later recounted. The two planes arrived on station just at sunrise and went into a lazy racetrack patrol pattern, loitering at 220 knots at 20,000 feet, alternately flying toward and away from the Libyan coast, timing their turns so that one plane had its radar pointing toward Libya at all times.

If today was going to be slow, Muczynski couldn't complain. For a peacetime pilot, he had already seen more than his share of action. Yesterday, he had run two intercepts on Libyan planes, rolling in right beside a MiG-25. Last year, on the night of the Iran rescue mission, he had been on deck alert in the Gulf of Oman, ready to launch air strikes against Tehran if the ground force got in trouble. That night, he had been issued a revolver to carry in case he had to bail out over Iranian territory. For the Gulf of Sidra, the Navy had not bothered to issue him a side arm.

By 7:00 A.M., Kleeman was beginning to run low on fuel. Before much longer they would either have to find another tanker or head back to the *Nimitz.* Kleeman turned toward the Libyan coast for one last run around the racetrack. Just then, David Venlet, Kleeman's radar officer, picked up a contact coming out of the south from the Libyan air base at Ghurbadiyah at the foot of the Gulf of Sidra. 102 has contact. 190 at 60, Venlet reported from the back seat, abbreviating their call sign, Fast Eagle 102, and giving the bearing in degrees and range in miles to the contact. The radio circuit was so busy with the other intercepts in progress, he didn't know if anybody heard him. Venlet watched as the contact climbed to 20,000 feet, accelerated to 550 knots, and headed straight for them.

Kleeman in Fast Eagle 102 and Muczynski in Fast Eagle 107 broke off their racetrack pattern and moved into a "loose combat spread," with Muczynski 8,000 feet above Kleeman and two miles off his right wing. From the back seat, Venlet told Kleeman to come right 20 degrees, beginning a long slow loop that would bring them in behind the Libyan "bogey." But the bogey changed course and continued to come straight at Fast Eagle 102. Venlet told Kleeman to come 40 degrees left. Again the bogey changed course to keep closing on Fast Eagle 102. The radar at Ghurbadiyah obviously was tracking Kleeman and passing his course and speed to the Libyan pilot.

Kleeman and Muczynski gave up their zigzag and headed straight for the Libyan. They pushed their throttles forward to 550 knots, barely cutting in their afterburners to burn off any tell-tale trail of black exhaust. They would execute an "eyeball/shooter intercept." Kleeman was the "eyeball," heading straight for the Libyan. Muczynski was the "shooter," circling into a position from which his heat-seeking Sidewinder missiles would have clear aim at the jet's exhaust. Muczynski told his radar officer to get the 35mm camera ready so they could take some pictures of the Libyan when they got close. That's what they had done yesterday, and, said Muczynski, "there was no reason to expect anything different from the day before."

Kleeman spotted the bogey when it was still eight miles away. Hank's got a tally, he reported. He could see that what looked like one plane on the radar scope was actually two planes flying close together in a "welded wing" formation. Kleeman identified the planes as Soviet-built SU-22 Fitters. The two formations were closing on each other at a combined speed of 1,100 knots. With a closure rate of 12 miles per minute, things began to happen fast.

Muczynski banked Fast Eagle 107 hard left, beginning a tight turn that would bring him in behind the Fitters. His "speed jeans"—a pair of inflatable chaps—filled with air to slow the rush of blood from his head as his body was torn by a force seven times that of gravity. An experienced pilot could take between eight and nine Gs before blacking out; the specifications for the F-14 recommended never taking the plane above six and a half Gs.

Muczynski could see the Libyan aircraft now. The lead Fitter was 1,000 feet in front of and 500 feet below Kleeman's Fast Eagle 102—nose to nose. "All of a sudden, the whole left side of the Libyan leader lights up," Muczynski recalled. At first he thought the Fitter had suffered some sort of explosion or fire. Then he saw the missile coming off its rail under the Fitter's wing. Skipper, he shot at you, Muczynski reported.

Kleeman saw it too, saw the missile coming off the Libyan's wing and then disappearing beneath him. The missile skittered across the sky, its sensors vainly searching for a heat source until its rocket motor ran out of fuel and flamed out.

Kleeman in Fast Eagle 102 broke left, directly over the top of the Fitter. "Hank and I are both in a left-hand turn," Muczynski said. "He calls me, 'Where are you going?' I said, 'I'm going for the leader.' He said, 'Okay, you go for the guy that shot at us. I'm going for the wingman.' I said, 'Roger that.'"

The lead Fitter went into a climbing left-hand turn. His wingman made a level turn to the right, heading south toward home. "It just looked like the wingman said, 'I'm outta here,'" Muczynski said. Kleeman's Fast Eagle 102 rolled in on the wingman's tail. Kleeman waited about ten seconds while his target passed through the glare of the rising sun, then he fired his Sidewinder at a range of three quarters of a mile. "The missile . . . struck him in his tailpipe area, causing him to lose control of the airplane, and he ejected within about five seconds," Kleeman said. Kleeman flew right by the Libyan pilot swinging in his parachute.

Muczynski in Fast Eagle 107 was on the lead Fitter's tail. He had to throttle back and put his speed brakes on to keep from flying past him. In his headset, he heard Kleeman yelling: Shoot, shoot, shoot.

The Rules of Engagement gave Muczynski all the authority he needed to shoot, but thoughts were racing through his mind. "I already had permission to shoot," he said later, "but let me tell you . . . this guy was no threat to me and no threat to the Skipper. . . . The guy I'm convinced never saw me. He was not maneuvering hard. . . . If I shoot, I'm going to kill this guy. If I shoot, I might start World War III. . . . What if I shoot, and the Skipper didn't shoot? What if I don't shoot?" Under the Carter Rules of Engagement neither Kleeman nor Muczynski would have fired. Under the Reagan Rules of Engagement, Muczynski squeezed the trigger.

Now a half mile behind the Fitter, Muczynski watched the missile track its prey at twice the speed of sound. "I can see the missile going right up his tailpipe," he said. "There was a big explosion and fireball and debris." Suddenly, Muczynski realized he was about to fly through that debris. "If you fly through this stuff, and it goes through your engine, you're finished. I said, 'My God, I've just shot myself down!' I just took the stick and buried it in my lap. I pulled straight up over the top, doing a seven-G pull-up."

Above the debris, Muczynski flipped his plane upside down so he could see what was left of the Fitter. "He was down underneath us, tumbling end over end. All the engine was gone, and all the tail was gone. . . . We saw him jettison his canopy. Then we saw the ejection seat. . . . He should have got a chute, but he didn't. All we can see is the guy, falling out of sight." Muczynski reported: Fox Two kill for Music.

It was over in a minute. Fast Eagle 102 and Fast Eagle 107 joined up and headed for the *Nimitz,* checking each other's tails to make sure there were no other Libyans around. Hey, Skipper, Venlet said to Kleeman from the back seat. What did we just do? . . . I bet the President gets woke up on this one.

Muczynski put his plane on autopilot and let it fly itself while he calmed down. "We were so pumped up . . . I literally was shaking uncontrollably." Kleeman was shaking too. Normally the best pilot in the squadron at landing on the carrier, Kleeman missed his first two approaches. As Muczynski shut down his engines, red-shirted ordnance men ran toward him, pounding on Fast Eagle 107 in celebration.

In Washington, the glee was more restrained but just as genuine. "We regret very much that the Libyans took this action and brought about these consequences," Defense Secretary Weinberger said, more in sorrow than in anger. Most officials were surprised that Qaddafi had challenged the Navy the way he did, but among themselves they called the shoot-down an unexpected dividend.

For the Fitter, a ground attack plane ill-equipped for the high-speed turns of a dogfight, taking on an F-14 had been suicidal. The F-14 was a swing-wing jet specifically designed for air-to-air combat, powered by the latest in jet propulsion, guided by the latest in electronics. Some of the pilots aboard the *Nimitz* took a look at the odds and concluded that the Libyan pilot had fired by mistake. Muczynski disagreed. He thought it was deliberate. Afterwards, he talked with the crew of an electronic eavesdropping plane that had monitored the shootdown. They told him the Libyan pilot reported he had fired without giving any indication it was a mistake. "My opinion is they were hoping for the one-time, fast, lucky, quick kill, and if it doesn't work, get the hell out of Dodge," Muczynski said. Nobody had told the Libyans that the rules had changed and there were no more free shots.

★   ★   ★

Within hours of the short-lived dogfight, the National Security Agency monitored a phone call to Qaddafi, who was visiting South Yemen, informing him of what had happened. Then and there, Qaddafi vowed to kill Reagan and boasted he had the means to do it. Qaddafi was already seething over a report in *Newsweek* magazine that the CIA was embarked upon "a large-scale, multiphase and costly scheme to overthrow the Libyan regime." According to the magazine, members of Congress who had been briefed on the plan thought it gave the CIA authority to assassinate Qaddafi. That report had been followed in short order by the visit to Washington of Qaddafi's arch enemy, Egyptian President Anwar Sadat and by the exercise in the Gulf of Sidra, which just happened to coincide with Egyptian maneuvers along the Libyan border. The administration's plans were neither as coordinated nor as ruthless as Qaddafi imagined, but just because he was paranoid didn't mean somebody wasn't after him.

The Reagan administration had started gunning for Qaddafi even before the President was inaugurated. While preparing for his Senate confirmation hearings as Secretary of State, Alexander Haig summoned to his transition office two top officials of the State Department's Bureau of Intelligence and Research, deputy director Herman Cohen and director for current intelligence Philip Stoddard. What can we do to hurt Qaddafi? Haig wanted to know.

This administration would see to it that America's enemies no longer slept soundly. "The game plan was to prove that we weren't going to be pushed around anymore," said Lillian Harris, the North African analyst in the State Department's intelligence bureau. "Qaddafi presented this marvelous target because you could fight the Soviets, you could fight terrorism, and you could fight evil Arabs."

If "swift and effective retribution" was to be the hallmark of the Reagan administration's campaign against terrorism, there was no better place to begin than with Qaddafi. According to the CIA, "the government of Colonel Qaddafi is the most prominent state sponsor of and participant in international terrorism." If the Soviets were the "grandparents" of terrorism, to use Bob Inman's term, Qaddafi was "the Daddy Warbucks of terrorism," to use Claire Sterling's phrase. "There has been a clear and consistent pattern of Libyan aid to almost every major international terrorist group, from the Provisional Irish Republican Army to the Popular Front for the Liberation of Palestine," the CIA said. "Libya's support for terrorism includes financing for terrorist operations, weapons procurement and supply, the use of training camps and Libyan advisers for guerrilla training, and the use of Libyan diplomatic facilities abroad as support bases for terrorist operations." When other Arab countries—first Algeria, then Jordan, and finally Iraq—closed down their training camps, Qaddafi was there to fill the void, opening new camps in Libya. By the start of the Reagan administration, there were between fifteen and twenty terrorist training camps in Libya.

In addition to his across-the-board support for terrorism, Qaddafi was openly conducting a campaign of assassination against his own people. "Early in 1980 [Qaddafi] warned Libyan exiles that they should return home, or they would be punished in place," the CIA reported. "During the remainder of the year, Qaddafi's assassination teams carried out his threats. Our records list fourteen attacks by Libyan assassination teams. They occurred in seven countries and resulted in eleven Libyan exiles murdered and one wounded."

One of those attacks had occurred in the United States. Faisal Zagallai, a graduate student at Colorado State University and a leader of the Libyan dissident community, had been left for dead, shot twice in the head at point-blank range with a .22-caliber revolver. Zagallai's assailant vanished into the night, but there was never any mystery about who was behind the attack. JANA, the official news agency of the Libyan government, announced that the Revolutionary Command Council had claimed responsibility for the shooting. Qaddafi was nothing if not indiscreet.

The FBI traced the gun to a former Army Green Beret named Eugene Tafoya, who turned out to be one of a number of ex-soldiers and intelligence officers recruited by Qaddafi. Both Zagallai, who miraculously survived the shooting, and his wife, who witnessed it, immediately identified Tafoya's picture. When Tafoya was arrested, his address book contained the names of other Libyan exiles living in the United States. Tafoya's arrest triggered the Reagan administration's first concrete action against Libya. On May 6, 1981 the State Department ordered the closing of the Libyan diplomatic mission in Washington and gave all Libyan diplomats five working days to leave the country.

Haig had much more in mind than simply declaring America off limits to Qaddafi's assassins. In Haig's mind, Qaddafi's machinations were a textbook case of Soviet-backed adventurism that could no longer be tolerated. In the fall of 1980, Qaddafi had sent 5,000 of his soldiers south across the desert into Chad to intervene in that country's fifteen-year-old civil war. Shortly thereafter, he proclaimed a union of the two countries. It was the fifth time Qaddafi had merged Libya with another state. If the union lasted, it would be the first.

The Carter administration had done nothing about Qaddafi's invasion of Chad, leaving the problem to the toothless Organization of African Unity. Given the strategic importance of Chad—a half million square miles of desert and grazing land in the middle of nowhere—that seemed a reasonable response, particularly for an administration hamstrung by the hostage crisis in Iran. To the Reagan administration, Qaddafi's intervention in Chad was another power grab by a Soviet client, one more name to add to the list of places like Afghanistan, Ethiopia, and Angola where aggression had gone unanswered by the United States. As Haig put it, "Our signal to the Soviets had to be a plain warning that their time of unresisted adventuring in the Third World was over, and that America's capacity to tolerate the mischief of Moscow's proxies, Cuba and Libya, had been exceeded."

To call Libya a Soviet proxy grossly corrupted the term. A proxy is authorized to act for another. While his anti-imperialist rhetoric and his taste for subversion often served Soviet purposes, Qaddafi was in no way authorized to act on behalf of the Soviet Union. By 1981, he had purchased an estimated $12 billion worth of Soviet arms, which made him a valuable source of hard currency. But serving as a cash cow did not oblige Qaddafi to follow the Kremlin line; if the Soviets did not want to do business with him, he could take his petrodollars elsewhere. To Moscow, as to the rest of the world, Qaddafi was a loose cannon rolling about the deck of North Africa. Anatoly Dobrynin, the veteran Soviet Ambassador to the United States, distanced his government from Qaddafi by privately telling Haig Libya was "an American problem."

Why Qaddafi spent so much money on Soviet military equipment was a mystery. With a population of just 3.5 million, Libya simply could not absorb all that hardware. The Libyan Air Force had more than 500 aircraft but only 200 pilots. The striking discrepancy between what Qaddafi bought and what he could use spawned a number of theories among intelligence analysts. A few believed the Soviets were prepositioning large stocks of weapons in North Africa. However, that theory foundered on the fact that most of the hardware was export quality—the kind the Soviets sold their friends but not the caliber they used themselves. Besides, it was hard to see what good the weapons, most of which had never been assembled or maintained, would do the Russians if war broke out. Nevertheless, Haig seemed wedded to the proposition that Libya was pockmarked with incipient Soviet bases. When Lillian Harris in the State Department's Bureau of Intelligence and Research wrote a memo challenging the notion, Haig scrawled in the margin: Oh come on, they've got 'em in droves.

If all that military equipment wasn't for the Soviets, whom was it for? Qaddafi spoke of Libya as the Arab arsenal for the war against Israel.

But Egypt, without whom war against Israel was unthinkable, was currently at peace with Israel and all but at war with Libya. In fact, Qaddafi maintained diplomatic relations with only two Arab nations, Syria and South Yemen. Was this the man who would some day lead a united Arab army against Israel?

The CIA attributed Qaddafi's profligate arms purchases to his megalomania, part of the same impulse that drove him to declare his support for liberation movements and revolutionaries all over the globe. By the State Department's count, Libya supported subversive movements in twenty countries from Europe to the Philippines. In Africa alone, the presidents of Niger, Mali, and the Sudan had all accused Qaddafi of attempting to overthrow them; Ghana had expelled Libyan diplomats on charges of subversion; and Gambia and Sierra Leone had broken diplomatic relations with Libya, citing Libyan attempts to recruit their citizens. One of Qaddafi's favorite tactics was to offer drought-stricken Muslim tribesmen jobs in Libya's oil fields and then press gang them into service in his "Islamic Legion." After three months of basic training, they would be infiltrated back into their countries of origin to conduct campaigns of sabotage and subversion.

Qaddafi was unquestionably a troublemaker, but was he a threat to U.S. interests? "These were the same acts that didn't seem upsetting enough to either the Carter administration or the French to do anything about," said Elaine Morton, the North Africa expert on State's Policy Planning staff. "Now they were looked upon in the context of things that shouldn't be tolerated."

Within days of Reagan's inauguration, the CIA had completed an assessment of Libya's vulnerabilities. Among other things, the study concluded that for all his psychological quirks, Qaddafi was in many ways a traditional Arab street politician whose authority flowed from his presence and his personality. If his charisma and his aura of invincibility could somehow be shattered, then his incompetent military and economic policies might catch up with him. "There was a strong feeling that Qaddafi was becoming in many ways his own worst enemy," said Philip Stoddard, State's director of current analysis. "His tide had been high before the October 1973 Arab-Israeli war, and it had been receding ever since. Therefore, he was not the menace some of the top people thought he was, but he also was vulnerable." Libyan opposition to Qaddafi was growing but haphazard, kept off balance by purges of the military and assassinations in the exile community. Still, there were grounds for hope that Qaddafi might someday leave the same way he had arrived in 1970—a junior officers' coup. "To create the conditions for an internal military coup was the best outcome we could imagine," said Frank Fukuyama of State's Policy Planning staff.

From the start, two issues dominated the administration's review of its Libya policy: oil and hostages. The United States could not credibly adopt a hard-line policy toward Qaddafi so long as it continued to pay him $7 billion a year for oil and so long as the estimated 2,000 Americans working in Libya provided him with a pool of potential hostages. Hostages, thanks to Iran, were on everybody's mind. Oil arose as an issue only after a reporter for *The Washington Post* asked Paul Wolfowitz, the State Department's new director of Policy Planning, why, with all the noise the Reagan administration was making about Qaddafi, the United States continued to buy his oil. "We could not answer the man," Wolfowitz's deputy, James Roche, said.

When Roche set out to find the answer, the department's Bureau of Economics and Business Affairs told him Libyan crude was particularly valuable to the American market because it was "light and sweet," meaning low in pollution-causing sulfur and well suited for making gasoline. Refineries in the northeastern United States made their living processing Libyan crude; a ban on Libyan oil imports could set off a mini-recession in the Northeast. Besides, cutting off imports of Libyan oil would not hurt Qaddafi since other customers, mainly in Europe, would quickly take up the slack.

Once again, the bureaucracy had produced its cherished reasons for doing nothing, reasons which overlooked the fundamental changes that had occurred in the oil market since the energy crisis of the 1970s. There was not yet an oil glut, but the market was definitely going soft. The European allies might not rush to fill the void left by an American boycott of Libyan oil. Europe now had convenient access to North Sea oil, which was also light and sweet. Nigeria alone had enough unused capacity to make up for the loss of Libyan oil, and Nigerian crude was selling for $1.50 a barrel less than Libyan. Oil experts could argue it back and forth, but Roche felt there was a much more fundamental issue involved. If the Reagan administration was serious about getting tough with Qaddafi, it would have to shoulder whatever economic burden the cutoff of Libyan oil entailed. At one meeting, Haig's counselor, Robert McFarlane, pounded his fist on the table and said, We must understand that this is a moral issue.

The oil issue dovetailed with the hostage issue since most of the 2,000 Americans in Libya were involved in oil production. American workers lifted about two thirds of Qaddafi's oil from the ground. Pulling them out would both eliminate the hostage pool and do at least temporary damage to Qaddafi's prime source of revenue. "One of the first things we had to do was invalidate passports for travel to Libya," Frank Fukuyama said, a step that would place Libya on a short list of pariah nations along with Cuba, North Korea, North Vietnam, and Albania.

The ominous, get-tough rumblings from the Policy Planning staff brought out a host of arguments from the professionals in the Near East Bureau, which had geographic responsibility for relations with Libya and would be charged with carrying out any changes in policy. The United States had the power to steam roll Qaddafi any time it wanted. As the Mideast specialists saw it, the challenge was to do that in a manner that did not destroy America's fragile credibility with the moderate Arabs. "One typical and very powerful argument used by the FSOs [the career Foreign Service Officers] was that . . . the way to treat Qaddafi was simply to ignore him or to laugh him off," Frank Fukuyama said. There was unquestionably an air of the ridiculous about Qaddafi, from his Gilbert and Sullivan uniforms to his pretensions as the prophet of Islam, but, said Fukuyama, "our feeling was he would be regarded as a fool and a joker until he got away with something big."

Something very big happened on October 6, 1981: the assassination of Anwar Sadat. The televised images of gunmen raking Sadat with automatic weapons fire while the American Ambassador dove for cover vividly captured the havoc terrorism could wreak. The one Arab brave enough to make peace with Israel was dead. Immediately, Qaddafi emerged as the prime suspect. He had been plotting to murder Sadat for years, and he openly gloated when the deed was finally done. "There was a major effort to find a Qaddafi link to the Sadat assassination," the CIA's deputy director, Bob Inman, said. The murder turned out to be the work of an internal Muslim group seeking revenge not only for Sadat's separate peace with Israel but also for his too cordial relations with the United States. Still, if Qaddafi was not directly responsible for Sadat's death, it was not for lack of trying. As Frank Fukuyama said, "It may not have been his people who did the actual shooting, but he was constantly sending people to Egypt to blow away Sadat." Although Qaddafi was acquitted of this particular crime, it stood as a prime example of why he should not be laughed off as a megalomaniacal fool.

Sadat's death also drove home the fragility of efforts to contain Qaddafi through the traditional instruments of American foreign policy. Elaine Morton of the Policy Planning staff concluded that, "from a cost-benefit analysis, it was beyond U.S. resources to strengthen neighboring governments like Sudan, Tunisia, and Morocco to the point where they could withstand all the subversion Qaddafi could support." Egypt already was receiving more than $1 billion a year in military aid, and it had not protected Sadat from assassins; indeed it may actually have egged them on. For the price of a few automatic weapons, Qaddafi could undo it all. "The leverage Qaddafi gets out of a small investment is very great," Fukuyama said. "How much does it cost to equip a hit squad?"

Even before Sadat's assassination, Haig had begun referring to Qaddafi in background sessions with reporters as "a cancer that has to be cut out," and on June 18, the President had signed a secret intelligence "finding" directing the CIA to provide "non-lethal" support and training to anti-Qaddafi exiles. In October, a former Libyan diplomat named Mohammed Mugharief founded the National Front for the Salvation of Libya, underwritten largely by the CIA with help from Saudi Arabia. Based in the Sudan, Mugharief's National Front established a radio station to broadcast a mixture of news and anti-Qaddafi propaganda into Libya and began casting about for other prominent exiles to join the campaign. Neither CIA director William Casey nor anyone else thought the exiles would be strong enough to topple Qaddafi, but they were a low-cost way to make trouble for him and a new source of intelligence on what was going on inside Libya.

On October 15, little more than a week after Sadat's assassination, Elaine Morton wrote a paper laying out the case for a trade embargo against Libya. As usual, the paper was circulated to the other branches of the State Department, and, as usual, they objected. Morton said her boss, Paul Wolfowitz, "took my paper and all the little memos objecting to it and clipped them together with a cover note and sent it to Haig, saying, 'Here's a good idea. Isn't it like the bureaucracy to say why it can't be done?' "

While the bureaucrats were haggling, a self-proclaimed terrorist walked into an American embassy in Africa and declared that he had been present at a terrorist training camp in Libya when Qaddafi personally approved plans to send hit teams to the United States to assassinate Reagan, Vice President George Bush, Haig, or any other high-ranking official. At first, there was every reason to doubt the story. The informant seemed to have walked away from the plot with remarkable ease, his story played off press accounts of Qaddafi's public threats against Reagan, and he was demanding money and asylum. It did not seem like a hot lead, but when he passed a lie detector test, he was sent to the United States for further questioning. The most striking aspect of the informant's story was that the plan he described—ambushing a motorcade with rocket-propelled grenades—was a dead ringer for an aborted Libyan plot to assassinate Hermann Eilts, the U.S. Ambassador to Egypt, in 1976. There was no good explanation for that coincidence—except either the informant had heard about the Eilts plot from someone else, which seemed unlikely since it had been a secret operation, or knew what he was talking about. His credibility suffered a temporary setback when he failed a second lie detector test, but his CIA examiners decided that was because they had asked him to tell more than he knew and he had tried to oblige, thinking that would secure him asylum in the United States. A third test was administered with the questions scaled back to cover only the part of the story he originally had volunteered. This time he passed.

Ever since the Gulf of Sidra incident when the NSA had overheard Qaddafi vowing to kill Reagan, the evidence of Libyan assassination plots against the President or his representatives had been growing. In Rome, Italian police uncovered an apparent plot to assassinate American Ambassador Maxwell Rabb. Seven armed Libyans were picked up and expelled from the country, while Rabb was whisked home to the United States so fast he didn't have time to take a change of clothes.

Neither the CIA nor the FBI was able to uncover any convincing evidence that hit squads had left Libya bound for the United States. Lillian Harris at State discounted the episode as mainly a "hysterical reaction" to unconfirmed intelligence and wrote a memo suggesting that the scare might have been a "third country disinformation scheme." Some officials suspected it had been cooked up by Israel to goad Washington into taking a tougher stance toward Qaddafi. A spurious report that "Carlos the Jackal" was leading the hit squads had come from the Israelis and mysteriously appeared in print a full day before the Mossad passed it to the CIA. Agency officials who knew the details of the defector's debriefings insisted he had to be taken seriously, even though, when challenged by the State and Justice Departments, they acknowledged they had no independent confirmation that he was telling the truth. What if the President had been assassinated? How would the CIA, FBI, and Secret Service explain why they had ignored a source who had passed two lie detector tests and whose story bore such a remarkable resemblance to the Eilts plot?

Real or imaginary, the hit squads had a dramatic effect on the Reagan administration's policy toward Libya. "The top people suddenly felt Qaddafi was coming after them personally," said Philip Stoddard. "They took umbrage at that." On November 30, at a meeting of the National Security Council, the President, in the words of a subsequent memo, "directed that plans be developed for a military response against Libya in the event of a further Libyan attempt to assassinate American officials or attack U.S. facilities." Following the meeting, Haig, Weinberger, and Casey recommended that contingency plans be prepared "to carry out military action against Libya in self-defense following a further Libyan provocation." The targets selected were Qaddafi's terrorist training camps and the piles of uncrated Soviet military equipment stored at Libyan bases.

Ten days later, on December 9, 1981, Deputy Secretary of State William Clark called upon "all Americans to leave Libya as soon as possible" and announced that "United States passports are being invalidated for travel to Libya, effective immediately." The accompanying public notice stated that "there is an imminent danger to the physical safety of Americans traveling to or present in Libya," a claim almost no one in government believed. Despite his plotting against U.S. officials and installations, "Qaddafi's attitude toward Americans was to go out of his way to make it clear that Libya was a good place to do business," said Elaine Morton. "The hidden agenda was that if you wanted to take military action, you couldn't because Qaddafi could take Americans hostage." "That was the intention all along," said Morton's colleague Frank Fukuyama, "to clear the decks."

The next day, December 10, the President signed National Security Decision Directive 16, which set up a task force to oversee the implementation of the new Libya policy. Additional measures were on the way. The administration already had decided to ban all purchases of Libyan oil and to crack down on the export of American goods to Libya. The actual announcement was delayed to give Americans in Libya time to leave and the allies in Europe time to join in. Haig was convinced that when the allies saw the quality of American intelligence on Libyan support for terrorism, they would fall into line. "He thought the stuff was so good and so impossible to deny that all we had to do was show it to the Europeans and they would go along," said Herman Cohen, State's deputy director of intelligence. Haig had his special assistant, Michael Ledeen, prepare a paper on Libyan support for terrorism to be presented to a meeting of NATO foreign ministers in Belgium. However, the NATO meeting was dominated by the declaration of martial law in Poland, and the job of rounding up international support for sanctions against Qaddafi fell to teams of intelligence analysts who were dispatched to Europe and Africa. In Africa, the Americans found themselves singing to the choir. In Europe, said one of the briefers, Herman Cohen, "Everybody took copious notes, but there was a total lack of interest in joining us."

By the time the oil import ban finally was announced on March 10,

1982, its effect was largely symbolic. Libyan oil was selling at such an inflated price that the market already had begun to turn elsewhere for light, sweet crude. American companies had cut back on the amount of Libyan oil they were lifting. The American market, which had imported more than half a million barrels of Libyan oil every day, was getting by nicely on just 150,000 barrels a day. As for the export ban, it applied only to those items already denied to Communist countries. Licenses would be required for all other exports to Libya, which at least would enable the government to keep track of what was still going there. "No question, it was a half-measure," Morton said.

★   ★   ★

Looking back on it several years later, Frank Fukuyama would claim that U.S. policy toward Libya was "one of the best planned out policies" of the Reagan administration. By that he did not mean that it was perfect, but that "all of the stages were well thought through" as the hard-line predilections of the new administration were filtered through the bedrock of the foreign policy establishment. "I can't emphasize enough the extent to which almost all the professionals in the State Department were against the policy," Morton said. It took fourteen months of bureaucratic maneuvering and a series of extraordinary events—the Gulf of Sidra incident, the assassination of Sadat, the reports of Libyan hit squads—for the Reagan administration to draft the bureaucracy into its slow-motion war against Muamar Qaddafi. Even then, few people were under any illusions that eliminating Qaddafi would put a stop to international terrorism or Soviet-sponsored adventurism, but it was a start. "It's true Qaddafi is not the source of all terrorism," Fukuyama said, "but he is the source of an identifiable large part—and furthermore we can deal with him because he is militarily and politically isolated." There lay the heart of the Reagan administration's fixation with Qaddafi. If the United States could not deal with him, with whom could it deal?

Qaddafi was the moral equivalent of a serial killer on the loose. He was armed and dangerous, a threat to the weak and unsuspecting, but he had no following and was bound, sooner or later, to self-destruct, a victim of the same impulses that made him so notorious. Unless he somehow got his hands on a nuclear weapon, he would never be more than a historical footnote.

The Ayatollah Khomeini, on the other hand, was history in the making. His overthrow of the Shah was among the most important political upheavals of the twentieth century. His vow to spread divine justice throughout the world was as portentous as Nikita Khrushchev's call for "wars of national liberation." The Shiites who heard Khomeini's cry represent only 10 percent of the world's 832 million Muslims, but during the Reagan era they would become perhaps the most powerful engine of change—and of instability—in the world. The Ayatollah, not the Colonel, would test the limits of American power. The first test came in Lebanon, which the Ayatollah himself said, "we consider . . . to be part of Iran."

★5★

THE SKY IS FALLING

Col. James Longhofer, the chief of the Army's Office of Special Operations, stood on the roof of the American Embassy in Cairo at midnight, monitoring the radio that linked him by satellite to way stations in the Sinai Desert and Israel. It was midnight, Friday, August 14, 1981.

Five hours earlier, two Hughes 500D helicopters attached to a secret Army unit called Sea Spray had lifted off from Cairo in the fading light and headed east into darkness toward the airfield at El Arish in the Sinai. There they topped off their fuel tanks and turned north toward Beirut, carrying Bashir Gemayel, the favorite son of Lebanon's most powerful Christian clan, his wife, and bodyguards on the last leg of a secret journey home from the United States. The crewmen who had loaded the Gemayel party's bags aboard the helicopters were sure they contained gold; nothing else could be so heavy.

Just north of Beirut, the helicopters, their running lights extinguished, turned east again and headed directly toward the coast of Lebanon, skimming the waves. On the beach, a car blinked its headlights. The helicopters settled to the ground, and the CIA's chief of station in Beirut welcomed Gemayel home. The entourage transferred to a fleet of waiting cars, and the helicopters departed, heading south to Israel to refuel before returning to Egypt.

Except for a patch of fog which forced the helicopters down briefly in the Sinai, the first mission flown by Sea Spray since the unit was created in the wake of the disastrous Iran rescue mission went off without a hitch.

Looking back, it was probably the last thing that went right for the United States in Lebanon. Within two years, Gemayel would be dead, and Ronald Reagan's administration would find itself embarked on the most disastrous military venture of his presidency.

★   ★   ★

At thirty-three, Bashir Gemayel, was perhaps the only man who could save his country from a slow and painful death. In the "black September" of 1970 some 9,000 PLO fedayeen had been driven out of Jordan and had moved into Lebanon, setting up bases in the southern part of the country from which they propelled rockets and terrorists toward the settlements of northern Israel. The Israelis fought back with air strikes and commando raids, blasting away at what was always a fragile stability in Lebanon. In 1975, the veneer of civilization that once had made Beirut the Paris of the Orient disintegrated into furious bloodletting as Christians and Muslims turned to violence to settle their ancient scores. An attempt by Lebanon's Christian militias to rid their country of the Palestinians escalated into a full-scale civil war, unleashing religious, ethnic, and political hatreds that had been festering for generations.

Syria, which saw Lebanon as a strategic buffer against Israel, intervened twice, first on the side of the Palestinians and then on the side of the Christian militias. In the first eighteen months of fighting, an estimated 40,000 people, most of them innocent civilians, perished. In 1978, the Israelis launched an operation of their own to root out the PLO, dispatching 10,000 soldiers on a sweep through southern Lebanon that sent 100,000 refugees fleeing north toward the shattered Lebanese capital. By 1981, the elegant and aptly named Place des Martyrs, once the heart of Beirut, was reduced to rubble. Sticks and string guided the occasional pedestrian through a minefield where once there had been a thriving marketplace, now a stark monument to the savagery of the militiamen, both Christian and Muslim. No one was immune from the fury. Bashir Gemayel's infant daughter was killed in an ambush meant for him.

Lebanon was not a nation so much as a battlefield onto which clans and sects poured their violent hatreds. Lebanon was governed—if that was the right word—by the National Pact of 1943, an unwritten agreement that allocated virtually every job from the presidency to the local postmaster along religious lines. Based on a 1932 census which changing demographics had long since rendered obsolete, the National Pact reserved the presidency for Maronite Christians like the Gemayel clan.

The prime minister was always a Sunni Muslim. The Shiites, long regarded as the rednecks of Lebanon, were left with a few powerless
portfolios, even though they were the largest and fastest growing sect.

To most Americans, the political landscape of Lebanon was incomprehensible. A country roughly the size of Connecticut, it was partitioned
among warlords and generals, militias and armies, much like the turf of
urban gangs. It was the Jets and the Sharks, the Diablos and the Sham-
rocks, but instead of chains, stilettos, and zipguns, they used automatic
rifles, mortars, and rocket-propelled grenades. The PLO ruled much of
Muslim West Beirut, collecting taxes, enforcing its own law, and raising
its own army. East Beirut was the province of Christian warlords like
the Gemayels. To the south of the capital, the downtrodden Shiites and
homeless Palestinians quarreled in the squalid suburbs that separated
Beirut from its seaside airport. In the Chouf Mountains which looked
down on the airport, the Druze, a Muslim sect, feuded with the Christians. Beyond the mountains, the Syrian Army controlled the fertile
Bekaa Valley and its population of Shiite Muslims. To the south, Israel
had carved out a security zone where Shiites, Palestinians, and Christians lived in mutual hatred.

Radiating through this war-weary and divided land were the tremors
of an earthquake whose epicenter was Iran, tremors which were largely
ignored by American intelligence analysts. "The thing everybody got
wrong was the Shiite revolution," said Francis "Bing" West, the assistant secretary of defense for international security affairs. "No one predicted that." Philip Stoddard, the State Department's director of current
analysis, agreed that "the tendency in the intelligence community was
to minimize the Shia influence and to ignore the situation of the Shia."

Evidence of the incipient alliance between the disenfranchised Shiites
and the Islamic fanatics in Iran was there for all to see. Beginning in
1981, posters showing the Ayatollah Khomeini and the Lebanese Shiite
idol Musa Sadr side by side began appearing in the southern slums of
Beirut. Born in Iran's holy city of Qom, well over six feet tall, strikingly
handsome and marvelously eloquent, Musa Sadr was a natural leader.
The American Ambassador had cabled the State Department that Musa
Sadr "is without debate one of the most, if not the most, impressive
individual I have met in Lebanon. . . . His charisma is obvious, and his
apparent sincerity is awe-inspiring."

In March 1974, Sadr had gathered a crowd of 75,000 in the Bekaa
Valley town of Baalbek and announced the creation of a new mass
movement to fight for the Shia's political and economic rights. He had
called it the "Movement of the Disinherited," which quickly was re-

duced to the acronym Amal. What does the government expect? Musa Sadr had asked the crowd. What does it expect except rage and except revolution? Within a year, the angry Shiites had raised an armed militia, just like every other sect.

From the start, Amal had two enemies—the Palestinians and the Israelis—who, as so often was the case in Lebanon, also were mortal foes of one another. The Palestinians used Shiite territory in southern Lebanon to launch commando raids and artillery strikes at settlements in northern Israel. The inevitable Israeli retaliation fell most heavily on the Shiites. Caught between the Palestinians and the Israelis, Musa Sadr turned to other Muslim nations for help in arming his Amal militia. On a visit to Libya in 1978, he disappeared, almost certainly murdered by Qaddafi for reasons that remain obscure to everyone but, presumably, Qaddafi.

After Musa Sadr disappeared, the leadership of Amal fell to an entirely different kind of man. Born in West Africa, educated in France, trained as a lawyer, Nabih Berri was more interested in political accommodation than Islamic revolution. "We support the Islamic revolution in Iran," he said, "but . . . we do not want an Islamic revolution in Lebanon." In cables back to Washington, the American Embassy portrayed Berri as a moderate who supported the Lebanese state and its army. His goal, according to the embassy, was to curb the power of the Christian minority and to allow the Shiites to exert the force of their numbers and thereby dominate Lebanese politics.

When Berri's brand of traditional politics failed to loosen the Christians' grip, disenchanted Shiites began to drift away from Amal to more radical factions which vowed to transform Lebanon into an Islamic republic modeled after Iran. These small splinter groups and their dogma of rage and revolution might have remained lost in the maze of sectarian strife had it not been for the Israeli invasion of Lebanon.

★　★　★

It was in October 1981 at the funeral of Egyptian President Anwar Sadat—himself a victim of spreading Islamic fundamentalism—that Israeli Prime Minister Menachem Begin first mentioned to Secretary of State Alexander Haig that Israel might sweep into southern Lebanon again to clear out the PLO. "If you move, you move alone," Haig told Begin. "Unless there is a major, internationally recognized provocation, the United States will not support such an action." To the Israelis, what Haig didn't say was more important. He did not threaten to cut off the supply of American military equipment that Israel needed to sustain an operation in Lebanon—especially if Syria entered the conflict with Soviet backing. Haig's omission created a vacuum, and Begin's Defense Minister, Ariel Sharon, rushed to fill it. "The entire U.S. tragedy in Lebanon was in large part an outgrowth of persistent misunderstanding and ambivalence toward Begin and Sharon," said Geoffrey Kemp, the Middle East expert on the National Security Council (NSC) staff. "I was part of it, so I'll take responsibility, but it was the most inconsistent policy toward any government I've ever seen."

The operation Begin described to Haig would simply have pushed the PLO 40 kilometers into Lebanon, where its rockets and artillery could not reach Israel's northern settlements. In fact, Sharon had an entirely different operation in mind, one whose objective was nothing less than the annihilation of the PLO—not the slaughter of every last fedayeen, but the elimination of the PLO as an independent political and military force in Lebanon. Sharon meant to drive Yasir Arafat and his fighters out of Lebanon forever, just as King Hussein had done in Jordan in 1970. Sharon and Bashir Gemayel had toured Beirut together and agreed upon a secret plan—secret even from the Israeli cabinet. Israel's army would drive north to the outskirts of Beirut and link up with Gemayel's militia, closing the ring around the PLO.

Sharon believed a Lebanon free of the PLO would be free to become the second Arab nation to sign a peace treaty with Israel. In Bashir Gemayel, he thought he had found the man to lead this new Lebanon. Sharon and other Israeli officials argued that Gemayel was a new Lebanese man, tired of civil war, disgusted by the Syrian and Palestinian occupation of his country, ruthless but willing to cooperate with rival sects.

American intelligence analysts and Lebanon experts were less impressed by Gemayel. The CIA's top Middle East analyst, Charles Waterman, was skeptical of the notion that Bashir Gemayel was a Lebanese first and a Christian second, and he warned against putting too many eggs in Gemayel's basket. The American Ambassador in Beirut, John Gunther Dean, despised Gemayel and refused to meet with him, and the embassy's political officers considered him more of a divisive force than a savior. "Bashir had no real friends at State," said Philip Stoddard. "He was the Aaron Burr of Lebanese politics. He was the first modern Lebanese politician but he was also a polarizing influence."

In what would become a trademark of the Reagan years, the advice of the experts was largely ignored. "There was no connection between the people who knew something about Lebanon and those who made the decisions at the top," Philip Stoddard observed. "It was part of the ideological baggage that the Reagan administration brought with it. They believed the bureaucracy was full of candy-ass wimps who were afraid to do anything." Added Stoddard's colleague Herman Cohen, the deputy director of Intelligence and Research, "Haig's view was that he was right and everybody else was wrong." The embassy in Beirut sent cable after cable to Washington, warning that an Israeli invasion would provoke terrorism and undermine America's standing in the Arab world, but not a word came back.

Haig was intrigued by the prospect of dealing a fatal blow to the PLO, which he considered little more than a tool of the Soviet Union. In February of 1982, Sharon sent his chief of military intelligence to brief Haig on the broad outlines of a plan to sweep into Lebanon, knock the Syrians aside if they dared to interfere and drive to the outskirts of Beirut. The Secretary repeated the same bland warning he had given Begin at Sadat's funeral about the need for an internationally recognized provocation and cautioned that the response should be proportional to the provocation. As soon as the briefing ended, Haig summoned his Assistant Secretary for the Middle East, Nicholas Veliotes, to his office. Sensing that something important was afoot, Veliotes brought along his senior deputy, Morris Draper. They found Haig sitting with a map of Lebanon.

Their plan is really very intriguing from a military point of view, Haig said. What? exclaimed a startled Draper. There are a million Shia in between!

If Sharon went crashing to Beirut, Veliotes argued, there would be nothing but pieces of American Middle East policy left to pick up. Furthermore, the veteran diplomat warned, Sharon was kidding himself if he thought he could destroy the PLO by crushing Arafat in Beirut. Even if Arafat and his top aides were all killed, Veliotes said, other Palestinians outside Lebanon would take up the cause of Palestinian nationalism.

"Haig's response was quite thoughtful," Veliotes recalled later. The Secretary of State asked Veliotes and Draper to draft a message for the U.S. Ambassador to Israel, Samuel Lewis, to convey to Begin, reiterating the cautions about adventurism in Lebanon he had made to Begin at Sadat's funeral. The Israelis, however, apparently interpreted the message delivered by Ambassador Lewis as a cover-your-ass communication and took Haig's earlier bland responses as the real signal.

Later in the month, Draper and Philip Habib, the President's special Mideast envoy, met with Sharon at the Israeli Defense Ministry and the beefy Israeli general got carried away with enthusiasm for his plan to tame Lebanon. The two American diplomats rushed back to the American Embassy and drafted a terse cable warning Haig what Sharon was up to, which was flashed to Washington on the Secretary of State's private "Roger Channel." In Washington, Veliotes's Near East bureau ignored the message: officials there knew Sharon was a schemer, but they blithely assumed that Menachem Begin and the rest of the cabinet would never approve an operation as reckless as the one Sharon had described to Habib and Draper. The envoys' Roger Channel cable went unanswered.

In May, Sharon himself visited Washington, and Haig again outlined the conditions he believed were necessary to justify an Israeli move. The State Department's Middle East experts felt Haig's attempts at subtlety were lost on Sharon. Begin would later claim that the Secretary of State had given Israel a green light, and Haig himself seemed to recognize that he had spoken too softly. In a speech trumpeted as a major policy statement, he offered the Israelis a list of reasons why they did not have to invade, but it was too little and too late.

On June 3, 1982, gunmen shot Israel's Ambassador to Great Britain, Shlomo Argov, outside London's Dorchester Hotel. The shooting, which left Argov gravely wounded, was an outrage, but it seemed clear that it was not the work of the PLO. Argov's assailants were armed with Polish-made machine pistols used almost exclusively by the renegade Palestinian terrorist Abu Nidal, a sworn enemy of Yasir Arafat and the mainstream PLO. One of the four gunmen was captured, and in time he led Scotland Yard to his accomplices, who revealed that their leader was a second cousin of Abu Nidal and that they had received their weapons from a military attaché at the Iraqi Embassy in London. None of that mattered to Sharon. To him, the shooting of an Israeli ambassador was not a mystery to be solved by Scotland Yard but the *casus belli* he had been waiting for. Measured by all that followed, the attempted assassination of Shlomo Argov was one of the most momentous terrorist attacks in history.

The next morning, Begin convened the cabinet to approve strikes against PLO arms caches in West Beirut. Israel's air force hit its targets that afternoon, and two hours later PLO artillery in southern Lebanon retaliated by opening up on Israeli settlements in Galilee. The next evening, after the end of the Sabbath, the Israeli cabinet met again and approved "Operation Peace for Galilee." According to minutes of the meeting, Sharon assured the cabinet that the operation was designed simply to drive the PLO's rockets and artillery out of range of the northern settlements. We're talking about a range of forty kilometers,

Sharon said. The stage I have spoken about is an operation that will take about twelve hours. Begin sent the same message to President Reagan and asked the United States to inform Syria that Israel would not engage Syrian military units in Lebanon unless Syria attacked first.

The orders to the Israeli Defense Forces directly contradicted both what Sharon had said to his own cabinet and what Begin had told the President of the United States. A division of Israeli paratroopers went ashore above the 40-kilometer line and immediately turned north toward Beirut. A second division was sent to cut the Beirut-Damascus highway, isolating the Syrian forces in Beirut from their bases in the Bekaa Valley. On June 8, while the President's Middle East envoy, Philip Habib, was in Damascus to deliver Begin's assurances that Israel was not looking for war with Syria, the Israeli Air Force knocked out fourteen Syrian antiaircraft missile batteries in the Bekaa Valley and, in one of the biggest air battles in history, shot down twenty-nine Syrian jet fighters that had been sent to defend the missiles. Within days, the Israeli Defense Forces destroyed a major portion of Syria's Soviet-supplied arsenal—89 aircraft, 19 missile batteries, and more than 350 tanks. All of us out here will live to regret this, Habib told Assistant Secretary of State Veliotes over the telephone.

Habib negotiated a cease-fire in place which was supposed to stop the Israelis at their avowed goal 40 kilometers inside Lebanon, but the Defense Forces simply kept rolling north toward Beirut. On June 14, an Israeli army unit linked up with Gemayel's militia and closed the ring around Muslim West Beirut. Operation Peace for Galilee, the 40-kilometer incursion against PLO strongholds in southern Lebanon, had become exactly what Sharon had intended from the start—the siege of an Arab capital.

Syria was humiliated; the PLO defeated. Israel had taken heavy casualties, 170 dead and 700 wounded. Haig believed that "in this tragic situation lay the great opportunity to make peace . . . to move all foreign forces—Syrian, Palestinian and Israeli—out of Lebanon and to return the country to the Lebanese." Acting on his own authority and without the knowledge of the President, Haig cabled Habib in Jerusalem and instructed him to inform the Israeli cabinet of his plan for seizing the opportunity to remake Lebanon. The key, Haig believed, was getting Arafat out of Beirut as quickly as possible, thereby removing the Israeli rationale for staying at the gates of the city.

In order to turn up the heat on Arafat, the Israeli Defense Forces sent spotters into West Beirut to track down the PLO leader and radio his position to Israeli planes circling overhead. Finding someone in Beirut is not easy, as the United States would soon learn. Arafat remained on the move, rarely staying more than thirty minutes in one place. Even so, the Israelis almost got him, once leveling a building two minutes after their quarry had left it. "Israel's objective was to create an atmosphere of pressure and threat that would persuade the PLO that it must either come to terms or be annihilated," Haig wrote in his memoirs. It almost worked.

Arafat, who at first had disbelieved the reports that the Israelis were in the suburbs of Beirut, panicked. On June 16, he asked a Lebanese official to send word to the Israelis that he was willing to leave the city in forty-eight hours. Some of his commanders began inquiring about taking asylum in foreign embassies, while PLO fighters stripped off their uniforms and burned their identification cards. "The PLO was going to be disarmed and probably leave the country," Haig wrote. "The siege of Beirut would be over." But just then, what Haig called "the constant bugaboo of the administration's foreign policy—divided councils, different voices," intervened.

Vice President George Bush and Defense Secretary Caspar Weinberger, in Saudi Arabia for the funeral of King Khalid and worried about the damage the invasion could do to America's position in the Arab world, told the new King, Fahd, that the United States would do everything it could to prevent the Israelis from entering Beirut. The next day, according to Haig, "we heard that the PLO was hardening its position: the Lebanese attributed this to Saudi advice, which was in turn based on what the Saudis had heard from the Vice President's party."

The Israelis, reluctant to send their troops into Beirut but determined to root out the PLO, laid siege to the city in earnest, killing hundreds of civilians. "They were bombing the shit out of the city day after day after day," Habib said. "The city was under siege. They'd turned off the water. They'd cut off supplies." When Reagan saw the carnage on television, he was deeply troubled. Since much of the killing was being done with American-made weapons, each day of siege was a day of damage to Washington's relations with other Arab countries.

Over the Fourth of July weekend, Habib sent a seventeen-page cable to Washington, suggesting that the Reagan administration send troops to Lebanon as part of a multinational force that would guarantee the safe retreat of Arafat's men to whatever Arab states could be persuaded to receive them. "I had to get the PLO out of Lebanon and that was the only way I was going to get them out," Habib said later. "They weren't going to walk out under the guns of the Israelis. You're not going to get a multinational force if you're not prepared to put your own troops in."

The Joint Chiefs of Staff (JCS) were already on record opposing the introduction of American forces into Lebanon. The very first document Gen. John Vessey had signed as chairman of the Joint Chiefs of Staff was a memo dated June 19, 1982, which urged Weinberger to tell the President that it would, as Vessey later put it, "be very unwise for the U.S. to find itself in a position where it had to put its military forces between the Israelis and the Arabs."

The choice of Vessey, an old-fashioned soldier who had enlisted in the Army and won a battlefield commission at Anzio in World War II, to succeed David Jones as chairman of the Joint Chiefs of Staff had been emblematic of the ascendancy of the military under Ronald Reagan. Fairly or not, Jones had been tagged as a political general, one who had trimmed his military advice to suit the Carter White House. As commander of U.S. forces in South Korea, Vessey had jeopardized his own career by bucking Carter's plan to withdraw 40,000 American troops. As chairman, Vessey could be counted on to give the President unvarnished military advice. Over the next four years, the plainspoken and unpretentious old soldier, a sort of Harry Truman in uniform, frequently would give Reagan advice those around the President didn't want to hear. Most of the time, Vessey would be backed up by the Secretary of Defense in cautioning against the use of military force. Exasperated members of the National Security Council staff would take to referring to Weinberger and Vessey as the one-two pillow.

In this case, however, Weinberger favored Habib's proposal. "I thought anything that could remove the PLO was a good thing to do," Weinberger said afterwards. "With the international force we could get out of Beirut a very volatile unpredictable group and that would remove any excuse the Israelis might have for moving into Beirut. Ultimately, then, we thought we could get some kind of peaceful conditions and return to previously existing borders. It seemed to me that it was a first step and a necessary step to take." The American debacle in Lebanon had begun, dressed in good intentions and humanitarian motives.

★　★　★

The Marines went ashore at dawn on August 25 to begin the evacuation of the PLO by sea. The Marines had been chosen because they were already in the Mediterranean and the European Command could commit them to Lebanon without any impact on its primary mission of defending against a Soviet invasion of Western Europe. Besides, the Marines carried less baggage than any other force. Their cooks, storekeepers, paymasters, medics, mechanics, even their tanks could remain aboard the ships offshore, making it easier to withdraw when the time came. "The JCS wanted it as impermanent as we possibly could," General Vessey said. Still, the Marines were a powerful symbol. By sending them, the United States was committing its honor and prestige to Lebanon.

Eight hundred Marines went ashore, along with contingents from France and Italy, to interpose themselves between 30,000 Israelis and 14,000 Syrians and armed Palestinians. The night before, the amphibious ships had stood off Beirut, eyeing their objective. "We intently watched the lightless Muslim West Beirut section from which thousands of rounds of ammunition were being fired into the air from many types of weapons," Col. James Mead, the commander of the Marines, wrote later. "It was an ominous sight."

"We didn't want to do it," said Gen. Willie Y. Smith, deputy head of the European Command, which had operational responsibility for Lebanon. "None of us felt that was the best way to use military force. We didn't know a lot about the environment ashore. We didn't know whether the PLO was going to cooperate. We were afraid we were going to get caught in the middle. We didn't want to do it, but we recognized we had to do it. We wanted to make sure we got in and got out as soon as we could."

The Marines had two missions. The first was to safeguard the evacuation of the PLO fighters as they boarded ships in Beirut harbor. The second was to uphold a promise made in an exchange of notes between the American and Lebanese governments. "Law-abiding Palestinian non-combatants remaining in Beirut, including the families of those who have departed, will be authorized to live in peace and security," the U.S. note said. "The U.S. will provide its guarantees on the basis of assurances received from the Government of Israel and from the leaders of certain Lebanese groups with which it has been in contact."

The last of the PLO, including Yasir Arafat, left Beirut without incident on September 1. "It's almost incredible," Vessey said, marveling at how well the evacuation had gone. "It worked very well," Weinberger agreed. "All the things happened that we predicted, that we hoped. We did not have problems. We got the PLO out. They used up a large portion of their ammunition, shooting it off in the air in that basically nonsensical way they have of behaving, and they left."

Ten days later, just seventeen days after they had landed, the Marines withdrew to their ships. "I wanted to get them out because the mission was over, and General Vessey certainly did, too," Weinberger recalled.

"Some people wanted them to stay. There was quite an argument internally."

Habib wanted them to stay. "I thought it would be desirable to help in the post-departure period," he said later. But he was overruled. When the Marines left, the French also decided to go. So did the Italians, who were stationed outside the Palestinian refugee camps south of the city.

★   ★   ★

Two weeks later, the new political order Israel had hoped to create in Lebanon went up in smoke. President-elect Bashir Gemayel—the man the United States was counting on to unify his country, the man Israel was counting on to sign a peace treaty—was killed by a bomb planted by a Syrian agent. The next day the Israeli Defense Forces moved into Muslim West Beirut in direct violation of the agreement under which the PLO had been evacuated, claiming it was protecting Palestinian civilians from revenge at the hands of Bashir's grief-crazed followers. In fact, Sharon was intent upon cleaning out the PLO terrorists and weapons caches he was certain Arafat had left behind. On the night of September 16, with Israeli Defense Forces' permission, Gemayel's Phalange militia entered the Palestinian refugee camps at Sabra and Shatila, ostensibly searching for the source of sporadic gunfire. When the Christian militiamen were finished, more than 700 unarmed Palestinians had been slaughtered.

Weinberger found no relation between the withdrawal of the multinational force and the massacre. "I don't think there's any connection," he said. Habib, who had promised Arafat in writing that the United States would guarantee the safety of the Palestinians left behind, disagreed. "The Italian force was right outside those camps," Habib said. "The Phalange troops would never have moved in there if the MNF [multinational force] had remained." The killing had been done by Lebanese militiamen while Israeli troops stood outside the camps, yet most American officials shared Habib's sense that, as Geoffrey Kemp of the NSC staff put it, "we had promised to protect the Palestinian civilians, it was our allies, the Israelis, who permitted the massacre to happen, and it was our boy Bashir Gemayel's troops that did the killing." Within forty-eight hours, the horrified Reagan administration agreed to a Lebanese request to send the Marines back to protect the people of West Beirut. "There was almost no debate," Kemp said.

"The second time I opposed going in," Weinberger remembered. "I thought we should not put people in on that kind of a mission that by definition could not be fulfilled unless you had an agreement to withdraw." If the mission was to protect the inhabitants of West Beirut from the Israelis and their Christian surrogates, the Marines would have to remain until the Israelis left and the Lebanese government was strong enough to guarantee the safety of the Palestinians.

Once Weinberger made up his mind, he rarely changed it. He was a gentleman in the best sense of the word—cultured, courteous, incorruptible—but he was stubborn as a man could be. Once he had taken a position, any further argument or suggestion of compromise fell on deaf ears. A short man, Weinberger joked about having been well over 6 feet tall when he took the job as Secretary of Defense, but more often than not it was he who wore the other person down. He had vast government experience, both as a member of the Nixon cabinet and as a California state legislator, but he was a self-acknowledged novice on defense. The armed services had welcomed Weinberger and the record defense budgets he brought with him. They had inculcated in him not only their needs for more and better weapons but also their determination never again to be sucked into an open-ended military action. The latter invariably became unpopular and undermined public support for the former. Over time, Weinberger's alliance with the military would drive other members of the Reagan administration to distraction, not only because it interfered with their agenda for redrawing the map of the world but also because it seemed so ungrateful for the Defense Department to be getting so much money and still be so reluctant to flex American muscle.

The Joint Chiefs were as strongly opposed to the second Beirut mission as they had been to the first. "We raised exactly the same arguments that were raised on the 19th of June," Vessey said, referring to his original memo to Weinberger. "I don't think anybody had any expectation we could turn it around. The guilt feeling affected us all. Still, we could see it's the wrong place to be."

A study by the Defense Intelligence Agency warned that "no one should be surprised if the peacekeeping force encounters intractable political and military problems on the ground." But if there was anything at all consistent about the administration's policy in Lebanon, it was that it routinely ignored the advice of the intelligence analysts. "If you kept raising problems, your access to the policymakers tended to dry up," said Phillip Stoddard, the State Department's director of current analysis. It is one of the paradoxes of the Reagan years that an administration so dedicated to rebuilding America's intelligence capabilities could be so contemptuous of the products they produced.

More than guilt was driving the Reagan administration. On September

1, the President had unveiled a new Middle East peace plan drafted by the new Secretary of State, George Shultz. Billed as "a fresh start," the plan sought to revive negotiations between Israel and its Arab neighbors, leading eventually to Palestinian autonomy in exchange for Arab recognition of Israel. So long as the Israelis occupied Lebanon, there could be no hope for progress on the peace plan. Reagan himself said the first steps on the road to peace would have to be taken in Lebanon.

"There were those of us saying that if we're going to do anything at all, now's the time to be bold," the NSC's Geoffrey Kemp recalled. "The argument was that we're a superpower. The Syrians have just been beaten, the Israelis are reeling, and the Lebanese are on their backs. Now's the time to send in real force. The idea was that the U.S. and France, and possibly Italy as well, would decide to introduce a major peacekeeping force into Lebanon—at least three American divisions and possibly two French—accompanied by ultimata to the Israelis and the Syrians to get their forces out of Lebanon." According to Kemp, the President liked the idea; so did his national security adviser, William Clark, and the deputy national security adviser, Robert McFarlane. Weinberger, of course, was unalterably opposed. It would not be the last time the staff of the National Security Council proposed a risky venture that appealed to the President but appalled the Secretary of Defense. The more Weinberger said no or stalled, the greater the temptation to bypass him became.

This time, Weinberger prevailed. "It never got anywhere," Kemp said. The brief debate over the expanded multinational force was another in what would become an endless series of struggles within the Reagan administration over the use of military power. "After the decision was made to go back in," Vessey said, "then we debated this business of what are we going to do. That was the question we never did get answered to our satisfaction. Perhaps it was our own pigheadedness that kept us from seeing what there was useful to do." The administration made up an answer by telling itself the Marines would be home soon. Reagan reported to Congress that the Marines would be needed in Lebanon "only for a limited period to meet the urgent requirements posed by the current situation." Assistant Secretary of State Veliotes told a Senate committee the end of the year was the "outer limit."

"We told CINCEUR [the Commander-in-Chief, Europe] to assume sixty days," Vessey said. "There might have been a little bit of wishful thinking on our part. The assumption that the Marines would only be there sixty days was based on: (a) we didn't want to be there in the first place; (b) we had a strong ally in the Secretary of Defense who didn't want to be there either; and (c) no goal or mission had yet been announced. We figured that once we got over our feeling of guilt and a little bit of law and order was established, the Marines would be withdrawn. I guess that was the fundamental wrong assumption in Lebanon—that things were going to get better."

The President caused a brief flurry when he suggested during a televised press conference that the Marines would not leave Beirut until all Israeli and Syrian forces had withdrawn from Lebanon. The White House rushed out a clarification explaining that the President really meant the withdrawal of all foreign forces was a goal, but not the criterion, for the successful completion of the Marines' mission.

The incident was passed over as just one more piece in the growing body of evidence that the President had a shockingly poor grasp of his own policies. Unwittingly, however, Reagan had exposed one of the fundamental weaknesses of his policy in Lebanon. No one, least of all the commander-in-chief, knew what it would take to declare victory. Unable to resolve the disputes within his administration, the President simply proceeded with a vague, ill-defined, and often deliberately ambiguous policy which each cabinet officer could interpret for himself. For his part, Weinberger said publicly that the Marines would withdraw the moment they encountered combat—an open invitation to anyone in Lebanon who wanted to get rid of the Marines.

★　★　★

The order sent out by the Joint Chiefs of Staff directed the Marines "to establish an environment which will permit the Lebanese Armed Forces to carry out their responsibilities in the Beirut area." The Marines were assigned to Beirut's international airport alongside the sea at the southern edge of the city. The other members of the multinational force, the French, Italians, and British, were located to the north of the Marines. For obvious military reasons, the Marine commander, Col. James Mead, wanted to occupy the hills just east of the airport, but for diplomatic reasons he couldn't. If he took the high ground, Mead explained, convoys resupplying Israeli Defense Forces' units in the mountains east of Beirut would have to pass through Marine lines, which the Muslims would perceive as cooperation between the multinational force and the Israelis.

The Marines had to settle for the low, flat ground at the airport. "We did not want to accept the position," Mead later testified, "but because of the low order of threat and the diplomatic requirements, it was acceptable and we felt that we could ensure the safety of the Marines." According to General Vessey, there was a more basic reason the Marines were left holding the low ground. "There's no high ground around the airport that's not dominated by higher ground to the east," Vessey explained. "Every time you got a piece of high ground there was always a next piece of higher ground than the one you just got."

Taking the higher ground would have required a larger force, and that was the last thing the Joint Chiefs wanted. They wanted the American military presence in Lebanon to be as innocuous as armed men can be. The Marine Amphibious Unit was a force of 1,500 men designed for the evacuation of civilians from trouble spots around the world. It was never intended to hold ground. It had only five tanks to its name. "Marines are supposed to get a beachhead and turn it over to somebody else," Adm. James Watkins, the Chief of Naval Operations, pointed out. Sending the Marines to occupy the airport was "like an incomplete amphibious operation," Watkins said. "It was a loser militarily."

But this was not a military mission. The order sent out by the Joint Chiefs on September 23 defined the mission as "presence," whatever that meant. When Ryan Crocker, the political officer at the American Embassy in Beirut, visited the arriving Marines aboard their ships, he asked them if anybody knew what a presence mission meant. If anyone does, Crocker said, please inform me, because the Department of State doesn't know either.

"Presence is what we do almost everywhere in the world in peacetime," Vessey explained. "The question is what is the purpose of our presence?" In Europe, American forces are present as a deterrent to Soviet aggression. Failing that, they are the first line of defense, a tripwire that would trigger an all-out military response. In Lebanon, the mission was to bear witness to the reestablishment of order. Failing that, well, nobody knew.

The sixty days that were supposed to mark the end of the American military presence in Lebanon expired, but the Marines went still deeper, conducting daily patrols through the city and training the Lebanese Army.

★ ★ ★

While the Muslim residents of West Beirut cheered the Marine patrols, Shiites from both Iran and Lebanon were converging on the crossroads town of Baalbek in the Bekaa Valley to begin plotting revenge against the Israeli invaders and their American patrons. Hussein Musawi, a former public school teacher who had become the military commander of the Amal militia, broke with the movement, accusing its leader, Nabih

Berri, of deserting Islamic principles. Moving to Baalbek, Musawi founded his own militia, which he called Islamic Amal. At almost the same time, a second group of Shiites formed around the radical cleric Sheik Hussein Fadlallah and called themselves Hezbollah, or Party of God. Iran was linked to both Islamic Amal and Hezbollah, in Hussein Musawi's words, as "a mother to a son."

Ever since the summer of 1980, Iran had been attempting to come to the aid of its Shiite brothers in Lebanon but had been restrained by Syria's Hafez Assad, who controlled the overland routes into the Bekaa Valley and who had no desire to see a fundamentalist revolution on his doorstep. All that changed, however, in the spring of 1982. When the Israelis invaded Lebanon in June, the Iranians dispatched a contingent of Revolutionary Guards to help expel the invaders. This time, Assad, furious that Israel had violated its promise not to attack Syrian forces, waved the Iranians through. "After the Israelis violated their promises, somehow the Syrians felt they had to let the Revolutionary Guards into Lebanon," said the State Department's Nicholas Veliotes. The engineers of this new alliance were Mohammed Mohtashami-pur, the Iranian ambassador to Syria, and Hosein Sheikholislam, the former Berkeley student and leader of the Tehran hostage siege.

The Iranians traveled overland to the Bekaa Valley along a dirt road that wound its way through the mountains from a holding camp inside Syria to Baalbek, an ancient city known for its Roman ruins and the quality of its hashish. Under the direction of Ambassador Mohtashami-pur in Damascus, the Iranians and their Lebanese Shiite allies moved into the Sheik Abdullah Barracks, a former Lebanese Army post which overlooks Baalbek from the south. The Revolutionary Guards established a command post in Baalbek's al-Khayyam Hotel and together with the local Shiite radicals took over a floor of what they promptly renamed the Ayatollah Khomeini Hospital. Soon posters of Khomeini and signs proclaiming "Death to America" began appearing in the streets of Baalbek, along with the more ominous message that "Martyrdom is the aim and hope of God's worshippers." Baalbek had become a forward base for bringing the Islamic revolution to Lebanon's one million Shiites, and the first goal was to drive out all Westerners. From his post in Iran's Foreign Ministry, Sheikholislam began sending messages to the Revolutionary Guard headquarters in the al-Khayyam Hotel, urging the shock troops of the revolution to prepare to confront America.

The first kidnapping of an American occurred on July 19, 1982 in the midst of the Israeli siege. As he was taking his afternoon walk David

Dodge, the acting president of the American University of Beirut, was hit on the head, and bundled into a car. Dodge, the most prominent American in Lebanon after the U.S. Ambassador, was turned over to the Iranian Revolutionary Guards, presumably in Baalbek, although he could never be sure since he was either blindfolded or drugged every time he was moved. His captors told him he was being held as ransom for the release of four Iranian diplomats who had been kidnapped by Christian militiamen in Beirut.

One of the missing Iranians was Ahmad Motevasselian, who Tehran said was an embassy political officer but who in fact commanded the Revolutionary Guards detachment that had just moved into Baalbek. Although political kidnappings were not new to Lebanon—nearly 2,000 Muslims, Christians, and Jews had disappeared during twelve years of civil war—Tehran was outraged to find its most important official in Lebanon on the wrong end of a hostage incident.

Dodge was as innocent of that crime as a man can be, but it is the tactic of terrorism to deliver a message by attacking the innocent. He was driven to Damascus in the trunk of a car and flown from there to a prison in Tehran where he was given adequate food, shelter, and medical care but never allowed to communicate with his family, who did not know if he was alive or dead. Motevasselian's disappearance sparked a new wave of kidnappings which began with Dodge and over time would cost more than 130 foreigners from 18 nations their freedom. At the time, the Reagan administration, preoccupied with trying to end the siege of Beirut, paid no attention to the plight of the four Iranians, but their kidnapping was the beginning of a sequence of events that would cost the administration dearly.

★   ★   ★

While the Iranian Revolutionary Guards were establishing their headquarters in the Bekaa Valley, the Soviet Union began rebuilding Syria's shattered air defenses. Syria's stunning defeat at the hands of the Israeli Air Force had exposed the perils of relying on Soviet military equipment, and Moscow was determined to repair the damage to its image. In October, the Soviets agreed to provide Syria with long-range SA-5 anti-aircraft missiles, which theoretically could hit planes over northern Israel. Five thousand Soviet military advisers arrived in Damascus to erect and run Syria's new air defense network. If there ever had been a moment when the United States could have coerced Syria into leaving Lebanon, it had passed.

Philip Habib had thought he could negotiate the Syrians out of Lebanon. "There was no reason to believe you couldn't negotiate a Syrian withdrawal," Habib said. "After all, I'd gotten the Syrians to withdraw out of Beirut, and President Assad didn't insist he was going to keep his forces in Lebanon." Once the Soviet military equipment started arriving, however, Assad was no longer dealing from weakness. "We could see the SA-5s moving into Syria," recalled the Pentagon's Lincoln Bloomfield, "and you had to change your calculus on the psychological equation. Once Soviet stuff started coming in, it was easier for him to say no and thumb his nose at the American effort." Robert McFarlane would later say it had been a "gross error" in tactics not to pressure Assad when Syria was weak and humiliated. "W. C. Fields was right," McFarlane said. "Never kick a man unless he's down."

Israel was no less intransigent, raising one procedural obstacle after another to the start of formal negotiations with the Lebanese, which only began December 28, three months after the Marines had arrived in Beirut for their sixty-day stay at the airport. "As early as January [1983], we could see clearly that the Israelis were dug in on the negotiations thing and were damned if they were going to go along with a model negotiation followed by withdrawal that would get all the moderate Arabs breathing heavily about a broader Middle East settlement," Lincoln Bloomfield said.

Stopping off in Washington during a visit to his relatives in Dearborn, Michigan, Amal leader Nabih Berri warned the State Department's Nicholas Veliotes that the longer the Israelis stayed in Lebanon, the stronger the forces of Shiite radicalism would become. Veliotes relayed Berri's warning to the Israelis, who ignored it. "The Israelis never wanted to believe it, never wanted to hear it," Veliotes said.

Intransigent or not, Israel was America's friend. On December 20, Congress raised U.S. military aid to Israel by $300 million, to a total of $1.7 billion in fiscal 1983, and tossed in another $250 million in loans that didn't have to be repaid. Although the administration officially opposed the aid increases, some officials were less than adamant in their testimony to Congress. If Israel sometimes behaved like a very bright, very spoiled child, the U.S. sometimes acted like an indulgent parent who scolded but rarely punished. The Reagan administration's fixation with containing the Soviets in the eastern Mediterranean made Israel an indispensable element of American national security policy. Cutting back aid to punish Israel was tantamount to reducing America's own defense budget, which to the Reagan administration was repugnant. The Israelis, on the other hand, never made the mistake of confusing their own interests with anybody else's.

With the chances for a negotiated withdrawal fading, the Reagan administration began betting more and more heavily on the Lebanese Armed Forces as the solution to the problem of bringing the Marines home. The sooner the Lebanese Army could fend for itself, the sooner the Marines could leave. In December 1982, the American Embassy opened an Office of Military Cooperation to oversee the equipping and training of the Lebanese Armed Forces.

"Actually, there was no army to rebuild," said Col. Arthur Fintel, the officer in charge of the program. The Lebanese Army had fallen apart in the civil war of 1975 and had been little more than a caretaker force ever since. At one point, only five people were showing up for work at the imposing marble and glass headquarters of the Ministry of Defense. When Fintel arrived, he found 10,000 men in uniform where the books showed 21,000. He found twenty-four warehouses full of unused military equipment—seven years' worth of deliveries that had never been issued to the troops. The Lebanese did not have the slightest idea what was in those warehouses since they had lost the computer code to the supply system.

Fintel's goals for modernizing the Lebanese Army called, in the short run, for bringing three brigades of 2,400 men each up to full strength. One brigade was to be deployed in south Lebanon to provide security along Israel's northern border if and when the Israeli Defense Forces withdrew. The other two brigades would keep the peace in Beirut. As the Lebanese Army grew to seven brigades, it would gradually expand its authority to the countryside—or so the plan went. A study conducted for the Joint Chiefs of Staff concluded that the Lebanese Army could take over internal security of the country in a year and a half and could patrol the borders within three years—provided the foreign armies withdrew and the Lebanese militias were disarmed; provided, in other words, that peace came to Lebanon.

Somehow, in all the planning, no one seemed to recognize that this effort to "Lebanize" the civil war would cost the United States its image as an impartial guardian of the peace. Increasingly the U.S. military and the Marines in particular would be seen as allies of the Christians who controlled the army and ran roughshod over the Muslim population. It was a vicious circle. The harder the United States tried to strengthen the Lebanese Army, the more hostile the Muslims became, and the more dangerous Lebanon became for Americans.

On March 16, 1983, someone hurled a hand grenade at a Marine patrol just north of the airport, slightly wounding five Marines. After that, the Marines began loading their weapons when they went out on patrol. Their commander, Colonel Mead, filed a situation report noting, "[Terrorist]-threat increases as diplomatic situation stagnates." The warnings didn't seem to travel very far up the chain of command. "I was down there the first week in April," the European Command's Gen. Willie Y. Smith recalled. "I remember riding through West Beirut—the Shiite sectors—and all the little children coming out and cheering and clapping. I went back and told people everything was going great. Ten days later our embassy was attacked."

★ ★ ★

"I got blown out a fifth-floor window," said Chief Warrant Officer Rayford Byers. One of the American trainers working with the Lebanese Army, Byers was in the finance office on the fifth floor of the embassy, picking up plane tickets back to the United States for himself and three other members of his team, when the bomb went off. He lost his left eye, suffered head injuries which required two craniotomies, broke both collar bones, his left arm, and all his ribs. "I never lost consciousness," Byers recalled. "I was hollering and screaming." That probably saved his life. A small Lebanese boy heard his cries and called for rescue workers, who pulled Byers from the rubble and rushed him to a hospital before he slipped into shock from his massive injuries. The other three members of his team, who had been having lunch in the basement cafeteria while Byers picked up the tickets, were crushed to death.

Maj. Joseph Englehardt was the luckiest man alive. He had stepped on the elevator to go down to the cafeteria for lunch, then changed his mind and gone back to his office to catch up on the morning message traffic. "I ordered my lunch from downstairs, bent over the traffic, and the embassy blew up," Englehardt recalled. Everyone in the cafeteria at the time the bomb went off was either killed or seriously injured.

A delivery van loaded with explosives had driven past a Lebanese guard post in front of the embassy, pulled under the front portico at the center of the V-shaped building, and detonated. The center section of the eight-story building collapsed like a house of cards, killing sixty-three people, seventeen of them Americans. "My first thought was that an RPG [rocket-propelled grenade] had hit either my office or next to it," said Robert Dillon, the American Ambassador. "I couldn't move." Dillon was pinned to the floor by a slab of masonry but otherwise unharmed. Had he stuck to his routine of jogging every day at noon, he would have been in the lobby when the van drove up, but a phone call detained him and probably saved his life. His bodyguard, Sgt. Terry Gilden of the Delta force, was killed, his military skills useless against a kamikaze driver in a delivery truck. In retrospect, the bombing of the American Embassy on April 18, 1983 was the first salvo in the Shiite holy war against the United States, but at the time, no one realized it. "Although it was a great tragedy," Vessey said, "it seemed like an inexplicable aberration."

The embassy bombing was the deadliest attack ever on a U.S. diplomatic mission. Americans in Beirut had been warned of an attack, but nothing like this. The National Security Agency had intercepted and decoded cables from the Iranian Foreign Ministry to the Iranian Embassy in Damascus, indicating a major attack on the multinational force in Beirut was being planned. The intercepts were of limited value because they did not reveal the time, the target, or the type of attack, but they confirmed that officials in Tehran had given permission to carry out the operation and had transferred $25,000 to their embassy in Damascus to pay for it.

The Lebanese subsequently arrested four suspects in the bombing, one of them a Palestinian employee of the embassy. With the help of a CIA officer, Keith Hall, the Lebanese extracted confessions from the four by beating them. Hall, who later was discharged by the CIA for taking part in the interrogation, acknowledged that his acts were "overly harsh." The Palestinian said his job had been to signal that Ambassador Dillon was inside the embassy so the attack could begin. The other three suspects admitted helping load the explosives into the van about a mile and a half from the embassy. Their confessions led Lebanese investigators to a fifth man who admitted recruiting the others and claimed he had escorted a Syrian intelligence officer into Beirut to wire the explosives into the van.

The trail ended there when the fifth man died in captivity, but U.S. intelligence already knew where it began. The messages intercepted by the National Security Agency clearly indicated that the home offices for Shiite terrorists in Lebanon were the Iranian Foreign Ministry and the headquarters of the Iranian Revolutionary Guard Corps in Tehran. The regional office was the Iranian Embassy in Damascus under the command of the ambassador, Mohammed Mohtashami-pur. "It's fairly clear this was run out of Damascus," said Noel Koch, the Pentagon's senior counterterrorist official. What was not clear was whether it had been run with the knowledge and approval of the Syrian intelligence services, which were headed by President Assad's brother, Rifaat.

The path from Damascus to the American Embassy in Beirut led through the Sheik Abdullah Barracks in Baalbek, home of the Revolutionary Guards and their Lebanese Shiite allies. Koch argued that "it's highly unlikely that they would have been able to move out of Baalbek through East Beirut and into West Beirut without the Syrians knowing what the target was." Specifically, Koch charged, "this couldn't happen without Rifaat Assad concurring."

Some U.S. intelligence analysts disagreed with Koch's conclusion, arguing that Mohtashami-pur had run the operation without clearing it with the Syrians. For what it was worth, Rifaat Assad called in the American Ambassador to Syria and vehemently denied the charge. A Syrian intelligence officer telephoned the Iranian Embassy in Damascus and complained that Iran should not have ordered the bombing without Syria's approval. Those who believed Syria was guilty dismissed the call, which was monitored by the National Security Agency, as a deliberate ruse intended for American ears. Other analysts believed the Syrians didn't know anybody was listening and thought the call was genuine.

More circumstantial evidence of Syrian-Iranian complicity appeared several weeks later with the return of the missing hostage David Dodge, who had been held in Iran but was released through the good offices of Rifaat Assad. Immediately after the U.S. Ambassador to Syria, Robert Paganelli, had complained that Iran was using Damascus as a base for terrorist operations, Rifaat Assad had dispatched a team to Tehran. He succeeded in convincing the Iranians that holding Dodge would not win the release of their four kidnapped officials in Lebanon, who in any event were almost certainly dead. Rifaat Assad had reported back to Paganelli that the Iranians had agreed to let Dodge go.

U.S. officials could never agree on what the episode said about Syria's hand in Shiite terrorism in Lebanon. To the Pentagon's Noel Koch, Rifaat Assad's intervention was "almost as if Syria was apologizing for having blown up the Embassy." To others, the Syrian role was mostly a product of Paganelli's cultivation of the powerful but unsavory Rifaat Assad. Conclusive proof never surfaced one way or the other, and the disagreement about whether the Syrians helped the Iranians blow up the embassy, or even knew about the attack in advance, remained unresolved. Dodge's release, however, did convince administration officials that one way or the other Syria held the keys to freeing hostages in Lebanon, an impression that was to linger for two years.

Partly because the evidence was so slippery and partly because the Reagan administration did not grasp the true significance of what had happened, there were no threats of retribution. "The emphasis was not on retaliation but on how to protect ourselves," General Smith of the European Command said. The State Department already had spent $1.5 million fortifying the embassy against attack—coating the windows with

Mylar to minimize the hazard of flying glass, installing a metal detector at the main entrance, constructing a heavy masonry wall with gun ports through which the Marine guards could flood the lobby with tear gas. But those were measures to deal with mob violence. Fortifying an existing building to withstand the blast of a 2,000 pound bomb was an entirely different proposition.

The only real defense against car bombs was to prevent them from getting close to their targets. The lone obstacle between the suicide bomber and the front door had been a checkpoint manned by Lebanese guards at either end of the short horseshoe drive leading under the portico. Security outside the embassy was a Lebanese responsibility, and Under Secretary of State Lawrence Eagleburger warned that if the United States were to take over "normal police functions which should appropriately be done by the host government, you begin to raise any number of questions about American imperialism."

After the bombing, that became a less pressing concern. A detachment of Marines from the airport took up sandbagged positions outside the British Embassy where American diplomats were temporarily housed until a new building could be located.

General Smith in Stuttgart dispatched Col. William Corbett, his special assistant for security matters, to Beirut to inspect the defenses that protected the 120 American soldiers assigned to the Office of Military Cooperation. "I was absolutely horrified," recalled Corbett, a raw-boned former Green Beret. "All the [Office of Military Cooperation] guys were living in one hotel" which had "an underground garage without a gate or a door or anything blocking it. Why they didn't take out the Cadmos Hotel along with the embassy I'll never know." Col. Arthur Fintel, head of the Office of Military Cooperation, didn't need Corbett to tell him how vulnerable his men were. He had been lobbying for physical barriers ever since he had arrived in Beirut to direct the reconstruction of the Lebanese Army. According to Fintel, "the embassy resisted my efforts and was upset when, in desperation, I put up concertina wire, sandbags, and fifty-five-gallon drums filled with sand as minimal measures." After the embassy bombing, Fintel erected a 10-foot-high earthen berm to protect the hotel—dubbed "the great wall of Cadmos." Behind the berm, a forest of concrete obstacles blocked the approach to the hotel. Anyone who successfully negotiated the maze would find himself staring down the barrel of a 106-mm recoilless rifle positioned at the hotel's main entrance.

Although General Vessey viewed the embassy bombing as "an inexplicable aberration," Corbett had no doubt that it signaled the start of a terrorist campaign against the American presence in Lebanon. On April

27, he reported to General Smith that the "bombing of Amembassy [American Embassy] removes any doubt of terrorist threat to U.S. interests in Lebanon. . . . Since such [terrorist organizations] are motivated by an ideology seeking long range ends, a single, random act of terrorism against U.S. interests in Lebanon is nonsensical. More applicable would be a series of terrorist acts, each, if possible, more spectacular and costly than the previous. Following Amembassy attack, U.S. military forces represent the most defined and logical terrorist target. . . . U.S. interests in Lebanon can expect an attack more spectacular than the action against the U.S. embassy."

Despite Corbett's warning, General Smith did not order any changes in security for the Marines at the airport. At a morning staff meeting, Smith told his operations officer: I want to make damn sure those Marines are secure. But nothing happened. Unlike the Office of Military Cooperation, which reported directly to Smith, the Marines were at the tail end of a marvelously convoluted chain of command which ran from Washington to NATO headquarters in Mons, Belgium, to the European Command in Stuttgart, to the commander of United States Naval Forces Europe in Naples, to the deputy commander of United States Naval Forces Europe in London, to the commander of the Sixth Fleet in Gaeta, Italy, to the commander of the amphibious task force off the coast of Lebanon, and finally to the commander of the Marine Amphibious Unit at the Beirut airport. It was a blueprint for losing things in translation and for passing the buck.

The first line of defense against any terrorist attack was good intelligence, and the Marines had repeatedly complained that they did not have good intelligence. "We have no foggy idea of what's going on right outside our gate," said Lt. Col. Donald Anderson, the commander of the Battalion Landing Team which had occupied the airport. "We have no capability of tapping that and understanding how those people out there are feeling about us, if there's anything going on. That's one of my biggest problems and that is one of the things I don't know exactly how we solve."

There were, of course, some Americans, like the European Command's William Corbett, who knew exactly what was going on outside the gate, who knew that in the past 13 months Hezbollah had mounted no less than 118 car bomb attacks against their many enemies, who knew that sooner or later the Marines would be a target for one of those attacks. But Corbett knew nothing about the tactical disposition of the Marines at the airport. He assumed they were spread out in bunkers around the perimeter, not, as it turned out, bunched into a single building. "The guys who knew the threat didn't know the circumstances, and the guys who knew the circumstances didn't know the threat," Corbett reflected.

The traditional source of intelligence, the local CIA station, was no more. The bomb at the embassy had exploded just as Robert Ames, by most accounts the CIA's best Middle East analyst, was convening a meeting in an office directly above the portico. Everyone in the meeting—all but two of the agency's officers in Beirut—was killed. The body of Kenneth Haas, the CIA station chief, hung in the wreckage for several days before workmen could finally reach it. The loss of the veteran Ames along with virtually the entire CIA station completed an intelligence disaster that had begun with the Israeli invasion.

Ames had for many years handled the CIA's extensive secret contacts with the PLO, which, both wittingly and unwittingly, had served as one of the agency's primary sources of intelligence about terrorist attacks against Americans. As part of his quest for legitimacy, Yasir Arafat had passed Ames information his own operatives picked up, always being careful to use a Lebanese intelligence officer as a go-between so both sides could deny any direct contact. What Arafat didn't volunteer, the National Security Agency often picked up by monitoring Palestinian phone calls. By dismembering the PLO, the Israeli invasion had destroyed much of the CIA's intelligence network in the terrorist underworld. Just as the threat of Shiite terrorism was beginning to mushroom, the intelligence community's ability to monitor and understand it had shrunk almost to zero.

Bereft of reliable sources, the intelligence community substituted quantity for quality, overwhelming the Marines with raw data of unknown reliability. It was not much help to the Marines, but it ensured that if something went wrong, somewhere in the reams of reports somebody could dig out a warning that had been ignored. Seeking to correct this abdication of responsibility, the Defense Department dispatched a small team from the Intelligence Support Activity (ISA), an officially nonexistent unit which had been created following the Iran rescue mission to do for the military what the CIA either could not or would not do. Among other things, the team recommended the creation of a "fusion center" that would help make sense of the flood of reports flowing into Beirut about possible terrorist plots. The European Command's reaction to the ISA recommendation consisted of assigning one intelligence officer to the Office of Military Cooperation.

The Pentagon's Noel Koch was scathing about the European Command's lackadaisical response to the ISA report. "Their report reflected adversely on people who outranked them and . . . had been submitted with no opportunity for the military system to sanitize their findings," Koch later wrote. "This led to denials, ass-covering, and all-around outrage that the survey had been done at all. Thus, it was decided that there were no problems and that even if there were, they had been fixed."

★   ★   ★

"Because of this latest crime," the President said in the wake of the embassy bombing, "we're more resolved than ever to help achieve the urgent and total withdrawal of all American forces from Lebanon—or, I should say, of all foreign forces. I'm sorry. Mistake."

Unfortunately for the Marines, it was a mistake. Once he got his lines straight, Reagan vowed "to press harder than ever with our peacemaking efforts." Against the advice of both Philip Habib and Nicholas Veliotes, the President dispatched Secretary of State Shultz to the Middle East to force the withdrawal talks to a conclusion. "I didn't want him to commit his prestige at that point because I wasn't sure it was going to work," Habib said. The CIA, the DIA, and the State Department's Near East bureau all said it wouldn't, and the American Embassy in Damascus cabled that staying in Lebanon was the only popular policy Syria's President Assad had. "Everybody—the Israelis, the CIA, the Syrians—realized this was a complete facade," Geoffrey Kemp said. "Every day the CIA came in with this excellent analysis that it wouldn't work."

George Shultz's impassive exterior and inscrutable demeanor earned him the nickname "Buddha." When one of his fingers accidentally got smashed in the door of his armored limousine outside London's Churchill Hotel, no one knew the mishap had occurred until he quietly sought out a State Department doctor, presented the injured digit, and inquired offhandedly whether anything should be done. And when he missed a Reagan motorcade in Brasilia because security officers barred him from entering an elevator with the President, a mishap which almost certainly would have sent Alexander Haig into orbit, Shultz simply clambered into an aging sedan and told the driver to follow the procession.

But beneath his bland facade, Shultz was a proud ex-Marine who valued his skills as a negotiator and who, once he had made up his mind, often was reluctant to change it. A thoroughly decent man who had been a team player as a blocking back at Princeton, Shultz was slow to anger, and when he did get angry he grew cold; his small eyes narrowed, his speech slowed to a deliberate cadence, and he seemed to grow dense and hard to budge, like water turned to ice.

Shultz was convinced that Assad was looking for a way out of Lebanon, that he was desperate to avoid another scrape with the Israelis, and that Saudi Arabia could provide enough financial sweetener to close the deal. Doggedly, he pressed on, shuttling back and forth between the Lebanese presidential palace in the hills above Beirut and Menachem Begin's modest home on a tree-shaded street corner in Jerusalem. Braving a wave of ailments that felled virtually the entire American delegation, Shultz hammered out an agreement for the simultaneous withdrawal of all foreign forces from Lebanon. Triumphant at last, he flew to Damascus for the first and only time in his shuttle mission to present the completed accord to President Assad.

Assad listened impassively as Shultz, speaking through an interpreter, briefed him at length on the details of what came to be known as the May 17 agreement. When he had finished explaining the accord, Shultz turned to the "side letters" between Israel and Lebanon, in which the Israelis made it clear they would not withdraw from Lebanon unless the Syrians did, too. Assad spoke for the first time, asking the Secretary of State to repeat his explanation of the side letters. As Shultz did so, Assad's face broke into a broad grin. He slapped the arm of his chair and exclaimed, The agreement is dead because we are not going to withdraw.

Assad confidently predicted that the Israelis would suffer serious casualties as long as they remained in Lebanon and that sooner or later they would withdraw regardless of what Syria did. "We were plowing ahead blindly without realizing the strategic environment had changed," said Peter Rodman, head of State's Policy Planning staff and a member of the Shultz delegation. "The agreement no longer fit the balance of forces. It wasn't tenable. The balance of forces in Lebanon had shifted under our feet. After Sabra and Shatila and the departure of Sharon [who had been relieved of his defense portfolio], we had a totally different Israel. The Syrians were throwing their weight around in Lebanon, and the Israelis did nothing. It was inexplicable."

On his way home from the Middle East, Shultz stopped off in Paris where Weinberger intercepted him. The two men met alone in a hotel room while their aides, Nicholas Veliotes and Richard Armitage, waited outside. Both Armitage and Veliotes knew exactly what Weinberger was saying to Shultz, and both of them agreed with him. The May 17 agreement had given Syria veto power over the Reagan administration's Middle East policy. As the Pentagon's Lincoln Bloomfield put it, "I developed this terrible image of Assad as Red Auerbach puffing away on his victory cigar."

The fundamental axiom of American Middle East policy—that Syria and Israel would withdraw from Lebanon—had been exposed for what it was, a naive hope. It was the assumption which governed the plans to rebuild the Lebanese Army and the assumption which determined how long the Marines would remain in Beirut. Without it, the rest of the policy had no underpinnings. Incredibly, the assumption would continue to govern the Reagan administration's policy in Lebanon until it was literally blown apart five months later.

★   ★   ★

Philip Habib, the President's Mideast envoy, was no longer welcome in Damascus after May 17. "If you can't talk to the Syrians, you can't do the job," Habib said. "Once I was declared persona non grata, I was useless." To replace Habib, the President turned to Robert McFarlane, the deputy director of the National Security Council (NSC) staff.

At the time, McFarlane was thinking of leaving government because he felt he wasn't doing anything of value. A retired lieutenant colonel who had led the first contingent of Marines into Vietnam in 1965, McFarlane yearned to help end the self-doubt and paralysis which he believed had crippled American foreign policy since the fall of Saigon. But McFarlane often seemed dogged by self-doubts of his own. He spoke in a monotone, which made him sound like a student who wasn't sure the answer he was giving was the right one, and he often lapsed into academic and military jargon which seemed calculated more to impress than inform the listener. Like his old mentor Alexander Haig, McFarlane was a prisoner of his service on Henry Kissinger's National Security Council staff, determined to eclipse the master but haunted by the fear that he could never measure up. Following in Kissinger's wake was a little like living in the shadow of a brilliant, successful father. The Reagan White House would become a deadly pressure cooker for McFarlane. The White House press corps, one of the cruelest institutions in America outside junior high school, cozied up to him in pursuit of leaks, then laughed at him behind his back.

Replacing Habib was McFarlane's chance to make a difference, and before long, many in the administration were complaining that McFarlane and his NSC staff had seized control of U.S. policy in Lebanon. In fact, even before he took on his new assignment, McFarlane made a secret trip to Damascus to test the waters, a trip Secretary of State Shultz found out about only after the fact. It was the first of several times that wheeling and dealing by the NSC staff would prompt the Secretary of State to tender his resignation.

When McFarlane became the Mideast envoy, the NSC staff became operational for the first time. "On the ground in Beirut, we figured out how to move the bureaucracy," said Howard Teicher, one of the NSC staffers assigned to work with McFarlane. Armed with a direct satellite link to the situation room in the White House basement, McFarlane and his aides were able to bypass State, Defense, CIA, and all the paralyzing arguments and discouraging assessments the bureaucracy could throw in the face of any new idea. "SATCOM [satellite communications], that's how you go operational," Teicher said. Understanding how to move the bureaucracy and understanding what was going on in Beirut were, of course, two different things.

McFarlane arrived in Lebanon on August 1. "I shouldn't even have gone if I had any sense," he said later. "The only hope was a naive one that we could get the Syrians and the Israelis out and let the Lebanese duke it out among themselves, and I clung to that."

For his part, Assad had taken the measure of the United States and knew it was in over its head. America is short of breath, Syria's Foreign Minister Halim Abdul Khaddam said. Why are you putting your trust in the Americans? Khaddam asked his Lebanese counterpart Elie Salam. The Americans are very, very far away. A few Marines will be killed, and they will leave.

McFarlane had been in Lebanon less than two weeks when he recommended that the administration suspend its efforts to broker a joint Syrian-Israeli withdrawal and concentrate instead on reconciling the various Lebanese factions. The Muslims had lost all patience with Amin Gemayel, who had ascended to the presidency following his brother's assassination. Gemayel's principal concern seemed to be not nation building but preserving the dominance of the Christian minority. He refused to so much as meet with Walid Jumblatt, the leader of the Druze, and a member of his cabinet. He ignores me, Jumblatt complained to an officer in the American Embassy. When the embassy managed to arrange a conciliatory phone call between the two, it quickly degenerated into a shouting match.

The Druze already had begun lobbying for a bigger share of political power by shelling the Beirut airport, the government's most important link to the outside world. On July 22, nearly a dozen mortar and rocket rounds landed inside the Marine perimeter. The Druze claimed they were merely firing on Lebanese Army positions at the airport, and the administration jumped at the excuse not to have to admit that the Marines had become targets. It was hard to tell exactly what the Druze were aiming at. One of their favorite tactics was to drive up in a Peugeot, haul a mortar out of the trunk, fire a few rounds in the general direction of the airport, and drive away.

After the first mortar rounds landed at the airport, two officers from the Defense Intelligence Agency drove across the runway and into the hills to the source of the fire. They confronted a Druze lieutenant and asked him what the hell he thought he was doing.

We were sending you a message not to get involved in our struggle, the Druze replied.

The American officers, one of whom spoke Arabic, warned him, The quickest way to Allah is to screw around with Americans.

Only later did they recognize just how empty a threat that was. After inspecting the Marines' positions, one of the DIA officers met with the new Marine commander, Col. Timothy Geraghty, and ticked off a list of security problems. Why, the intelligence officer wondered, didn't the Marines have their weapons loaded? Why wasn't there a barricade at the entrance to their compound?

Why do you think? Geraghty shot back.

Because you have orders, the DIA officer replied. That was the end of it.

Everybody was shooting in the direction of the Marines. Sometimes it was the Druze, sometimes Shiite snipers in the slums around the airport, sometimes Christians trying to provoke the Marines into firing at the Druze. To get a better idea of just who wanted them dead, the Marines brought in a special Army radar designed to pinpoint the source of incoming rounds.

When mortar rounds began landing at the airport on the morning of August 29, they "walked" in textbook fashion straight toward Alpha Company's First Platoon. The fourth round scored a direct hit on the platoon's command tent, instantly killing Sgt. Alexander Ortega; 2d. Lt. George Losey died of his wounds as he was being medivaced to one of the amphibious ships offshore. The Marines returned fire with illumination rounds to show they knew where the mortar shells were coming from. When the shelling continued at the rate of one round every fifteen seconds, the Marines fired their first shots in anger—six 155-mm high-explosive rounds, which reportedly killed three Druze and wounded fifteen more.

A few days earlier, Capt. Morgan France, the commander of the amphibious task force offshore, had said, "As soon as we start firing, we've lost our mission here." The Reagan administration wasn't ready to admit that yet, but it had to come up with some sort of response to a sudden flood of congressional charges that its peacekeepers had become engaged in combat. Vice President Bush and Defense Secretary Weinberger flew back to Washington from vacation in Maine to meet with Shultz. As he stepped off his helicopter, Weinberger told reporters that the fire which killed the Marines "appears to have been directed at the Lebanese Armed Forces' positions." It was all a terrible mistake, in other words. At the airport in Beirut, Marine Capt. Paul Roy knew better. "We were taking direct fire from the hill," he was quoted as saying.

The distinction made no difference to the dead Ortega and Losey, but it was crucial to determining whether the Marines in Lebanon were covered by the War Powers Act. Under the act, the President is required to notify Congress when American forces are sent "into hostilities or into situations where imminent involvement in hostilities is clearly indicated by the circumstances." Once Congress is notified that the War Powers Act applies, the forces must be withdrawn within sixty days unless a law is passed allowing them to remain. After deliberating for a day, Reagan sent Congress a letter which split the difference between accident and hostilities by saying the Marines were involved in "sporadic fighting."

The semantics did nothing to alter the fact that the Marines were finished as a neutral peacekeeping force. On September 1, Amal leader Nabih Berri issued a statement that the Marines had "turned into a fighting force against Muslims in Lebanon." That same day, Druze leader Walid Jumblatt told a press conference in Damascus that "the mere fact that they are providing the Lebanese factional army with logistic support, expertise, and training is enough for us to consider them enemies."

Just as the Marines were being sucked into Lebanon's factional fighting, the Israelis were preparing to bow out. As Assad predicted, Israel had lost its stomach for occupying Lebanon and was about to pull its forces out of the Chouf Mountains east of Beirut to more defensible positions south of the Awali River. The Israeli withdrawal would create a military vacuum in the heights above Beirut that could only lead to more bloodshed when the rival militias rushed in. Indeed, much of the fighting that had erupted around the Marines in August had been preliminary jockeying for position in anticipation of the Israeli withdrawal.

Knowing the Lebanese Army was in no condition to fill that vacuum, McFarlane recommended that the Marines and the other members of the multinational force move into the Chouf as observers and advisers to the Lebanese. To back up this show of American resolve, McFarlane told two of his aides, Howard Teicher and Navy Capt. Philip Dur, to suggest ways of bringing more American firepower to bear in Lebanon. Over dinner, Teicher and Durr came up with the idea of having the battleship

New Jersey with its 16-inch guns join the U.S. flotilla standing off the airport. The next day, as a joke, the two wrote their suggestion on a small scroll and presented it to McFarlane on a silver platter.

Weinberger and the Joint Chiefs were willing to send the *New Jersey,* since it represented no increased risk to American personnel and might even help protect the Marines. But they were adamantly opposed to exposing the Marines to even greater danger by having them fill the vacuum left by the Israelis. Israeli Defense Forces' convoys attempting to resupply Israeli units in the Chouf had been ambushed repeatedly. What reason was there to think the Marines would fare any better? "It's not like the militias have never seen a modern fighting force," said Maj. Joseph Englehardt, the Army attaché in Beirut, who was sent out to find the best sites to deploy the Marines. Most military officers saw the proposal as a deliberate attempt by the NSC staff to push the Marines beyond the point of no return in Lebanon.

The Marines remained at the airport while the Reagan administration begged the Israelis to delay their withdrawal until the Lebanese Army was ready to move into the Chouf. The policy, which all along had been predicated on the withdrawal of all foreign forces, was now turned on its head.

The Israelis were scheduled to begin their withdrawal in the first hours of Sunday morning, September 4. On Friday, the Americans made a last-ditch effort to win a delay. At ten o'clock that night, Gen. Ibrahim Tannous, the commander of the Lebanese Armed Forces, hosted a dinner for Israeli and American military officers at his home. Before dinner, Tannous tried to impress upon the Israelis that his army had made progress but needed more time before it could move into the Chouf. The Israelis refused to listen, several times rudely cutting Tannous off in mid-sentence. After dinner, Tannous tried to make his case again. This time, Gen. Moshe Levy, the Israeli chief of staff, invited Tannous to join him in the next room.

While Tannous and Levy talked in private, Maj. Mark Gatanas, McFarlane's military assistant, accosted General Ehud Barak, Israel's chief of military intelligence. The Lebanese commander is trying to give you a plan, and you don't let him get past the first sentence, Gatanas complained. Washington is anxiously awaiting the results of this meeting, and you know who's going to write the cable, don't you?

You, Mark? replied Barak. Write it well.

What am I going to say? Gatanas asked.

Say it was a good dinner, Barak suggested.

After fifteen minutes alone with Tannous, the Israeli chief of staff reappeared and said it was time to go. Gatanas grabbed Barak by the elbow and demanded, What do you want me to say?

Barak pulled away from Gatanas, trying to make his exit. Gatanas followed Barak into the garden. General Barak, the only thing I can say is that the Israelis refuse to listen. That's the truth. Do you want me to put it in those terms?

Mark, the political decision has been made, Barak said.

Unless we get a commitment to another meeting, it's going to look bad in Washington, Gatanas threatened.

Two hours later, before Gatanas could transmit the cable to Washington, the Israelis sent word that the new Defense Minister, Moshe Arens, would meet the following day with Richard Fairbanks, a senior member of McFarlane's party. The meeting took place as promised just hours before the withdrawal was to begin, but Arens refused to budge. Israel wanted its sons home in time for Yom Kippur.

★   ★   ★

Within twenty-four hours, rocket, mortar, and artillery fire began raining down on the Marine positions. Two Marines were killed in a rocket barrage just before dawn on September 5. The next day, more than 120 rounds landed inside the Marine perimeter. On September 7, aircraft from the carrier *Eisenhower* flew their first reconnaissance mission over Lebanon, and on September 8, the destroyer *Bowen* fired its 5-inch guns in support of the Marines—two more milestones on the slippery slope of American military involvement in the killing fields of Lebanon.

Col. Timothy Geraghty, the commander of the 24th Marine Amphibious Unit now stationed at the airport, sent a situation report warning of "the increasing involvement in direct and more frequent combat actions." The "stakes are being raised weekly," Geraghty reported, "and our contribution to peace in Lebanon since 22 July stands at four killed and twenty-eight wounded." In another message, Geraghty reported that "morale remains high, but the bunkers are getting deeper."

On the ridgeline above the airport, Druze militia, backed by Syrian artillery fire, had routed the Christian militia. General Tannous was left with a Hobson's choice. If he tried to drive the antigovernment forces off the ridgeline, he risked destroying the army that was supposed to be the vehicle for unifying Lebanon. If he allowed the Druze and their allies to dominate the high ground over Beirut, the government's position would become untenable.

Tannous sent the 2,100 men of the Eighth Brigade to hold the ridge at a small market town called Souk al Gharb. Although Lebanese intelligence officers insisted the ridge was under attack by up to 25,000 hostile troops, there was hard evidence of only 2,500 enemy soldiers, mostly Druze militiamen with about 300 Palestinians and 100 Iranian Revolutionary Guards, supported by thirty old Soviet-made T-54 tanks donated to the cause by Libya's Muamar Qaddafi. The attackers were receiving heavy artillery support from Syrian gunners, and a total of sixty truckloads of supplies rolled in from Syrian-controlled territory. Almost immediately, the commander of the Eighth Brigade, Michel Aoun, began calling for reinforcements, warning the Defense Ministry he could not hold Souk al Gharb for more than a few hours.

It was difficult to know precisely what was happening at Souk al Gharb. McFarlane felt Aoun was "not at all above doctoring the intelligence." The Lebanese had every reason to portray the fighting as a Syrian and Palestinian attack on Lebanon and to paint the bleakest picture possible in order to draw the United States more deeply into the conflict. Cloud cover interfered with reconnaissance flights from the carrier offshore, so McFarlane's military aide, Mark Gatanas, was sent to Eighth Brigade headquarters to see for himself.

On Saturday night, September 10, the Lebanese reported that five truckloads of militiamen charged up the hill at Souk al Gharb and literally chopped up a company of the Eighth Brigade, hacking the commander to pieces with axes. Some American intelligence analysts later concluded that the slaughter had been an inside job by members of the company led by a treacherous Lebanese lieutenant and that the story of the militiamen storming the hill was fiction. Col. Arthur Fintel, who later interviewed some of the Lebanese soldiers involved in the fighting, was told that the attackers did not speak Arabic and were probably Iranians from Baalbek. Whatever the truth, the story of the ax attack had a powerful impact.

The next day, Sunday, September 11, McFarlane met with his advisers in the library of the American Ambassador's residence in the hills overlooking Beirut. Incomplete casualty figures from the previous night showed the Eighth Brigade had suffered seven dead, forty-three wounded, and more missing. The brigade still held the ridge, but Brig. Gen. Carl Stiner, the representative of the Joint Chiefs of Staff and an expert on small unit warfare, warned that another attack could turn into a rout. The Pentagon had sent Stiner to Lebanon to keep an eye on McFarlane and the NSC staff, to act as a military counterweight to whatever schemes they came up with. Weinberger and Vessey weren't about to rely on McFarlane's advice. Stiner impressed everybody with his cool. The hotter the situation, the slower his Tennessee drawl became. Trim and muscular, Stiner was a real soldier, a paratrooper who'd been wounded in combat. If he was worried about a rout, it was time for everybody else to worry about a rout. If that happened, there would be no time for the United States to react. The ambassador's residence was just five kilometers from the front, guarded by a total of fourteen Marines. There was a brief discussion about reinforcing the Marines at the residence, but doubling or even tripling the guard would not stop a company-sized attack complete with tanks and artillery.

McFarlane and Stiner believed it was time to change the Rules of Engagement to allow the Marines and the naval task force offshore to fire in support of the Lebanese Army. "When you sat at [the ambassador's residence] and saw this phenomenal flotilla offshore, to open fire with five-inch guns seemed the very least we could do," Geoffrey Kemp of the NSC staff recalled. "Given what we had available, it was an exercise of colossal self-restraint."

McFarlane turned to his secretary and began dictating a message to Washington that was undoubtedly the most dramatic document in the sad history of the American involvement in Lebanon. Within the Reagan administration, it came to be known as the "sky is falling" cable. "There is a serious threat of a decisive military defeat which could involve the fall of the Government of Lebanon within twenty-four hours," McFarlane began.

Last night's battle was waged within five kilometers of the Presidential Palace. For those at the State Department, this would correlate to the enemy attacking from Capitol Hill. This is an action message. A second attack against the same Lebanese Armed Forces unit is expected this evening. Ammunition and morale are low and raise the serious possibility that the enemy brigade, which enjoys greater strength and unlimited fire support and resupply, will break through and penetrate the Beirut perimeter. In short, tonight we could be in enemy lines.

Faced with this threat which cannot be contained by the LAF [Lebanese Armed Forces], we must decide whether the U.S. will, by withholding direct support, allow the fall of the GOL [Government of Lebanon]. The new element which should be seriously addressed in our calculus is that for the first time the threat is unambiguously foreign. Specifically, the attack last evening was conducted by a PLA [Palestine Liberation Army] brigade. It is comprised of Palestinian soldiers commanded by Syrian officers and is directly controlled by the SARG [the Syrian general staff]. In short, this represents foreign aggression against Lebanon.

Our ROE [Rules of Engagement], as amplified by the NSDD [National Security Decision Directive] approved 10 September, allows the use of U.S.

military force only in self-defense. In considering the threat now posed to Americans (the multinational force, other U.S. military personnel in Beirut, and the U.S. diplomatic presence), we must recognize that to wait until an attack tonight is at our doorstep before responding would be too late. This requires a certain amount of judgment on the scene to be able to deal in a timely fashion with a clear and present danger. In my judgment, danger to Americans would exist if the PLA captures Souk al Gharb. Consequently, it is within our current ROE in my judgment not to allow such a loss to occur. To state clearly the significance of what I am saying, I am recommending that the U.S. Government support the LAF with fire support to include the use of TACAIR [tactical aircraft].

It is important to understand, as we have stressed in recent weeks, that this is not a civil conflict. This reality was underscored in last night's attack by the fact that there were no Lebanese involved in the attacking ground forces. There, forces were comprised of a PLA brigade and Iranian elements. The battle was savage and included ax fighting and hand-to-hand fighting of a brutality equal to the worst atrocities of Vietnam. I do not say this to be melodramatic, but to make clear that the GOL is threatened with impending takeover by an uncivilized foreign force.

I am very conscious of the difficulty of taking such a decision in a climate of public and congressional ignorance such as exists in the U.S. today. The fact is that we may well be at a turning point which will lead within a matter of days to a Syrian takeover of the country north of the Awali [River]. It is requested that this situation be considered by the NSC and guidance provided within the next four hours so as to facilitate the necessary planning and coordination so that a new ROE can be approved. Needless to say, if a cease-fire does not come into effect and an attack takes place, we must be prepared to carry out an immediate evacuation.

It is conceivable that tonight's attack will be contained, that Syria will discontinue its support and that a cease-fire can be established. That seems unlikely to me and even though we might get by tonight, unless we see a change in Syrian policy today the survival of the GOL is a matter of days. As you know, I am not given to handwringing and [I understand] that competing demands in Central America and elsewhere may have led us to a decision to cut our losses. If so, I would like to know so I can deal in good faith with GOL and the protection of U.S. personnel.

The doubts McFarlane and the others at the table had about the quality of the intelligence they were receiving on the fighting at Souk al Gharb had vanished. The way McFarlane now put it, the Reagan administration had no choice but to fire in support of the Lebanese Army. Although the fighting in the Chouf had been started by the Christian militia, McFarlane portrayed the battle for Souk al Gharb as a clearcut case of aggression by a Soviet client state. It was a message perfectly tuned to the ear of a President who boasted that not one inch of territory had been lost to the Communists on his watch. Suddenly, the battle for Souk al Gharb was exhibit number one in what Reagan called "Soviet-sponsored aggression against Lebanon." Even Weinberger, who had opposed the entire venture from the start, now warned that the collapse of the American peacekeeping effort would result in a "Soviet-controlled enclave throughout the whole of Lebanon." The Reagan administration had a pronounced tendency to see local crises as skirmishes in the global struggle between the United States and the Soviet Union, which the President dubbed "an evil empire." That, of course, was also how the administration had first addressed the issue of international terrorism, only to discover that the Soviet role was both problematical and irrelevant.

In addition to so clearly defining the enemy, McFarlane's cable implicitly suggested how the administration could fight the good fight without running afoul of Congress and the War Powers Act. As McFarlane described it, firing in support of the Lebanese Army would be a simple exercise in self-defense that entailed no new commitment to the government of Lebanon, just a slight loosening of the Rules of Engagement. Everyone involved could simply deny the significance of what was about to happen. When the Joint Chiefs of Staff transmitted the President's decision to modify the Rules of Engagement, the order stated that "nothing in this message shall be construed as changing the mission for the U.S. multinational force."

The order left the decision to fire on Souk al Gharb to Col. Timothy Geraghty, the commander of the forces ashore. Rugged and crew cut, Geraghty looked as though he had stepped right out of a Marine recruiting poster. Headquarters did not pick just any officer to command a Marine Amphibious Unit [MAU]. There were only six MAUs in the entire Corps, and only the best officers got to command them. Geraghty, who had not been present that Sunday afternoon in the ambassador's library when McFarlane dictated his cable, opposed any change in the Rules of Engagement as "a departure from our normal peacekeeping role." McFarlane recognized that firing in direct support of the Lebanese Army would irrevocably strip the last vestiges of neutrality from the Marines, but he did not have Geraghty's appreciation of the consequences. Geraghty was surrounded at the airport by increasingly hostile forces that held all the high ground and already had killed four of his men. In retrospect, Mark Gatanas, McFarlane's military assistant, concluded that Geraghty was right. "I think there was overreaction on the

11th," Gatanas said. "We were all caught up by events. If anything, the guy with the most realistic perspective was Geraghty. He was saying, 'If I take sides, I'm done for.' "

Geraghty resisted the entreaties to fire on Souk al Gharb for a week, and still the Eighth Brigade, the same brigade which McFarlane had said probably wouldn't last the night, held the line. Finally, on September 19, under great pressure, Geraghty gave the order. The daily assault on Souk al Gharb had begun with an artillery barrage at 2:00 A.M., and the Lebanese were in a panic. At 3:30 A.M., Simon Cassis, Lebanon's chief of military intelligence, awakened Gatanas with an alarming report—without American help Souk al Gharb would fall in half an hour. Gatanas awakened General Stiner, the representative of the Joint Chiefs, and they rushed to the Defense Ministry. Other than the night duty officers, no one was there. Gatanas was furious. He searched about for Cassis, finally locating him by phone at about four-thirty. I think this is piss poor, Gatanas told Cassis. If the world is caving in on you, it doesn't look like it. Everybody's asleep. Gatanas said he was going back to bed. Cassis pleaded with him to stay. Soon, Lebanese officers began drifting into the Defense Ministry.

Gatanas borrowed a helmet and went to the Eighth Brigade command post where he found the commander, Michel Aoun, almost beside himself. "He was smoking three cigarettes at the same time," Gatanas recalled—one in the ashtray, one in his hand, and one in his mouth. The commander reported he was all but out of artillery shells.

"The reason he was running low was that he had been squandering it," said Col. Arthur Fintel, who was back at the operations center in the Defense Ministry. Aoun's men were shooting three times what American military doctrine called for in high-intensity combat with the Soviets in Europe. To make matters worse, a maritime accident had thrown off the schedule for replenishing the brigade's ammunition. The ship carrying the shells—just one load of the nearly $900 million worth of military equipment the United States would sell to Lebanon in 1983—had rammed a pier in Italy.

By now, five hours had passed since Simon Cassis had told Gatanas Souk al Gharb would fall in half an hour without American help. Gatanas asked Aoun where the main threat was coming from. "He says, 'Everywhere!' " Gatanas recalled. Gatanas tried to explain to Aoun that not even the United States could fire everywhere. "Gradually, we developed a picture," Gatanas related. There was hand-to-hand fighting on the southern flank, but the main threat was coming from the north. "It became apparent we were going to have to fire in support," Gatanas said.

More than the tactical situation, it was the sight of the frantic Aoun which convinced Gatanas that the United States would have to open fire. "There was a breakdown in the leadership system of the brigade," Gatanas said, "a beginning of the crumbling of the brigade."

Using a secure voice radio provided by the CIA, Gatanas called Stiner at the Defense Ministry. "I couldn't raise a damn soul," Gatanas remembered. He picked up a phone and dialed the ministry. "The first couple times I called, the number was busy." Finally, he got Stiner on the line, telling him that whatever he did, he should not hang up. "I said to Stiner, 'They're really in a bad way. The leadership is edgy, and I don't know if they can hold on.'"

Col. Arthur Fintel, who had his own sources within the Lebanese Army, told Stiner that reports from platoon and company commanders did not indicate any panic in the ranks. Fintel, who had spent so many months trying to rebuild the Lebanese Army, hated to see the American military forced to come riding to the rescue. "The Lebanese Army had fought its enemies to a standstill for almost three weeks—against unanimous predictions to the contrary—and I didn't want them to lose credit for it," Fintel said later. The attacks usually didn't last past ten o'clock in the morning. If this one ended on schedule, there would be time to resupply Aoun's brigade with ammunition.

Stiner did not share Fintel's proprietary interest in the Lebanese Army. If Aoun was in a panic, the whole thing could come unglued from the top. Stiner relayed Gatanas's end-is-near message to Geraghty, who finally relented. "The Lebanese had run quite low on ammunition, and it would have been unconscionable for us not to have provided support at a very crucial time for them," Geraghty said afterwards.

At 9:45 A.M., Gatanas received permission to call in naval gunfire. Nineteen minutes later, the cruiser *Virginia* opened fire. To spot the fall of shot, Gatanas had to rely on a Lebanese artillery observer who spoke no English and was using a French map in a different scale from the American charts. Afraid of hitting Lebanese positions by accident, "I must have called the first rounds six hundred meters away from friendly positions," Gatanas said. "But it turned out he was a good enough spotter that we could call in the rounds within fifty meters of friendly positions."

During the course of the day, the *Virginia* and three other Navy ships fired a total of 360 rounds on the Souk al Gharb ridgeline. "They didn't hurt anybody," Fintel said. To hit the advancing troops, the shells had to land on the back side of a hill, always a difficult shot. They "just hunkered down and looked up and watched the shells pass overhead,"

Fintel said. "It was really noisy and great, but it didn't cause any damage." Nevertheless, Gatanas said, "the effect of the fire was that the brigade held and was able to resupply."

In apparent retaliation for the American intervention, shells started falling on the ambassador's residence, setting off fires. The residence, which had served as a makeshift headquarters ever since the April bombing of the embassy, had to be evacuated. Only the Marine guard and the radio operators remained. For the first time, a Marine report referred to the antigovernment forces as "the enemy." The Marines were peacekeepers no more.

On September 23, McFarlane left Beirut for Damascus and another meeting with Assad. As usual, he got nowhere, but as he rose to leave, McFarlane told the Syrian leader, President Reagan asked me to let you know that the battleship *New Jersey* will be arriving in a few days. On September 25, one day before the *New Jersey* was scheduled to arrive off the coast of Lebanon, all sides agreed to a cease-fire. The airport was reopened, and soon more than seventy international flights a day were arriving and departing. The American show of force seemed to have worked. "We packed our bags and left in early October, and everything was hunky-dory," Geoffrey Kemp of the NSC staff said. "There was a lot of optimism in Lebanon after the cease-fire."

McFarlane and his aides seemed convinced that the American show of force had carried the day. When he returned to Washington, McFarlane sent a handwritten note on White House stationery to the Joint Chiefs of Staff directing the Marines and the ships offshore to commence "offensive peacekeeping." According to W. Hays Parks, an Army lawyer assigned to review the order, McFarlane's directive would have meant that "fire directed at the Marines would be answered by salvos by the battleship *New Jersey* and air strikes, even if it resulted in the destruction of entire villages and the loss of hundreds of civilian lives." The Joint Chiefs of Staff unanimously refused to carry out the order, which Parks said was "manifestly illegal."

With its concern for legalities, the United States was playing by rules which nobody else in Lebanon followed. The Marines had become another militia without the advantages the real militias had. The United States was playing by Clausewitz's rule that war is a continuation of politics by other means. In Lebanon, terrorism was a continuation of war by other means.

★ 6 ★

DEAD. ALL DEAD

Lance Corp. Eddie DiFranco heard it first. He looked up from his sandbagged guard post outside the headquarters of the Battalion Landing Team and saw a yellow Mercedes Benz stakebed truck about the size of a dump truck ramming through a 5-foot-high roll of concertina wire. It made "just a popping sound, just something snapping, like somebody walking on twigs," he recalled. "I knew what was going to happen."

On orders from his commanding officer, DiFranco's M-16 wasn't loaded. By the time he had chambered a round and shouldered his weapon, the truck was past him. As it roared by, DiFranco recounted, the driver, a young man with bushy black hair and a mustache, "looked right at me . . . and smiled." The driver shifted gears, picked up speed, passed through an open gate in the chain-link fence surrounding the headquarters, and headed straight for the four-story concrete building where some 350 Marines were sleeping late this Sunday morning. DiFranco picked up his field telephone to alert the sergeant of the guard, but already it was too late.

Sgt. Steve Russell was in the guard shack at the entrance to the building. He, too, heard "a sort of popping or crackling sound," but he did not turn to investigate until he heard the roar of a diesel engine. The yellow truck was coming straight for him at about 30 miles per hour. Russell bolted across the lobby and out the back door, screaming, Hit the deck, hit the deck! Looking back over his shoulder, Russell saw the truck smash into his guard shack, sending it "like a huge wave of water rushing into the lobby." The truck ground to a halt in the center of the lobby. Still running, Russell looked back in time to see "a bright orange-yellow flash at the grill of the truck." He felt "a wave of intense heat and a powerful concussion" as he was blown 15 feet through the air. When he regained consciousness and saw what had happened, he began yelling, Oh my God, I can't believe it! over and over again.

Experts from the Federal Bureau of Investigation later said the explosion was the largest non-nuclear blast they had ever seen, equivalent to 12,000 pounds of TNT. The bomb dug an 8-foot crater through a 7-inch floor of reinforced concrete. It lifted the entire building upward, shearing the support columns off at their base. Corp. Joseph Martucci, who was sleeping on the roof, said, "We saw the center of the building actually lift, blow out. . . . The building . . . was going down in approximately three or four seconds. . . . We rode the roof down." Martucci was lucky. Two hundred forty-one American servicemen were killed, crushed beneath hundreds of tons of concrete. Some died instantly. Many suffered for hours, trapped in a concrete tomb, bleeding to death. For the Marines, it was the greatest loss of life in a single day since the assault on Iwo Jima in 1945.

Col. Arthur Fintel was lying in his apartment five miles away, trying to decide whether to get up or sleep late this Sunday morning. "Suddenly, there was a tremendous concussion," he recalled. "My first thought was that we had a round land outside my apartment building." His second thought was that terrorists had blown up the Cadmos Hotel where his men were staying. "I jumped up and ran straight out on the balcony." Looking across Beirut and out to sea, he couldn't see any sign of an explosion. Then he leaned out over the railing and looked south. "I could see this huge mushroom cloud. I could see the dust wave coming out of it. It was big enough I almost thought it was a nuclear weapon. Then right in front of me there was a flash and a big cloud of black smoke and that was the French going up." A second suicide bomber had driven into the headquarters of the French contingent of the multinational force, killing fifty-nine soldiers.

Col. Timothy Geraghty, the Marine commander, had been up for an hour, working in his office on the second floor in a building 100 yards from where the Battalion Landing Team was quartered. The blast blew out all the windows in the headquarters building. Geraghty ran downstairs and out the door but all he could see was "a heavy fog and debris . . . still floating down." He ran to another building, searching for the source of the blast. "And it was just then . . . the fog was clearing, and I turned around and the BLT building, the headquarters, was gone. I can't explain to you my feelings then. It was just unbelievable." Geraghty ran back to get his executive officer, Lt. Col. Harold Slacum. Good God, the BLT is gone! Geraghty cried. You won't believe it, the building is gone!

"Explosion at BLT 1/8 Hq," the flash message sent to Washington read. "A large explosion at BLT 1/8 Hq Bldg collapsed the roof and leveled the building. Large numbers of dead and injured . . . BLT Hq destroyed. Amplifying info to follow." That did not begin to describe what had happened.

"The thing that struck me is that it was deathly silent," Lieutenant Colonel Slacum said. "This was perhaps three, four minutes after the explosion . . . and there was a gray dust over everything you could see, as far as you could see. The concrete . . . from this collapsed building, that had once been three–four stories high was now down to one story. . . . You could make out which was the first story and then just another ten to fifteen feet of rubble piled on top of that. . . . I first looked around and that's when you started to see the first bodies."

"Books, seabags, scraps of paper, running shoes, torn sleeping bags, parts of uniforms and shredded mosquito netting were strewn everywhere," Lance Corp. Michael Petit later wrote.

Jeeps had been crushed and tossed around like children's toys. The plywood outhouses 20 meters from the building were splintered and macabre streamers of toilet paper fluttered from the trees. Everywhere I looked I saw bodies sprawled in gruesome positions. One Marine, still in his sleeping bag, hung from a tree. The decapitated body of another was under a Jeep, his arms twisted at an impossible angle. The legs of yet another jutted from beneath a huge slab of concrete. . . . The building had folded in upon itself like an accordion, and the men hadn't had a chance.

My foot kicked something soft and yielding. I glanced down. A severed hand, palm up, lay next to my boot. It wore a wedding ring . . . I saw unattached arms, legs, and heads. Some of the faces wore looks of shock and pain, but those who had been sleeping when the bomb exploded were frozen in a bizarre repose of tranquility. All were caked with blood and dirt. Some were crushed, the bodies twisted beyond the recognition of human form. A few were little more than lumps of charred flesh. The smell of blood, the reek of vomit and urine and excrement, the bittersweet odor of death, hung in the air. I turned my back on the carnage, gasping for air to keep from retching.

Maj. Joseph Englehardt, the Army attaché who had so narrowly missed being killed in the embassy bombing six months before, drove up and jumped out of his car. "The smell of explosives and powdered cement is a powerful smell," Englehardt said. "I remembered it from the embassy bombing. It just buckled my knees—like that."

They found Lt. Col. Howard Gerlach, the commander of the Battalion Landing Team, lying unconscious outside what used to be his second-floor office. A Lebanese ambulance rushed him to a Shiite hospital where doctors saved his life. He had a concussion, a punctured eardrum, a face crushed by falling debris, a broken right leg, and a broken left arm. The doctors didn't realize it then, but his neck was broken, too.

When they carried him into the hospital, Gerlach saw Lebanese faces looking down at him. He thought he heard one of them ask, What is your mission? Peacekeeping, he mumbled. He was convinced he'd been taken prisoner, and until he lapsed into a coma, he refused to give his rescuers anything but his name, rank, and serial number.

It was nearly two months before Gerlach realized what had happened. By then, he had been transferred to Bethesda Naval Hospital in the suburbs of Washington, D.C. He had been there once before, when he had taken a North Vietnamese round through his abdomen. Then, he had been engaged to Patty. Now, they were married with two children—and he was paralyzed from the neck down.

Patty tried to tell him what had happened, but he didn't understand. She left the television on, hoping he would get the news that way, but he didn't pay much attention. He was still seeing double. It started to dawn on him the day the television networks showed what was left of his unit coming home to Camp LeJeune, North Carolina—a wrenching scene of tears for the dead and joy for the living. Then, one day, he asked for Mike Haskell, his weapons officer. Is Mike okay? he asked. No, Patty replied. Is he dead? Gerlach asked. Yes, said Patty. He asked after each of his staff officers. Each time Patty's answer was the same. Dead. All dead.

★   ★   ★

What happened at the airport in Beirut at six-thirty Sunday morning, October 23, 1983 was almost beyond comprehension. "From a terrorist perspective," a Pentagon commission later wrote, "the true genius of this attack is that the objective and the means of attack were beyond the imagination of those responsible for Marine security."

Whose fault was it that so many young Americans had been slaughtered in their sleep? Judging by the punishments handed down, Geraghty and Gerlach were to blame. The commission headed by retired Adm. Robert Long recommended that they be punished for "failure . . . to take

the security measures necessary to preclude the catastrophic loss of life."
The Secretary of the Navy gave "letters of instruction" to both men.

According to the Long Commission report, Geraghty and Gerlach
had failed to observe the fundamental military principle of dispersion.
They had concentrated nearly one quarter of their 1,200-man force in a
single building and had failed to erect adequate defenses around it. The
gate in the chain-link fence was left open, and the sentries outside the
gate did not have their weapons loaded. Geraghty had ordered the
sentries to keep their magazines in their ammunition pouches as a precaution against an accidental or over-eager discharge of a weapon that
might kill or wound one of the thousands of Lebanese civilians who
visited the airport daily.

For what it was worth, Gerlach had disagreed with Geraghty. "I'm
old school," said Gerlach, who had enlisted in the Marines when he was
eighteen. "If a Marine's on post and he has a weapon, I think a weapon
ought to be loaded." But, Gerlach added, "it wouldn't have made any
difference." Even if the gate had been closed, even if the sentries had their
rounds chambered and their safeties off and had opened fire the instant
they spotted the truck, they probably could not have saved the building.
The Long Commission concluded that it would have collapsed even if
the truck had exploded in the parking lot.

Geraghty and Gerlach had inherited the building from preceding
Marine units which had occupied it ever since they had arrived at the
airport in September 1982. After the embassy bombing in April, the
Marines had erected the concertina wire fence and sandbagged the sentry
posts to keep car bombs away. But car bombs weren't killing Marines;
rockets, mortars, artillery shells, and small arms fire were. The headquarters building offered the best protection against incoming rounds, so
Geraghty and Gerlach had moved another 150 men into its reinforced
concrete walls. "We had tents outside," Gerlach explained, "and we had
a building made of concrete with steel reinforcing rods in it." Marine
Commandant Gen. P. X. Kelley pointed out that "during the earlier
fighting for Beirut it endured furious Israeli artillery barrages without
being destroyed." The Israelis had been impressed enough to use it as
a field hospital. Four stories high, it also served as an excellent observa-
tion post and as a platform for mounting communications antennas.
Even the Long Commission recognized that "the building was an ideal
location for the command post of a battalion actively engaged in fulfilling
a peacekeeping and presence mission."

That, of course, was where Geraghty and Gerlach had gone wrong.

They had persisted in trying to carry out the mission they had been assigned. Geraghty "perceived his mission to be more diplomatic than military, providing presence and visibility . . . to help the Government of Lebanon achieve stability," the Long Commission said, but "by late summer 1983, the environment changed to the extent that the conditions on which the [peacekeeping] mission was initially premised no longer existed." Geraghty could see the conditions had changed. It was his men, after all, who were being killed. But his orders were never modified to reflect the changing conditions. Even when Geraghty was authorized to fire in support of the Lebanese Army at Souk al Gharb, the order from Washington specifically stated that "nothing in this message shall be construed as changing the mission."

If ever a military commander had been left out on a limb, it was Col. Timothy Geraghty. He had been assigned a piece of territory, the airport, not for its military merits but for its political and diplomatic symbolism. Once the shooting started, occupying the low, flat ground at the airport was, in Weinberger's words, like "sitting on a bull's-eye."

Sitting there with orders to fire only if fired upon, Geraghty had been provided with intelligence totally inadequate to his needs. Between May and October, he was inundated with more than one hundred warnings of impending car bomb attacks, sometimes with the color, make, and license number of the vehicle. But most of the warnings were so vague and unreliable that they were useless. The Long Commission said Geraghty "received volumes of intelligence information but none specific enough to have enabled the prevention of the attack or provide him other than general warning."

Buried in those volumes, waiting to be discovered and pieced together, lay clues that might have saved the Marines. Months later, the Office of Naval Intelligence conducted a review of all the data collected prior to the bombing in an effort to determine if better analysis could have predicted the attack. "We concluded the chances were pretty good we would have been able to predict," said Rear Adm. John Butts, the director of Naval Intelligence. The reason Naval Intelligence failed to provide Geraghty with adequate warning was simple—despite all the high-level rhetoric about combatting terrorism, not a single analyst was assigned to work full time on the terrorist threat to the Marines in Lebanon.

Beyond the unrealistic Rules of Engagement, beyond the inadequate intelligence, there was a much more fundamental reason why so many Marines died that Sunday morning. As the Long Commission concluded, the Marines were "not trained, organized, staffed or supported to deal effectively with the terrorist threat in Lebanon." The Marines at the airport had been given exactly one hour of classroom instruction in combatting terrorism, far less training than they received in countering much more unlikely threats such as nuclear, chemical, and biological warfare. The armed forces of the United States were simply not prepared to combat terrorism.

Despite all the circumstances beyond his control, Geraghty was the commander on the scene. He was responsible for the lives of his men, and he had, in effect, permitted his position to be overrun without firing a shot. If no combination of available obstacles could have stopped the truck, surely there was some combination that could have made the attack more difficult, perhaps so difficult that the driver and his accomplices might have decided to look for an easier target.

Howard Gerlach was in a Veterans Administration hospital which specialized in spinal cord injuries when he received his "letter of instruction" from the Secretary of the Navy. He already had heard about it on the evening news, had heard how it would ruin his career. That made him laugh; he was more concerned about regaining even the partial use of his arms and legs than he was about making colonel. Lying there in traction, Gerlach had thought and thought about what he might have done differently. "I look back on it and say, 'Yeah, I think I probably could have done better,' " he reflected. "But against an attack of that magnitude with the resources I had available and given what our mission was, I don't think I could have stopped it."

Gerlach looked at the letter of instruction and thought of a summer twenty-four years before at Marine boot camp at Parris Island. The drill instructor had made his recruits lie in the mud and rain, then yelled at them for getting their uniforms wet and dirty. Then, as now, there was only one right answer. Sir, no excuses, sir.

There would be no courts-martial for what happened in Lebanon. President Reagan, the commander-in-chief, declared that "if there is blame, it properly rests here, in this office, with this President." It was one of the President's most trusted tactics, one he would use over and over again throughout his administration—accepting responsibility without confessing error, taking blame without admitting error, stopping the buck without telling the whole truth. This time his acceptance of responsibility was enough to head off courts-martial that would have replayed in public the whole pathetic story of his disastrous policy in Lebanon.

Not since the Japanese attacked Pearl Harbor on another Sunday morning forty-two years before had the United States military and its civilian leaders been caught so utterly by surprise. The Long Commission concluded that "the Department of Defense needs to recognize the importance of state-sponsored terrorism and must take appropriate measures to deal with it." Nearly four years after another act of state-sponsored terrorism, the seizure of the American Embassy in Tehran, had all but paralyzed the foreign policy of the United States, the Defense Department, with its record budgets, still had not recognized the importance of this new brand of warfare. It was a failure of both military and civilian leadership that in 1983 the armed forces of the United States were as unprepared to defend themselves against terrorism as they had been to rescue American hostages in Iran in 1979.

The Japanese eventually suffered grievous consequences for their sneak attack. Aside from the driver of the truck, none of the terrorists responsible for the bombing of the Marine barracks suffered any consequences at all for their act of war. Within four months, the Marines would be withdrawn from Lebanon as the United States ran from a war it was not prepared to fight.

★ ★ ★

Howard Teicher of the National Security Council staff had been in the Battalion Landing Team building the night before it was blown up, waiting for a plane to take him to Jordan for another meeting in the endless round of negotiations aimed at achieving a more equitable distribution of power in Lebanon. When he arrived back at the Beirut airport at eleven-thirty Sunday morning, fires were still burning and Marines were being stuffed into body bags. Teicher hurriedly reported to President Gemayel on the results of his meeting in Jordan, then returned to the ambassador's residence to find a secure phone to call Washington. When he got a line, he dictated a memo for McFarlane, who had just been promoted to national security adviser, recommending that the United States proceed immediately with plans to retaliate for the slaughter at the airport.

"It was clear in my mind the U.S. had to answer this immediately," Teicher said. "I argued we should hit targets associated with Syrian-sponsored terrorism in Lebanon." Teicher had no way of knowing what evidence, if any, linked Syria to the attack. But he saw no need to inquire too deeply. "This is a consistent pattern of Syria in Lebanon over the years," he maintained. "It was clear they were trying to blow us out." President Assad, after all, was doing everything he could to frustrate American attempts to rebuild Lebanon, and his intelligence officers and troops controlled much of eastern Lebanon, including Baalbek where most of the Shiite radicals and their Iranian allies were headquartered. Most of the evidence, however, indicated that the government of Iran had directed the bombing while Syria looked the other way.

A previously unknown group called Islamic Jihad, or Holy War, claimed responsibility for the bombing. "We are the soldiers of God and we crave death," a statement published in Beirut newspapers read. "Violence will remain our only path if they [the multinational forces] do not leave. We are ready to turn Lebanon into another Vietnam. We are not Iranians or Syrians or Palestinians. We are Lebanese Muslims who follow the dicta of the Koran." The driver of the truck was reported to be a member of a group called the Hussein Suicide Commandos, headed by a cousin of Hussein Musawi, the former schoolteacher who had left the mainstream Amal and formed his own radical Shiite group, Islamic Amal, with headquarters in Baalbek. According to one unconfirmed account, the driver had been blessed by Sheik Fadlallah, the spiritual leader of Hezbollah. Both Hezbollah and Islamic Amal swore allegiance to Iran.

The National Security Agency had intercepted and decoded cables from the Iranian Foreign Ministry to Mohammed Mohtashami-pur, the Iranian Ambassador in Damascus, urging a major attack against the Americans. Other intercepted conversations revealed that the Iranian Revolutionary Guards in Baalbek had asked the embassy in Damascus for permission to launch the attack. A week before the bombing, Hosein Sheikholislam, the veteran of the U.S. Embassy siege in Tehran who now worked out of an office in the Iranian Foreign Ministry, had checked into the Sheraton Hotel in Damascus. He checked out on October 22, the day before the bombing. In Beirut, the Lebanese intelligence service reported that the Iranian Embassy there had been evacuated early on Sunday morning, just before the bombing.

There was no smoking gun, no conclusive evidence that could convict the Iranians in a court of law, particularly since much of the evidence consisted of highly classified communications intercepts. But the Reagan administration knew to a moral, if not a legal, certainty who was responsible for the massacre of the Marines. The plot had been conceived in Tehran, born in Baalbek, and wet-nursed at the Iranian Embassy in Damascus.

A team from the Intelligence Support Activity (ISA) was sent to reconnoiter a list of targets developed by the Pentagon for a retaliatory strike. The team cased everything from the personal residences of Sheik

Fadlallah to Syrian antiaircraft positions and considered everything from conventional air raids to "black" operations that could not be traced to the United States.

Just as after the embassy bombing in April, the ISA team was sent to Lebanon without the knowledge of the European Command, which had operational responsibility for Beirut and would be charged with carrying out any retaliatory strike. The new deputy European commander, Gen. Richard Lawson, was outraged when he found out. "I didn't even know ISA was there until I found out accidentally during a walk through a building after the bombing," he said. "I threw them out. Just three more Americans that could be captured." There were a lot of American military men in Beirut that Lawson didn't know about. An investigation turned up thirty-one "stovepipe" operations in Beirut—units reporting directly to the Pentagon without following the chain of command. It was symptomatic of the chaos that passed for policy in Lebanon.

★   ★   ★

Reagan vowed that "those who directed this atrocity must be dealt justice, and they will be." But thoughts of retaliation were swallowed up by the invasion of Grenada two days after the bombing in Beirut. Grenada was a textbook study in the application of overwhelming military force, but it also demonstrated the risks inherent in any military operation that depends on surprise. The helicopters carrying Delta force took off late from Barbados 80 miles to the northeast, and arrived in Grenada after daybreak, making them easy targets for small arms fire from the scattered defenders. Several members of the force were badly wounded; others were injured when their helicopter crashed after its pilot was shot through the head. The timing had become snarled when someone misconverted the Greenwich Mean Time in the operation plan to the local time in the Caribbean. The transport planes carrying the helicopters from the United States had gotten off late, then spent three times longer than planned trying to unload their cargo. Even so, Delta had fared better than the Navy SEALs assigned to ferry ashore the Air Force's John Carney—the same John Carney who had landed at Desert One in 1980—to set up the drop zone for the paratroopers. Four SEALs drowned because the seas and winds were higher than forecast. Any thought of a lightning retaliatory raid against those responsible for the Beirut bombing would have to take account of the dismal performance in the Caribbean.

A retaliatory raid would require precise intelligence, and the experience in Grenada had not been encouraging. The CIA had only one agent on the island. In the hours before the invasion, the Army's Office of Special Operations had tried desperately to infiltrate another one. Col. James Longhofer, the same officer who had stood on the roof of the American Embassy in Cairo and monitored the secret journey home of Bashir Gemayel, flew to Barbados carrying a briefcase filled with $100,000 in cash to pay the agent. A civilian transport plane brought in a small Hughes 500D helicopter to airlift the agent to Grenada, but at the last moment the spy got cold feet.

When the main invasion force struck on the morning of October 25, its commanders did not realize that the American medical students they were supposed to evacuate were scattered at different locations around the island. As a result, it took more than thirty-six hours to round them all up. Locating Islamic terrorists in Lebanon would be a lot harder than finding American medical students in Grenada.

★　★　★

While the Army was mopping up the remaining defenders on Grenada, a small cabal in the Pentagon was developing a "Navy only" option for striking back at the terrorists who had massacred the Marines in Beirut. "The Navy staff came up with the idea that the only thing that was needed was to go bomb Baalbek into oblivion," the European Command's General Lawson said. Hitting the Sheik Abdullah Barracks, the former Lebanese Army post now in the hands of Hezbollah and the Iranian Revolutionary Guards, offered the best chance of killing the perpetrators of the Marine bombing.

The Navy claimed that with precision-guided munitions its pilots could put a bomb through a window of the barracks. Lawson, a former bomber pilot who had once commanded the Eighth Air Force, knew air strikes were never as surgical as advertised. "One of the oldest temples in the world [the Roman temple of Mercury] is three quarters of a mile from the Sheik Abdullah Barracks," Lawson said. "I knew sure as hell they were going to hit that temple." Besides, Lawson had a more fundamental problem with the retaliation option. "My feeling was I didn't think in the whole damn Middle East there's a target that demonstrates the quid pro quo for two hundred-odd Marines." But Lawson didn't have much say in the matter, even though he was the theater commander. The entire retaliation plan was put together without his knowledge. He found out about it only after the fact.

The military's chain of command was a complete mystery to most outsiders and to many insiders, but few subjects aroused more intense passions among the cognoscenti. The heads of the four military services—the Chief of Naval Operations, the Commandant of the Marine Corps, the Army Chief of Staff, and the Air Force Chief of Staff—were responsible for manning, equipping, and training the forces but had no authority to issue operational orders to troops in the field. As members of the Joint Chiefs of Staff, they could offer advice as to how the troops should be employed, but the actual control of those troops belonged to the so-called unified commanders—the Commander-in-Chief Atlantic, Commander-in-Chief Pacific, Commander-in-Chief Europe. This division of labor was a source of never-ending frustration to the service chiefs, since, in the case of Europe, the Chief of Naval Operations had to sit still while his ships were ordered about by an Army or Air Force general. The temptation to meddle was overwhelming, and no service succumbed to it more than the Navy.

The "Navy only" option was drawn up by Vice Adm. James "Ace" Lyons, the deputy chief of naval operations for plans, working directly with Rear Adm. Jerry Tuttle, the commander of the naval task force off the coast of Lebanon. Lyons and Tuttle were two of the Navy's best known "warriors"—a term used to connote not only courage and cunning in combat but also an all-out style of operating that bordered on recklessness. They were indispensable in war but could be troublesome in peace. Lyons, a brilliant strategist who had the disconcerting habit of saying what he thought and saying it loudly, had seen his career take off when his next-door neighbor and friend John Lehman became Secretary of the Navy. There were those in the Navy who felt Lyons owed his high rank to cronyism, but the truth was that his break-all-the-china style was exactly the kind of talent Lehman prized most. Tuttle, a former carrier pilot who called himself Sluf, for "short little ugly fucker," was caustic and hard-driving—the kind of man you either loved or hated. He drove no one harder than himself, somehow getting by on about three hours' sleep a night.

The strike plan drafted by Lyons recommended an eight-plane strike, but Tuttle added four more planes, just to be sure. Only after the final operations plan had been hand-delivered to Tuttle by a courier from the Pentagon did he inform his immediate superior in the chain of command. It was, to say the least, highly irregular, and it spoke volumes about the loss of discipline among the forces committed to Lebanon.

At the same time, another Navy officer, Rear Adm. John Poindexter, who was assigned to the White House as McFarlane's deputy, made contact with the military adviser to French President François Mitterand. The French contingent of the multinational force in Lebanon had been hit by a suicide bomber on the same morning as the Marines, and it made sense for the two countries to coordinate their actions.

On board the carriers, the air wings were poised to strike. George Wilson, a reporter for *The Washington Post,* was aboard the *Kennedy.* "I sensed the tension all around the carrier and saw the loading of the A-6 bombers," he later wrote. "Several times the crews were awakened from a sound sleep, ordered to dress in their flight and survival gear, briefed on the strike and ordered to the roof [the flight deck] to man up the airplanes. . . . The alerts for the strike and the accompanying tension climbed night after night. Higher Authority each time called off the raid at the last minute." In Stuttgart, General Lawson, the putative commander of these forces, knew nothing about the hair trigger they were on. He had not issued any alert orders to the fleet. The orders were coming straight from the jury-rigged "Navy only" chain of command.

In Washington, Higher Authority couldn't make up its mind. First Grenada, then a presidential trip to Asia intervened, but to bureaucratic veterans like Under Secretary of State Lawrence Eagleburger these just seemed to be convenient excuses for putting off a tough decision. Eagleburger later said that when he heard Vice President Bush, Defense Secretary Weinberger, and White House chief of staff James Baker all argue that the United States could not launch a retaliatory raid with the President out of the country, "I knew that was the end of it."

Along with Shultz and McFarlane, Eagleburger favored retaliation on the ground that force was the only language terrorists and their sponsors understood. In Lebanon, "we always got a few days relief after the Navy opened up, even if they didn't hit anything," Eagleburger argued. He had little patience for the sometimes Jesuitical debates over pinpointing responsibility for the attack on the Marines. "We constantly tended to think of the problem in terms of who was the perpetrator and where was he located," Eagleburger recalled. "It made very little difference whom you clobbered, so long as you clobbered somebody who had it coming. They all talk to each other."

Weinberger took precisely the opposite view. "I'm not an eye-for-an-eye man," he said afterwards. "You've got to have a purpose, and if your purpose is just to kill a lot of people, that's easy enough to do. . . . There was a lot of blind rage and everybody shared that," he continued, "but some people felt we should just go bomb anything we could find or thought that because there was some feeling that the origin of the activity had taken place in Baalbek we should go up and bomb Baalbek. I have no objection to bombing Baalbek if you're going to accomplish something with it, if you're going to stop future terrorism with it. . . . But we didn't have the conclusive kind of target information that I think is essential."

The Joint Chiefs of Staff were split. It was one thing to tell the President a mission *could* be carried out. General Vessey had no doubt that bombing the Sheik Abdullah Barracks "was easy to do—just an exquisite nighttime radar target." It was quite another to tell the President the mission *should* be carried out. The nation's military leaders still had not sorted through the moral dilemmas of fighting this new kind of war. Adm. James Watkins, the Chief of Naval Operations, wanted to retaliate. "I wanted to go because I felt the confluence of information was almost overwhelming," he said later. "We could do the job and do it right." P. X. Kelley, the Marine commandant for whom October 23 had been "the hardest day of my life," cared only for the safety of the Marines still hunkered down at the airport, and feared that retaliation, successful or not, would put them in even greater danger.

With the chiefs split, the chairman became the swing vote. "Everybody would have been happy to retaliate had we been able to select a target that made sense, that would reduce the prospect of further terrorism against Americans and would further U.S. objectives in the area," Vessey said afterwards. "But it came back to the fact that we didn't have conclusive proof that the guys we would bomb in Baalbek were the people who did the Marine barracks business."

At a meeting of the National Security Council on November 14, Vessey told the President the Navy was ready, willing, and able to launch a strike against the Sheik Abdullah Barracks, but he warned that American pilots might be shot down by Syrian antiaircraft batteries in the vicinity of Baalbek and that retaliation probably would increase the likelihood of further attacks against the Marines at the airport. Despite Vessey's warnings, the President indicated he wanted to proceed with a strike.

The next day, the commander of the French battle group off Lebanon arrived on board the carrier *Eisenhower* carrying a letter from the French chief of staff requesting Rear Admiral Tuttle to assist in planning a joint strike against Baalbek. Tuttle replied that he could help plan the raid but he could not execute it without a direct order from Washington. According to McFarlane, the President and his advisers were agreed that a strike would take place on the 16th. Early that morning, the White House Situation Room telephoned McFarlane at home and assured him the strike was still on. The *Eisenhower* and the *Kennedy* were in position, but the execute order had not yet been given.

When McFarlane arrived at the White House early on the 16th, the execute order still had not been transmitted, and Poindexter told him, I don't think they're going to do it. A short time later, Vessey's assistant, Vice Adm. Arthur Moreau, called Poindexter to tell him that Weinberger had ordered the fleet to stand down. McFarlane called the Defense Secretary, demanding to know what had happened. According to McFarlane, Weinberger said, We just don't think the conditions are right, and explained that there had not been enough time to coordinate the raid adequately with the French. Finally, McFarlane recalled, Weinberger declared, I just don't think it's prudent.

As McFarlane saw it, the Defense Secretary had disobeyed a direct order from the President. When he told Reagan what had happened, the President balled his hand into a fist, pounded his desk, and said, Damn, I sure wish we could do it.

The French did do it, or at least they attempted it, launching planes against the Sheik Abdullah Barracks. Reconnaissance photos revealed that they missed everything. "The French accomplished nothing whatever with that raid," Weinberger said. "They probably made some people feel good . . . but that's not really a basis for military action."

Weinberger's recollection of the affair differed sharply from McFarlane's. According to Weinberger, there had been nothing more than "some discussions in a very inconclusive way of possibly taking an air raid, sort of a single shot raid, just to do some damage in Baalbek." As Weinberger told it, the French Defense Minister, Charles Hernu, called one morning and announced that the French were going to attack targets in Baalbek in one hour. "In effect, all we could say is good luck," recalled Weinberger, who said he has "no memory" of the President authorizing a joint attack on the Sheik Abdullah Barracks.

It was not unusual for two of the President's closest advisers to come out of a meeting with completely different impressions of what Reagan had decided. Although he projected the image of a strong leader, Ronald Reagan frequently relied on ambiguity to resolve—or bury—the conflicts within his administration. Never one to master the intricacies of a problem, he was dependent upon his advisers to tell him not only the facts but also what they meant. When his advisers gave him conflicting opinions, when the time came for him to make a complex and truly difficult decision that only the President could make, he frequently failed. The President's involvement in foreign affairs was episodic, anecdotal, impulsive, and rarely decisive. It was no wonder that the staff of the National Security Council later concluded that the best way to serve Reagan was to do his job for him.

Unable or unwilling to retaliate, the American Gulliver was being run ragged by Lilliputian terrorists. The two aircraft carriers—a force no other nation, including the Soviet Union, could muster—were scrambling to protect themselves against reported terrorist threats ranging from kamikaze planes to hang gliders to rubber boats loaded with explosives. On the *Kennedy*, George Wilson of *The Washington Post* wrote that the "air wing was sent out on one false alarm after another to head off terrorist attacks." The catwalks of the *Kennedy*, arguably the most powerful ship in the world, had to be rigged with .50-caliber machine guns to defend against this new threat. The carrier became a symbol of the musclebound superpower, its high-tech weaponry useless in the face of a low-tech threat. The huge ship with its eighty-five aircraft could have prevented every plane in Lebanon from taking off, every boat from setting to sea, but that would have required the indiscriminate use of force. The *Kennedy*'s mission was to defeat the terrorists, not imitate them.

To protect the Marines, the carriers were launching daily reconnaissance flights over Lebanon, searching for signs of impending attacks against the airport. On December 3, an F-14 Tomcat headed inland at 600 miles per hour at an altitude of 3,500 feet, a camera pod mounted under the fuselage. Below, its crew saw the usual twinkle of antiaircraft guns blazing futilely away. Suddenly, a series of smoking corkscrews rose toward the plane, the trails of heat-seeking SA-7 antiaircraft missiles. They missed, and the F-14 returned safely to the *Kennedy*, but this time the United States was determined to strike back. As Admiral Watkins explained, "There was a feeling at the time that a response in kind was a legitimate thing. In other words, if you're shot at, you shoot back." Having failed to shoot back when 241 Americans were blown up, the Reagan administration had no difficulty deciding to retaliate against a few shoulder-fired missiles that had missed.

Before the day was out, the Joint Chiefs recommended and the President approved an air raid against Syrian antiaircraft sites in Lebanon. The chiefs considered and rejected using the *New Jersey*'s 16-inch guns. They had the range to reach targets behind Syrian lines, but without forward observers to spot the fall of shot they were not accurate enough. "Here in Lebanon we had a very complex environment, a peacetime environment where collateral damage [i.e., civilian casualties] is a very big concern to us," Watkins said. "So my feeling was that it was the right decision to recommend using airplanes from the carriers rather than employing the 16-inch guns of the *New Jersey*." Unlike everyone else in

Lebanon, the United States was willing to risk the lives of its own men to protect the lives of non-combatants.

It was nine-thirty at night by the time the order worked its way through the chain of command to Rear Admiral Tuttle, the task force commander, now on board the carrier *Independence,* which had relieved the *Eisenhower.* Tuttle put together a strike that would simultaneously hit three different targets behind Syrian lines. One was a French-built early warning radar complex; the other two were simply geographic coordinates within which as many as twenty-eight Syrian gun positions were located. To cover that many aim points, Tuttle would need to use both carriers. "With all the aim points that were in those targets, we probably were still short on aircraft" even with two carriers, Tuttle said later. He dispatched pilots to the Naval Air Station at Sigonella, Sicily, to pick up extra aircraft that had been undergoing maintenance.

Aboard the *Kennedy,* George Wilson looked at the reconnaissance photographs of the Syrian gun sites. "On the photos they looked like little metal washers lying in the dust," he wrote. The gun positions were too small to reflect radar beams, so the pilots would have to go in low enough to locate their targets visually, exposing themselves to Syrian, Druze, and Palestinian antiaircraft fire. "They weren't great military targets," Tuttle said.

At three-thirty on the morning of December 4, Tuttle submitted an operations plan which called for launching the strike at midday when there would be no shadows to mask the targets and the Syrian antiaircraft gunners would have to look straight into the sun. He then lay down to catch a few hours sleep while his operations plan was being reviewed in Washington. While Tuttle slept, the Joint Chiefs issued an order calling for an "early morning strike" so that the retaliation would occur within twenty-four hours of the attack on the reconnaissance mission. "The twenty-four-hour deadline wasn't hard and fast," Vessey recalled. "It was a general guideline for tying the retaliation to the event so we could point to the world and to Syria and say that this was retaliation."

The time, in other words, was suggested for political reasons, but it was to have profound military consequences. With the morning sun low in the east, the targets would still be in shadow and the pilots, not the antiaircraft gunners, would be looking directly into its glare. Somehow, somewhere in the convoluted chain of command between Washington and Beirut, the vital point of timing became lost or garbled. Exactly where the mistake occurred is impossible to pinpoint, but the result was clear. The chiefs in Washington and General Lawson at the European

Command in Stuttgart were proceeding on the assumption that the planes would strike at dawn. Tuttle and his carrier pilots were planning to strike at midday.

At 5:33 A.M., dawn in Lebanon, Lawson issued an execute order specifying a time over target of 7:30 A.M. When Tuttle was awakened by a phone call telling him the order had been released, "I said no way in hell we could make it." Tuttle requested a delay but was denied. "I told them three times I couldn't make it, and they said you've got to make it," he recalled.

As the *Kennedy*'s pilots filed into the briefing room, Cdr. John Mazach, who would lead the strike, told them, You've got only a few minutes to go over this stuff because your target time for launch is 0720. Most of the fliers had been through so many false alarms that they did not take Mazach seriously. Each air crew—pilot and bombardier—was handed a strike folder containing maps and pictures of his target.

On the flight deck, Lts. Tom Corey and Bill Davis walked to their A-6 bomber to begin the pre-flight checks. They stopped and looked at each other in disbelief—there were no bombs under the wings. The cluster bombs that could spray shrapnel over an area the size of a football field were still in their crates below decks. "Throw some bombs on there," Corey told the ordnance men, pointing to some 1,000-pound "iron" bombs stacked nearby on the flight deck. The 1,000 pounders had tremendous concussive force, ideal for collapsing the walls of a building, but they weren't accurate enough for small targets like the Syrian gun sites. Rolling in from 12,000 feet, Corey and Davis weren't likely to hit much with their iron bombs, but it was better than going into battle unarmed.

The ordnance men had time to clamp just two of the bombs under the wings before Corey lit the engines. Most of the other planes weren't much better off. The only plane carrying a full load of munitions belonged to Lts. Mark Lange and Robert Goodman. Since they were the last in line to launch, there was time to arm their A-6 with six 1,000-pound bombs. As Cdr. John Mazach's aircraft was hooked to the catapult, he saw the Soviet intelligence trawler which routinely shadowed the *Kennedy* standing a half-mile off the port side. I wonder what that guy is thinking, Mazach said to his bombardier. Almost certainly, the Soviets would recognize the difference between routine flight operations and this helter-skelter launch and would warn the Syrians that trouble was headed their way. Lt. Robert Goodman, the bombardier in the last plane to launch, wasn't worried about the Soviet trawler; he was thinking about the lookouts posted in the mountains the planes would have to cross. Using binoculars, a lookout could see the aircraft swarming like bees as they massed for the strike. The planes were easy to spot: the rising sun was shining on them like a spotlight. To make matters worse, the Israeli Air Force appeared over the target area just before the American strike was launched, ending any remaining chance of catching the Syrians napping.

Catapulted off the deck, Mazach climbed to 12,000 feet to rendezvous with the rest of the *Kennedy* strike group. Over his radio, he could hear the voice of Cdr. Ed "Honiak" Andrews, the leader of the *Independence* strike group. Tuttle came on the circuit from his command post aboard the *Independence.* "This is Alpha Bravo," Tuttle radioed. "You're a go." Twenty-three planes, a combination of A-6s and lighter A-7s, staggered in sections of two and three, headed east toward Lebanon, into the morning sun.

The bombers from the *Independence* were the first over the beach. In his headset, Mazach could hear the sounds of pilots being shot at by surface-to-air missiles. "SAMs! SAMs! SAMs! . . . I'm hit. I'm hit." Andrews in the lead plane was on fire. "Mayday. Mayday," he radioed. "I'm proceeding out over the water now . . . I got 250 knots."

"How are you doing back there?" his wingman asked.

"I'm fine," Andrews replied. "Almost clear right now."

"We're looking for you right now," his wingman said.

"Honiak out of here," said Andrews as he punched out of his flaming A-7.

"Good chute, good chute," his wingman reported. "Did you get a good tally on him?" he asked the rescue helicopters.

"Searching for him in the harbor area," one of the helicopter pilots responded. A Lebanese fisherman got to Andrews first and turned him over to the French, who quickly returned him to the *Independence.*

The *Kennedy* strike group was not so lucky. Behind schedule and anxious to catch up, some of the pilots had not wanted to waste time climbing to the assigned altitude of 12,000 feet. As the mountains of Lebanon rose to meet them, they came within range of the SA-7 missiles. "I remember scanning the horizon, looking down and seeing small puffs of smoke," Goodman said later. "I remember seeing one smoke trail behind me, a kind of corkscrew trail of white smoke that went up and past the airplane, then feeling this violent jolt."

"Fireball! Fireball!" Lange and Goodman had been hit. Their A-6, the only fully armed plane to launch from the *Kennedy,* tumbled out of control, smashing into the side of a ridge and sending flaming chunks of wreckage cartwheeling down the slope. Somehow—Goodman does not remember how—they managed to eject, smashing through the plastic canopy into a 450-mile-per-hour windstream. At those speeds, ejecting is only slightly better than going down with the plane.

Lange's parachute had barely opened when he hit the ground. Somewhere between the violent ejection and the brutal landing, his left leg was severed. He bled to death before the Syrian gunners who shot him down could or would apply a tourniquet. Goodman also landed hard, breaking a rib, separating a shoulder, and tearing up his left knee. When he came to, the Syrians had taken his watch and ring and were tying his hands and feet. "The only thing I remember is thinking I was going to lose my fingers because my hands were going numb," he recalled. The Syrians blindfolded him and threw him in the back of a truck bound for Damascus.

Two planes had been lost, one pilot killed and his bombardier captured. Lange and Goodman never had a chance to drop their bombs. Mazach's bombs had hung up and refused to drop. The other eight planes from the *Kennedy* were so lightly armed that a single A-6 could have carried the entire load. Two Syrian gun emplacements were knocked out, and the building at the radar site was damaged. Two days later, the radar was operating again. "A lot of people over here felt it was not worth the price," Gen. Lawson said.

It had been a knee-jerk, tit-for-tat response made needlessly dangerous by the political requirement to launch at first light, a decision for which no one was willing to take responsibility. Afterward, the chain of command did its best to cover up what a fiasco the raid had been. Vessey himself did not learn what had happened until he visited the fleet over Christmas and talked to the pilots. "To go out to the carrier and find it was a Chinese fire drill was quite a shock," Vessey said. Worst of all, the strike had been launched in support of a policy that now was doomed to fail, and probably had been from the start. There had been nothing to gain, only more to lose. The Sixth Fleet took the lesson to heart and quietly stopped flying reconnaissance missions over the most dangerous parts of Lebanon.

★   ★   ★

Public support for the Reagan administration's policy in Lebanon had begun to disintegrate even before the attack on the Marines. On September 29, an increasingly skeptical Congress grudgingly had authorized the Marines to remain in Beirut for another eighteen months, but in exchange the Democrats had forced the administration to promise that it would not try to expand the Marines' role, relocate them, or otherwise change their mission without congressional approval. After the bombing of the Marines, congressional opposition to the deployment welled up in earnest, no doubt convincing the Syrians that time was on their side, as indeed it was.

"All the goals we had espoused were by that time untenable by the means we had chosen," said Lincoln Bloomfield, the Lebanon desk officer at the Pentagon. "The two things were used up—introducing a military presence to restore calm and forcing all the parties to sit down and work things out. That was gone. There was nothing good left. There were only two ways of looking at it. One is you could in effect go to war. The other is you could just sit there in Lebanon and get bloodied out of pure humanitarianism." Flatly and publicly, Weinberger ruled out going to war, saying, "We'd have to put in about fifteen divisions." Still, there were some in the administration who continued to believe that force was the answer to the loose coalition of Syrians, Iranians, Druze, Palestinians, and Lebanese Shiites bent upon driving the United States out of Lebanon.

"One of the ironies of our Mideast policy was that the Defense Department always came across as the diplomats in the proceedings," Geoffrey Kemp of the NSC staff said. "The seventh floor of the State Department always came across as the gung-ho hawks. The NSC position was even stiffer. If you're a superpower, if you've got all these goddamned forces that you've built up for one reason or another, and you can't use them in a situation like this, then you've got a weak country." In the Pentagon, debates over the use of military force dealt with more basic questions. "It's difficult to talk with a military man when you want to talk political symbolism," the Pentagon's Francis "Bing" West said. "The military man wants to know what he should do if a 155-millimeter shell lands near him." "The question Shultz raised many times was why don't you shoot?" Vessey recalled. "He couldn't understand why we weren't shooting. Our answer was after you shoot today, what do you want to do tomorrow?" For his part, Shultz said, "I think you can make out a strong case that our position deteriorated when we did not return fire more aggressively." Howard Teicher remembered flying into Damascus on the day the *New Jersey* fired its 16-inch guns for the first time against Syrian positions. "Khaddam [the Syrian Foreign Minister] was a changed man," Teicher said. "This man was sweating. This man was nervous." There were, of course, other reasons why Khaddam might be nervous, not the least of which was that Syrian President Assad had suffered a heart attack, setting off furious jockeying for power in Damascus amid rumors of his imminent demise.

Even if the *New Jersey* had caught the Syrians' attention, that did not answer Vessey's question—today the *New Jersey;* tomorrow, what? Col. Fadlo Massabni, the U.S. defense attaché at the embassy in Beirut, was with Gen. Ibrahim Tannous, the Lebanese Armed Forces commander, when the *New Jersey* fired for the first time. Massabni was sitting with his back to the window when Tannous looked over his shoulder and exclaimed, Fadlo, that's the *New Jersey.* As they watched, the big battlewagon turned broadside and began to fire. After a few rounds, the ship was wreathed in black smoke and Tannous was ecstatic. He hugged the American officer. Then, he turned pensive. Fadlo, he said, What are the Americans going to do next? Are they going to fly B-52s wingtip to wingtip over Lebanon?

The *New Jersey,* with its ability to hurl a 2,000-pound projectile more than 20 miles, was a fearsome weapon, but without forward observers to correct the fall of shot, it was dreadfully inaccurate. "The *New Jersey* at that time was a great psychological weapon, but I hated to see it used," Massabni said. "I thought it was senseless, just senseless shelling. You don't throw a projectile that size without having somebody watch where it falls." The United States already had lost any hope of achieving its objectives in Lebanon. The question now was whether it would lose its humanity as well.

At a luncheon meeting in the White House on the day before Christmas, McFarlane presented the outline of a seventeen-page paper written by Dennis Ross, the deputy director of the Pentagon's Office of Net Assessment. In his paper, Ross argued that the best the United States could do in Lebanon was to negotiate concessions from the Syrians in return for the withdrawal of the Marines. But first Assad had to be convinced that the Marines would stay in Lebanon for as long as it took. Assistant Defense Secretary Richard Armitage, Vice Adm. Arthur Moreau, and several other second-tier officials listened as McFarlane made the case for moving the Marines to a safer place such as Christian East Beirut or Juniyah, north of the capital. McFarlane concluded the meeting by asking each of the departments represented to submit papers analyzing the options for redeploying the Marines—for coming up, in other words, with a policy the administration could sustain. When Armitage and Moreau returned to the Pentagon with their marching orders from the White House, Weinberger vetoed the entire exercise.

Weinberger didn't want the Marines in a safer place in Lebanon; he wanted them out. "Having gone in reluctantly, they stayed reluctant," Under Secretary of State Lawrence Eagleburger said of the Pentagon. "They never gave any thought to how they could change the circumstances on the ground."

Still stuck at the airport, the Marines moved underground. They lowered trailers into trenches and covered them with dirt. They walked from post to post in covered trenches. "They lived like moles," said Fadlo Massabni. Doggerel scrawled on the doorframe of one underground bunker summed it up nicely:

> They sent us to Beirut
> To be targets who could not shoot.
> Friends will die into an early grave
> Was there any reason for what they gave?

Vessey toured the airport over Christmas. "I became convinced that we just had to get the Marines out of there," he said. "I could see that the whole situation had changed drastically."

Opposed to the deployment from the start, the Joint Chiefs had, until now, been afraid to advance but unwilling to retreat. As late as September of 1983, Admiral Watkins had told Congress, "It is the opinion of the Joint Chiefs of Staff that withdrawal of the multinational force at this time probably would have a devastating effect and could plunge Lebanon into total anarchy." Until now, the chiefs had not had the courage of their conviction that Beirut was the wrong place for the Marines to be. "It sounded almost disloyal and inhumanitarian to suggest they be withdrawn," Vessey explained. "It's kind of like being against gambling when fifty percent of the parish money comes from the Bingo game. None of us marched in and told the President that the U.S. is going to face disaster if the Marines didn't withdraw. Those of us who were concerned about our military presence in Lebanon realized we might be wrong. There was always this underlying hope this might work out."

But by January, all hope was gone. "We were desperate to get out," said Assistant Defense Secretary Richard Armitage. "If we could get them on the ships, we could see no reason why we would ever have to return." Weinberger preferred to call that a "redeployment," not a withdrawal, but a retreat by any other name was still a retreat.

As Congress returned to work in January 1984, the Democrats immediately began pressing resolutions to withdraw the Marines. "When Congress went home for Christmas after that bombing, it was over," Lincoln Bloomfield said. "All those congressmen going to church on Christmas Eve. They were just different when they came back from the holiday break. All tolerance or acquiescence was gone." Even Republican loyalists like Mississippi Congressman Trent Lott were backing away from the administration's policy. You make sure the Secretary knows that even though we voted for eighteen months, we meant three months, Lott told Assistant Secretary of State Veliotes.

Congress, Weinberger's unremitting adversary when it came to the defense budget, was now his most valuable ally. Congress, of course, was merely reflecting public opinion. The polls showed that in December 48 percent of the public favored withdrawing the Marines from Lebanon; by January, 57 percent believed the United States should get out.

The collapse of public and congressional support for the administration's policy coincided with the disintegration of the Lebanese Army. Despite the influx of nearly $1 billion worth of American military equipment, the army had failed to become a unifying force. Instead, as both the CIA and DIA had predicted, Amin Gemayel had used it as a bulwark against giving the Shiites and the Druze a greater voice in government. Druze leader Walid Jumblatt called on all Druze soldiers to desert the army, and Shiite leaders began putting pressure on Shiite soldiers to lay down their arms. Muslim soldiers, who made up 60 percent of the army, continued to serve at their own peril. Gassan Chamas, a Shiite who continued to serve in military intelligence, watched over the ensuing months as four of his fellow Muslim intelligence officers were picked up and murdered for the crime of working for the government. He would have been murdered, too, except that on the day his car was ambushed, only his driver was inside. The driver would spend eighteen months as a hostage and four more in the hospital recovering from his beatings. Chamas finally fled Lebanon for his life.

For the first time, even George Shultz was privately admitting the policy had failed. If I ever say send in the Marines again, he told a meeting of the National Security Council, somebody shoot me. Robert McFarlane reluctantly had come to the same conclusion, although for different reasons. "I guess I was most moved by the untenable tension between Cap [Weinberger] and Shultz," McFarlane explained. Even Howard Teicher, that tireless advocate of force, was resigned to the fact that the Defense Department would do whatever was necessary to block any attempts to change the situation on the ground in Lebanon. "When you have a cabinet officer with the power to foil the President's will, it was crazy to have people exposed," he said.

Teicher wrote a paper which called for making more liberal use of naval gunfire and airpower while at the same time gradually withdrawing the Marines from the airport. Sprinkling the paper with phrases like "more with less," "umbrella of protection," and "redeployment" took some of the sting out of what was in essence a proposal to quit and go home. "That was an idea whose time had come," said Dennis Ross, the

Pentagon analyst. "Defense accepted it because it was the first chance to get the Marines out."

Shultz knew he had lost, but he was still opposed to a precipitous withdrawal that would leave Lebanon to the not so tender mercies of Syria. When Shultz departed on a long-scheduled trip to Latin America, it fell to the Under Secretary of State, Lawrence Eagleburger, to fight a rearguard action. At the next meeting with the President, Eagleburger made an impassioned argument for staying the course in Lebanon. Weinberger countered by telling the President the administration's policy was still hitched to a dead horse—Shultz's May 17 withdrawal agreement. Heatedly, Eagleburger responded that the United States could not negotiate an agreement and then walk away from it after less than a year without doing serious damage to the nation's credibility.

Eagleburger left the meeting thinking he had carried the day. "President Reagan felt we shouldn't get out with our tail between our legs," he remembered. Indeed, in an interview with *The Wall Street Journal,* Reagan said withdrawal "would mean the end of Lebanon" and a "pretty disastrous result" for American foreign policy. Asked about House Speaker Thomas "Tip" O'Neill's campaign to get the Marines out, Reagan said, "He may be ready to surrender, but I'm not." In his weekly Saturday radio address on February 4, 1984, the President maintained that "our efforts to strengthen the Lebanese Army . . . are making sure and steady progress," and added that the dangers and frustrations of Lebanon were "no reasons to turn our backs on friends and cut and run."

At the same time the President was vowing not to cut and run, Nabih Berri was calling on the Shiites in the army to lay down their arms. The commander of the largely Shiite Lebanese Sixth Brigade, which kept what peace there was in West Beirut, pulled his remaining forces into the barracks as Muslim militiamen took over the streets. "It was an intolerable situation," said Maj. Joseph Englehardt, the Army attaché. "With the Lebanese Army gone, you realized just how thin a line a Marine amphibious battalion really is. We were surrounded by hostile militias, and we either had to get serious about defending ourselves or we had to get out. There was no more good to be done." The embassy began evacuating Americans, the *New Jersey* started firing in support of what was left of the Lebanese Army, and the Marines sent the engineers who had been helping them dig in back to their ships.

George Shultz had arrived at his hotel overlooking the beach in Rio de Janeiro late Sunday afternoon. It was to be his only free evening on a typically grueling trip, so the American Ambassador led the Secretary and his entourage to a local nightspot. They had been there about an hour when Raymond Seitz, Shultz's executive assistant, got a call from the hotel that Rear Adm. Jonathan Howe, the State Department's director of Politico-Military Affairs, was urgently trying to reach him. Seitz excused himself and returned to the hotel to talk to Howe on a secure telephone line. Howe told him the Vice President would table a proposal for withdrawing the Marines at a meeting scheduled for Monday. McFarlane also favored withdrawal, Howe said, so there was no one but Eagleburger left to fight for staying the course. When Seitz told Shultz the news, the Secretary repeated his belief that the United States could not cut and run. Shultz added that he doubted it was mere coincidence that the decision to pull out was being brought to a head while he was out of town.

★　★　★

When the National Security Planning Group (NSPG) met for a final discussion of the Marines, President Reagan was flying west to his California ranch, leaving George Bush to preside over one of the administration's most important foreign policy decisions. The intense congressional pressure already had helped convince Bush that the Marines had to leave, and he gave short shrift to Lawrence Eagleburger's final pleas that abandoning the Lebanese government would undercut America's credibility all around the world. Bush called Reagan aboard Air Force One and told him: All your senior advisers except State think we should get out, and I agree with them. It was one time that the usually invisible Bush made a difference. Had he sided with Shultz and Eagleburger and presented the question to Reagan differently, the President might not have been persuaded to reverse himself and approve the withdrawal.

As it was, Reagan accepted the recommendation. The NSPG drafted a withdrawal announcement and relayed the text to Air Force One. When the blue and silver jet landed near Santa Barbara, the President strode to the Marine helicopter waiting to take him to his ranch, while his press aides handed out a statement announcing "decisive new steps" in Lebanon, including "the redeployment of the Marines from Beirut airport to their ships offshore." It was probably the closest Ronald Reagan had come to being decisive during the entire eighteen-month agony of the American crusade in Lebanon.

Shultz had flown on to Grenada, his first visit to the island since the invasion. There, at the end of a hectic day, in a shabby corrugated tin shed where a secure communications link to Washington had been set up, Bush and McFarlane told the Secretary of State the decision to withdraw the Marines had been made. To his watching aides, George Shultz looked like a man who had just been mugged.

The job of telling Amin Gemayel the United States was abandoning him fell to Donald Rumsfeld, the latest of the President's Middle East envoys. A week earlier, he had assured Gemayel that although the United States might reduce its forces in Lebanon it would continue to stand behind the Lebanese government. Now, Rumsfeld and his aides, along with Ambassador Reginald Bartholomew, all wearing sidearms, arrived in Gemayel's antiseptic white bunker in the basement of the presidential palace. Upstairs, constant artillery fire had long since shattered the glass walls of the president's office. Rumsfeld told Gemayel the decision to withdraw the Marines had been made; it was final and would be announced shortly in Washington. The boyish Lebanese president asked a number of questions, but he took the news philosophically, which only deepened the sadness and shame the Americans felt. "I just felt terrible," Rumsfeld recalled. "I felt sick to my stomach."

It happened so fast that Brig. Gen. Jim Joy, the new commander of the Marines in Lebanon, heard about it on the BBC before he received the withdrawal order from the Pentagon. The next day, the Marines began withdrawing to their ships as the *New Jersey* blasted away with its 16-inch guns. The gunners did not know what they were shooting at, much less what they were hitting. There were no forward artillery observers to verify that the coordinates provided by the Lebanese were bona fide targets. "We're still looking for where the *New Jersey* rounds hit," said Gen. Lawson of the European Command.

In a nine-hour period, the battleship fired 288 16-inch rounds, each one weighing as much as a Volkswagen Beetle. In those nine hours, the ship consumed 40 percent of the 16-inch ammunition available in the entire European theater. It was as if the military was trying, in one burst of wretched excess, to make up for its reluctance to shoot during the past eighteen months. It was, said Geoffrey Kemp, "the most absurd thing of all. Weinberger, having resisted for months and months the use of force, now agrees to bombardment as the price he had to pay to get the Marines out."

Early in the barrage, Michael Burch, the Pentagon spokesman, went up to Weinberger's office to find out what was happening. He encountered Vessey coming out of the Defense Secretary's office with maps and charts under his arm. "I asked him, 'Why are we firing?'" Burch recalled. "Vessey said, 'Well, it's up to the theater commander to decide how many rounds.'" Burch then asked Weinberger what the *New Jersey* was firing at. Weinberger said the targets were communications facilities, ammunition dumps, and terrorist camps. Burch, a former Air Force officer, knew what a 2,000-pound shell could do. It was inevitable, as Navy Secretary John Lehman indelicately put it, that the *New Jersey* would kill "the odd shepherd." When the number of rounds climbed past 150, Burch went upstairs to see Weinberger again. "I said, 'Is this really necessary? That's one hell of a lot of iron,' " Burch recalled. "Weinberger picked up the phone and called Vessey and said, in effect, enough is enough."

The last elements of the Battalion Landing Team left the beach at 12:37 P.M. on February 26. At a brief ceremony turning the airport over to the Lebanese Army, the Marines struck the American flag. The Lebanese liaison officer suddenly grabbed his country's flag and presented it to the Marines. Well, you may as well take our flag, too, he said. Then he asked if they could give him a helicopter ride back to the Ministry of Defense—he was a Christian and could not get through the Muslim checkpoints. The Marines dropped him at the Ministry of Defense and flew out to the ships offshore, leaving behind the more than one million sandbags they had filled during their occupation of the airport. Within minutes of the Marines' departure, the Shiite Amal militia began occupying the vacant positions.

Three days later, Weinberger, who would never forgive himself for what happened to the Marines, flew to the U.S.S. *Guam* to tell them "that this is a lot better place to be than sitting down in a little hole." Weinberger was much too loyal to the President to reveal how strongly he had opposed sending the Marines to Lebanon, but now that they were out he came as close as he ever would to speaking his mind in public. "It was, I suppose, one of the toughest and most miserable tasks that was ever assigned," he said. "You couldn't do any of the things you were trained for. You couldn't move out or take high ground or improve your position." The Marines had no idea how often Weinberger had vetoed proposals to do just that.

In a macabre sort of way, it was fitting that the last Marine to die at the airport in Beirut had accidentally shot himself with his own pistol. America's involvement in Lebanon had been a misuse of military power from beginning to end. The President had dispatched a token force to a vulnerable corner of Beirut thinking an American military presence would somehow transform Lebanon from a battlefield into a nation. The military had been given an impossible job to do and had done it badly.

"The question that has nagged at me ever since the bombing of the Marines is how much did our opposition to being there affect our performance in ways that may have permitted the bombing," Vessey said later. "How much did our hopes to get out of there affect our ability to protect ourselves." The military's reluctance had been compounded by the confusion and inefficiency of the chain of command between Washington and Beirut. Even when the spirit was willing, the flesh was weak, as in the case of the disastrous December raid on Syrian positions in Lebanon.

The attack on the Marine barracks had exposed the fundamental error in committing American fighting men to Lebanon. It was not vital to American interests, not worth a single American life. American freedoms were not at stake in Lebanon. Incredibly, said Eagleburger, "the fundamental question—to what degree is Lebanon fundamental to the security interests of the United States—was never asked." The salvation of Lebanon was unquestionably a worthy cause, but that was not enough to justify the sacrifices Lebanon demanded. Not even Israel was willing to make the sacrifices Lebanon demanded.

"What was our mission?" asked Lance Corp. Nick Mottola. "I'll tell you what our mission was. A lot of people died for nothing and then we left."

★　★　★

The Marines were gone, but for the Americans who stayed on, the war in Lebanon was far from over. Islamic Jihad, the catch-all name used by the network of Iranian and Lebanese Shiites who had blown up the Marines, was determined to rid the Middle East of every trace of Western influence. To Islamic Jihad, every American, no matter how innocent, how well meaning, or how fluent in Arabic, was an enemy to be eliminated. Even before the Marines departed, Islamic Jihad had claimed responsibility for the murder of Dr. Malcolm Kerr, who had replaced the kidnapped David Dodge as president of the American University of Beirut. Two young men had waited by the elevator outside his office and shot him twice through the head. The cold-blooded murder of a genial gentleman sympathetic to the Arab cause was a warning that no American was safe in Lebanon any longer.

On the morning of March 16, 1984, William Buckley, the CIA station chief in Beirut, left his apartment and was heading down the cul-de-sac where he lived on his way to work when he was grabbed and stuffed into the trunk of a white Renault. The kidnapping or assassination of intelligence officers was a tactic most nations had long since foresworn. But the Shiite radicals were breaking all the rules. They had seized an American Embassy and held its occupants hostage for more than a year. They had launched a suicide attack that had been beyond the ability of Western minds even to grasp, much less defeat. Now, with the abduction of Buckley, they were resorting to kidnapping an intelligence officer who supposedly enjoyed diplomatic immunity.

Buckley had gone to Beirut to begin rebuilding the agency's intelligence network after the bombing of the embassy had wiped out virtually the entire station. Now, for the second time in less than a year, the CIA station was shattered by a terrorist attack. The agency immediately evacuated all its officers from Lebanon on the assumption that everything Buckley knew would soon be pried out of him. That assumption quickly gained credence when some of the CIA's Lebanese agents disappeared or were murdered. Eventually, the CIA replaced its officers in Lebanon, this time stationing them in Christian East Beirut, which was marginally safer but provided less access to the Muslim community. For Americans in Lebanon, the primary mission was now survival.

Buckley was more than just a CIA officer; he had become, in many ways, the agency's point man in the war against terrorism. In earlier assignments, he had trained Anwar Sadat's bodyguards and served as the Agency's liaison to Delta and as the CIA representative to the Interagency Group on Terrorism, which coordinated the Reagan administration's counterterrorism policy, such as it was. A lifelong bachelor, he frequently told colleagues they could never be serious about fighting terrorism if they had families to worry about. When Kenneth Haas, the previous station chief, had been killed in the embassy bombing, Buckley had volunteered for duty at the front.

It was a disastrous assignment. Embittered by the Marine pullout from Beirut, he called CIA headquarters on a secure telephone line in early February, complained that he no longer knew who the United States was supporting in Lebanon, and demanded that someone at the Agency get the National Security Council staff to explain the administration's policy. Now he was in the hands of terrorists determined to extract from him not only the secrets of U.S. intelligence operations in Lebanon but also the details of the Reagan administration's policy and tactics for combatting terrorism.

The CIA identified Buckley's kidnappers as members of a cell within the Iranian-backed Hezbollah, headed by a young Shiite named Imad Mugniyah. Handsome, charismatic, and educated, Mugniyah came from a large middle-class family in southern Lebanon. He was not a devout Muslim, but like so many other Shiites radicalized by the twin shocks of the Iranian revolution and the Israeli invasion, he had joined Amal and drifted into Hezbollah, rising through the ranks to become the commander of Sheik Fadlallah's bodyguards. Mugniyah's brother-in-law was one of seventeen terrorists who had been tried, convicted, and sentenced for a bomb attack against the American and French embassies in Kuwait in December of 1983.

Buckley was one of three Americans kidnapped by the Mugniyah clan early in 1984 in an effort to ransom their comrades and relatives imprisoned in Kuwait. Hezbollah and its Iranian patrons had discovered that a handful of live Americans could be at least as valuable as hundreds of dead ones.

Americans were being killed and kidnapped with seeming impunity. The Pentagon drew up contingency plans for attacks on targets inside Iran, including the headquarters of the Revolutionary Guards and the Taleghani Center, where many of the revolutionary cells maintained offices. Like most contingency plans, they went nowhere, stymied by concerns that Iran would fall into the arms of the Soviet Union and by the dispute that continued to rage within the administration over the use of military force. The only action the Reagan administration had taken after all that had happened in Lebanon was to add Iran to the State Department list of terrorist nations—an action which, among other things, prohibited the sale of weapons to the Iranians. It was a meaningless action: Jimmy Carter had instituted an arms embargo against Iran in 1979 which had never been lifted.

★　★　★

The withdrawal of the multinational force from Lebanon had answered the tactical question of where to put the Marines, but the strategic question of how to use force was no closer to resolution than it had been on the day the Marines had landed. After the withdrawal, George Shultz ruminated about the problem for months and commissioned a paper on the relationship of power and diplomacy. His thinking was influenced in part by the Israeli model and by Benjamin Netanyahu, a compelling young diplomat who served as Israel's Ambassador to the United Nations. Netanyahu's older brother, Jonathan, had died leading the Israeli rescue mission at Entebbe in 1976. In his memory, Benjamin had helped create the Jonathan Institute, an international think tank devoted to the study of terrorism. In March, soon after the last Marine departed from the Beirut airport, Netanyahu visited Shultz and presented him with copies of a book summarizing the Institute's first international conference on terrorism.

On April 3, 1984, Shultz gave a speech blaming what happened in Lebanon on the military's inability or unwillingness to take more aggressive action. "It was precisely our military role in Lebanon that was problematical, not our diplomatic exertion. Our military role was hamstrung by legislative and other inhibitions," Shultz declared, without elaborating on what those "other inhibitions" were. Anyone familiar with the history of the Marines in Lebanon knew exactly who and what he meant.

"It is often said," Shultz continued, "that the lesson of Vietnam is that the United States should not engage in military conflict without a clear and precise military mission, solid public backing, and enough resources to finish the job." That, of course, was what Weinberger had been saying all along. "This is undeniably true," Shultz conceded, "but does that mean there are no situations where a discreet assertion of power is needed or appropriate, for limited purposes? Unlikely. . . . The need to avoid no-win situations cannot mean that we turn automatically away from hard-to-win situations that call for prudent involvement. . . . Few cases will be as clear or as quick as Grenada. On the contrary, most other cases will be a lot tougher. . . . But we cannot opt out of every contest. If we do, the world's future will be determined by others—most likely by those who are the most brutal, the most unscrupulous, and the most hostile to our deeply held principles." It was a melancholy view of the world, but one which accurately described Lebanon.

On the same day Shultz spoke, the President signed National Security Decision Directive 138, which codified the administration's strategy for combatting terrorism. Work on NSDD 138 had begun back in the late summer of 1983 when the President had reacted emotionally to a grisly attack by Armenian separatists against the Turkish Embassy in Lisbon. Although no Americans had been killed, the Pentagon's Noel Koch had seen in the President's reaction a window of opportunity through which to push a tougher policy. "I called Ollie and said, 'This is our chance,' " Koch recalled. Oliver North, the NSC staff member responsible for counterterrorism, needed no prodding. I'm already working on it, he responded.

North's draft of NSDD 138 included a passage authorizing operations to "neutralize" terrorists. To some, particularly John McMahon, the deputy director of the CIA, that sounded too much like "assassinate," which was against the law. As with most disputes in government, it came down to haggling over words, but the issue was fundamental. Should the United States conduct pre-emptive operations against terrorists—hit them before they hit you? Even the Long Commission said, "it makes little sense to learn that a state or its surrogate is conducting a terrorist campaign or planning a terrorist attack and not confront that government with political or military consequences if it continues forward." The bureaucracy finally decided "proactive" was a sufficiently palatable term. On April 3, 1984, the President signed NSDD 138.

The preamble to NSDD 138 declared that "the U.S. government considers the practice of terrorism by any person or group in any cause a threat to our national security." That said more about the emotionalism surrounding the issue of terrorism than about the threat it posed. The Reagan administration had built terrorism into something it was not. As horrendous as it was, the suicide bombing of the Marines had not threatened the national security. To the contrary, it had forced the realization that Lebanon was not vital to American interests. Terrorism was a threat not to the national security but to the government's ability to protect its citizens. The threat to American lives was enough to justify taking up arms against terrorists, even to launch pre-emptive strikes, but NSDD 138 did little to clarify the administration's thinking on the subject of terrorism.

Only two-and-a-half pages long, NSDD 138 was intended to create a mechanism for managing the war against terrorism—a need first identified after the Dozier kidnapping in 1981. Since then the federal bureaucracy had taken only a few halting steps. It had at last created the "fusion centers" that both the Intelligence Support Activity and the Long Commission had recommended as a means of bringing intelligence from all sources into a single nexus. At CIA director William Casey's suggestion, a computer network called "Flashboard" had been set up to link all the analysts working on terrorism in all the government agencies. Still, no one could agree on who was in charge.

According to Noel Koch, NSDD 138 "was simply ignored. No part of it was ever implemented. The President's signature on a document meant no more to the conflicted elements of his administration than his pro forma threats against terrorism meant to the terrorists."

Knowing that NSDD 138 was not the cure for the administration's paralysis, Shultz continued his public campaign for a tougher policy against terrorism. On June 14, speaking to a conference of the Jonathan Institute, Shultz asked, "Can we as a country—can the community of free nations—stand in a solely defensive posture and absorb the blows dealt by the terrorists? I think not. From a practical standpoint, a purely passive defense does not provide enough of a deterrent to terrorism and the states that sponsor it. It is time to think long, hard, and seriously about more active means of defense—about defense through appropriate preventative or preemptive actions against terrorist groups before they strike."

The administration was still thinking when at midday on September 20, 1984, a van bearing diplomatic license plates skillfully navigated around three concrete barriers in front of the U.S. Embassy annex in Christian East Beirut and exploded. Two American military officers and twelve Lebanese were killed.

Ninety minutes after the explosion, an anonymous caller claiming to represent Islamic Jihad telephoned Agence France-Presse and declared in Arabic, "The operation goes to prove that we will carry out our previous promise not to allow a single American to remain on Lebanese soil." Although just two Americans were killed, the annex blast was, in some ways, the most graphic example yet of American incompetence and impotence in the face of terrorism.

Following the April 1983 bombing of the U.S. Embassy, the American diplomatic presence in Lebanon had been reduced to twenty-seven people, working out of a building in West Beirut that belonged to Great Britain. Guarded by a force of one hundred Marines, the building was considered all but impregnable to terrorist attack. But it was a miserable life for the diplomats, who were separated from their families and virtually held prisoner behind the embassy barricades. The new ambassador, Reginald Bartholomew, was anxious to move, to stop imposing on the British, to start leading a more normal life. He leased two buildings, one to serve as the embassy in Muslim West Beirut and one as an annex in Christian East Beirut. Col. William Corbett, the European Command's security expert, inspected the buildings and was convinced that they could be defended, but he strongly recommended against making the move until after new barriers had been erected, complete with a sand-bagged automatic weapon on the roof. "I told them, 'They're going to bring a bomb in here,' " Corbett said of the East Beirut annex. " 'They're going to find a way to get a truck bomb in here.' " Bartholomew couldn't wait. By the end of July, the move had been completed, and all but fourteen of the embassy's Marine guards had been withdrawn and replaced by hired Lebanese militiamen.

On September 8, after the United States vetoed yet another United Nations resolution condemning the continuing Israeli occupation of southern Lebanon, Islamic Jihad telephoned Agence France-Presse, this time to warn that it would attack "one of the vital American installations in the Middle East." During September, the Defense Intelligence Agency issued two specific alerts, warning of threats to American personnel in Beirut. Intelligence also picked up the fact that Iran was shipping explosives into Lebanon through its embassy in Damascus.

Despite all the warnings, much of the new equipment designed to protect the embassy building had yet to be installed. A heavy steel gate that was to block the road leading to the annex was still lying on the ground, leaving only the obstacle course created by the three concrete barriers to slow down a would-be bomber.

Within twenty-four hours of the blast, the CIA produced conclusive evidence of where the bombing had been planned and who had planned it. A review of reconnaissance photographs of the Sheik Abdullah Barracks in Baalbek revealed a mockup of the concrete obstacles that had been erected in front of the annex. A closer look revealed tire tracks running through the obstacles: the suicide driver had practiced navigating his way through the maze. "We had them dead to rights," national security adviser Robert McFarlane said.

Yet when the National Security Planning Group met to consider the evidence, Weinberger and the Joint Chiefs remained unconvinced, arguing, among other things, that it was impossible to know whether the terrorists still in the Sheik Abdullah Barracks were the same terrorists who had conducted the bombing. "It's an impossible standard that you have to have the guy who lit the fuse or drove the truck," McFarlane fumed. That was particularly true in the case of suicide bombers. Given the risks of losing an American plane, of causing civilian casualties, and of triggering increased terrorist attacks in Lebanon, not to mention the possibility that one or all of the American hostages might be incarcerated in Sheik Abdullah Barracks, Weinberger concluded that the evidence was not compelling enough. Reagan was unwilling to force the issue, and within a week communications intelligence suggested the terrorists had realized the danger they were in and moved on.

The failure to retaliate infuriated Shultz, who once again took to the lectern to air his views. The United States must be prepared to use military force, he said, even though "we may not have the kind of evidence that can stand up in an American court of law," and even though some innocent people might be killed. "We cannot allow ourselves to become the Hamlet of nations, worrying endlessly over whether and how to respond."

Waiting until after the presidential election, Weinberger returned Shultz's broadsides with a speech of his own. "Employing our forces almost indiscriminately and as a regular and customary part of our diplomatic efforts would surely plunge us headlong into the sort of domestic turmoil we experienced during the Vietnam war, without accomplishing the goal for which we committed our forces," Weinberger warned. "The commitment of U.S. forces to combat should always be a last resort." Put in Shultz's terms, Weinberger wanted the United

States to worry, if not "endlessly," then at least long and hard over whether and how to respond.

The differences between the President's two top foreign policy advisers were stark. At White House meetings they deliberately ignored each other, speaking to the President as if the other weren't in the room. Shultz considered force an essential element of policy; Weinberger considered it a last resort to be used only when the nation's vital interests were at risk. It was a potentially endless debate in which Weinberger, who controlled the forces, could always frustrate Shultz. Only the commander-in-chief could resolve the issue, an act of leadership which Ronald Reagan, whom *Newsweek* had dubbed the "disengaged President," was either unwilling or unable to perform. Instead, he had tried to split the difference between Shultz and Weinberger and had succeeded only in widening the gap between America's ends and the means it was willing to use to achieve them. "American power and influence is based on firm leadership and the will to act, not rhetoric or the size of the defense budget," said Howard Teicher. "Because he was unwilling to exercise leadership or to enforce discipline within his own cabinet, history will judge Ronald Reagan a weak and indecisive man." It would take a series of extraordinary events—and the deaths of more innocent Americans—to force the issue to a head.

★ 7 ★

"A BLOODY CIRCUS"

TWA Flight 847 was overbooked and an hour late taking off from Athens. Most of the passengers aboard the Boeing 727 were already worrying about making their connections in Rome. Afterwards, only one passenger, James Hoskins, would claim to have had a sense of foreboding. Hoskins and his girlfriend Kathryn Davis had just placed their carry-on luggage on the X-ray machine when an agitated Arab dressed in a Palm Beach suit rushed up and stuffed his bag between theirs. Hoskins told him to take it easy, but the Arab didn't seem to hear. A second Arab, who was just behind Hoskins going through the metal detector, set off the alarm. The second Arab removed a pen and a cigarette lighter and walked through the metal detector a second time. Again, he triggered the alarm. The third time he walked through the detector backwards without setting it off. He grabbed his bag and pushed through the crowd to the front of the line waiting to board the bus that would take the passengers to the plane. Hoskins told his girlfriend he had bad vibes. "He didn't want to get on the plane," Kathryn Davis recalled, "but he thought he was being paranoid."

The two Arabs took their seats in the last row of the plane, next to Peter Hill, an irascible tour operator from Chicago. While still waiting for the rest of the passengers to board, Hill recalled, "the one sitting next to me stands up with . . . a canvas traveling bag, like an athletic bag." Hill was sitting on the aisle, right next to the lavatory. "He starts to step over me," Hill continued. "I push my legs aside, and the stewardess says, 'Sir, please sit down. We're still boarding.' He says, 'Toilet, toilet.' And he just went ahead into the toilet." Hill next heard "a tremendous crash, a smashing of glass . . . like a hundred crystal goblets breaking on the floor—a high, ringing, tinkling smash." Shortly afterwards, the Arab returned to his seat, stepping over Hill again, and began whispering to his companion.

Flight 847 took off at 10:00 A.M. local time on Friday, June 14, 1985. There were 153 passengers and crew on board, 135 of them American. It was a short flight to Rome, so the pilot, Capt. John Testrake, switched off the "Fasten Seatbelt" sign sooner than usual to give the flight attendants time to complete their meal service. The seatbelt sign had just gone off when, as Hill related it, the two Arabs "both stood up and jumped— literally jumped—over me and started running up the aisle. One of them slipped on the way up to the forward cabin because of the angle of ascent." The lead Arab planted a flying karate kick square in the chest of one of the flight attendants, Uli Derickson, knocking her to the floor. "Each of them had a hand grenade," another passenger, Arthur Toga, said. "They were the button type of hand grenade. They had pulled the pin and were holding down the button." Kurt Carlson, an Army reservist returning from temporary duty in Cairo, watched as the two men pounded on the door to the cockpit. "They were literally jumping up and down now, screaming something in Arabic, then, in broken English, 'Come to die! Americans die!' " They banged Uli's head against the cockpit door, stuck a grenade in her face and a gun in her ear.

Inside the cockpit, Christian Zimmermann, the flight engineer, heard the commotion and got up to look through the peephole in the door. We've got a hijack, Zimmermann said. Phil Maresca, the co-pilot, didn't believe him at first, but the banging continued. Maresca radioed Athens radar control they were being hijacked and punched in the numbers "7500" on the cockpit transponder, sending out an international code that would tell all air traffic controllers that TWA 847 had been hijacked. Uli Derickson's voice came over the intercom, Captain, we're being roughed up back here. Please open the door. Testrake told Zimmermann to let them in.

They burst into the cockpit, yelling Algera, Algera. After a moment's incomprehension, the crew realized the hijackers were demanding to be taken to Algeria. Maresca found the proper chart and quickly calculated that they did not have enough fuel. No Algiers, Testrake said. No fuel. Algera, the hijackers repeated. Testrake pointed to the fuel gauge and pantomimed running out of gas, but the hijackers only repeated their demand. Testrake, who at fifty-seven was old enough to be their father, lost his temper. If you want to keep going this way, I'll put you in the ocean somewhere off of Tunis, he snapped, because that's where I'm going to run out of fuel.

The hijackers didn't speak enough English to understand him, but fortunately there was a translator. Uli Derickson had lived two years in Saudi Arabia and spoke enough Arabic to understand the obscenities the hijackers were screaming at "the Americans." Trying to divert them, Uli said she wasn't American but German, and one of the hijackers stunned her by breaking into flawless German. With Uli serving as interpreter, Testrake persuaded the hijackers they should head for Cairo. While Maresca was plotting a course for Cairo, the hijackers changed their mind and yelled, Beirut! Fuel only! The hijackers took the change in plans out on Zimmermann, beating him with an arm rest and the butt of a revolver. "You could see blood coming through his shirt," Testrake recalled. Testrake changed course and headed southeast toward Beirut, 700 miles away.

Testrake knew he and his passengers were in grave danger, but he felt no fear. His life had been stricken by misfortunes worse than this. Many years ago, his infant son had been killed in an automobile accident; he had lost his first wife to cancer; and another son had committed suicide. In grappling with his losses, Testrake had become a devout Christian who believed in "God's loving care and guidance and how He rescues us just when we've come to the end of ourselves and have no choice but to turn things over to Him." Now, it was his turn to face death, but it held no fear for him.

★   ★   ★

It was seven minutes to four in the morning Washington time when the first word of the hijacking reached the communications center of the Federal Aviation Administration, relayed by telephone from TWA's international operations center in New York. After several minutes spent verifying the few details available—flight number, type of aircraft, destination, number of Americans aboard—the FAA watch officers began waking people up. Even before he was fully awake, Billy Vincent, the FAA's chief of security, knew "this is a bad one." He threw a few extra changes of underwear in his gym bag and headed downtown.

With 3 million people taking 22,000 international flights each day, the chances of being the victim of a terrorist attack—a hijacking or, worse, a bombing—were infinitesimal, particularly while flying aboard an American airliner. In all of 1984, for instance, there had been just two hijackings and no bombings of American airliners on international flights. Despite the reassuring numbers, Vincent had become increas-

ingly convinced that a major terrorist attack against an American airliner was only a matter of time. The terrorists were getting better while
the airlines were standing still, reluctant to take security precautions that
would cost money or inconvenience passengers.

In August, 1982, a bomb under a seat cushion had gone off as a Pan
Am jet approached Honolulu on a flight from Tokyo. The occupant of
the seat, a young Japanese student, had been killed, and fifteen passengers injured. The incident did not receive much public attention, but for
Vincent it was "a signal event." A terrorist had built a bomb complex
enough to be triggered by a change in cabin pressure, yet small enough
to fit beneath a seat cushion. "From a technical standpoint, it was the
most sophisticated device yet run across in aviation," Vincent said. Two
weeks later a similar device—about the size of a reporter's spiral notebook—was found by a clean-up crew on a Pan Am plane that had just
landed in Rio de Janeiro. Mercifully, it had failed to go off.

In the spring of 1983, another device was found in a hotel in Geneva,
this one secreted in the lining of a suitcase. The CIA had been alerted
to it by a courier who got cold feet. The CIA passed the warning to Swiss
authorities, who sent a bomb squad to the hotel. The squad's bomb-
detecting dogs sniffed the suitcase but could find no scent of explosives.
The Swiss reported back to the CIA that the courier was a fraud. The
courier insisted he was telling the truth, and the CIA persuaded the Swiss
to look again. This time, they took the suitcase apart and found the
explosives molded into the cardboard lining. The quarter-inch thick
plastic explosive smelled like cocoa butter and was not detectable either
by dogs or X-ray equipment. It was the closest thing to an invisible bomb
anyone had ever seen.

According to a State Department document, the bomb was the work
of the May 15 group which took its name from the date of Israel's
independence and was led by Mohammed Amri, a Palestinian who called
himself Abu Ibrahim and was grudgingly acknowledged to be an "expert
bomb maker." The State Department paper reported that a Jordanian
and his Moroccan wife "supposedly had been trained by Abu Ibrahim
at his headquarters in Baghdad and were allegedly given five bombs in
special suitcases which were to be given to unwitting couriers to travel
by air."

May 15 was one of a number of terrorist groups set up by the PLO's
Yasir Arafat, who was so adept at concealing his links with them that
intelligence officials dubbed him "the Teflon terrorist." In addition to
Abu Ibrahim, PLO groups led by close associates of Arafat and calling
themselves Force 17, Col. Hawari, and Fatah (Western Sector) staged

a number of bombings, leaving some intelligence officials fearful that the PLO had decided to begin attacking Americans instead of concentrating almost exclusively on Israelis, as it had done in the past.

"It became so obvious to me that this was escalating quite a bit that I started putting pressure on the U.S. airline industry to react to it," Vincent recalled. "I was rebuffed at every turn." Finally, on December 23, 1983, Vincent gave up his efforts at persuasion and ordered airlines to upgrade their security by issuing a series of emergency amendments to the Standard Air Carrier Security Program. Six days later, as if to emphasize the point that tighter security was needed, Turkish security agents at the airport in Istanbul picked up a suitcase bomb about to be put on an Alitalia flight to Rome. The timer was set to detonate the bomb several hours later, after the suitcase had been transferred to a Pan Am flight bound for New York.

Security at the Istanbul airport was among the best in the world, but even the tightest security—Israel's—was apparently no match for Abu Ibrahim. That same month, a young Englishwoman flew from Athens to Tel Aviv to pick up some curios for her Jordanian boyfriend. From Tel Aviv, she took an El Al flight to London, where she sold the curios before returning to Athens. Only several months later did she learn that the suitcase her boyfriend had given her had contained a bomb wired to go off on the Tel Aviv to London leg of her journey. Suspecting the boyfriend was a terrorist, a CIA officer broke into the woman's apartment in Athens and took photographs of the booby-trapped suitcase, which fortunately had failed to detonate. The CIA showed the pictures to Greek authorities, who arrested the Jordanian. According to a State Department document, the Jordanian "is believed to be linked to seven planned terrorist attacks using suitcases rigged with explosives." Despite the suspicions, he was quickly released, ostensibly for lack of evidence, more likely because Greece was notorious for accommodating terrorists in return for exemption from attacks.

In May, 1984, one month after this latest suitcase bomb was discovered, the FAA issued a confidential notice to all airlines, warning of "baggage carried by innocent victims and improvised explosive devices which were secreted under the bag lining, thus making them very difficult to detect by hand search or cursory X-ray examination." The notice went on to warn that the "most likely targets" for these bombs were "U.S. [and] Israeli airlines and airlines serving Athens, Greece," where the government was willing to let suspected terrorists go free and the airport was known for its lax security.

Athens had been the starting point for the 1976 Air France hijacking which had ended in Entebbe with an airborne raid by Israeli commandos. Since then, Greek authorities had done almost nothing to improve security. If anything, the situation had become worse. After the Israelis drove the PLO out of Lebanon in 1982, some of the displaced Palestinian fighters ended up working for ground crews at the Athens airport. Vincent and a team of aviation experts inspected the airport early in 1985, and, according to a State Department memo, concluded that "the level of danger to commercial aviation in Greece . . . appears to be high" and "is likely to remain high for the foreseeable future." Airport security was "lax," baggage inspection was "spotty," and guards were neither trained nor equipped to do even "an adequate job." In its May 1985 issue, *Frequent Flyer* magazine warned that Athens was the airport from which "you are most likely to be hijacked."

★ ★ ★

The hijackers of TWA 847 eventually would be identified as Mohammed Ali Hamadi and Hasan 'Izz-al-Din, although those were not the names they traveled under. The passengers would come to know them as Castro and Said. Along with a third man named Ali Atwa, they had left Beirut the preceding day on a Middle East Airlines flight and had spent the night in the Athens terminal. All three had attempted to book space on the Athens to Rome leg of Flight 847, but Ali Atwa had been unable to get a seat. Kurt Carlson, the Army reservist, described Castro as about twenty-four years old, slight of build and short of stature, with a round face and black mustache; he spoke fluent German and carried a 9-mm pearl-handled pistol. "The hammer was cocked and there wasn't any safety on the gun," another passenger, Arthur Toga, recalled. "The slightest mistake would have killed someone." The other hijacker, Said, looked to be about twenty years old and about 5 feet 9 inches tall. "He had the uncanny ability to move each of his eyeballs separately," Carlson later wrote. "They darted around like Ping-Pong balls. He had the look of a real live bogeyman."

As the plane turned toward Beirut, Castro told Uli Derickson to move the first-class passengers to the rear. With every coach seat already filled, some passengers had to squeeze four abreast into rows only three seats wide. They were told to remain silent, put their hands behind their heads and their heads between their knees. "It was the most eerie feeling," Derickson said later, "to look back into a cabin that you know contains over one hundred forty passengers and not be able to see them." The hijackers were doing everything by the book. Having cleared out a command post in first class, they began moving passengers around, placing abler-bodied males in window seats where they could not get at the hijackers.

They were also scaring the wits out of the passengers, knowing that terror was the best way for two lightly armed men to dominate more than 150 people. "If anyone moved or uttered a sound," Carlson wrote, Castro "pounced, karate-chopping people across the backs of their necks, striking some with the barrel of [his gun]. With a screaming leap three feet in the air, he kicked one elderly woman in the face, shattering her glasses." Castro tried to convince Derickson there were more than just two hijackers, that three "sleepers" were hidden among the passengers, but she didn't believe him. "Everyone was so obviously scared to death," she said.

Castro ordered Derickson to collect all the passports and bring them up front. He told her to pick out the Israeli passports, but she said there were none. He told her to select the Jews, but she said American passports do not show religion. Then Castro had her read the names out loud from a passenger list. When she came to what sounded to him like a Jewish name, he ordered her to find that passenger's passport. After finding about seven he thought were Jewish, Castro shifted his attention to the military ID cards Derickson had collected from Carlson and six Navy divers returning from an underwater construction job in Greece. Castro and Said went back to coach class and forced the divers to move to widely separated seats, yelling "Marines" and "New Jersey" at them.

As Testrake steered the plane past Cyprus, Maresca made contact with Beirut. "Beirut control. TWA 847. Request landing instructions," Maresca said. "I am unable to give you landing instructions due to the closure of the airport," the controller replied. Testrake continued his descent toward the airport. "Beirut, the hijacker has pulled the pin on his hand grenade," Maresca warned. "He will land at Beirut. He is desperate." The tower tried to say something in Arabic to the hijackers, but Maresca broke in. "He has pulled a hand grenade pin and is ready to blow up the aircraft if he has to. We must, I repeat, we must land at Beirut. We must land at Beirut. No alternative." Testrake turned onto the final approach. The runway is in view and is being blocked with barricades, he reported to the passengers over the intercom. After landing you will probably hear crashing sounds toward the front of the plane. The tower asked TWA 847 to hold for ten minutes. "That is negative," Maresca responded.

Later, Maresca confessed, "it was as much a bluff as anything else. We felt the authorities no more wanted us to crash on their runway than we wanted to crash." The tower watched as the plane continued inbound over the rooftops of Beirut. "Understand that you are landing without permission," the controller scolded. "Be advised we have no choice. We must land," Maresca replied. The tower relented. "Okay, sir. Land. Land quietly." At the last moment, the barricades were removed, and TWA 847 touched down—so hard that Kurt Carlson thought all the tires would blow.

As Testrake braked to a halt, he passed the wreckage of a Royal Jordanian Airlines plane that had been hijacked and blown up just two days before. The hijackers instructed Uli Derickson to tell the passengers to look out their windows and see what would happen if anybody tried anything. The hijackers then ordered the shades drawn, and the passengers sat in silence under the noonday Mediterranean sun. "The air had become hot and stale," Carlson wrote. "It smelled, too, as not everyone had been able to repress nature's call."

In the cockpit, "the hijackers were yelling frantically into the radio that they wanted fuel," Maresca recounted. Castro and Said "were very jumpy and nervous . . . because this was unplanned for them," Testrake recalled. "They were afraid of a foul-up, especially when we had to move off the runway and go to the refueling pits. They didn't like that at all because it was a more confined area. They were very much afraid, I think, of something going on." As Testrake taxied toward the fuel pits, Castro "stood in back of me with his cocked pistol held against my head. In his other hand, he held a hand grenade, with its pin pulled, directly in front of my face. . . . His hand in front of my face made it impossible to see where I was going. I figured that all I had to do was hit one chuckhole, and it would be the end of the ride for everyone." The hijackers kept screaming for fuel, but no one came.

In the cabin, Carlson saw Said "pulling one of the young Navy men from the center seat. It was Bob Stethem . . . I'll never forget the look on his face—pure fury, rage, way beyond anger . . . I don't know how he was chosen by the hijackers. Maybe he was just closer to the front of the plane than the other Navy men." Said took Stethem into the first-class cabin and bound his hands behind his back with elastic "bungi" cords. Ruth Henderson watched "as they kicked him in the head. They kicked him in the face and kneecaps and kept kicking him until they had broken all his ribs. Then they tried to knock him out with the butt of a pistol. They kept hitting him over the head, but he was very strong, and they couldn't knock him out."

Maresca frantically radioed the tower, "They are beating the passengers! They are beating the passengers! They are threatening to kill them now! They are threatening to kill them now! We want the fuel now. Immediately.'' The tower responded, ''I am doing my best.'' Maresca shouted, ''He says if he doesn't get fuel in three minutes he's going to kill an American that he has tied up in the cockpit.'' Finally, workmen appeared and began refueling the plane. The hijackers dumped Stethem, sobbing and bleeding, into the seat next to Ruth Henderson. Uli Derickson pleaded with Castro to let her untie Stethem's arms which had lost circulation. Castro relented, but it took Derickson a long time to undo the elastic cords because they were so deeply imbedded in Stethem's arms.

In anticipation of the long flight to Algeria, Testrake took on all the fuel the plane could hold. With a full load of passengers, TWA 847 was now some 15,000 pounds overweight. Using that as an argument, Testrake and Uli persuaded the hijackers to let some of the women and children go. Seventeen women and two children were allowed to leave by sliding down the emergency escape chutes.

Releasing passengers reduced the number of people the hijackers had to control, but it also gave away intelligence about what was happening aboard the plane. Until now, the crisis management teams gathering at the FAA, Pentagon, State Department, and White House Situation Room had only the sketchiest details. The crew of TWA 847 was able to pass some information by radio, but they could only talk when they were left alone in the cockpit and they did not know what was going on behind them in the passenger cabin. The released passengers remained the best source of intelligence—they had firsthand knowledge of conditions aboard the plane and could be debriefed at length. But it would be hours still before the released passengers could be flown to Cyprus and interviewed by American officials.

One of the most critical pieces of information—what the hijackers wanted—finally spilled out in a long, rambling diatribe that Castro delivered in Arabic over the radio. He wanted more than seven hundred Lebanese Shiites released from an Israeli prison, seventeen Shiites freed from a Kuwaiti prison, two from Spain, and two more from Cyprus. Beyond that, he wanted Israel to withdraw from southern Lebanon, the United States to admit responsibility for a recent car bombing in Beirut, and the world to condemn America for its support of Israel. It was, obviously, an impossible list of demands. It was just as well that the crew of TWA 847 had not understood a word of it. Testrake roared down the runway, coaxed his overweight jet aloft, and headed west toward Algeria, 1,800 miles away.

★   ★   ★

It was six-thirty in the morning in Washington, and the Reagan administration was still trying to organize itself to deal with what the FAA's
Billy Vincent called "the most significant terrorist attack against U.S.
aviation since the early 1970s, maybe the most significant ever." Despite
the momentous nature of what was unfolding, President Reagan had not
yet been awakened. The rest of the crisis management system seemed
overwhelmed. At the State Department, the operations center was
deluged with phone calls from relatives of the passengers. That, plus the
need to establish contact with the governments of every country within
range of the TWA plane, was more than the system could handle. There
was no one to man the phone linking the State Department operations
center with its counterparts at the White House, Pentagon, and FAA.
"We tried and tried and tried to get them to keep someone on the other
end of the line, and they kept putting the phone down," Donald Engen,
the head of the FAA, said. Finally, Billy Vincent left the FAA operations
center and went over to the State Department to find someone to answer
the phone.

Engen was a retired admiral who had spent much of his life flying the
Mediterranean as a carrier pilot. He knew off the top of his head the
locations of all the air traffic control centers that might have a track on
TWA 847. He tried calling them, but with no success. He was either
unable to reach anyone in authority or else they were not even aware a
hijacking had occurred. "I recall vividly . . . I could get no information,"
Engen said. "It was a very maddening feeling. If I've ever felt not in
control, it was during the TWA 847 hijacking. I waked up to the realization that as a nation we had not thought out how to deal with an
international hijacking. It was not a sense of failure. It was more a sense
of revelation." By the time Engen found out TWA 847 was on its way
to Algiers, the plane was already nearing Tunisia.

★   ★   ★

It was midday in Algiers, a sleepy Friday during the Muslim holiday of
Ramadan, when the telephone rang in the second-story study of the
American ambassador's residence. Michael Newlin picked up the receiver and heard the voice of a watch officer at the State Department:
We want to inform you that a United States airliner has been hijacked,
and we believe it is headed toward Algeria. Newlin was directed to
contact Algerian President Chadli Benjedid with two requests in the
name of President Reagan: first, to make an exception to its ironclad

policy that hijacked aircraft not be allowed to land; and second, not to permit the plane to take off again. A personal message from Reagan would follow.

Ambassador Newlin despaired of being able to rouse the Algerian government on a holiday. Most of his own staff had already fled the dusty city for the Mediterranean beaches two hours away. But much to his amazement, Newlin got right through to Benjedid's chief of staff. Forty-five minutes later, the Algerian called back to say TWA 847 would be permitted to land "on humanitarian grounds." To the crew of TWA 847, "it didn't make any difference because we were going to land anyway," Maresca said afterwards. TWA 847 had less than thirty minutes of fuel remaining.

Newlin wanted to be at the airport when the plane arrived, but he was stuck at the embassy, scribbling down the promised message from Reagan to Benjedid as it was dictated over the telephone from Washington. This is too long, Newlin complained. The message droned on about the importance of cooperation in the fight against terrorism and about how President Reagan looked to the Algerians to convince the hijackers to surrender. Newlin thought it was a lot to ask from a government which Reagan had never bothered to thank for its help in negotiating the release of the Americans held hostage in Iran. When the message finally ended, Newlin told his secretary to type it up, have it translated into French, and delivered to Benjedid immediately. By the time Newlin arrived at the airport, TWA 847 already had landed and twenty-one more passengers—eighteen of them American—had been released.

The freed passengers were bused to Newlin's residence where the ambassador's wife took charge of calming them down and confirming their names. They were in a state of shock—some frantic about their relatives still on the plane, others preoccupied with questions about refunds and what would happen to their bags. They couldn't agree on either the number of hijackers or their locations aboard the plane. The hijackers' tactic of forcing the passengers to bend forward with their heads between their knees had had its intended effect: they hadn't seen much. They all agreed, however, that Uli Derickson was the only thing standing between the passengers and a bloodbath.

On board the aircraft, the remaining hostages still sat hunched over in the "847 position," sweltering in the heat. Outside, Algerian military vehicles surrounded the aircraft. Kurt Carlson felt a tap on his shoulder and looked up into the barrel of Castro's pearl-handled pistol. Castro marched Carlson forward into the first-class compartment. "Yanking my arms behind my back, he tied my hands together with a silk tie, so tightly that it cut into my wrists," Carlson later wrote. "Then he blind-folded me with a handkerchief that stank of vomit." Castro threw Carlson, bound and blindfolded, onto the floor of the cockpit. Carlson could hear Testrake asking the tower to summon the American ambassador and deliver a full load of fuel. The tower stalled, telling Testrake the ambassador had taken the day off and that there were no facilities for refueling a 727. The hijackers responded to the stall tactics by pummeling Carlson with an armrest. "I had willed myself to be silent when the beating started but now realized they wanted me to make noise," Carlson wrote. "Screams might convince the tower to refuel us. I yelled."

Newlin and the Algerian security chief appeared on the tarmac just outside Testrake's window. Castro stuck his head out the window, waving his pistol. Inside the cockpit, Testrake realized that with Castro leaning out the window, "one push—one very slight push—and we could be minus one hijacker." Testrake looked at Zimmermann. They were both thinking the same thing. "In two seconds, we could have grabbed that guy's legs and tossed him about forty feet onto the runway below," Testrake wrote. "I wanted to do it so badly I could hardly restrain myself." But that would still leave Said and his hand grenades back in the passenger cabin. "It just wasn't worth the risk," Testrake concluded.

Three refueling deadlines came and went. Still bound and blindfolded, Carlson could hear Castro chanting, One American must die. Testrake pleaded again for fuel, but the tower had fallen silent. Carlson could feel one of the hijackers hovering over him. "He let out a piercing scream: 'Marine.' I felt something smashing into the top of my head—once, twice, three times. . . . He kicked my head back to see if I was still conscious. I guess I was because I heard the tower crackling through the radio, 'Your fuel is coming.' " Still, there was no fuel truck. Castro dragged Carlson to the airplane door. "With the gun barrel pressed against my head, just behind the right earlobe, he held me at the open door and yelled again, 'One American must die.' Abruptly, he dropped me to the floor, closed the door, and stalked toward the cockpit. . . . And then I blacked out."

When he came to, Carlson heard Testrake shouting, "I see the fuel truck. . . . The fuel truck is coming." But the driver would not start pumping until he had been paid. TWA did not fly to Algiers, so it did not have an account with the airport. The driver wanted a credit card—a Shell credit card. "The poor guy who was driving the fuel truck was only doing his job," Maresca said later with much more empathy than he felt at the time. Uli Derickson rummaged about in her purse, found her personal Shell card, and tossed it out the window. She was later billed for 6,000 gallons of jet fuel at one dollar a gallon.

Once the refueling was completed, TWA 847 took off again and headed east, back toward Beirut. Once aloft, the erratic Castro embraced the groggy Carlson, telling him, I love you. Easing Carlson into a seat, Castro helped him to a drink of water while Derickson untied his hands. Using her to translate, Castro told Carlson that he, too, had a wife and baby, but they had been killed by American bombs. His rage spent, Castro asked Derickson to sing to him in German. As TWA sped east on its lunatic voyage, she sang "Patty Cake, Patty Cake" and Brahms's "Lullaby" to a dewy-eyed Castro.

★   ★   ★

At about the same time, another jet, a C-141 transport, was heading east from Andrews Air Force Base just outside Washington, carrying a twenty-man Emergency Support Team (EST), the vanguard for a rescue mission. Led by the State Department and made up of specialists from State, CIA, and Delta, the team's mission was to advise the local American Ambassador. If it was asked, it also would assist a friendly government in mounting its own rescue mission, or lay the groundwork for the insertion of U.S. forces. Despite the attention focused on the Delta commandos, the EST was probably the most important facet of the nation's counterterrorist capability. Certainly, it was the most used. By 1985, it had become clear that for all its skills Delta might never be used. The variations of terrorist attacks were endless, but the precise mix of circumstances which would permit Delta to act—a cooperative host government, isolated terrorists caught off guard—was extremely rare.

In their own countries, counterterrorist teams worked wonders. In London in 1980, the British SAS had stormed the Iranian Embassy, rapelling from the rooftop, sneaking along ledges, killing five terrorists who had been holding the embassy employees hostage. At the time, one month after Delta's failed attempt to rescue the hostages from Tehran, the SAS operation had been held up as evidence that the British knew how to do things right while the Americans were nothing but bunglers. In fact, SAS commandos had succeeded where Delta had failed because they had total control of the environment. They controlled all the communications into and out of the embassy. They lifted fingerprints from the box lunches sent in during the siege until they were certain exactly how many terrorists they were dealing with. They even redirected aircraft out of Heathrow Airport, using the noise of low-flying jets to cover their movements. SAS could have done none of that if it had been operating in hostile territory.

The Joint Special Operations Command (JSOC), which controlled America's counterterrorist forces, was prohibited by law from operating inside the United States unless the President first invoked "posse comitatas," declaring the situation an emergency local law enforcement officials couldn't handle. JSOC had been prepared to intervene if terrorists seized hostages during the 1984 Olympic Games in Los Angeles, and had gone so far as to pre-position both Delta and SEAL Team Six, the Navy's version of Delta, along with all the helicopters and communications equipment needed to support a hostage rescue mission. The rescue force remained on alert throughout the Games armed with videotapes of every room at every Olympic site, showing every entry and exit, every view from every window. It had been a massive undertaking, requiring months of advance planning with the FBI, the Los Angeles Police Department, and more than a dozen local law enforcement agencies in Southern California—the kind of coordination possible only in the United States and even then only with the luxury of having several months lead time.

JSOC tried to make similar preparations for terrorist incidents overseas, sending its operatives traveling around the world to videotape airports. But advance planning could not overcome the aversion of sovereign nations to permitting a foreign military force to operate on their territory. Most self-respecting countries were willing to accept advice, but nothing more.

In its advisory role, JSOC had scored some notable, though unpublicized, successes in helping other countries deal with terrorist incidents. In March 1981, JSOC officers had consulted by long-distance telephone with Indonesian commandos who were about to storm a hijacked airliner on the runway at Bangkok's international airport. Following JSOC's advice, the commandos had climbed onto the wings and stormed the plane, killing four of the five hijackers and rescuing all fifty-five passengers and crew. In the summer of 1983, JSOC had secretly assisted the Sudanese national police in finding and freeing five relief workers, two of them American, taken hostage by antigovernment guerrillas. The JSOC team had gone equipped with a satellite communications set and a laser facsimile machine that could reproduce copies of overhead reconnaissance photographs sent from Washington. Using satellite pictures and communications intercepts, JSOC had helped the Sudanese track the guerrillas to the hideout where they were holding the hostages. Again, in 1984, JSOC had provided impromptu training to Venezuelan commandos about to storm a hijacked airliner in Curaçao. The two hijackers were killed and all seventy-nine hostages escaped unharmed. Even that modest level of assistance had set off a small storm. By actually training rather than simply advising the Venezuelan commandos, JSOC had exceeded its authority.

Most countries were grateful for the help, as long as it was kept secret. Others wanted nothing to do with American counterterrorist teams. In 1982, when six tourists, including two Americans, were kidnapped by guerrillas in Zimbabwe, a JSOC team spent a week in isolation on Ascension Island in the south Atlantic waiting to be given permission to enter the country. They never were allowed in. The rebels eventually killed their hostages.

Dispatching an Emergency Support Team (EST) would seem to be a routine matter; either a country wanted assistance, or it didn't. But nothing in the war against terrorism was simple. Much of the past four and a half years had been wasted on bureaucratic wrangling over who would be in charge of the team. The CIA had argued it should run the EST on the grounds that the advance party was nothing more than an augmentation of the intelligence capabilities of the local CIA station. Besides, CIA personnel invariably made up the bulk of the teams. The Pentagon, which provided transportation and communications for the teams, did not like the idea of taking orders from the CIA. The State Department had insisted that it be in charge since it had been designated the "lead agency" for all terrorist incidents overseas. The issue had gone all the way to the President without ever being satisfactorily resolved.

★　★　★

On the afternoon of June 14, 1985, David Long, a Middle East specialist assigned to State's Office for Combatting Terrorism, was picked to head the support team handling the TWA hijacking. Long had been on Capitol Hill briefing members of Congress when the first news of the hijacking reached Washington. He was ordered to rush home, pack his bags, and report to Andrews Air Force Base immediately. "We were flying by the seat of our pants in those days," Long recalled. "Those days" happened to be exactly five years after the Holloway Commission had concluded that the Iran rescue mission had failed because United States forces were not properly organized to deal with terrorism, eighteen months after the Long Commission had warned that "U.S. military forces lack an effective capability to respond to terrorist attacks."

The EST did not take off from Andrews until nine hours after TWA 847 had been hijacked, more than twice as long as it was supposed to take. With a stop for refueling, it would be another ten hours before the team reached the Mediterranean. The plane headed for the British air base at Akrotiri on the island of Cyprus. From there, Long planned to fly by helicopter to East Beirut, but he didn't have the slightest idea what he could do once he got there, other than advise the ambassador and report developments to Washington.

★   ★   ★

It was after two o'clock in the morning in Beirut when TWA 847 began its second approach to the now blacked-out airport. Once again, the control tower refused permission to land. "From a technical point of view this was probably the most difficult [moment] of the entire trip," Maresca recalled. "There was a fairly low cloud cover, and the authorities had turned off all the navigational aids and the runway lights." Denied permission to land, Testrake told the tower, "I'm exhausted. My airplane is in distress. . . . We're in deadly danger. I implore you to open your airport and let us land." The controller replied, "Unfortunately my superiors do not care about your problems." Testrake told the hijackers that if they tried to land, they would crash. "Good," one of them replied. "That will save us the trouble of blowing it up." Testrake told Uli Derickson to prepare the passengers for a crash landing.

"Uli began pulling blankets and pillows from overhead," Carlson wrote. "Testrake's voice barked over the intercom. 'We are going in. Prepare for a crash landing. We are low on fuel, and we have to land. If we can find the airport, we will land on the ground beside the runway. Otherwise, we'll have to land in the water. . . . We have fuel for only one approach.' " TWA 847 broke out of the clouds at 500 feet over downtown Beirut, about ten miles from the airport. With about three miles to go, the runway lights blinked on, and the tower told Testrake he was cleared to land. TWA 847 touched down at 2:20 A.M. Saturday morning.

The hijackers ordered Testrake to stop in the middle of the runway, well away from any buildings. Castro and Said began talking to the tower in Arabic, their voices rising in anger as they demanded that reinforcements be allowed to board the plane. "I don't want to talk to you," one of them said to the controller. "I'll only talk to the Amal. You are trying to gain time. You don't believe me. Well, take this Marine."

Castro had his choice of two hostages: Robert Stethem and another Navy diver named Clinton Suggs who had been trussed up during the approach to Beirut. Castro grabbed Stethem and dragged him to the door of the airplane. Derickson's voice came on the intercom. "You will hear some noise. Don't look up or it will be your fate." Desperately, Maresca called the tower: "He's about to shoot a passenger." Blindfolded, Clinton Suggs could only listen helplessly to Stethem's final moments. "I could hear him screaming and yelling and he was just in sheer agony. And then I heard the gun go off." Castro shot Stethem in the head and dumped his body onto the tarmac. "He just killed a passenger. He just killed a passenger!" Maresca yelled into the radio. Castro grabbed the microphone from Maresca. "You see. You now believe. There will be another within five minutes." "Isn't it a shame, killing an innocent passenger," the tower remonstrated. "Did you forget the Bir al Abed massacre?" Castro shot back. The reference to a car bomb set off near the residences of Sheik Fadlallah, the spiritual leader of Hezbollah, was convincing evidence that Castro and Said were members of that radical Shiite group.

Castro ordered Testrake to taxi to the refueling pits. "As I began moving down the runway," Testrake recounted, "I turned the wheels sharply to avoid running over the young serviceman's body." In the refueling area, the silence of death fell over the plane. "You could hear a pin drop," Uli said. "All the window shades were closed—it was pitch dark. I felt my heart beating wildly. . . . Breaking the silence, one of the two men, I don't know which one it was, began singing a song. . . . It was a song of celebration."

Clinton Suggs was to be the next victim. "The hijacker came back where I was, and he was kicking me and hitting me and calling me 'American pig.' . . . I thought I was dead. I prayed. I asked the Lord to receive me in His arms . . . and then the stewardess rushed over, and she talked to him and said, 'No. Please. Please.' . . . I could feel her right next to me." Suddenly, the blindfolded Suggs "heard many voices screaming. Many people came on the plane. . . . The next thing I heard was, 'Stand up. Stand up.' And that's when I thought it was my turn. And they rushed me to the back end of the plane, and they told me to sit down again."

According to Kurt Carlson, "the tail door sprang open and ten or twelve militiamen ran into the plane, screaming and shouting, all brandishing automatic weapons. They seemed to be friends of the hijackers, hugging them and slapping them on the back." Reinforcements had arrived. "Personally, it was good news," Maresca said. "One of them, a fellow who called himself Jihad, spoke English. He indicated he thought the hijackers were crazy. I considered him more rational. I was a little less concerned about some hothead doing something abrupt."

Maresca had no way of knowing that this newly arrived voice of reason was one of Lebanon's leading terrorists. His name was Imad Mugniyah, and he, as much as any man, was directly responsible for the terror visited upon Americans in the Middle East. If Sheik Fadlallah was the spiritual leader of Hezbollah, Mugniyah was the enforcer. Among other things, he had orchestrated the kidnapping of Americans in Beirut as hostages for the return of his brother-in-law, a convicted terrorist under a death sentence in Kuwait for building a bomb used to attack the U.S. Embassy there. Mugniyah may have seemed more reasonable than Castro or Said, but he was every bit as ruthless.

Kurt Carlson, Clinton Suggs, three other Navy divers, a Greek singer named Demis Roussos and his secretary were ordered into seats in the last two rows. "And then right after that," Suggs said, "we all stood up and we were rushed off the back of the plane onto a truck." The hijacking of TWA 847 had just turned into a kidnapping as well. A second group of five passengers was taken off the plane—two men, Richard Herzberg and Robert Trautmann, with Jewish-sounding names, another Navy diver and two other passengers apparently chosen at random.

The truck carrying Carlson and six other hostages left the airport, driving past two Lebanese Army soldiers at the gate who simply looked the other way. After careening up and down back alleys and passing through militia checkpoints, it pulled up in front of a four-story building. "We were herded into a basement . . . about 12 by 20 feet," Carlson wrote. Roussos and his secretary were taken to an upstairs room while the five military men were left in the basement. "As the door closed behind us, we heard the roar of a jet taking off from the airport a short distance away," Carlson wrote. "We knew it had to be Flight 847."

★　★　★

It was daybreak Saturday when TWA 847 took off again from Beirut and headed west toward Algiers. The hijacking was now in its second day, and the Joint Special Operations Command had at last been deployed. Two separate teams were en route to the Mediterranean: the twenty-man Emergency Support Team headed by David Long and a rescue force headed by Brig. Gen. Carl Stiner, formerly the Joint Chiefs' man in Beirut, now the commander of JSOC. Long's team had been launched Friday afternoon while TWA 847 was en route back to Beirut. Stiner and the Delta force had not taken off until early Saturday morning after Stethem's body had been dumped onto the Beirut tarmac. Both teams were bound for the British base of Akrotiri on Cyprus.

By the time Stiner was airborne, more than twenty-four hours had elapsed since the start of the hijacking, and there were still ten hours to go before the rescue force arrived in the Mediterranean. At its first meeting on Friday morning just six hours after word of the hijacking had reached Washington, the administration's Terrorist Incident Working Group had recommended that Delta be dispatched at once, but the Pentagon had wanted to keep its rescue forces at home rather than have them shuttle about the Mediterranean waiting for TWA 847 to stand still. "The military felt extremely strongly that until they knew exactly where they were going, they would be better off at Fort Bragg," the NSC's Howard Teicher recalled. "That would preserve the 'integrity of command' and they would not have to move all the hardware from place to place." To Teicher, that sounded like just another of the military's excuses for doing nothing.

With TWA 847 now headed back to Algiers, both the Emergency Support Team and the rescue force would be woefully out of position if they continued on to Cyprus. After pulling out the charts and consulting his team, David Long recommended diverting to the NATO base at Sigonella, Sicily. The State Department scrambled to get permission from the Italian government. When Long stepped off the plane at Sigonella, he told the American base commander, Navy Capt. William Spearman, that his quiet little domain was about to become busier than Tempelhof Airport during the Berlin airlift. All told, JSOC would bring in six planeloads of equipment, everything from helicopters to first-aid kits, and between 200 and 300 people, everybody from commandos to mechanics. When the commandos arrived, they were loaded on buses and driven to a vacant hangar where they remained out of sight, waiting for their orders.

★　★　★

In Algiers, Ambassador Michael Newlin had just fallen asleep after tucking the twenty-one freed hostages into a hotel when he was awakened by another call from the State Department operations center. TWA 847 was headed his way again. This time, the State Department wanted Newlin to ask the Algerians for permission to bring in Long's Emergency Support Team. Newlin thought it was a bad idea. He thought the Algerians would consider the support team a rescue mission, and he knew they would never permit that. "A rescue attempt would have been impossible," Newlin said later. "The Algerians are very good and might have tried themselves if they thought that was the only way to save the hostages. But they were not about to stand aside and let us try. Our people would have had to fight their way through the Algerians to get to the plane." Both Long and General Lawson, the deputy commander of U.S. forces in Europe, agreed. "My advice was that sending JSOC into Algiers would tear it with the Algerians for some time to come," Lawson said.

Despite the bleak prospects, Long proceeded with plans to send in elements of his team. In an effort to cause as little offense as possible, Long pared the team down to a third of its original size. Since neither the Algerians nor the hijackers would take kindly to an American military plane landing next to TWA 847, Long and his pared-down traveling squad would have to fly commercial. The nearest airport with direct flights to Algiers was in Marseilles, so Long headed north to France while Delta and the rest of the support team waited in the hangar at Sigonella.

For the Delta commandos, perhaps the most important piece of information after the location of the plane and the number of hijackers on board was the model of the aircraft they would have to storm. The Boeing 727 was a standard model, and Delta knew it well, but every airline laid out its cabin differently. TWA agreed to fly a duplicate of 847 into Sigonella that Delta could use both as a practice vehicle and as a Trojan horse to fly into Algiers under the pretext of bringing in a fresh crew for TWA 847. As the second 727 flew toward Italy en route to Sigonella, the pilot turned off his transponder and the plane simply disappeared from air traffic control radars.

★　★　★

TWA 847 landed in Algiers for the second time at 7:50 local time Saturday morning. The hijackers had spent the trip systematically looting the remaining 113 passengers and crew. According to Peter Hill, the passenger who had sat next to Castro and Said on takeoff from Athens, "everyone was brought forward in front of the original two hijackers and stripped of all their valuables—children, women, the men—all their jewelry, the watches, their money and so on. The original two hijackers took all the cash and jewelry, and the rest of the bandits helped themselves to everything else"—everything but credit cards. The hijackers just tossed the cards on the floor, making the aisle slippery with plastic.

Over the radio, the hijackers demanded the release of their accomplice Ali Atwa, who had been arrested at the Athens airport. If he was not released, the hijackers threatened, they would start killing the Greek passengers. That afternoon an Olympic Airways jet took off from Athens bound for Algiers with Ali Atwa on board. The hijackers originally had promised to release only the Greek passengers in return for Atwa, but the Algerians parlayed him into a deal which freed everyone except the

American male passengers and crew. "The Algerians were absolutely superb," Newlin said. "They made the hijackers pay for everything."

Under questioning by police in Athens, Atwa had claimed that his accomplices had smuggled their weapons past the airport X-ray machines by wrapping them in fiberglass insulation. On board TWA 847, Peter Hill had made a slightly different discovery. When the passengers were finally allowed to go to the bathroom, Hill searched the lavatory for the remnants of that loud crash he had heard just before takeoff from Athens. "I got down on the floor, and in the corner . . . I found two pieces of evidence: two bits of glass of different thickness," Hill recounted. "The weapons had to have been encased in a special sort of glass. I'm convinced it was crystal, with a high lead content, that made it possible for them to get the bag through two X-ray checks."

The pistol and grenades were now reinforced by a small armory of weapons that Imad Mugniyah and his men had brought on board in Beirut. "They had M-60 machine guns, ammunition boxes in the aisle," the Pentagon's Noel Koch said. "The fucking plane was a flying arsenal." That plus the fact that some of the passengers had been taken off the plane and were being held in Beirut meant "there was no Delta option," Koch said. Negotiations were the only way out.

The hijackers were focusing their demands on the release of the 700 Shiites held prisoner in Israel. The Shiites had been picked up for "security offenses" during Operation Iron Fist, the Israeli Defense Forces' answer to a deadly campaign of ambushes and car bombs mounted by the Amal militia against the Israeli invaders. About 1,000 young Shiites had been sent to Atlit Prison south of Haifa in clear violation of the Fourth Geneva Convention, which prohibits the transfer of civilians to the territory of an occupying power. Even the United States, Israel's closest friend, had protested. Israel wanted to rid itself of the prisoners and escape the international opprobrium. About 300 Shiites already had been freed when the kidnapping of some United Nations soldiers in southern Lebanon had prompted Israel to suspend the releases. The trick was to find a way for the Israelis to resume the prisoner releases without the appearance of giving into the hijackers' demands. "It seemed to me the ingredients of a settlement were there," Newlin recalled. When Newlin left the Algiers airport in the small hours of Sunday morning, he was confident the Algerians, with help from the International Committee of the Red Cross, would settle the crisis without further bloodshed.

A few hours later, Newlin was awakened by a call from one of the embassy's communications officers who was monitoring the conversations between the cockpit and the tower. The hijackers were once again demanding fuel. Newlin called the secretary general of the Algerian presidency, a combination chief of staff and national security adviser, and repeated the American position that everything possible should be done to keep the plane on the ground, even if that meant shooting out the tires. The Secretary General told Newlin his government would do what it could to prevent the plane from leaving. A few minutes later, the embassy communications officer called Newlin back and said TWA 847 was taking off. Newlin called the Algerians again and asked what had happened. He was told the hijackers had threatened to blow up the plane. Later, the Algerians told him they had heard radio reports that the Delta force was on its way and speculated that the hijackers had heard the reports, too.

★   ★   ★

In their nightly newscasts on Friday, the first day of the hijacking, both ABC and NBC News had reported that Delta had been dispatched from Fort Bragg. The reports were technically inaccurate since Delta did not take off from Fort Bragg until several hours later, but the substance had been correct—the United States was positioning a rescue force. The reports were picked up by a number of other news organizations and before long the whole world knew Delta was moving. None of the Americans aboard TWA 847 could remember hearing any radio reports about Delta, but there was a lot happening in Arabic that they didn't understand. Other than the comment by the Algerian, there is no evidence that news reports of Delta prompted the hijackers to break off negotiations. By their actions, the hijackers had shown themselves to be worried about a rescue attempt from the very start, and they did not need a radio to tell them they had been on the ground too long in Algiers.

Of all terrorist organizations, Hezbollah was perhaps the best prepared to stay one step ahead of Delta, since by now Imad Mugniyah's men had been holding William Buckley, one of the CIA's leading experts on terrorism, for more than a year. "The terrorists had adapted to the Western CT [counterterrorist] capability, and I think that all came from Buckley," Noel Koch said.

Even without Buckley, terrorists knew from Mogadishu and Entebbe that the longer they stayed in one place the more vulnerable they were to a rescue mission. They also knew that the chances of a military operation increased dramatically once they murdered a hostage. By moving frequently and splitting up the hostages, the terrorists multiplied the obstacles facing a rescue force. Most of these tactics were obvious, and that was the point—it was relatively easy for terrorists to foil the best laid plans of a counterterrorist force. Terrorists didn't convene blue ribbon panels like the Holloway and Long commissions, but they were at least as capable of learning from their mistakes as governments. Unfettered by bureaucracy or the law, they were probably more capable of applying the lessons they learned.

★　★　★

In the cockpit of TWA 847, Mugniyah told Testrake, We want to play a little game here. We need to convince the airport to bring us fuel. Mugniyah brought twenty-two-year-old James Hoskins, the youngest remaining hostage, into the cockpit and told him to scream into the microphone as if he were being beaten. "He was petrified and didn't scream too well," Maresca recounted. "One of the hijackers sort of looked at me, so I grabbed the mike and started screaming." According to Testrake, "the fuel truck arrived within minutes to fill our tanks, but it was the same driver who had fueled us the day before . . . and he asked again for a credit card." Maresca told the driver he already had the only credit card he was ever going to get from TWA 847. This time the driver relented, and while the plane was being refueled, Testrake and Mugniyah discussed their destination. Mugniyah said he wanted to go to Aden in South Yemen; Testrake responded that a 727 couldn't fly that far without refueling. Testrake suggested stopping in Cairo; Mugniyah countered with Beirut. The hijackers talked among themselves in Arabic, and Testrake thought he heard the word "Tehran," the one place he knew he didn't want to go. Mugniyah turned to Testrake and said in English, We will fly back to Beirut for fuel. Then we will go somewhere else.

TWA 847 took off for Beirut shortly past 8:00 A.M. after spending more than twenty-five hours on the ground in Algiers. A half hour later, an Air Algérie plane arrived from Marseilles carrying David Long and five members of his Emergency Support Team. Long and his team never would see TWA 847; it was gone from Algiers forever.

Testrake and his crew decided that once they landed in Beirut a third time, they were not going to take off again. "The final trip to Beirut was going to be for the purpose of refueling in order to continue on to Tehran," Maresca recalled. "We said to ourselves: this is it, we're not going to Tehran." Left alone in the cockpit for the first time since the hijacking began, the crew discussed among themselves and by radio with TWA officials in New York what they should do next.

Officials in Washington knew exactly what TWA should do. "We wanted to divert the plane to Larnaca [on the island of Cyprus], where Delta could get at it," Koch said. The idea was never communicated to the crew of TWA 847. "We had very clear reception directly to our operations center in Rome," Maresca said. "They could have relayed suggestions from the company in New York or the government in Washington . . . but we never got any feedback." It was probably just as well, Maresca continued, because "if Washington or New York had told us to go to Cyprus, I'm not sure we would have done it."

The crew of TWA 847 didn't want to be rescued, they wanted to be released. That was their best chance of getting out alive. "What we were trying to do is not precipitate anything," Maresca explained. "We decided that Beirut was the best alternative we had open to us."

As TWA 847 made its final approach into Beirut, Christian Zimmermann pointed excitedly at one of the cockpit gauges, warning that they were about to lose an engine. As the plane touched down, Zimmermann closed the fuel valve and tripped the electrical power to engine number two, setting off a display of flashing lights on the instrument panel. Testrake informed Mugniyah that TWA 847 could not fly again until a new engine was brought in from the States. It was 2:25 Sunday afternoon in Beirut, 7:25 Sunday morning in Washington.

★　★　★

The Reagan administration was now more than forty-eight hours into its worst hostage crisis, yet the President remained at his Camp David retreat, to all appearances taking the weekend off. One of the first decisions of the crisis had been to keep the President out of it. Everyone remembered how in the early days of the Iran crisis President Carter had made himself a virtual hostage by publicly dedicating his every waking moment to securing the release of the Americans at the embassy in Tehran. Reagan attempted to keep his distance by sticking to his regular schedule, giving a speech in Baltimore on Friday and going on to Camp David for the weekend. The administration didn't want the hijackers to know they had seized the attention of the President of the United States. It was a forlorn hope. With the lives of so many Americans at stake, no President could feign business as usual.

The charade ended on Sunday, shortly after the hijackers cut off the negotiations in Algiers and returned to Beirut. Reagan left Camp David ahead of schedule and returned to the White House for an afternoon meeting in the situation room. Stopping on the White House lawn to answer the shouted questions of reporters, Reagan said, "We're doing everything we can, but I'm not going to talk about details." That revealed nothing, but it was news—the President had talked about the hostage crisis.

By the time Reagan sat down with his advisers in the White House Situation Room, the chances for an early end to the crisis had all but vanished. Not only had the hijackers broken off talks in Algiers, but Israel had vastly complicated the situation with its first public reaction to the demand for the release of the 700 Shiite prisoners. Following a meeting of the Israeli cabinet, an official who refused to be identified by name read reporters a brief statement. "Israel itself will not enter into any negotiations for an exchange of Lebanese Shiite detainees for the American hostages held by the terrorists," the unidentified official said. "However, if the United States government, on a senior level, will turn to the Israeli government and request that it release the detainees, the government of Israel will consider such a request." With two sentences, Israel had shifted the onus for making concessions from itself to the United States. That was particularly galling because those Shiite prisoners were part of the bitter legacy of Israel's 1982 invasion of Lebanon which had triggered the chain of events leading to the Marine massacre.

The President opened the meeting in the situation room by reading the text of a handwritten message to him from the thirty passengers still on the plane. "We implore you not to take any direct military action on our behalf," the message read. "Please negotiate quickly our immediate release by convincing the Israelis to release the 700 Lebanese prisoners as requested. Now!" One of the passengers, Peter Hill, had signed his name "Peter Hell." Reagan was determined to end this outrage quickly. The public will demand satisfaction, he said, according to notes taken at the meeting.

General Vessey, chairman of the Joint Chiefs of Staff, briefed the President on the forces that could be used to go after TWA 847. Delta and the Blackhawk helicopters needed for a rescue attempt could be moved to Cyprus, 100 miles from Beirut, but that was only slightly better than leaving them at Sigonella. The Beirut airport was an armed camp occupied by the Amal militia. Delta alone did not have the firepower to go in there. A much larger force, one that included Army Rangers, would be needed to establish a perimeter around the plane while Delta went after the hostages. Vessey felt the chances of moving those kinds of forces into position and still preserving the element of surprise were extremely poor. In short, the prospect of a successful rescue mission was virtually nonexistent. The discussion of military options ended with some inconclusive talk about cratering the runway if it looked like the plane was about to take off for Tehran. The carrier *Nimitz* already had been diverted toward the coast of Lebanon, but that did not change the fact that while the United States had overwhelming military power, the terrorists held all the cards.

The President turned to the prospects for a peaceful settlement. Release the hostages and we'll get the Israelis to release the Amal prisoners, the President suggested, according to the notes. Secretary of State Shultz had to argue strenuously to convince the President that the administration's policy of not making concessions to terrorists included not encouraging others to make concessions. Don't force the pace, Shultz counseled. Buy time, Robert McFarlane, the national security adviser, added.

The immediate danger to the hostages seemed to have passed. The first hours of any hostage crisis are the most perilous—the moments of true terror when both hijacker and hostage are scared and confused. In the case of TWA 847, the terror had ended and the siege had begun when Amal leader Nabih Berri agreed to represent the hijackers in the negotiations. Berri "saw an opportunity here to elevate his own standing within the Shiite community by winning the release of the prisoners in Israel," McFarlane said later.

Unlike the hijackers, Berri was a known quantity—a lawyer who had once lived in Dearborn, Michigan, and whose family still lived there, he was a politician who thought not of Islamic revolution but of power for himself and benefits for his constituents. McFarlane had met Berri in the fall of 1983 during his brief, ill-fated tour as the President's Middle East envoy. If there was a silver lining to America's disastrous involvement in Lebanon, it was McFarlane's firsthand knowledge of the factions and their leaders. McFarlane had that rare and precious commodity—a feel for the situation on the ground in Beirut. The TWA 847 crisis was to be his finest hour.

At about two o'clock Monday morning, Washington time, McFarlane placed a long-distance call to Berri. Speaking from a carefully scripted text, McFarlane told Berri the United States would not make concessions or encourage others to do so, effectively ruling out the Israeli suggestion that President Reagan had only to ask and the Shiites would be released. As McFarlane later explained it, "Berri's strategy fundamentally was [to] use the Americans to leverage Israel. So you had to . . . disabuse him of that belief that his strategy would work here."

The other message McFarlane tried to get across to Berri in that early morning phone call was that this was his game to win or lose. "We believe he is the key to the solution," White House spokesman Larry Speakes told reporters several hours after the phone call, reading from a statement drafted by McFarlane. By declaring Berri the key, McFarlane hoped to increase the pressure on him to find a solution or at least to make it difficult for him to walk away from the crisis and leave the hostages in the hands of Hezbollah. Not incidentally, shining the spotlight on Berri might take some of the heat off the President.

None of these tactics, adroit as they were, could mask the bleak prospect that this hijacking-turned-kidnapping could drag on for days, weeks, or even months. After all, Hezbollah had been holding other Americans hostage in Beirut for more than a year. TWA 847 had every chance of becoming for Ronald Reagan what the Iran hostage crisis had been for Jimmy Carter.

★　★　★

One of Berri's first acts was to order the rest of the passengers off the plane. Jimmy Palmer sensed something was about to happen when the cabin lights were turned off for the first time since the hijacking began. It was about four o'clock in the morning, and he quickly dozed off in the darkness. Suddenly, he was awakened and loaded into a windowless van with the rest of the passengers. "It looked like a death van to me," passenger Thomas Cullins said afterward. "I felt sure we were going to be trucked out to some bunker and just peppered. One of our group asked both the Catholic priests with us to say some prayers. We all said the Lord's Prayer together." They were driven into the slums of Beirut and led by the hand into the pitch-black basement of an apartment building. "They turned on the lights and there were, I guess, a half dozen soldiers standing at the other end with automatic weapons," Jimmy Palmer said. "I think everybody there thought, well, this is it. They are fixing to snuff us out here." Instead, their captors passed out blankets and led the passengers in groups of four to a building across the street.

At a press conference later that same day, Berri confirmed that the last of the passengers had been removed from the plane "on my personal orders." Berri was taking control, but he wasn't buying the McFarlane line that he was the key to a solution. "I believe that the problem now is an American problem," Berri said, referring to the Israeli statement that they were only waiting for a request from Washington to free the Shiite prisoners. Release of the Shiites in Israel had been only one of the hijackers' original demands, but Berri had shrewdly stripped away the others, leaving himself with a strong case to argue. The Shiites had been, in Berri's words, "kidnapped on and taken from Lebanese territory." As he put it, "the Israeli authorities violated the law . . . just as does any hijacking operation, whether it involves an airplane, a ship, or a ground action." That, of course, did not justify the hijacking of TWA 847, but Berri's point was a sound one.

★   ★   ★

Perhaps more than any other event, TWA 847 gave terrorism a human face, revealing that behind the murderous ravings of Castro and Said there lay real grievances. This particular grievance—the holding of 700 prisoners in violation of international law—was simple and easy to understand. It was not imbedded in the long and tangled history of Arab and Jew, a history charged with hatreds only those who had lived it could fully understand. On the other side of this clear and simple wrong done to the Shiites of south Lebanon were forty Americans entirely innocent of the crime for which they were held hostage. The employees at the American Embassy in Tehran and the Marines at the airport in Beirut had at least been official representatives of a hated American policy. The passengers aboard TWA 847 were private citizens minding their own business. The combination of genuine grievances and innocent victims put even more pressure on the Reagan administration to bring the crisis to a quick and peaceful end.

Once the television networks reached the passengers who had been released and the relatives of those still being held, the administration's no-concessions stance began drowning in a wave of human emotion. Television is a medium of images, not ideas, and as McFarlane's press secretary Robert Sims later put it, "TV served to focus public concern on the hostages' human anguish without similar coverage that would have balanced the immediate problems of the hostages' safety with the long-term problems that Americans will face if [terrorists] perceive that their violence works." Lloyd Cutler, counselor to President Carter, had experienced a similar effect during the Iran hostage crisis. "The most harmful effect of television news," Cutler said, "is its tendency to speed up the decision-making process on issues that television news is featuring and to slow down and interrupt the process of deciding other important issues that get less television attention."

The White House could try to downplay events, could try to keep the President above the fray, but there was no stopping the networks. The CBS Evening News devoted nearly two thirds of its air time to the crisis. During a similar period in 1979, the Evening News had spent only half of each show covering the Iran hostage crisis. TWA 847 was surely not a more important story than the taking of the embassy. The difference was that the networks were technologically capable of doing more in

Beirut in 1985 than in Tehran in 1980. As ABC's Ted Koppel, who had been catapulted to stardom by the Iran crisis, put it, "Sometimes, we must admit, we end up doing things simply because we can, and not because we should."

The tendency to be stampeded by the networks was even more pronounced in the Reagan administration because the President was a man of images, not ideas. Reagan was a master of the medium of television, but in terrorism he had met his match. Terrorism offered a means for the underdogs of the world to break into prime time by creating a human drama no network could resist. Terrorists could shoot their way onto the air and the networks would take it from there as they spared no expense in the competitive battle to be the first to break the news. Newspapers did the same thing. The difference was that print deadened the drama while television enhanced it. It was one thing to read about the odyssey of TWA 847, quite another to hear Phil Maresca's frantic cry, "He just killed a passenger!" Maresca's cry could be played again and again, while the President's statement that "we're doing everything we can" got old fast. "I was struck as a government spokesman . . . by the ability of the hijackers and their friends to create news and have their message enhanced through repetition," Robert Sims said.

On Tuesday night, the President held a televised press conference—a significant news story under any circumstances, a major event in the midst of a crisis. On Wednesday morning, the President's remarks were eclipsed by an even bigger event in Beirut—a cockpit interview with Testrake and the crew of TWA 847 by Charles Glass of ABC News. It was the television news "scoop" of the year, not just exclusive information but exclusive pictures of the men in the cockpit who until that moment had been disembodied voices pleading with the Beirut tower.

The content of the interview was unexceptional. Testrake said they were being treated fairly well and that nothing much had happened since the last of the passengers had been taken off. But the drama of this first glimpse of the crew was exceptional—complete with a made-for-TV ending when Castro put his hand over Testrake's mouth and pulled him back into the cockpit, waving his pistol at Glass on the tarmac below. As if that were not enough, there was the pathos of flight engineer Christian Zimmermann sending a message through the camera to his father that "everything's okay," not knowing his father had died of a heart attack upon learning that his son had been hijacked.

ABC's coup turned a highly competitive story into what Michael O'Neill, the former editor of the New York *Daily News* and president of the American Society of Newspaper Editors, disdainfully called "an orgy of overkill that exploited the hostages, their families, and the American people." The next day Amal produced five of the hostages for a press conference that turned into what one of them, Peter Hill, called "a bloody circus." The sight of the hostages set off such a shouting and shoving match among the assembled reporters that one journalist actually apologized to the terrorists on behalf of the press corps.

More than any single event of the entire crisis, the press conference created a moral equivalence between Hezbollah's kidnapping of 40 Americans and Israel's abduction of 700 Shiites. In an opening statement, Allyn Conwell, a Texas oilman the hostages had chosen as their spokesman, said, "We understand that Israel is holding as hostage a number of Lebanese people who undoubtedly have as equal a right and as strong a desire to go home as we do. . . . We condemn hijacking or terrorism of any sort or nature irregardless of the perpetrator or the circumstances." Nabih Berri couldn't have said it better himself.

If President Reagan would not negotiate with Berri, then Berri would negotiate directly with the American people, and the networks were only too willing to oblige. David Hartman, the host of ABC's Good Morning America, ended an interview with Berri by asking, "Any final words to President Reagan this morning?" Each morning, network anchormen called Berri from New York to negotiate the day's news story, beginning with a request to talk to the hostages, or, failing that, an interview with Berri himself. The result was an undeniable tilt in favor of the terrorists. Nearly two thirds of the time ABC's World News Tonight devoted to the crisis consisted of interviews with Berri, the hostages, or their families—who cared only about meeting the hijackers' demands so everybody could go home. By contrast, Reagan administration officials armed with arguments against making concessions to terrorists showed up in only 12 percent of the crisis coverage on World News Tonight.

It was easy to say this was not television's finest hour, not so easy to say what it should have done differently. Reflecting on his network's coverage of the crisis, Lawrence Grossman, president of NBC News, said there was "virtually nothing I would take back." Whether the television networks made the Reagan administration's job easier or harder was simply not the right way to judge their coverage. The networks do not work for the government; they are supposed to work for the public.

The public wanted to know where the hostages were and how their families were bearing up, and the networks told them. Sometimes, however, news of the hostages was manufactured. One of the freed hostages, Arthur Targontsidis, was "reunited" with his parents on Good Morning

America—then "reunited" again on NBC's Today Show and a third time on the CBS Morning News. But mostly television dispensed information to all the different parties to the hijacking. Kurt Carlson later wrote that "throughout the ordeal . . . the State Department provided absolutely no information to [my brother] Mark, who became disgusted with them. CBS, on the other hand, phoned constantly, anytime there were new reports about the hostages in general and especially about [me]."

Television coverage invariably told the administration things it needed to know. Charles Glass's interview with the TWA crew confirmed that all the passengers had been taken off the plane—a vital piece of information in weighing the prospects for a rescue mission. "Our best intelligence is invariably the media," the Pentagon's Noel Koch said. "One of the first things we do is tune in CNN [Cable News Network]," the FAA's Donald Engen added. "You learn just about as much real time intelligence from watching the networks as you do from what's coming through the [official] pipeline." David Gergen, at one time the White House director of communications, remembered how in the hours immediately following the assassination of Sadat, Washington had to rely on CNN for its information. "We literally didn't know what was happening from minute to minute, even though we had an open telephone line to the embassy," Gergen said. "The networks were so far ahead it was embarrassing. Everyone thought we were sitting on a lot of information or lying, but the fact was the networks knew a lot more than we did." The networks weren't necessarily smarter, but sometimes they had better access. "CNN runs ten minutes ahead of NSA," said Oliver North of the NSC staff.

Television also withheld information. Early on, the mother of Clinton Suggs told a local reporter her son was in the Navy. The Pentagon asked the networks and other news organizations not to repeat the story or to reveal the military affiliations of the other passengers. Everyone complied, although it didn't do Robert Stethem or Kurt Carlson any good because the hijackers already had confiscated their military ID cards.

Critics claimed that excessive television coverage prolonged the crisis by giving Amal a new chance to voice its grievances every day. But Jeremy Levin, a reporter for CNN who had been kidnapped and later had escaped from Beirut, pointed out that the longest-running hostage crisis was the least covered hostage crisis—the Americans who had disappeared almost without a trace from the streets of Beirut.

The maddening thing about the press was that you could never tell whether it was for or against you. In the hours immediately following

the 1983 Marine bombing, some of the survivors had threatened to shoot
television cameramen if they did not stop taking pictures of the carnage;
other Marines ran in front of the cameras so their families back home
could see they had survived the blast. Relatives of the TWA hostages
resented the intrusions but welcomed the coverage which made it impossible for the White House to ignore the hostages' plight. The administration cried foul when NBC and ABC reported the movement of Delta on
the first day of the crisis. Yet in the final days, the administration was
encouraging news reports of American military movements as a means
of applying pressure on Berri.

★   ★   ★

If a crisis like TWA 847 exacerbated the tensions in the adversarial
relationship between press and government, it also brought to a head the
unresolved disputes within the Reagan administration. They were some
of the same disputes—the ambivalence toward Israel, the tension between the NSC staff and the rest of the bureaucracy—that had paralyzed
policy toward Lebanon in 1982 and 1983, and they threatened to do so
again. The pullout from Lebanon had settled nothing. It merely had
provided a respite until the next crisis again revealed the administration's
internal contradictions.

Policy disputes were not, of course, peculiar to the Reagan administration. What was peculiar about the Reagan administration was the way
it dealt with them. The staff of the NSC was supposed to be the mechanism by which disputes were, if not resolved, at least managed. In the
Reagan administration, the NSC staff often was the engine of dispute.

One way or another, Israel always seemed to be a party to those
disputes—if not directly as in Lebanon and TWA 847, then indirectly
as a role model for those looking to break out of the post-Vietnam
syndrome of self-doubt and indecision. American support for the Jewish
state was a political and moral imperative, yet Israel's disastrous policies
in Lebanon had helped bring the fury of the Shiites down upon the
United States. From the Shiite point of view, the United States was
Israel's accomplice in Lebanon. American economic and military aid
supported the Israeli state. American-supplied weapons killed Shiites,
sometimes wantonly, in Lebanon. American diplomats at the United
Nations vetoed resolutions calling for sanctions to restrain Israel. The
United States already had paid dearly for its support of Israel. Now
Israel's illegal detention of Shiite prisoners at Atlit had become the focal
point of a hostage crisis that threatened to cast a pall over the remaining
years of the Reagan era. "The rest of government, except for Shultz,

wanted to beat up on the Israelis for the prisoners at Atlit," Howard Teicher of the NSC staff recalled. "It was a whole lot easier to beat up on the Israelis than to pressure the Syrians."

Teicher was Jewish, a strong supporter of Israel, and an ardent foe of Syria. With his dark beard, he bore a physical resemblance to the terrorists he was tilting against. Like most of them, he was young, tireless, committed, and sometimes cocky. He had followed Robert McFarlane from the State Department to the National Security Council staff, and as he rose through the ranks, his religion and his abrasiveness made him a catalyst for the ugly feud between Arabists and supporters of Israel in the U.S. government. Middle East experts in the State Department, the NSC staff, and some Washington think tanks conducted a tireless whispering campaign against him, intimating that he was an Israeli agent. During a visit to Lebanon in 1983, McFarlane had asked CIA station chief William Buckley for a briefing. The often abrasive Buckley replied that he would oblige McFarlane, but not with Teicher present. It'll get right back to the Israelis, Buckley said. In the absence of any evidence, Teicher was no more guilty of working for the Israelis than his accusers were of working for Syria or the PLO. Still, there was little doubt where his sympathies lay. He delighted in showing other members of the NSC staff a film made by the Israelis which showed Syrian officials slaughtering animals and drinking their blood—proof, Teicher maintained, of what barbarians they were.

As far as Teicher and other members of the NSC staff were concerned, the road to freedom for the TWA hostages led through Damascus, not Jerusalem. Syria's President Assad could be counted on to do one thing and one thing only—act ruthlessly in his own interest. If the Reagan administration could convince Assad that an end to the hijacking was in his interest, then the crisis would be resolved. The NSC staff came up with one proposal to get Assad's attention by launching a cruise missile attack against the Syrian Ministry of Defense in downtown Damascus. It was, even its proponents acknowledged, a high-risk gambit that might well make matters worse.

The standoff between the NSC staff and the rest of the government produced exactly what the Reagan administration had found so repugnant about the Carter administration—a strategy by default which shied away from bold initiatives. *The Wall Street Journal* captured the administration's predicament with an editorial entitled "Jimmy Reagan." As the first week of the TWA hijacking stretched toward the second, the Reagan administration did not seem to be solving the crisis—or even managing it.

The point was brought home to the President by a four-year-old magazine article written by Peter Rodman, a former aide to Henry Kissinger who by 1985 had returned to government as director of Policy Planning at State. Entitled "The Hostage Crisis: How Not to Negotiate," the article dissected Jimmy Carter's conciliatory negotiating tactics during the Iran hostage crisis, tactics that according to Rodman "only guaranteed that Iran paid no price for perpetuating the crisis." Rodman noted that on the second day of the Iran crisis, Carter's press secretary Jody Powell had "stunningly announced . . . that the use of force had been ruled out." According to Rodman, "the first lesson to be learned from the hostage crisis is that to announce that force is ruled out is to consolidate the adversary's victory and to relinquish control over events." Reagan already had violated Rodman's first rule by all but ruling out the use of force when he told a nationally televised press conference that "I have to wait it out as long as those people are there and threatened and alive and we have a possibility of bringing them home."

Shultz brought Rodman's article to a White House meeting and recommended it to both McFarlane and the President as required reading. McFarlane said later the article had no impact on the handling of the crisis, but the turnabout in the administration's tactics was unmistakable. On Tuesday, June 25th, the eleventh day of the crisis, Reagan chaired another meeting in the White House Situation Room. Something had to be done. Not only did Amal still hold forty Americans but terrorism was breaking out all over, as if the jackals of the world knew they had nothing to fear. Four off-duty Marines and two American businessmen had been gunned down at an outdoor café in San Salvador. A bomb had gone off in the terminal at Frankfurt Airport, killing three people, two of them children. The President was talking tough again, warning that "our limits have been reached," but where was the action to back up these words?

There had been some slight progress in the TWA standoff, but progress that suggested the United States was doing exactly what it had said it would not do—pressure the Israelis to release the Shiites. The Israelis had released thirty-one Shiites, as if in down payment for the larger swap of American hostages for Lebanese detainees. Israel's Prime Minister Shimon Peres claimed with a straight face that the release had nothing to do with the hostage crisis, that it was simply an administrative action taken in response to petitions filed by some of the prisoners. However, Peres gave the game away by admitting he had called Shultz at two o'clock in the morning to inform him personally of this unrelated administrative action.

The United States had, in fact, been applying secret pressure on Israel. With the knowledge and approval of the administration, Thomas Ashwood, chairman of the security committee of the International Federation of Airline Pilots Association, had met with Amiram Nir, the adviser on counterterrorism to Israel's prime minister, and had offered to call for an international boycott of Ben Gurion Airport as a means of putting pressure on Israel to release the Shiites. Nir rejected the idea but got the message: the release of the thirty-one Shiites followed shortly.

After eleven days of waiting it out, the United States was no closer to dominating events than it had been in those early hours when Castro and Said were in control of TWA 847. Berri, not Reagan, seemed in control. So far, Reagan, like Carter in Iran, had not given Berri and his Shiite constituents any reason to believe they would have to pay a price for holding the hostages. Reagan actually seemed to be pursuing a softer line than Carter. At a similar point in the Iranian crisis, Carter had suspended oil imports from Iran and frozen Iranian assets in the United States. Worse, the President, just like Carter before him, had become hostage to the crisis. On Monday, the President had been forced to cancel a ten-day vacation at his California ranch.

At that Tuesday meeting in the situation room, the President and his advisers decided, in McFarlane's words, to "alter the climate in which Berri makes decisions." The time was long overdue for Berri to start worrying that he might indeed have to pay a price for holding Americans hostage. The price McFarlane had in mind was an economic blockade of Beirut. "If you can cut off goods and services into Beirut, that really does have an effect," McFarlane argued. The Shiites made money off the airport and the entire community depended on the port. "The opinion makers, the leaders, the people that make money, do so through that port in a very major way," McFarlane said. "Both the illegal . . . and the normal commerce through there are very central to the day-to-day well-being of the heavies in Beirut." According to McFarlane, Reagan wasn't ready to order a blockade but said instead, Let's make it clear that we're considering it so that it gets the attention of those people and Nabih Berri.

After the meeting broke up, White House spokesman Larry Speakes told reporters the President had reviewed a wide-ranging series of options that could be applied to the situation should the hostages be held much longer. "The President will let diplomacy run its full course before taking further steps, but he is prepared to take whatever actions are necessary," Speakes said without elaborating. Just one week before, the President had said, "I have to wait it out." Now, his spokesman was saying the President was only going to wait "a day or two" longer. It was the first major change in administration tactics since the crisis began.

Berri now faced a situation where, if Reagan made good on his threats of economic and military reprisals, the Shiites of Lebanon could be even worse off than they had been before the hijacking. Berri had milked the crisis for all it was worth and more. It had, after all, made him and his movement household words in the United States, had lifted the plight of the Lebanese detainees out of obscurity into the international limelight. Now it was time to bring the bloody circus to an end before the law of diminishing returns set in.

The next day, Berri released Jimmy Palmer for health reasons and offered to transfer the remaining thirty-nine hostages to a neutral embassy in Beirut or to Syria, the pending release of the Lebanese detainees—to put them in escrow, so to speak. That was the first real break in the crisis—the first sign that Berri was looking for a way out, and more importantly, the first sign that his most powerful backer, Syria's Assad, was actively engaged in the search for a solution. Having permitted—and perhaps encouraged—his client Berri to take control of the hostage drama, he could ill afford to let his best friend among Lebanon's Shiites fail. But the original hijackers, Castro and Said, weren't loyal to Berri; they were members of Hezbollah with allegiances to the Iranians, and that is where Assad now turned.

He asked Hashemi Rafsanjani, the speaker of the Iranian parliament, to stop in Damascus on his way home from an arms-buying trip to Libya. Although much remains murky about the machinations among Syria, Iran, and Hezbollah, the conditions for the release of the hostages almost certainly were established at a meeting in Damascus between Assad and his vice president Abdul Halim Khaddam on one side and Rafsanjani and two of the prime movers of the Iranian terror network on the other—Mohammed Mohtashami-pur, Iran's Ambassador to Syria, and Mohsen Rafiq-Doust, the minister in charge of the Revolutionary Guards. After the meeting, Rafsanjani publicly criticized the hijacking: "Had [Iran] known in advance about this kind of action, it would have acted to prevent it," he said. While in Damascus, Rafsanjani also met with Sheik Fadlallah and other Hezbollah mullahs who were in Syria as part of a delegation of Shiite leaders. With Assad and Rafsanjani engaged, the Reagan administration declared a news blackout in Washington—a sure sign that the posturing had ended and the dealing had begun.

★   ★   ★

The administration seemed so confident of a resolution that it added a new demand. In a speech Wednesday night in San Francisco, Shultz said, "We insist on release of our hostages, all forty-six of them immediately." Suddenly, the seven "forgotten hostages" who had been kidnapped from the streets of Beirut over the preceding year were given equal status with the TWA thirty-nine. Almost from the beginning of the crisis, relatives of the seven had been clamoring for equal time, and finally they had succeeded.

During a trip to Chicago, Reagan met privately with the family of Father Lawrence Jenco—the first time the President had met with any relatives of the forgotten seven. Jenco's family had not been invited to a meeting with the relatives of the TWA hostages in the Chicago area, but when they heard about it they pressed for an audience of their own and with the help of their congressman they got one. When they asked Reagan why he couldn't negotiate for their loved one, he replied with the standard line that to do so would only encourage the terrorists and put other Americans in greater danger. But as the TWA crisis continued to unfold, that line was being stretched to the breaking point.

The President's meeting with Jenco's relatives was "intense," McFarlane said, and "you could see that he was really affected by it." Afterwards, while the President stood in a holding room waiting to give a speech, he stared into space, pursed his lips, and said, I really understand how they feel. I wish there was something more we could do. In time, the emergence of the seven from the limbo to which the administration had so assiduously assigned them would prove to be one of the more lasting effects of the TWA hijacking.

Despite the new demand, Berri remained upbeat in his public statements. "I think we're in the end of this thing," he was quoted as saying. The emerging deal was now obvious to everyone. Syria would take custody of the hostages and release them to the United States with the understanding that Israel would promptly free its Shiite prisoners. Unlike any Western intermediary, Syria could convince Berri that Israel would deliver if only he didn't make freeing the Shiites a precondition for the release of the TWA hostages.

The understanding that Israel would release the Atlit prisoners was the product of a secret backchannel Secretary of State Shultz had opened to Benjamin Netanyahu, Israel's Ambassador to the United Nations. Netanyahu had previously been the number two man at the Israeli Embassy in Washington and had worked closely with Charles Hill, then the State Department's head of Arab-Israeli affairs and now Shultz's executive assistant. Tiptoeing along the edge of his no-concessions policy, Shultz inquired of Netanyahu about Israel's plans for releasing the Atlit prisoners once the TWA passengers were free. Netanyahu assured Shultz that the release of the TWA thirty-nine would remove the only obstacle to Israel's plans to send the Shiites home. Netanyahu was making a commitment on behalf of his government and tacitly authorizing Shultz to give Syria his word on it. The no-deal deal was confirmed by an exchange of letters between Reagan and Peres in which the President asked and was assured that Israel's previously announced plans for releasing the Shiite prisoners still stood.

The release of the hostages was virtually sealed by Friday when Reagan sat down to lunch with community leaders in Chicago Heights, Illinois. Then, in response to a question about a statement by hostage spokesman Allyn Conwell that it would be a mistake to link the TWA thirty-nine with the forgotten seven, Reagan said, "I don't think anything that attempts to get people back who have been kidnapped by thugs and murderers and barbarians is wrong to do." Given all that was to follow, that remark was undoubtedly more prophetic than the President intended. For the moment, it threatened to undo the no-deal deal. For all the problems the press had supposedly created for the administration during the course of the crisis, nothing caused more trouble than the reporting of what the President said. When word of what Reagan had said reached Beirut, "our guards were steaming," John Testrake later wrote. "They were so unpredictable you never knew what they might do next . . . including the possibility that they might march us out, line us up against a wall, and shoot us. I didn't think they would. But they were angry."

Testrake went to sleep Friday night stretched across a row of seats, wondering if Reagan's remarks would queer the guards' promise to let the crew take a shower at the airport firehouse. Shortly after midnight, they were shaken awake, crammed into a car, and driven through the mazelike streets of Beirut to an apartment. Expecting to find a television interviewer, Testrake was delighted to see instead mattresses on the floor. "When I saw those mattresses," Testrake wrote, "I realized for the first time that something big was happening." It looked as though he would not be spending another night on the plane. More delightful still, he was allowed to shave and shower. Then he lay down to sleep, worrying about having left all the systems running on the airplane.

Reagan was just returning to the White House from Chicago when thirty-two of the hostages gathered at the Summerland Hotel overlooking the Mediterranean for what had all the trappings of a farewell party. For Kurt Carlson and the four Navy divers, it was the first time since they'd been taken off the plane that they'd seen any of the other hostages. When his guards gave him their addresses and asked him to mail them visas so they could come work for him in America, Carlson began to believe for the first time that he was going home. As reporters and cameras clustered round, Amal brought out a spongecake decorated with the words: "Wishing You All a Happy Trip Home." Beneath the frivolity and good cheer lay apprehension that something could still derail the release. "Reagan was right when he called these guys a bunch of thugs, but he was stupid to say it when he did," one hostage whispered to the *Time* magazine correspondent. "Can you believe an American President would say such a thing when American citizens are being held hostage?"

Testrake was awakened at seven-thirty the next morning and driven to a walled schoolyard. "When the gate swung open, a cheer went up," Testrake wrote. "There . . . were all of the other passengers—or at least most of them. . . . The courtyard was also filled with newspaper and television reporters. Cameras were whirring, flashbulbs were going off, and it looked like the high society event of the year." There in the middle of the southern suburbs of Beirut, surrounded by the bombed-out buildings and pathetic refugee camps of a war that had sucked them into its vortex, the TWA hostages waited in expectation. "We're on the way home," the Rev. James McLoughlin said.

Shortly after four o'clock in the morning Washington time, Larry Speakes came into the White House briefing room to tell reporters that Red Cross vans carrying the hostages "are now departing" for Damascus. The State Department already had begun calling families to tell them the hostages were en route to Damascus. A C-141 transport took off from Andrews Air Force Base with a team of FBI agents, intelligence experts, psychiatrists, and doctors to debrief the hostages when they arrived in Frankfurt; another C-141 had already left Frankfurt to pick up the hostages in Syria. In Damascus, the United States Ambassador, William Eagleton, headed for the border with Lebanon to become the first American official to greet the hostages on their way to freedom. In Jerusalem, Shimon Peres went through with Israel's part of the bargain, saying, "If the hostages reach their homes, we won't have the obstacles that we have had until now" against freeing the Shiite prisoners.

But a cloud had gathered over the schoolyard. Four of the hostages— Robert Brown, Richard Herzberg, Jeffrey Ingalls, and Robert Trautmann—did not answer the roll call. Sitting in a basement just a few blocks from Berri's home, Brown had heard a BBC broadcast the night before about the dinner for the hostages at the Summerland and their imminent transfer to Damascus. "That makes us the insurance policy that the Israelis will release the prisoners," Brown wrote in a diary he was keeping. According to Berri, Hezbollah was holding on to the four because of Reagan's remark the day before about "thugs and murderers and barbarians." To put the release back on track, the United States would have to guarantee that there would be no retaliatory strikes after the hostages were released. "Guarantees must be given to Syria," Berri said. "If those guarantees are provided tonight, they will be released tonight. If not, we are not in a hurry. Tomorrow, the day after, who knows?" Berri went home to bed, and the hostages were sent back to their apartment prisons.

McFarlane couldn't believe Hezbollah was serious. "They know darn well they are not vulnerable to reprisals," he said. "Hezbollah lives in urban areas. It is manifestly infeasible, and they know it, to conduct violent raids against them." McFarlane thought Hezbollah was using the President's remarks as a pretext for backing out of a deal which made Berri, their main rival for the soul of the Shiites in Lebanon, look too good. Whatever the motive, the deal had stalled.

Assad moved quickly to salvage his reputation as the Middle East's answer to Machiavelli. His vice president telephoned the Iranian Revolutionary Guard command post at the al-Khayyam Hotel in Baalbek with the message that Hezbollah could release the hostages or get out of the Bekaa Valley. At the same time, Assad dispatched Brig. Gen. Ghazi Kanaan, an intelligence officer who served as Syria's viceroy in Lebanon, to Beirut to oversee the final transfer. The choice of Kanaan was an unmistakable signal to Hezbollah that Syria meant business.

Assad also promised to sell Iran Scud long-range, surface-to-surface missiles for its war with Iraq. The Soviet-built Scuds, with a range great enough to reach downtown Baghdad, would allow Iran to retaliate for the air raids which Iraq had recently launched against Tehran. There is no evidence that Assad tied the shipment of Scuds directly to the release of the hostages, but the hostages were released and the missiles were shipped—on a clandestine flight over Soviet territory.

Howard Teicher was in the situation room eating pizza when the cable came in from Damascus. McFarlane and his wife were upstairs having dinner and watching the movie *Rambo* with the President and First Lady. The message said that if the United States would reissue a statement affirming its respect for the sovereignty of Lebanon—a piece of boiler plate that appeared in virtually every administration policy statement—Hezbollah would accept that as a no-retaliation pledge. McFarlane came down to the situation room and told Teicher to direct the State Department to release the statement. At 10:00 P.M. the State Department put out a one-sentence statement: "The United States reaffirms its long-standing support for the preservation of Lebanon, its government, its stability and security, and for the mitigation of the suffering of its people."

That was sufficient. At three-thirty Sunday morning Washington time, McFarlane received a cable from the American Embassy in Damascus quoting Syrian officials as saying "Syria has solved" the problem. Dropping his stone-faced resolve, McFarlane walked over to a small refrigerator and passed out beers all around. This time there were no hitches. This time the four missing hostages were brought to the schoolyard along with all the rest—except for the forgotten seven who had fallen by the wayside in the last-minute scramble to put the no-deal deal back together. It was late afternoon in Beirut by the time the Red Cross convoy pulled out of the schoolyard and headed for Damascus and freedom. Teicher watched as CNN broadcast the pictures of the convoy pulling out of the schoolyard while the intelligence community continued to report it could not confirm the hostages' departure.

That night the President went on national television. "The United States gives terrorists no reward and no guarantees," he said. "We make no concessions. We make no deals."

In his speech, the President also announced the creation of a panel chaired by the Vice President to review American policy against terrorism. The staff director of the panel was the former Chief of Naval Operations, Adm. James Holloway, the same man who had headed the Carter administration's investigation into the failure of the Iran rescue mission. The war against terrorism was coming full circle—but with a difference. No matter what the Bush Commission determined or recommended, members of the NSC staff already had concluded that the bureaucracy was too decrepit, too cowardly and too leaky to combat terrorism. None of the organizations—the Terrorist Incident Working Group, the Joint Special Operations Command—the bureaucracy had created to fight terrorism was of any use in the TWA crisis. "The NSC ran this," Teicher claimed. "The NSC staff developed the strategy. If the NSC hadn't done it, the State Department never would. We got things done, and in this administration that counted for something."

The next day, Reagan placed a phone call to Assad, who had let it be known he was disappointed at the lack of gratitude for his efforts in freeing the TWA passengers. Working from a script drafted by Teicher and Oliver North, Reagan perfunctorily thanked Assad, but then launched into a vehement monologue which caught the Syrian president by surprise. Reagan demanded that Syria produce the seven other hostages and bring the hijackers of TWA 847 to justice, so that he would not have to act further. Assad tried to break in, but Reagan wasn't listening. It was plain murder, Reagan told Assad. Tell him it was murder, he repeated to the interpreter. Assad started to speak but Reagan cut him off. This is murder. Tell him it was murder. He didn't want to hear excuses about how the hijackers had vanished into the slums of Beirut. We know you have ways of finding out who they are, he said.

★   ★   ★

Reagan's outburst flew in the face of protocol. Vice President Bush, appalled by the discourtesy, sent his own conciliatory thank-you note to Assad. Reagan's attempt to hold Assad accountable also flew in the face of what the United States now knew about Iran's role in ending the crisis. Without Iran's blessing, even the ruthless Syrian president could not have delivered the four hostages held by Hezbollah. If Assad could not deliver those four hostages, how could he free the other seven Americans held captive by Hezbollah somewhere in Lebanon? The fate of TWA 847 marked a turning point in the administration's thinking about terrorism in Lebanon. Not only did the Iranians hold the keys; for the first time, they had been willing to turn one of them.

The first instinct among some military officers in the Pentagon was to punish Iran. A golden opportunity soon presented itself when U.S. intelligence learned that the entire high command of the Iranian Revolutionary Guards, including its leader, Mohsen Rafiq-Doust, was planning to hold a meeting with its Lebanese allies at the Sheik Abdullah Barracks in Baalbek. Aides to the Joint Chiefs of Staff drew up a proposal to attack the barracks with conventionally-armed cruise missiles fired from a submarine in the Mediterranean. The terrorists would never know what hit them, or so the proposal went. But when officers from the Defense Intelligence Agency and the JCS staff presented the plan, the Joint Chiefs rejected it out of hand, saying it was too barbaric and too technologically risky. Two days after the gathering took place, intelligence officials learned that Hosein Sheikholislam, the principal architect of the Iranian Foreign Ministry's terror network, also had attended the meeting.

Instead of attacking Iranian terrorists, the Reagan administration decided to try making friends with them.

8

PRISONERS OF GOD

The Rev. Benjamin Weir overheard his guards chattering excitedly, but he could not make out what they were saying, even though he spoke excellent Arabic. Later, he figured out they had been talking about a TWA jetliner that had been hijacked in Greece and forced to land at Beirut International Airport, not far from the apartment in the city's southern suburbs where he lay chained and blindfolded. In the distance, Weir could hear the whine of jet engines.

Weir, a Presbyterian missionary who had lived in and loved Lebanon for thirty-one years, had spent the past fourteen months with a succession of young Lebanese Shiite guards. For much of the time, other hostages had been chained close by, but because they were blindfolded and forbidden to speak, the captives were seldom sure who lay just out of reach, beyond the plastic shower curtains or the crude fiberboard partitions. Four months before, Weir had whispered briefly with two other American hostages and now, in mid-June of 1985, he was certain other prisoners were nearby. For one thing, the guards frequently took his precious Bible away from him, as if it were being shared with others he could neither see nor hear.

The hostages' lives were changing for the better, but they did not know why. Until now, it had seemed that their captors didn't much care whether they lived or died. In the months since they had been snatched one by one from the streets of Beirut, all of them had endured endless hours of quiet desperation punctuated by intervals of stark terror, usually when they were bound and shoved into cars to be shuttled from one prison to another or when one of the guards pulled the trigger of his pistol on an empty chamber.

Then, suddenly and without explanation, a doctor appeared and wrote prescriptions—dyazide for high blood pressure and terramycin for eye infections. The hostages were permitted to take daily baths, although they had to share the same towel and the same tub of water, which put a premium on getting to the bathtub first. The guards brought flak vests and ordered the hostages to put them on and leave them on, despite the hot, humid summer weather in Beirut. One of his captors told Weir the vests had cost more than a hundred dollars apiece and had been purchased for the hostages but not for the guards. When the gunfire from Lebanon's still raging civil wars came too close, Weir and the others were led blindfolded to a room in the center of their prison, away from the danger of stray rounds.

Their captors seemed to want them alive and perhaps even well.

★   ★   ★

Over time, it would become clear that the kidnapping of Americans in Lebanon had been triggered by a ninety-minute bombing spree in Kuwait on December 12, 1983. Suicide bombers had unleashed a coordinated attack against six targets, including the American and French embassies, a huge petrochemical plant, and an apartment building housing employees of the Raytheon Corporation. The bombings had been a replay of the suicide attacks against the Americans and French in Lebanon two months before—even to using explosives packed around gas cylinders to enhance the force of the blast. This time, fortunately, the results had been far less horrendous. Five people had been killed and eighty-six injured. Almost immediately, the Kuwaitis had arrested seventeen men in connection with the attacks, fourteen of them members of an Iranian-backed group called al-Dawa which had its headquarters in Tehran. The other three were Lebanese followers of Sheik Fadlallah and Hezbollah. One of the three was the brother of a woman married to the rising young Lebanese Shiite terrorist Imad Mugniyah, who at the age of twenty-five already had earned a reputation as Hezbollah's most feared enforcer.

Family ties were everything in Lebanon, and Mugniyah was determined to free his brother-in-law in Kuwait. As the Kuwaitis prepared to try the Dawa prisoners, Mugniyah and his Hezbollah cell had begun snatching Americans off the streets of Beirut. Their first victim was Frank Regier, a professor at the American University of Beirut, kidnapped on February 10, 1984, the day before the trial opened in Kuwait.

The second was Jeremy Levin, a reporter for the Cable News Network, taken on March 7. The third was William Buckley, the CIA station chief in Beirut, who was kidnapped March 16. In short order, Mugniyah had grabbed three Americans, one each for his brother-in-law and the other two Lebanese prisoners in Kuwait. When rival Shiite militiamen found Regier and freed him, Mugniyah promptly restocked his hostage pool by seizing Reverend Weir. Mugniyah's terrorists did not grab another American for eight months, until after another attempt to free the Kuwaiti prisoners, this time by hijacking a Kuwaiti jetliner to Tehran, had failed to produce results. Some American intelligence analysts thought that was more than coincidence.

Benjamin Weir had read about the Kuwaiti bombings and the trial of the suspected terrorists before he was kidnapped, but he had not linked them to his own predicament until one of his guards gave him a pen and paper and told him to copy down a message. "To his Eminence, the Prince of Kuwait," it began, going on to explain that whatever happened to the seventeen prisoners in Kuwait would happen to Weir. If they were executed, he would be executed. If they were freed, he would be freed. "Here for the first time was the reason for my kidnapping," Weir later wrote. He was marched into a room and told to read the message before a video camera. Later, after he'd been returned to his chains, Weir heard someone else reading in the next room. He assumed other hostages were making similar appeals.

As the days slid into weeks and the weeks into months, Weir stole occasional glimpses of the world outside. Reaching to the limit of his chain, he peeked through a window and looked westward toward the snow-covered Lebanon mountains where well-to-do Beirutis went skiing. From one of his cells, he could see the ruins of an ancient Roman temple. He was in Baalbek, in the heart of the Bekaa Valley, in a villa next to the Sheik Abdullah Barracks, headquarters for Hezbollah and the Iranian Revolutionary Guards. He was certain that his captors would hold hostages there only with the permission of the Iranians.

Occasionally, Weir could hear antiaircraft guns on a nearby hilltop firing at what he assumed were Israeli reconnaissance planes. Weir didn't know it, but he and the other hostages did not have to worry about dying in an Israeli air raid. The United States had quietly asked the Israelis to refrain from hitting Hezbollah strongholds in the Bekaa Valley for fear that the hostages might be there. The hostages were valuable to Hezbollah in more ways than one.

★ ★ ★

The hostages' plight, and their country's inability to end it, made a mockery of Ronald Reagan's vision of a world made safe for Americans. During a meeting with his foreign policy advisers before he took office in 1981, Reagan had recalled that during the Manchurian War between Japan and China in the 1930s, Americans had been able to cross both sides' lines simply by wearing an American flag. He was determined to restore the respect for the United States that had made it possible for Americans to travel virtually anywhere without fear. It was dubious history, which played more to emotions than intellect, but that was Ronald Reagan, a man of images and instincts, vignettes and visions.

One of his more powerful visions, one that had helped him defeat Jimmy Carter, was of a world in which terrorist thugs cowered at the prospect of American retaliation. On January 29, 1981, the President had been asked at a press conference whether he was prepared to take action to back up his tough talk about "swift and effective retribution" against terrorists. "People have gone to bed in some of these countries that have done these things to us in the past confident that they can go to sleep, wake up in the morning, and the United States wouldn't have taken any action. . . . Anyone who does these things—violates our rights—in the future is not going to be able to go to bed with that confidence."

If anything, however, Imad Mugniyah was sleeping better with three American hostages in his pocket. Not only had the United States failed to free the hostages or to retaliate for their seizure, it also had asked Israel to exercise restraint. The inconsistency between rhetoric and reality seemed to bother neither Congress nor the press. The hostages were few in number, and more importantly they were all but invisible to the American public.

★　★　★

One hostage, however, was anything but invisible to his colleagues at the Central Intelligence Agency or to his boss, William Casey. By volunteering for Beirut, William Buckley had made himself a hero to Casey. Buckley's kidnapping had summoned up the CIA director's memories of his own experiences running secret agents behind the lines in Europe during World War II.

Buckley's performance in Beirut, however, had been less than exemplary. To the consternation of his colleagues, he had failed to observe basic security precautions. He had lived at the end of a cul-de-sac, and he had gone to work at the same time and by the same route each morning. So many of the CIA's Lebanese agents vanished or turned up dead on the heels of his capture that U.S. analysts concluded Buckley had been carrying his list of CIA agents with him on the morning he was taken. For the second time in a year, CIA operations in Lebanon ground to a halt just when the United States desperately needed good intelligence.

Buckley was far more than simply the CIA station chief in Beirut. Because the United States had no embassies in Iran or Iraq and because the entire CIA network in Iran had been destroyed when the embassy in Tehran was seized, the agency's secret operations in the northern Persian Gulf region had been run out of the Beirut station. The secrets compromised by Buckley's kidnapping extended far beyond Lebanon, into the heart of the Iranian revolution itself.

To find Buckley had become the CIA's top intelligence priority in Lebanon, a hunt that led down one blind alley after another. "Beginning in 1984, when the great burst of early hostages were taken . . . we began to receive feelers," remembered Clair George, the CIA's deputy director for operations. "It is a brutal, ugly story, but people were selling information, selling hostages, selling their rings, selling their clothes, selling letters from them, trying to make money out of the hostage business." The CIA had little choice but to listen to all the sordid pitches. "In the hostage business . . . unlike many other intelligence activities, you have to follow up on your leads, as silly or as impractical or as unprofessional as they sound," George explained.

George had witnessed more than his share of brutal, ugly stories during a lifetime in the CIA's Operations Directorate. In the 1970s, he had been the station chief in Beirut when Ambassador Francis Meloy and the embassy economic counselor were kidnapped and then shot. From there, he had gone to Athens to take the place of Richard Welch, the chief of station, who had been gunned down by assassins. Just short of six feet tall and stocky, George always seemed to shout at subordinates when he was displeased, and these days he was shouting a lot.

Locating the hostages was "sort of a hit and miss activity inside the United States government, and everybody was running around doing their thing," George recalled. William Casey made a secret trip to Damascus to enlist Syria's help in finding the hostages. The American and Syrian intelligence organizations, bitter rivals in the Middle East, agreed to share some of what they knew about Imad Mugniyah and his operations, but the Syrians never produced anything of value. The administration also considered kidnapping Mugniyah, but the idea foundered on a host of legal questions, not to mention the fact that his whereabouts were almost as elusive as the hostages'.

Casey also contemplated contacting the Kuwaitis to ask if the seventeen Dawa prisoners could be released. Casey's freelance bid never got anywhere because both the CIA station chief and the American Ambassador, Anthony Quainton, who formerly had been the head of the State Department's Office for Combatting Terrorism, kept urging Washington to support the Kuwaitis' hard line. The administration did, however, ask the Kuwaitis not to execute the five Dawa prisoners, including Mugniyah's brother-in-law, who had been sentenced to death. Oliver North of the National Security Council staff—a man already famous within the bureaucracy for coming up with a hundred ideas a day, a few of them inspired but most of them bad—suggested that the United States might try to break the Dawa prisoners out of their Kuwaiti prison and offer to trade them for the hostages in Lebanon. It might even be possible, North thought, to trick Mugniyah into releasing the Americans while his brother-in-law and the other Dawa prisoners still could be retrieved and sent back to jail. The idea never even made it to a formal interagency meeting. It was easier to shoot down bad ideas than to come up with good ones.

While the Reagan administration grappled unsuccessfully with the hostage problem, the terrorists tried a new approach of their own to freeing their confederates in Kuwait. On December 3, 1984, a Kuwaiti airliner en route from Dubai to Karachi was hijacked and flown to Tehran. As the Iranian government stood idly by, the hijackers murdered two Americans, William Stanford and Charles Hegna, both of whom worked for the Agency for International Development. Sadistically wielding a lighted cigarette, the hijackers bound, beat, and tortured two other American passengers, all the while demanding the release of the Dawa prisoners.

Through it all—the kidnappings, the hijacking, the American schemes—the Dawa 17 remained in jail. Kuwait understood that the real enemy was not Imad Mugniyah but Iran, and the Kuwaitis understood, as the Reagan administration did not, the dangers of appeasing their Persian neighbor.

★   ★   ★

Although the Iran hostage crisis had helped catapult Reagan into the presidency, Iran had never been near the top of the administration's foreign policy agenda. In 1981, Iran had seemed a society on the verge of self-destruction, under attack from without by Iraq, which was killing Islamic youth by the tens of thousands, and from within by an armed resistance whose spectacular terrorist attacks had killed several senior government officials, including the chief justice and the premier. Analysts at both the CIA and the State Department noted, however, that the regime had been able to replace its fallen leaders and to persevere in the face of all enemies, foreign and domestic. Despite appearances the Ayatollah had succeeded in institutionalizing his Islamic revolution.

The truth was that the United States, having lost virtually all its intelligence sources to the revolution, knew almost nothing about what was going on in Iran. Caution seemed the best policy, at least until the CIA could develop a bigger and more reliable intelligence network inside Iran. Caution, however, was not what William Casey had in mind. Casey was a man of omnivorous intelligence, a man who hungered for new ideas, who believed in taking risks, a man who had learned the craft of intelligence during the World War II days of the Office of Strategic Services when no scheme was too far-fetched. His appearance and his voice were a perfect match. Perpetually unkempt, he mumbled in a heavy New York accent that at times was all but unintelligible. But appearances were deceiving, and so was William Casey. Throughout his career, he had been a corner-cutter, a trimmer, a clever man whose penchant for action was stronger than his scruples. As Director of Central Intelligence, he was determined to be one of the architects of the Reagan administration's foreign policy, not a mere technocrat who decided how many spy satellites the United States needed.

Frequently he found himself at odds with much of the intelligence bureaucracy and especially with those CIA officers who had suffered through the traumatic exposés of the seventies and who were determined never to be called rogue elephants again. Increasingly, Casey had begun to ignore the cautionary notes sounded by the professionals, especially his own deputies, first Bob Inman and then John McMahon, and to rely instead on a handful of upwardly mobile aides who shared his enthusiasm for high-risk, high-gain covert operations.

Inman, who looked and acted like the whiz kid of American intelligence, resigned in 1982 and left McMahon to try to ride herd on Casey. With white hair and a round Irish mug that flushed beet red when his temper flared or when he laughed hard, McMahon looked more like an affable bartender or a stereotypical New York cop than a veteran CIA officer. Just turning fifty-three when he took over the second-highest job in the American intelligence community, he took himself and his work very seriously. He tried to balance his loyalties between the Agency and its director, once arranging for Casey to receive a prestigious intelligence award while at the same time attempting to put the brakes on Casey's riskier schemes. Some of Casey's friends told the CIA director he should fire McMahon and find a deputy who shared his zest for covert action, but Casey would not hear of it. He knew that if McMahon was a bit of a goody-two-shoes, he was also popular on Capitol Hill, where the CIA needed all the friends it could get.

In 1981, Casey had convinced the President to approve a modest amount of "non-lethal" covert aid to Iranian exile groups in an effort to unify the moderate opposition into an alternative government. From the beginning, some officials had qualms about the program, which was based on the dubious premise that the mullahs could not survive. When a CIA operations officer named Chuck Cogan brought a copy of the secret plan to the State Department, Assistant Secretary of State Veliotes was skeptical.

I don't know enough about the situation. Do you? he asked Cogan.

Cogan, a veteran covert operator with a reputation for doing his job well and by the book, didn't answer. All he said was: Casey wants this.

The CIA put the plan on hold for a few months while it sought to learn more about developments in Iran. But the Agency came up with almost no new information and President Reagan signed the finding in the spring with no significant changes.

As part of the program, the CIA planned to finance a radio station in Turkey and to provide aid to a royalist faction led by the late Shah's twin sister, Princess Ashraf, and to two paramilitary groups, one led by Rear Adm. Ahmad Madani, the former commander of the Shah's navy, and the other by Gen. Bahram Aryana, who had been the Ayatollah's first Defense Minister.

The plan got off to an inauspicious start. The CIA wanted the exiles to kick off their campaign against the Khomeini regime early in 1982 with an announcement that they had formed a unified opposition front, but the idea of a public declaration was scrubbed after the exile factions began bragging to one another that they had the backing of the CIA. "I think we've had some experience that the words 'Iranians' and 'confidentiality' are mutually exclusive," Veliotes said later. The CIA payments to exiles went ahead anyway, and the experience, unfortunately, was quickly forgotten.

Another potential path to renewed influence inside Iran had been obvious, and Israel, which also mourned the fall of the Shah, had been the first to try it. In the fall of 1980, with Iran scouring the world for the military equipment to beat back the Iraqi invaders, Israel began selling the Ayatollah spare tires for American-made F-4 Phantom jets. When Jimmy Carter found out about it, he sent Ambassador Samuel

Lewis to protest, and Menachem Begin promised to stop any Israeli arms sales to Iran as long as the Americans were held hostage at the embassy in Tehran. But Begin also argued that when the crisis ended, Israel and the United States would have to cultivate friends in Iran.

Even before the hostages were home or Ronald Reagan had taken office, Menachem Meron, the defense attaché at the Israeli Embassy in Washington, had asked Morris Amitay, head of the powerful American Israel Public Affairs Committee, to sound out the incoming national security adviser Richard Allen about the new administration's attitude toward Israeli shipments of military spare parts to Iran. According to Amitay, Allen responded to the feeler by saying, Tell your friend you told me about it and I heard what you said. As Allen later insisted, that was something less than an endorsement, but Amitay interpreted it as "a wink and a nod." He told Meron, If you ask me what this means, to me it's a go-ahead—an amber light.

As it had demonstrated in its 1982 invasion of Lebanon, Israel did not stop at yellow lights. Moshe Arens, Israel's Ambassador to the United States, would later claim his government had received permission to sell arms to Iran from "almost the highest levels" of the Reagan administration. In fact, American policy had not been nearly so definitive as that. Secretary of State Haig had discussed the subject with Israeli Defense Minister Ariel Sharon, and while he had never approved arms sales to Iran, his responses had been so artfully phrased that Sharon could interpret them almost any way he wanted. Only the Defense Department and the Joint Chiefs of Staff had stood four square against allowing arms to make their way to the Iranians. The chiefs had argued that even a passive policy of turning a blind eye to arms shipments "would intensify the war with Iraq" and "would be perceived by the moderate Arab states as an action directly counter to their interests." Despite that warning, the administration had decided that to do nothing was the best policy. On July 21, 1981, the Senior Interdepartmental Group on Iran had met and concluded that "U.S. efforts to discourage third country transfers of non-U.S. origin arms would have only a marginal effect on the conduct and outcome of the [Iran-Iraq] war, but could increase opportunities for the Soviets to take advantage of Iran's security concerns and to persuade Iran to accept Soviet military assistance."

That same month, the Iranian Ministry of Defense had signed a contract for $132 million worth of American-made arms with Israeli arms dealer Yaacov Nimrodi, who had once been the Israeli military attaché in Tehran. Only after a chartered Argentinian plane carrying U.S.-made arms to Iran had gone off course and crashed—or had been shot down —in the Soviet Union had the rest of the U.S. government begun to suspect what was going on behind its back.

Casey's covert operations and Israel's secret arms sales bore no fruit. Admiral Madani retired in Europe; the CIA cut back its support for the exiles and their radio station; and Haig finally told the Israelis in no uncertain terms to stop selling arms to Iran. As the debacle in Lebanon deepened with the slaughter of the Marines, American policy toward the Islamic republic lay moribund, a feckless combination of neglect and contempt which ignored the strategic importance of Iran and the danger its revolutionary acolytes posed to Americans.

Finally, on January 13, 1984, just one month before the Marines' ignominious retreat from Beirut, Geoffrey Kemp, the Mideast expert on the NSC staff, sent a memo on Iran to his boss, national security adviser Robert McFarlane. In it, Kemp suggested it was time for the United States to reassess its policy toward Iran in light of the intelligence which indicated the Iranians had sponsored the attack on the Marines. Kemp argued that the Khomeini regime was a menace to American interests, a threat to the West's supply of Persian Gulf oil, and a danger to Saudi Arabia and the moderate sheikdoms of the Gulf. He proposed that the CIA revive its covert action program against Iran, and he offered the names of some exiles who claimed that with American financial assistance they could exploit divisions within the Islamic republic and begin to reverse the revolution.

McFarlane was receptive. The newly installed national security adviser believed the administration was not prepared for the succession struggle that inevitably would follow the Ayatollah's death, and he was worried that the Soviets might seize the inside track. Nobody, least of all Ronald Reagan, wanted to see a pro-Soviet state sitting atop the Persian Gulf oil fields, next door to Soviet-occupied Afghanistan.

The Kremlin's interest in Iran was undeniable, and although the Iranian revolutionaries claimed they hated both superpowers equally, they seemed to chant "Death to America" with much greater frequency and fervor than they shouted "Death to the Soviet Union." The United States, after all, had backed the Shah almost to the end, armed his military and helped train the hated SAVAK, the Shah's secret police. Still, the Soviet Union seemed no better positioned than the United States to influence events in Iran. Without Soviet weapons, Iraq's invasion of Iran would not have been possible. Moreover, the Communist party in Iran, the Tudeh Party, had barely survived the revolution, and a purge in the spring of 1983 had all but wiped it out. A Soviet official in Tehran had defected to the British with details of Moscow's links to the Tudeh Party, and the CIA had passed the intelligence back to the Iranian government, which knew exactly what to do with it. Some two hundred suspected Communists were executed, most of the balance of the Tudeh leadership was thrown in jail, and eighteen Soviet diplomats were expelled from Iran. By the end of 1983, the Soviets' ability to expand their influence in Iran was all but nonexistent, especially given the historic animosity between Persians and Russians and the even sharper conflict between the theocrats in Tehran and the atheists in Moscow. But the Reagan administration would never take so complacent a view of the Soviet threat.

Just as the administration had been drawn to Lebanon and Libya by fear of Soviet inroads, so it was dragged into the morass of Iranian politics by the desire to keep the Russians out. It was another of the paradoxes of the Reagan years that while the President regularly consigned Communism to the ash heap of history and celebrated its dismal record both at home and abroad, he and his advisers continued to behave as if Marxism-Leninism was still on the march around the globe. When the emotional issue of the hostages became intertwined with the administration's determination to resist Soviet expansionism, when the war against terrorism merged with the war against Communism, the Reagan administration went haywire, as if its circuits had overloaded. The bad habits the administration had acquired during the bitter experience in Lebanon—the disregard for the opinions of the intelligence community, the resentment of the Pentagon's reluctance to act, the excessive deference to Israel, the detachment of the President himself, and the growing penchant of CIA director Casey and a few members of the NSC staff to take matters into their own hands—combined to produce disaster.

★   ★   ★

On December 3, 1984, kidnappers struck again, seizing Peter Kilburn, a librarian at the American University of Beirut. Kilburn, U.S. intelligence concluded, was grabbed by a group of thugs who hoped to sell him to the highest bidder. He was chosen, it seemed, because he had picked a Christian over two Shiites for a job in the university library. A month later, Imad Mugniyah abducted Father Lawrence Martin Jenco, the head of the Catholic Relief Services in Beirut.

In an effort to coordinate the hunt for the hostages, the administration established a Hostage Locating Task Force, which included representatives from CIA, DIA, NSA, FBI, the State Department, the Drug Enforcement Administration, the Customs Service, the Immigration and

Naturalization Service, and even the Commerce Department. The task force held weekly meetings, but all too often there was nothing to report. Then, six weeks into 1985, the administration got a break.

★   ★   ★

One winter morning, Benjamin Weir and Lawrence Jenco both were awakened by the shouts of obviously excited guards. "It was clear from the confusion that [a] hostage was not in the room anymore," Weir later wrote. "He had escaped." Peeking from behind his blindfold, Jenco saw two blankets tied in a knot on a mat where CNN correspondent Jeremy Levin had slept. He marked the date by scratching its significance in a tile: "February 14, Feast of St. Valentine's Day."

Without his glasses, Jeremy Levin made his way from his prison in a villa adjacent to the Sheik Abdullah Barracks to a Syrian Army checkpoint about a mile away. He courageously tried to lead a Syrian patrol back to free the strangers he called "my brothers," but without his glasses he couldn't tell where he was, much less where he had been. Giving up his search, he was taken to Damascus where he was released to the American ambassador, William Eagleton.

For the first time, the Reagan administration knew where the hostages were—or at least where they had been. At the American hospital at Weisbaden, West Germany, Levin's photographic memory thrilled his debriefers. He had been held in ten different places, but his description of the villa from which he'd escaped was precise. He knew the layout of the building, and he remembered the approximate number of guards who manned it. He also reported that William Buckley was ill. McFarlane and Casey wanted to launch a rescue mission at once. With the help of a computer, intelligence analysts used overhead reconnaissance photographs to draw side views of the building, which would be helpful in devising a plan of attack.

Once again, McFarlane remembered, the Pentagon was reluctant to act. Both Defense Secretary Weinberger and General Vessey, the chairman of the Joint Chiefs of Staff, warned that Levin's information could not be confirmed and already was out of date. Given the concentration of armed Hezbollah terrorists and Iranian Revolutionary Guards around the Sheik Abdullah Barracks, not to mention the Syrians and their antiaircraft missiles, a rescue mission would require a huge force and was likely to cause numerous casualties. Weinberger and Vessey were right to be cautious. The hostages were moved long before any rescue mission could have been launched. Laundry disappeared from the roof of their villa, suggesting to American photoanalysts that the building had been vacated. A rescue mission would have been a replay of the 1970 Son Tay operation in which a specially trained force descended on a North Viet-namese POW camp only to find all the prisoners gone.

In fact, on the evening of the day Jeremy Levin escaped, Reverend Weir was taken out of the villa, shoved into a car, driven a very short distance, and led into an underground cell which contained only a bed, a bowl, and a spoon, with a bare lightbulb overhead. After about an hour, Weir was shoved into another vehicle, which drove through rain and sleet for forty-five minutes before depositing him in a modest apartment. The following night he was moved again. Father Jenco, too, was moved out of the villa next to the Sheik Abdullah Barracks. Leaving his glasses behind, he was stuffed in the trunk of a car for an hour and a half and delivered to a house he later concluded was an abandoned summer home in the mountains. "That was the first time I feared for my life," he later recalled.

The hostages were together again, this time in a large, bare room with paper covering the windows and guards sleeping at one end. The next morning, the guards set to work constructing little stalls for the hostages out of lumber and fiberboard. Weir could hear children playing just outside. The guards told him not to cough or even clear his throat, and they warned Jenco not to peek through the cracks in the crude partitions.

That afternoon, Weir tried to make contact with the hostage he could hear in the next stall. My name is Ben Weir, a Protestant pastor. Who are you? he whispered.

Back came another whisper: Lawrence Martin Jenco, Catholic priest.

The two men began to pray for one another, and for the other hostages they sensed were nearby. The next day, from a distant stall, Jenco and Weir heard another whisper: I am Buckley . . . William Buckley. Who are you?

Shortly afterwards, Jenco was wrapped like a mummy and dumped in the trunk of a car again. Guards stuffed a cloth in his mouth and put tape over it, but when the others weren't looking, one of the younger guards, whom Jenco later recalled was "a gentle, kind man," ripped off the tape and pulled out the rag. When Jenco finally was able to lift his blindfold enough to look at his latest prison, he noticed a yellow, waxy, conical object which was connected to some haphazard electrical wiring. One of his guards explained that the building had been rigged with explosives and added that if the Syrians or the Americans tried to rescue the hostages, he and his comrades would detonate the explosives, killing themselves along with their prisoners. We couldn't care less, the guard told Jenco.

Benjamin Weir had been moved into the same prison. He noticed the explosives, too. Desperate to stop the guards from blowing up the building, Weir waited for his chance and peeled back the paper from a window. In the distance, he could see two men trying to start a car. He yelled for help. One of them paused a moment, then went back to his chore. A guard stormed in and beat Weir, kicking him and threatening to break his arms and legs. When he was finished, he taped Weir's arms behind his back and chained his feet to the wall.

In mid-March, Jenco recalled, he was moved to still another prison, this one in Beirut, this time with a black plastic bag over his head. For weeks, he was chained in a closet that was about 2 feet deep and 6 feet wide. He could stand up and "you could basically lie on your back," but he was never allowed to shower or shave or brush his teeth. Spring was coming to Lebanon, and Jenco could hear the birds outside. Peeking through a crack in the door, he could see a new hostage, Terry Anderson, an Associated Press correspondent, chained hand and foot to a squeaky bed. For two weeks, Jenco recalled, Anderson remained "in a trauma," unaware that another prisoner was nearby. "He got mad at the bed every time it squeaked," Jenco remembered.

Finally, Jenco's captors removed the bag from his head to cut his hair. Standing behind him, one of the guards cuffed Jenco on the side of the head, then asked if the priest knew why he'd been hit. When Jenco said no, the guard explained: You looked. Later, he was struck again when he hid his spoon under his mattress in an attempt to keep it clean.

In late April, Jenco was moved again, this time to an apartment belonging to one of his guards, a young Shiite who was nicknamed Haj and who sometimes entertained guests with chicken dinners while his prisoners were chained in the next room. Blindfolded, Jenco was shackled to a wall. Another hostage was chained to a bed 2 feet away behind a plastic shower curtain. Whenever his neighbor pulled at his chains, Jenco awakened. "It was very annoying," Jenco recalled.

Jenco shared Haj's apartment with both Terry Anderson and William Buckley. "The guards treated Buckley quite well," Jenco recalled. He saw no sign that Buckley had been tortured. Indeed, he recalled that the guards sometimes were more considerate of Buckley than they were of their other prisoners. Sometimes, Jenco remembered, Buckley would remind a guard named Said that he owed him a couple of favors. Sometimes the CIA man talked with his young captors about America and other places he'd lived.

But when Buckley's health began deteriorating that spring, his captors did nothing to help him. Pictures and videotapes of Buckley released by Hezbollah showed a steady deterioration in his condition, suggesting to

CIA analysts that he was being tortured or else had fallen seriously ill and was being neglected. Casey and Oliver North decided Buckley had been tortured, and North later gave congressional investigators an especially gripping account of his torture. Other officials at the CIA, the State Department, and the FBI said that although Buckley's condition was clearly deteriorating, the skimpy evidence didn't indicate why.

Before and after snapshots of Buckley were posted on the walls of the Hostage Locating Task Force's offices at the CIA, mute testimony to the administration's helplessness. The knowledge of Buckley's condition tore at CIA director Casey, at the agency's deputy director John McMahon, at everyone who knew about it. Buckley's fate was "an issue on Mr. Casey's, Mr. McMahon's, and my plate every day of the week of every month of that horror," Clair George later testified. "I think the emotionalism of the hostage issue throughout the entire affair, with Bill Casey, with the President, with me—people didn't want to stop. They wanted to get the hostages, and it led them to do and run operations that are now after the fact foolish."

★ ★ ★

William Dwyer and Frank Tarallo, two agents for the Drug Enforcement Administration, came up with a Lebanese Druze informant who claimed he was in contact with someone who could deliver the hostages—for a price, of course. The members of the hostage task force were skeptical. The minutes of a March 6 task force meeting recorded the reaction: "We are dealing almost on a daily basis with individuals who are contacting us in order to 'sell' information about the hostages." But Edward Hickey, the chief of security at the White House and a neighbor of William Dwyer, was enthusiastic. "Hickey was really hot on this idea and might try to put pressure on the Agency," the minutes warned. Oliver North was hot on the idea, too.

On March 12, 1985, a member of the task force called North to talk about the "Hickey problem—Independent action," as North recorded it in one of the spiral notebooks he kept on hand. "Payoffs," North jotted down. "AmCits [American citizens] will be delivered. Fundamental decision. Do we pay ransom?" That afternoon, North discussed the problem with deputy national security adviser John Poindexter, and they agreed to proceed cautiously and in secret.

"This was hocus pocus," said Clair George, the CIA's director of operations, who had assigned his own officers to investigate the DEA's informant. "We came to the decision that . . . it was a scam. No big surprise. There was nothing to get excited about. We were scammed regularly on the hostage business and others. This was a scam. . . . This is life." The DEA's own representative on the hostage task force, a cigar-smoking veteran agent of Lebanese extraction named Abe Azzam, was even more dubious. "It stunk," he said.

Azzam demanded that the two DEA agents produce some proof that their informant could deliver. The informant produced a Lebanese newspaper with Buckley's initials scrawled on it. But Buckley's middle initial was wrong, and when a secretary at the CIA who had worked with him for eight years was shown the paper, she said: Some raghead's ripped you off. The CIA then drafted a list of questions which only the hostages could answer, but the informant refused to return to Lebanon to submit the questions. Azzam threw out the newspaper and shut down the operation—or thought he did. It was hard to shut down Oliver North. On May 22, Dwyer and Tarallo reported that their source could produce the hostages if he was given $200,000 to bribe Lebanese officials and another $2 million to free the captives.

North accused Abe Azzam of being "negative" and lobbied to have him removed from the hostage task force. Operating through McFarlane and Attorney General Edwin Meese, North arranged to have Dwyer and Tarallo detached from the DEA and assigned to work full time on the hostage case. In the name of secrecy, he ordered them not to prepare any written reports of what they were doing.

If the DEA and CIA didn't have the nerve to finance the operation, North would find someone who did. With McFarlane's approval, he called H. Ross Perot, the Texas billionaire he had tapped in 1981 for half a million dollars to aid in the search for the kidnapped Gen. James Dozier in Italy. Perot immediately agreed to pay the informant to come up with concrete proof that he could deliver the hostages. He sent $200,000 and told North he would provide more if needed. Dwyer and Tarallo knew that DEA rules prohibited them from handling funds not appropriated by Congress, so Dwyer recruited his brother to carry the cash. North also prevailed on Adolfo Calero, a leader of the Nicaraguan contras, to fork over $50,000 worth of traveler's checks to serve as "walking around money" for Dwyer and Tarallo. Calero took the money from a $32 million contribution which Saudi Arabia secretly had made to the contras. It was the first time North dipped into one of his secret projects to help finance another. "Ollie North always sort of implied when we were talking about the hostages that if I ever thought that I needed money and that policy dictated it, but I didn't want to take it from CIA funds because they were congressionally controlled, he could get money," said CIA operations director Clair George.

On June 1, the two DEA agents brought their informant to meet North. According to North's notes of the meeting, the informant said all the hostages were alive and had been moved near the Syrian border. North wrote a memo to McFarlane reporting that Tarallo "believes that the hostages can be bribed free for $1 million apiece." North had solved the fundamental question of "do we pay ransom" by calling it bribery. The ever-resourceful Marine proposed renting a yacht for transferring the hostages at sea and a safehouse on Cyprus "as a temporary holding location in the event that all hostages are not recovered in the first attempt." McFarlane went to Meese and to the President, who approved North's plan.

The informant was unable to produce his "contacts" for a scheduled meeting in Cyprus, but that did not deter North, Dwyer, and Tarallo. Between June and September, Tarallo, Dwyer, and Dwyer's brother cashed three of Adolfo Calero's traveler's checks for a total of $25,300, and the two agents would continue to pursue the case for another year before it finally collapsed. "Ollie was grandstanding," said Abe Azzam of the DEA. "He saw it was the only thing going and he was throwing a Hail Mary pass and hoping he could get all the hostages standing in front of the White House wrapped in a ribbon." At the CIA, Clair George, who also had opposed the operation from the start, was more philosophical. "If someone decides in the White House that they do not like my opinion on an operation . . . they can do it," he said.

★　★　★

While the two DEA agents were trying to deliver the hostages, another operation, this one concocted by the CIA and not the White House, met with disaster. Late in 1984, CIA director Casey persuaded the President to approve a $10 million to $15 million program to train Lebanese intelligence officers in counterterrorist tactics in hopes that local agents could do a better job of penetrating, and perhaps attacking, the tightly knit Shiite cells. It was, everybody recognized, risky business. In the past, similar proposals had been rejected. In 1983, when two Marine officers suggested giving sniper training to selected Lebanese Army units, the notion was quickly vetoed by other officers who wondered how they could be sure some of the Lebanese wouldn't start sniping at the Marines at Beirut Airport. But now, with Buckley in captivity and with no real prospect of locating, much less freeing, the hostages, the administration was more willing to take a chance.

McFarlane later said he warned Casey that Simon Cassis, the head of Lebanese intelligence, was not to be trusted and had provided bad information during the fighting for Souk al Gharb in 1983. John McMahon, the CIA's deputy director; Clair George, the operations director; and Robert Oakley, the State Department's director of counterterrorism, all worried that since most of Cassis's operatives were Christians, they might use American aid to pursue their private vendetta against the Shiites. Nevertheless, Casey was determined to get his man back or at least to try taking the war to the terrorists who had seized Buckley. CIA officers and agents located and surveyed all of Sheik Fadlallah's half dozen residences in south Beirut and the agency provided communications and other specialized equipment to Lebanese intelligence officers. CIA officers also complained to their Lebanese counterparts that Sheik Fadlallah was a meddlesome priest, which deliberately or not left some of the Lebanese with the impression that Washington, or at least Langley, Virginia, wanted Fadlallah eliminated.

In late February, William Buckley's replacement as the CIA station chief in Beirut sent a cable warning that the Lebanese were proving difficult to control. CIA deputy director John McMahon seized upon the warning as proof that he had been right to question the plan and as another opportunity to pull the plug on it. Before he could, however, Cassis's operatives set off a bomb outside one of Fadlallah's apartment buildings near the Bir al Abed mosque in south Beirut. Fadlallah escaped injury, but eighty people died. Hezbollah retaliated against the Lebanese it thought had planted the bomb, killing eleven and sending others fleeing for their lives. The CIA flatly denied that anyone it had trained was involved. The chief of the CIA's Near East operations division, Bert Dunn, assured McMahon the bomb had gone off before the CIA had trained any of the new Lebanese recruits. But when *The Washington Post* linked the agency's covert training plan to the bombing, the damage was done. Three months later, just after he dumped Navy diver Robert Stethem's body off TWA Flight 847, the hijacker called Castro screamed: "Did you forget the Bir al Abed massacre?"

Despite the disaster at Bir al Abed, Casey, McFarlane, and Shultz had lost none of their enthusiasm for "proactive" counterterrorist measures. Within six weeks of the bombing, both the national security adviser and the CIA director gave speeches vowing, in identical language, that the United States "cannot and will not abstain from forcible action to prevent, preempt, or respond to terrorist acts where conditions merit the use of force. Many countries, including the United States, have the specific forces and capabilities we need to carry out operations against terrorist groups." Having the forces was one thing; using them was another, and the Bir al Abed bombing did nothing to make proactive measures any more palatable to Weinberger or the Joint Chiefs.

★   ★   ★

The hostages' families were growing increasingly frustrated. Over the Christmas holidays, President Reagan sent Benjamin Weir's wife, Carol, a telegram saying he and First Lady Nancy were praying for them. Carol Weir appreciated the expressions of concern, but she wanted results, and she decided the only way to get them was to take her case to the public. In March 1985, she held a press conference and called her husband's kidnapping a cry of desperation from Shiites who had been radicalized by their own suffering, some of which she said had been caused by America's involvement in Lebanon and its support of Israel. She ended the press conference by summoning the dread spirit of the Iran hostage crisis. "Do I have to wait 444 days for Ben's release?" she asked.

After that, Secretary of State Shultz agreed to meet with Carol Weir for the first time. The session did not go well. When she suggested that the United States should negotiate with the kidnappers, Shultz replied that such people heard voices from God and were deranged. He was angered by her suggestion that the kidnappers had legitimate grievances. The meeting ended with Shultz repeating that the administration's policy was not to make concessions to terrorists.

As Shultz and Carol Weir talked past each other, a few blocks away at the White House Oliver North and deputy national security adviser John Poindexter were discussing the DEA's scheme to ransom the hostages for $1 million apiece. North's handwritten notes of the meeting that day record what was fast becoming the norm: "Nobody at State knows." That same afternoon, again without anybody at State knowing, North met with a consultant to the NSC staff named Michael Ledeen, and an even more controversial scheme to free the hostages began taking shape.

★   ★   ★

Ledeen's proposal was modest enough. He wanted to make a trip to Israel on behalf of national security adviser Robert McFarlane. A European intelligence officer, recently returned from Iran, had told Ledeen the situation there was more fluid than the United States realized and had suggested comparing notes with the Israelis.

The issue of what to do about Iran had been inching its way through the bureaucracy ever since January of 1984 when NSC staffer Geoffrey Kemp had sent McFarlane his memo urging a reassessment of the administration's policy toward the Ayatollah. The only thing that had come of the deliberations was a tightening of restrictions on American exports to Iran and a campaign, dubbed "Operation Staunch," to halt the flow of arms to Iran. For officials concerned about the almost total absence of American contacts and influence in Iran, the administration's policy seemed to be going in exactly the wrong direction.

A Special National Intelligence Estimate on Iran had been completed in October 1984, but it had found little new under the sun. According to the estimate, the United States had "no influential contacts" in the Iranian government, little hope of establishing any, and only a slim chance of enhancing its position through covert action. By December, the State Department had distilled the report into a draft National Security Decision Directive, but it, too, had been a sterile document. It merely had directed the bureaucracy to be prepared to exploit any opportunities that might arise and had reaffirmed the existing policy of stopping the flow of arms to Iran. The entire effort had "produced no ideas which any of us involved in it considered to be of great value in terms of significantly affecting our posture in the region," said Howard Teicher of the NSC staff.

When Michael Ledeen walked into North's cluttered office on the afternoon of March 16, 1985, the Reagan administration was desperate for new ideas on Iran and the hostages. If the bureaucracy couldn't come up with any, maybe the Israelis could. Donald Fortier, the NSC's senior director for politico-military affairs, sent a note to McFarlane saying that while he disapproved of using a consultant as the primary channel for working with the Israelis, he thought Ledeen could usefully carry two messages to Prime Minister Shimon Peres. Wrote Fortier: "1) The White House feels it is essential to begin to develop a more serious and coordinated strategy for dealing with the Iranian succession crisis—a crisis that is almost certain to turn on outside involvement of one kind or another; and 2) we would like his [Peres's] ideas on how we could cooperate more effectively. The last point is a hard one for us to ask our intelligence community to communicate, since we suspect they may be part of the problem."

Ledeen traveled to Israel in May, and Peres told him he would be happy to cooperate with the United States in developing better intelligence on Iran. According to Ledeen, Peres also asked him to query McFarlane on whether the administration would permit Israel to ship a small quantity of artillery pieces or shells to Iran. Peres's timing was far better than he possibly could have known.

On May 17, Graham Fuller, the CIA's National Intelligence Officer for the Near East, sent William Casey a five-page memo painting a dire picture of events in Iran. "In bluntest terms," Fuller wrote, "the Khomeini regime is faltering and may be moving toward a moment of truth. We will soon have a struggle for succession. The U.S. has no cards to play; the USSR has many. . . . Our urgent need is to develop a broad spectrum of policy moves designed to give us some leverage in the race for influence in Tehran."

Fuller, short, rumpled, with a fringe of long hair which made him look like a medieval monk, was known in the intelligence community as an agent provocateur, a man who liked to write unconventional papers and was not afraid to take risks in his analysis. He concluded his memo by writing that the most sensible way to cultivate influence in Tehran was to allow friendly nations to sell modest quantities of arms to the Iranians, enough to convince them that they had alternatives to Soviet aid, but not enough to give them a decisive edge in the war against Iraq.

Casey hand-delivered Fuller's memo to Secretary of State Shultz, who passed it to his top aides. Both the Near East bureau and the intelligence bureau wrote scathing denunciations of the memo. Morton Abramowitz, the director of the Bureau of Intelligence and Research, was appalled by what he considered a senior intelligence officer's attempt to write a policy recommendation instead of an intelligence assessment. But the analysts who prospered under Casey were those whose analysis usually supported Ronald Reagan's policies. The director of Central Intelligence himself frequently abandoned any pretense of providing unvarnished opinions and concentrated instead on trying to make foreign policy.

Working with Howard Teicher at the NSC, Fuller outlined his ideas for an opening to Iran in a draft of a formal intelligence estimate. When it was circulated to the rest of the intelligence community, the draft met with objections from every agency, including the DIA, which was not known for underplaying the Soviet menace. Intelligence analysts at the State Department circulated a memo containing a strong rebuttal of Fuller's theory that Iran was about to collapse and the Soviets were preparing to move in. The memo noted that while relations had begun thawing at the beginning of 1985, they had plunged back into the deep freeze in April, when Iraq began attacking Iranian cities with Soviet-supplied Scud missiles. In other words, the State Department memo said, Fuller's new estimate already was behind the curve. But when the National Foreign Intelligence Board met to debate the new estimate, Casey resisted the footnotes the State Department and the DIA tried to insert and only minor changes were made in Fuller's and Teicher's draft.

The estimate was published on May 20 under the title "Iran—Prospects for Near-Term Instability." According to this now official Special National Intelligence Estimate, Iran's leaders had concluded that "improvement of relations with the USSR is now essential to Iranian interests. . . . The United States is unlikely to be able to directly influence Iranian events, given its current lack of contact or presence in Iran. European states and other friendly states—including Turkey, Pakistan, China, Japan, and even Israel—can provide the next most valuable presence or entrée in Iran to help protect Western interests. The degree to which some of these states can fill a military gap for Iran will be a critical measure of the West's ability to blunt Soviet influence."

Donald Fortier sent a message to McFarlane on the NSC's computer network calling Fuller's estimate "one of the best yet," and adding, "I think the Israeli option is one we have to pursue, even though we may have to pay a certain price for the help."

★　★　★

But as usual the terrorists were moving faster than the administration. In late May, Father Jenco recalled, the hostages were joined by a new man—American University Hospital administrator David Jacobsen, who was kidnapped May 28. William Buckley was dying and still his captors would not lift a finger to help him, or even to ease his suffering. He was racked with vomiting and dry heaves, burning with fever, and raving with delirium. My God, Jenco heard him say, I've been through so much, why this? Mercifully, Buckley's raging fever already was transporting him to a better place than the miserable cubicle where his life was slipping from him. Once, Jenco remembered, Buckley in his delirium said politely: I'd like some poached eggs on toast.

The guards asked the newcomer Jacobsen, the hospital administrator, what to do, but they would not let him see the dying hostage. When Jacobsen told them to take the man to a doctor, they said they could not. Blindfolded, Jacobsen, Jenco, and Terry Anderson listened to William Buckley retching in his delirium until, on the night of June 3, 1985, the noise stopped. "There was just a long, long silence," Jacobsen remembered. "When you're in a small room . . . there are certain noises that are associated with death."

The next morning, Jenco asked one of the guards, named Said: How is he?

He died, Said replied. The next day, Said told Jenco he had been kidding; the other hostage was well.

Six days later, Imad Mugniyah's thugs kidnapped another American,

Thomas Sutherland, the dean of agriculture at the American University of Beirut.

★ ★ ★

After Buckley's death and the TWA hijacking, all the hostages held by Imad Mugniyah—Benjamin Weir, Father Jenco, Terry Anderson, David Jacobsen, and Thomas Sutherland—were brought together in one room for the first time. Their isolation was ending, at least for a while, although they still could not see each other because of their blindfolds. When one of his guards offered Weir a chance to watch television, he was delighted. Still blindfolded, he was led through a succession of passageways into a room and told to sit on a mattress on the floor. Then came the real surprise.

"You have a friend next to you," the guard said. "Take his hand."

Weir groped until he felt another hand. Then the guard told him to remove his blindfold. Blinking from the light, Weir saw another man with a full beard just like his own, but when the guard asked who the man was, Weir said he didn't know. Despite all the months under the same roof, neither man had seen the other's face until this moment. Still forbidden to converse with his fellow captive, Weir sat in silence watching a video cassette about Muslim prayers, all the while wondering who was sitting next to him. Then he was ordered to put his blindfold back on and he was led back to his room. He and Jenco both went to sleep pondering what had happened.

In the middle of the night, Weir was awakened and told he was going to be moved. A guard led him outside, along a walkway, and upstairs, where he was told to sit on a mattress and chained once again to the wall. The guard left. When Weir lifted his blindfold, he saw chained to the opposite wall the man with whom he had watched the videotape. In a whisper, he asked the man who he was. "Father Martin Jenco," the man replied.

It had been more than six months since Jenco had been kidnapped. "Just seeing another man's face was a gift," he remembered. As grateful as they were for human contact, Weir and Jenco could not help wondering why, all of a sudden, the guards had allowed them to be together. Weir was afraid they would be separated again, then pumped for information about one another.

He spotted a suspicious object and whispered to Jenco, "I think that this place is bugged! Look at that thing down by the wall."

After a moment, Jenco reached out, picked up the object, and examined it. Then he shrugged and said, "It's just a solid air freshener to make the room smell better."

For the first time in months, Reverend Weir and Father Jenco laughed. They laughed until their sides hurt.

The two men, who had come to Lebanon to serve the Lord and had been imprisoned by men serving Allah, prayed together and then fell asleep. When they awoke, they exercised for half an hour and wondered whether the noises they heard outside meant other hostages were nearby. By the next morning, Jenco and Weir were convinced that there were other hostages in the building. The guards were banging on the walls, perhaps bolting new rings to them in order to chain new prisoners.

One of the guards came and ordered Jenco to follow him. The priest was led into the room next door to hear confession from Terry Anderson, who had been seized four months earlier as he was returning to his apartment from a game of tennis. Jenco found Anderson deeply depressed. When he heard the journalist's confession and looked him in the eyes for the first time, both confessor and priest broke down and wept. After confessing his sins, Anderson told Jenco he had been reading the Bible to David Jacobsen, who did not have his glasses, and that they both had been pestering the guards to let all the hostages worship together. When Jenco returned to his room, he and Weir began making the same request.

Beginning in July, the hostages were allowed to hold weekly religious services in what Weir called "the church of the locked door." They were all being held in the same 10- or 12-foot-square room now, each chained to the wall. In the mornings, they propped their mattresses against the walls to make room to exercise. Anderson and Jacobsen introduced the others to their practice of taking "walks," marching rapidly in place for thirty or forty minutes in the morning and again in the afternoon. Thomas Sutherland taught the others about his academic specialities, animal husbandry and genetics. Anderson fashioned a chess set from small pieces of aluminum foil scavenged from the breakfast servings, but when he asked for a piece of cardboard to make a chessboard, the guards deliberated for days before announcing that a religious ruling had been issued. Prisoners and guards were permitted to play checkers, but not chess, even though it is a Persian game. It wasted too much of their time. Anderson next used a ballpoint pen and some empty cheese cartons to make a deck of cards. When one of the guards found the hostages playing hearts, he confiscated Anderson's deck and ripped it up. Card playing, too, was forbidden. Anderson was not one to give up easily, however. He made a pinochle deck and hid it from the guards.

About the only things the hostages had in common were their nationality and their bad luck. Anderson and Jacobsen occupied opposite ends of the political spectrum, with Jacobsen being a devout conservative. The two of them "fought constantly," said Jenco. In such close quarters, each prisoner inevitably rubbed the others the wrong way at times. When one went to the toilet, the other four would gang up and "ventilate" their feelings about him, Jenco said. But when bedtime came, the five Americans always gave each other what Jenco called "the kiss of peace."

The guards began bringing Arabic newspapers which Weir translated for the other four hostages. Anderson started studying Arabic, using the cheese cartons to make flashcards with Arabic phrases on one side and their English translations on the other. Sometimes, when the guards disagreed with Weir's translations, they would take over the teaching. Sutherland knew French and translated the occasional French-language newspaper that came the hostages' way. "We even took imaginary trips," Weir wrote. One evening, Jacobsen took his four friends to his apartment and cooked them a meal. Jenco led the group on a tour of Rome which ended at his Servite Order's house on a feast day. Sutherland led an expedition to Scotland, where he had been born, and recited lines from Robert Burns. Anderson took them to Japan.

"I believe that the guards brought us together because they saw it had a positive impact on us," Weir later wrote. "Their job was to keep us alive and healthy. The worship obviously contributed to this goal. It was also easier to manage five happy people than to control five angry or depressed prisoners." Still, some of the fifteen or twenty guards who watched over them were unpredictable. They frequently lied to the hostages about when they would be fed next, and one of the guards sometimes forced the five to march up and down the hall in lockstep, chanting, "God is great" in Arabic.

★　★　★

At the White House, Donald Fortier had set about turning the new intelligence estimate on Iran into a National Security Decision Directive (NSDD). On June 11, 1985, he and Howard Teicher submitted the first draft of the NSDD to McFarlane. First on its list of proposals was to "encourage Western allies and friends to help Iran meet its import requirements so as to reduce the attractiveness of Soviet assistance and trade offers, while demonstrating the value of correct relations with the West. This includes provision of selected military equipment as determined on a case-by-case basis." The draft NSDD listed a number of strategic goals, including establishing links to "Iranian leaders who might be receptive to efforts to improve relations with the United States" and ending the Iran-Iraq war. It never mentioned the hostages in Lebanon.

On June 17, three days after TWA Flight 847 was hijacked, McFarlane circulated the draft NSDD to Shultz, Weinberger, and Casey. Two days later, Weinberger recorded his reaction in a memo. "This is almost too absurd to comment on," he wrote. "The assumption here is 1) that Iran is about to fall and 2) we can deal with them on a rational basis. It is like asking Qaddafi over for a cozy lunch." Several days later, Shultz wrote McFarlane that the draft NSDD exaggerated the Soviets' advantage over the West in Iran and underplayed "the inherent limits on the Iranian-Soviet relationship." The proposal to permit or encourage arms sales to Iran, Shultz wrote, "is contrary to our own interests." He added, "We should not alter this aspect of our policy when groups with ties to Iran are holding U.S. hostages in Lebanon."

Casey heartily approved of the draft NSDD, particularly when intelligence picked up the fact that Hashemi Rafsanjani, the speaker of the Iranian parliament, had played a role in freeing the four TWA hostages held by Hezbollah. However, since Shultz and Weinberger, the President's two principal advisers on matters of national security, both opposed selling arms to Iran, Casey and McFarlane reluctantly abandoned their effort to redirect official U.S. policy. They had already found a way to approach the Iranians that did not require any official changes in policy.

On July 3, two days after the TWA hostages at last had been freed, David Kimche, the director general of the Israeli Foreign Ministry, met with McFarlane in the West Wing of the White House. Kimche, a former head of the Mossad station in Tehran, said some influential Iranians were growing fearful of Soviet pressure and were interested in a dialogue with the United States. The Iranians, Kimche said, had suggested that they might be able to exert some pressure on Hezbollah to release the American hostages in Lebanon, but he warned that they probably would want something in exchange. The something, Kimche told McFarlane, probably would be arms. Kimche explained that his information came from an Iranian named Manucher Ghorbanifar, a former agent of the Shah's secret police who now claimed to be an adviser to Iran's prime minister. Ghorbanifar had provided the Israelis with transcripts of taped telephone calls with the prime minister and a list of a thousand Iranian military officers and officials who allegedly sought closer ties to the United States.

McFarlane asked Casey to assess Kimche's presentation, and the CIA director personally endorsed Ghorbanifar's intelligence, apparently without bothering to check with his own operations staff. Ghorbanifar already was well known to the CIA. Five years before, the agency had tried to use him to gather intelligence on the hostages at the American Embassy in Tehran, but, as Clair George put it, his "intelligence, regardless of the subject, was inaccurate, incomplete and dishonest." In July of 1984, the CIA had given up trying to deal with Ghorbanifar and had taken the unusual step of issuing a "burn notice," warning all its officers that this man was not to be dealt with because he was a liar. "You have to work at it pretty hard . . . to get a burn notice out of the operations directorate of the CIA," Clair George said.

Ghorbanifar, who was nothing if not persistent, had kept trying to get America's attention, through a retired CIA officer, through Army intelligence, and then through the State Department. Each time he had failed, and late in 1984 Richard Murphy, the new Assistant Secretary of State for Near Eastern and South Asian Affairs, and Robert Oakley, the Department's top counterterrorism official, had dismissed a Ghorbanifar proposal to ransom the hostages as a "scam."

It didn't matter. Ghorbanifar and the Israelis had said the magic words—"hostages" and "Russians"—in the same breath. The President was obsessed with the hostages. He asked about them almost every day, usually at his morning national security briefings. Reagan had been moved to tears by his visit to Robert Stethem's grave, and he couldn't forget the anguish of Father Jenco's relatives, whom he had met in Chicago during the final days of the TWA hijacking. When McFarlane briefed him on what Kimche had said, the President was enthusiastic. He was intrigued by the strategic overtones of an opening to Iran, but, McFarlane said later, "it is very clear that his concerns here were for the return of the hostages."

On July 13, the day the President had a cancerous polyp removed from his large intestine, NSC consultant Michael Ledeen brought McFarlane another message from the Israelis. It, too, had originated with Ghorbanifar, and it said his Iranian contacts thought they could arrange the release of the hostages in exchange for 100 TOW antitank missiles. McFarlane transmitted the proposal to Secretary of State Shultz, who was en route to Australia. Shultz cabled back a recommendation for "a tentative show of interest without commitment." Almost immediately, Shultz began to have second thoughts. The State Department turned up a biographic file on Ghorbanifar which labeled him "a talented fabricator," and the conflict between what the CIA and his own department were saying about Ghorbanifar gave rise to "grave doubts about the objectivity and reliability of some of the intelligence I was getting."

The Secretary of State, to put it bluntly, was being deliberately deceived. When Samuel Lewis, the American Ambassador in Israel, got wind that Ledeen was on a "secret mission for the White House" and asked Shultz if he knew "what was going on," the Secretary of State had to confess that he did not. Demanding an explanation, Shultz received a cable from McFarlane assuring him that Ledeen's trip had been "an Israeli initiative," that Ledeen had been acting "on his own hook," and that "I am turning it off entirely."

Instead, McFarlane relayed the TOWs-for-hostages proposal to Reagan in the hospital on July 18. According to White House chief of staff Donald Regan, the President asked a few questions and then authorized McFarlane to pursue the matter. Delivering a few antitank missiles to Iranians who wanted to change their country's policies was not the same as paying off terrorists, Reagan said. He was willing to take the public heat if the effort failed.

On August 2, Israeli diplomat David Kimche returned to Washington and met with McFarlane again. The Israelis wanted to know if the United States was willing to provide weapons to help strengthen moderate factions within the Iranian military. When McFarlane said the United States was unlikely to ship arms to Iran, Kimche asked what the Reagan administration would do if Israel sold some of its American-made hardware to the Iranians. McFarlane asked why Israel would sell arms to the Ayatollah, and Kimche forthrightly replied that his country wanted to ensure a stalemate in the war with Iraq, get the United States back into Iran, and moderate Iranian policies. Israel needed to know, Kimche continued, whether the Reagan administration would sell Israel new weapons to replace any it shipped to Iran.

Well, that really isn't the issue, McFarlane replied. Israel has bought weapons from the United States for years and always will, so you don't need to ask whether you can buy more weapons.

Given the relationship between the two countries and the depth of congressional support for the Jewish state, that was a statement of fact. Still, Kimche said he needed a more concrete promise. He got it after an August 6 meeting between the President and his top advisers, when Reagan telephoned McFarlane and told him that despite strong objections from Shultz and Weinberger he would agree to replenish small amounts of American-made defensive weapons sold to Iran from Israeli stocks.

Later that month, Amiram Nir, the Israeli prime minister's new adviser on counterterrorism, came to Washington for two weeks of get-acquainted meetings. Nir, a former television reporter, was an outsider among the intelligence officers who traditionally ran Israeli counterterrorism programs, and he was eager to outflank his colleagues by forging strong links to the Reagan administration. Nir and Oliver North hit it off immediately. Their relationship paralleled the partnership one rung above them between McFarlane and Kimche. In short order, Nir began visiting Washington secretly, sometimes telephoning American officials from North's office and asking them: Don't tell my embassy I'm here.

Nir and North soon had a lot to talk about. On August 27, the Iranian central bank deposited $1.2 million in a Swiss bank account. Three days later, McFarlane asked the State Department to issue North a passport in the name of "William P. Goode" for "a sensitive operation to Europe in connection with our hostages in Lebanon." On August 20, Israel delivered ninety-six TOW missiles to Iran, and on September 4, Reginald Bartholomew, the American Ambassador to Lebanon, reported to the State Department that "North was handling an operation that would lead to the release of all seven hostages" and that a covert debriefing team had been deployed to Beirut. Brig. Gen. Carl Stiner, the head of the Joint Special Operations Command, was standing by with Delta in case the opportunity for a rescue attempt suddenly presented itself amid the last-minute maneuvering for the hostages' release.

★ ★ ★

Near the end of the first week in September, as Weir remembered events, the senior guard, the one who went by the nickname Haj, came into the hostages' cubicle, sat down on a mattress, and began talking, using Weir as an interpreter. Haj said the guards were considering whether to release one of the hostages, and he asked the five Americans to decide who should be set free. Haj explained that the freed hostage would carry a message to the U.S. government demanding that it put pressure on Kuwait to release the seventeen men imprisoned for the December 1983 bombings of the American and French embassies there. The one let go would also be expected to encourage the American public to pressure the Reagan administration to respond to the Lebanese kidnappers' demands, Haj told his captives.

The next morning, the five hostages told Haj they believed Terry Anderson, the newsman, was the best choice to carry the messages. Haj did not seem to agree, but he said little. Nothing happened for a week.

★ ★ ★

The middleman Ghorbanifar had an explanation: the ninety-six TOW missiles had been seized by the commander of the Iranian Revolutionary Guards. In what was to become a familiar ritual, Ghorbanifar explained that the "moderates" for whom the weapons had been intended wanted their TOWs before they produced any hostages. On September 14, with President Reagan's blessing, the Israelis shipped another 408 TOWs to Iran. McFarlane was told he could select any hostage except Buckley to be released. Buckley, Ghorbanifar said, was too sick to be freed. Buckley, of course, was dead.

★ ★ ★

On the evening of September 14, Haj returned, this time with another guard named Said. In Arabic, he told the blindfolded prisoners that Weir was going to be released that night.

"You mean right now?" Weir asked in Arabic.

"Yes, you will be released right now," replied Haj.

"Well, I would like to go, but are you sure I am the one who is most helpful and in need of release?" asked Weir.

"You are the one chosen," said Haj.

"If you want someone to take a message, Terry Anderson is more capable because he is a newsman and has connections," Weir protested. "If you want someone who needs to be released, I think of Father Martin, who is not in as good physical condition as I am."

"No, you are the one who is going to go," Haj declared. "You will have your hair trimmed by Said, you will take a shower, and then you will go."

"Oh God, what can I do?" exclaimed Weir, this time in English. He translated the decision to the other four, who were dumbstruck but quickly congratulated him.

"For my part, I wanted to live and return to my family; I was glad," Weir later wrote. "But at the same time I was in deep consternation. Could I do anything to bring about the release of my brothers? I doubted that and felt helpless. But there was no time to reflect."

Said trimmed Weir's beard. The fortunate hostage took a shower, put on a jogging suit and a pair of rubber slippers, and pulled a ski mask over his face. He hugged Anderson, Jacobsen, Jenco, and Sutherland. As he started down the stairs, Said shoved a fistful of notes the other hostages had written to their families into the minister's pocket. Weir was led to the rear door of a car and told to lie face down on the seat. Haj sat in front next to the driver.

As they drove, he told Weir, "You are to do two things. First, tell the American government that they are to put pressure on Kuwait for the release of the men being held here. Second, say you have been released as a sign of our good intention of solving this situation and to do it quickly and without publicity."

After about twenty minutes, Haj said, "Be ready now to get out of the car when it stops. Take off your ski mask as you step out and don't look back. You will know where you are."

When the car stopped, Weir took off his mask and climbed out. The car sped away. It was midnight, and the street was deserted. He looked around and saw he was near the American University. He was free.

★ ★ ★

Oliver North immediately arranged for Weir to be taken to a CIA safehouse in Virginia where he could be debriefed about the condition and whereabouts of William Buckley and the other hostages. But Carol Weir refused to let her husband be locked up again, even if it was by his own government. After being reunited with his family at a hotel in Norfolk, Virginia, Weir agreed to meet with CIA and FBI officials. He described how Father Jenco and the others had heard what they assumed was William Buckley's death. When his debriefers asked him to describe where he had been held and the identity of his guards, Weir balked. "I was afraid they might try to rescue the other prisoners by force, so I refused to say anything that might endanger them," Weir later explained. It didn't matter. The Shiite slums of south Beirut where Weir and the other hostages had spent the summer were a rabbit warren, and he had no idea exactly where he had been imprisoned.

When President Reagan called him from Air Force One, Weir delivered the messages Haj had given him, saying the captors expected Washington to press Kuwait for the release of the Dawa prisoners and that his freedom was intended as a gesture of good faith. Imad Mugniyah had succeeded in delivering his message directly to the President of the United States.

★ ★ ★

Another year would pass before Weir and the rest of the world learned the price the Reagan administration had paid for his freedom. Like the families of the other hostages, the Weirs had blamed the American government for doing too little to free their loved ones. In fact, the President and a handful of his aides had been doing far too much. The hijacking of TWA Flight 847 finally had given the "forgotten hostages" the visibility their relatives had been clamoring for all along, and when the administration was forced to confront the issue of the hostages, its system for making national security policy had begun to break down.

For Weir, the nightmare was over. For the President and his advisers, it was just beginning. Without realizing it, or at least without admitting it, even to themselves, they had crossed a threshold. They had begun making concessions to terrorists. There was enough window dressing— the notion of an opening to moderates in Iran—and enough subterfuge— the pretense that the Israelis did it—to deny even to themselves the true nature of what they were doing.

The cold hard fact was that the United States had for the first time given Hezbollah and its Iranian patrons concrete evidence that there was something to be gained by holding Americans hostage. The deal had been made largely out of compassion for the hostages and their families, but it would have a cruel effect on other Americans who now were such tempting targets for terrorists eager to extract concessions from the United States. There wasn't much time to dwell on it, however. Terrorism was breaking out on all fronts.

The wreckage of the failed Iran rescue mission became a symbol of the Carter administration's impotence in the face of terrorism. *Photo credit: AP/Wide World Photos.*

"Chargin' Charlie" Beckwith, commander of the Delta force that attempted to rescue the hostages in Tehran. Afterward he said, "If the U.S. ever gets caught like that with its pants down again, somebody's ass ought to burn." *Photo credit: AP/Wide World Photos.*

National Security Adviser Robert McFarlane. His melodramatic "sky is falling" cable from Beirut helped drag America deeper into Lebanon's civil war. *Photo credit: AP/Wide World Photos.*

The Marines belatedly mount a guard at the wreckage of the American Embassy in Beirut. The suicide blast killed the CIA's top Middle East analyst and all but two of the agency's officers in Lebanon. *Photo credit: AP/Wide World Photos.*

Left: A giant mushroom cloud towers hundreds of feet into the sky moments after a suicide bomber crashed into the Marine barracks. FBI experts called it the largest non-nuclear blast they had ever seen. *Photo courtesy of Howard Gerlach.*

One of the lucky survivors. Weeks later, when the Marine commander regained consciousness and asked his wife what had happened to his staff, she replied, "Dead, all dead." *Photo credit: AP/Wide World Photos.*

Ronald Reagan was unable to resolve the bitter dispute between Secretary of State Shultz and Defense Secretary Weinberger. As a result, his National Security staff started trying to do his job for him. *Photo credit: AP/Wide World Photos.*

The blood of murdered Navy diver Robert Stethem stains the side of TWA 847. The 17-day ordeal revealed that the Reagan administration was no better equipped to rescue hostages than the Carter administration had been. *Photo credit: AP/Wide World Photos.*

4339

Two of the hijackers of TWA Flight 847. Iran's role in ending the crisis helped convince some U.S. officials that Tehran held the key to freeing American hostages in Lebanon. *Photo credit: AP/Wide World Photos.*

Father Lawrence Martin Jenco, one of the "forgotten hostages." The President's meeting with Jenco's relatives brought Reagan face to face with their suffering for the first time, with disastrous results. *Photo credit: AP/Wide World Photos.*

The kidnapping of CIA officer William Buckley drove his boss, William Casey, to "try almost anything" to get him back. Despite claims by administration officials, there is no hard evidence that Buckley was tortured to death. *Photo credit: AP/Wide World Photos.*

Church of England envoy Terry Waite. Oliver North wanted to use him as an unwitting pawn in a plot to kill Qaddafi, but Waite ended up as a hostage in Lebanon. *Photo credit: AP/Wide World Photos.*

Leon and Marilyn Klinghoffer. The attempt to capture his murderers led to a near shoot-out with Italian troops. *Photo credit: AP/Wide World Photos.*

Looking like a character out of a Gilbert and Sullivan operetta, Muamar Qaddafi heads for his self-proclaimed "line of death" in the Gulf of Sidra. *Photo credit: AP/Wide World Photos.*

Aftermath of the U.S. raid on Libya. Air Force bombers tore up this Libyan frogman's school, but U.S. pilots were disappointed with their performance. *Photo credit: AP/Wide World Photos.*

Three of the architects of the Reagan administration's Libya policy—Secretary of State Shultz, National Security Adviser Poindexter, and Deputy National Security Adviser Fortier—brief President Reagan on the results of the Libyan bombing. Meanwhile, Poindexter was keeping Shultz in the dark about secret U.S. arms sales to Iran. *Photo credit: Bill Fitzpatrick, the White House.*

Hezbollah terrorist Imad Mughniyah. His many attempts to free his brother-in-law from a Kuwaiti prison led to some of the grisliest terrorist incidents of the 1980s. The U.S. tried but failed to kidnap him. *Photo credit: Alfred, SIPA-Press.*

Marine Lt. Col. Oliver North, the ultimate can-do officer. His friend Richard Secord said, "They treated him like the Marines treat their mules. They kept piling the work on his back until he broke down." *Photo credit: AP/Wide World Photos.*

★ 9 ★

"A MOST RIDICULOUS THING"

President Reagan's initial reaction was to call it "a most ridiculous thing." The SOS had been picked up first in Göteborg, Sweden—an improbable location for an improbable call from an Italian cruise ship hijacked off the coast of Egypt. The *Achille Lauro* had set sail from Alexandria that morning, Monday, October 7, 1985, after dropping off most of its 750 passengers for a bus tour of the Pyramids. It was to pick them up that night in Port Said before continuing on to Israel, midpoint in a Mediterranean voyage that had begun four days earlier in the *Achille Lauro*'s home port of Genoa.

Ninety-seven passengers—many of them elderly or infirm—had decided to skip the bus tour, bypassing the rigors of a fourteen-hour day in the Egyptian heat for the more sedentary pleasures aboard ship. Some of the stay-behinds, like Rene Sprecher of Switzerland, delighted in the prospect of having the 633-foot liner virtually to themselves. They were just finishing lunch in the ship's dining room when two men stormed in from the kitchen, firing bursts from their machine guns in the air. "Women cried, Italians were screaming, two crew members cried and screamed and one even wet his pants," Sprecher said afterwards. "Shards of glass and bullets flew about. Many passengers fell on the floor or ran for the kitchen."

The ship's captain, Gerardo de Rosa, was in his cabin when the second officer ran in with word that terrorists were on the loose. "I rushed out, heard the sound of machine-gun fire, took the service stairs to the navigation room and found two of them there," he recounted. "Then we went to the bridge where the officers had been forced to lie down, and [the terrorists] told me they had taken control of the ship." One of the terrorists "fired some shots in the deck and screamed in Arabic and told me to head to Tartus," a Syrian port 400 miles away. The terrorist also told de Rosa he had twenty men on board. In fact, there were only four—four men in command of a 24,000-ton vessel with 344 crew members and 97 passengers on board. Most of the crew were Italian, while the passengers were an international mix of travelers.

Lying on the dining-room floor, some of the terrified passengers recognized their assailants. They were part of a group of four young men who had boarded the ship along with everyone else in Genoa. A few of the passengers had thought them strange from the start; they looked like Arabs, but they carried Argentinian, Portuguese, even Norwegian passports. They didn't talk much—indeed, none of them seemed to speak the native language of his passport—and they spent most of the time locked away by themselves in Cabin 82. One of the ship's stewards had become suspicious and had decided to take advantage of the lunch hour, when he assumed the four men would be in the dining room, to search their cabin. Instead of an empty stateroom, he found the four men cleaning their weapons, thus forcing them into action before they reached their intended target in Israel.

The crime—the hijacking of an Italian ship on the high seas—was a crime against the state of Italy. The outrage was against Americans, most of them retired couples from the New York area who had known each other and vacationed together for years. Marilyn Klinghoffer, who just the night before had celebrated her fifty-eighth birthday in the same dining room, was the youngest. Her husband, Leon, was eleven years her senior, confined to a wheelchair by two strokes that had left him partially paralyzed. They ignored his infirmity as best they could—refusing to retreat into old age, continuing to travel, remaining an outgoing couple even though Leon's slurred speech made conversation difficult. There were, of course, limits. They couldn't attempt a tour of the Pyramids; they couldn't negotiate the ship's ladders. His weakened condition was to cost Leon Klinghoffer his life.

In the dining room, "they started to threaten us and show us their power," Viola Meskin, another of the Americans, recalled. "They had hand grenades in their hands, and they would remove the pins and play with them." Judge Stanley Kubacki said the hijackers forced his wife Sophia and two other women to hold live grenades with the pins pulled. Reagan no good, Arafat good, the terrorists proclaimed in broken English, occasionally loosing a burst of machine-gun fire into the ceiling.

They demanded to know who among the passengers was American. "When no one responded, they commanded that the Austrians come forward," Marilyn Klinghoffer said later. "An elderly couple got up and was brought to the front of the room. The terrorists demanded to know if they were Jews. The man said he was and was knocked on the ground by a rifle butt blow to his chest. He was struck repeatedly while he lay on the ground." The Americans, some of whom were also Jewish, could remain silent, but eventually their passports would give them away. The twelve Americans, along with the two Austrians and six women from a British dance troupe, were separated from the other passengers and marched to the ship's lounge as the *Achille Lauro* steamed north toward Syria.

★　★　★

In Washington, the Terrorist Incident Working Group convened in the White House Situation Room. Chaired by John Poindexter, its members included Oliver North from the NSC staff, Robert Oakley from the State Department, and Noel Koch from the Pentagon. Poindexter opened by saying the first thing that had to be done was to get a passenger list so they could find out exactly how many Americans were on board. "I said, 'John, wait a minute, the first thing we need to do is alert Six and get them out there," Koch recalled. "Six" was SEAL Team Six, Navy frogmen assigned to the Joint Special Operations Command. This is the best one we've had yet, Koch argued, pointing out that as long as the ship remained at sea it was isolated and vulnerable. In contrast to TWA 847, all the hostages were in one place and that place was not in the middle of hostile territory. We can take that sucker down, Koch said.

David Long was sent home from the State Department to pack his bags for another trip to Europe as head of the Emergency Support Team. It was after midnight, more than twelve hours after word of the hijacking reached Washington, before the twenty-man team took off from Andrews Air Force Base. "It seemed like forever," Long said. At almost the same time, Brig. Gen. Carl Stiner and the main force of the Joint Special Operations Command (JSOC) were taking off from Fort Bragg.

In theory, the support team was supposed to precede JSOC, helping the local American ambassador manage the situation, surveying the crisis scene, and radioing back advice on what special equipment and personnel the situation required. In practice, the flying times to Europe and the Middle East were such that JSOC could not afford to wait for a report from the team. James Holloway, the former Chief of Naval Operations who directed the work of the Bush Commission appointed by Reagan in the aftermath of TWA 847, had been appalled to find out how long it took to get JSOC moving. At one point he even said to Stiner, If you can't improve your deployability, let's get rid of the outfit.

In past episodes, like TWA 847, there had been what Terrell Arnold, a member of the Bush Commission staff, called a "seemingly unconscionable delay" in deploying JSOC. The primary cause of delay, in Arnold's words, "appears to be the need to make a host of last-minute decisions about team composition, weapons, dress, communications, and related issues, and then to rehearse the team in coping with detailed aspects of the specific incident in progress." The men and equipment to storm a hijacked airplane in Beirut were different from what was needed to rescue Americans from a ship on the high seas—and different again if that ship should pull into port. Once all the equipment had been loaded and airlifted to Europe, it still had to be unloaded, reassembled, and put in operating condition. Then, JSOC would have to wait for nightfall, since operating in darkness was one of its primary methods for achieving surprise. According to Arnold, "it may take as much as seventy-two hours to get a team ready for a specific mission." By then, the team could be facing an entirely different set of circumstances from those at the time the decision to deploy JSOC was originally made.

When Stiner took off from Fort Bragg in the early morning hours of Tuesday, he had with him not only SEAL Team Six but Delta as well. He headed for the NATO airfield at Sigonella, Sicily, which he would use as his main operating base while at the same time sending some of his forces forward to the British base at Akrotiri on the island of Cyprus. Since Stiner had to be prepared to assault the ship both in port and at sea, he needed a dozen transport planes, including four giant C-5s, to bring in all his equipment, along with about 500 men. It was almost more aircraft than the single 8,000-foot strip at Sigonella could handle.

★   ★   ★

The support team and JSOC were still airborne by the time the *Achille Lauro* arrived off the Syrian port of Tartus on Tuesday afternoon. For most of the night, no one had known where the vessel was. The Sixth Fleet had been trying to fix its position for nearly twenty-four hours, sending out long-range patrol planes from the aircraft carrier *Saratoga*. But the terrorists had gone into a communications blackout, and the *Achille Lauro* had simply vanished into the Mediterranean night. It was not found again until it arrived off the coast of Syria and broke radio silence with a request to dock at Tartus.

Vulnerable to an attack that could come from any point on the compass, the terrorists desperately needed a haven where they could hole up and begin negotiating. They were demanding the release of fifty Palestinians being held in Israeli prisons. Unlike the Shiite detainees of the TWA 847 crisis, these prisoners were convicted terrorists, members of the Palestine Liberation Front, men like Sami Kuntar who in a 1979 raid on an Israeli settlement had bashed in the head of a five-year-old girl.

Alone on the high seas, leveling an impossible demand, the hijackers were dealing from a position of weakness. After checking with the United States and Italy, Syria rejected the hijackers' request to dock at Tartus. Again, Hafez Assad was acting in his own interest. Having identified the hijackers as members of the pro-Arafat Palestine Liberation Front, Assad saw another opportunity to undermine Arafat, whom he despised as a "capitulationist" toward Israel. The hijackers demanded that the ambassadors whose citizens were held hostage be brought to Tartus to act as intermediaries. Syria stalled.

So close to land, the hijackers feared an attack more than ever. They decided to move their eighteen American hostages out of the lounge onto an open deck where anyone who approached the ship could see the danger they were in. To get there, the hostages had to climb a narrow staircase. "I attempted to push my husband in his wheelchair in the direction of the staircase," Marilyn Klinghoffer recounted. "The terrorists ordered me to leave him. I told them that I couldn't leave him and begged them to let me stay with him. They responded by putting a machine gun to my head and ordered me up the stairs. That was the last time I saw my husband."

Along with the Austrian couple and the British dancers, the Americans were paraded into the midday sun, their hats and sunglasses taken away from them. There they would sit for the next four hours, surrounded by cans of fuel which the terrorists threatened to ignite.

On the bridge, the leader of the hijackers, Majed Molqi, was talking by radio with the unyielding Syrian port authorities, threatening to kill passengers if his demands were not met. "We have no more time," Majed warned. "We will start executing at three P.M. sharp." As the clock ticked toward three, he warned, "We have five minutes only." Then, "We can't wait any longer. We will start killing."

Majed left the bridge and wheeled Leon Klinghoffer to the starboard side of the ship. There, he shot him once in the head and once in the chest, toppling him onto the deck. "He was flat on his face with the wheelchair turned over," one of the ship's waiters, Joaquim da Silva, said. Majed ordered da Silva and Ferruccio Alberti, the ship's hairdresser, to throw the body overboard. "So Ferruccio and I picked up the old American by the armpits and turned him around. He was all covered with blood, so much that we couldn't figure out where he was hit. We picked him up. He was already almost cold. The ship hadn't moved for some time, and there was no noise from the engine room. We threw the body overboard, and I tried not to look. I heard it fall in the water."

Captain de Rosa heard the shots. "They told me, 'Now we have killed one,' " he said later. "They made me write it down and told me to call it to Tartus." The hijackers already had selected their second victim, Mildred Hodes, from the pile of American passports they had collected. She was outside on the deck, sweltering in the sun.

"What are the developments, Tartus?" Majed, his clothes spattered with Leon Klinghoffer's blood, asked over the radio. "We will kill the second. We are losing patience." But Tartus refused to yield.

Before they could kill another passenger, the hijackers received a message over Radio Monte Carlo, an Arabic-language station on Cyprus. It was from "Abu Khaled," a common code name among Palestinians. In Washington, intelligence analysts were feverishly trying to determine who "Abu Khaled" was. The question was important since there was more than one faction of the Palestine Liberation Front. If the pro-Arafat faction headed by Abu Abbas was responsible for the hijacking, as Syrian President Assad claimed, the terrorists probably would return to Egypt, where the authorities almost certainly would set them free rather than risk a contretemps with the PLO. But if a breakaway faction which was on the outs with Arafat had seized the ship, the Reagan administration might have no choice but to let Carl Stiner's men try a rescue mission. The renegade PLF faction had nowhere to go and nothing to lose. A hurried check by intelligence analysts at the State Department revealed that only one PLF leader, Abu Abbas, a close associate of Arafat and a member of the PLO's executive council, had ever used the name Abu Khaled. In contrast to the popular image of intelligence analysts poring over reports from spies and satellites, the experts at the State Department were doing what they usually did whenever there was a terrorist incident—ferreting through stacks of public reports on the whereabouts and declarations of terrorist groups and leaders. "Abu Khaled's" message directed the hijackers to treat the passengers kindly and head back to Port Said. It came too late to save Leon Klinghoffer, although the hijackers now did their best to pretend the murder never happened. At gunpoint, Captain de Rosa broadcast a plea for any would-be rescuers to stay away. "I have only one message— please, please, don't try anything on my ship. Everybody is very good on the ship."

Despite de Rosa's disclaimer, the Reagan administration was convinced that the hijackers had indeed killed one and possibly two Americans. The administration was in a rage, determined to put an end to this wanton killing, determined not to spend another seventeen days at the mercy of terrorists. Within hours, Maxwell Rabb, the American Ambassador to Italy, was in Italian Prime Minister Bettino Craxi's office. Rabb said his government believed the reports of the killings and considered the situation aboard the ship untenable. According to Craxi, Rabb "informed me of the decision to set in motion a military action the deadline for whose initiation the Americans had set as Wednesday night." Stiner's JSOC team was only now approaching Cyprus and would not be ready to go by Tuesday night.

With darkness once again descending on the Mediterranean, the *Achille Lauro* headed south, as Abbas had directed, back to Port Said. Once again, the reconnaissance aircraft from the *Saratoga* could not find it, and some intelligence analysts in Washington thought it was bound for the Cypriot port of Larnaca. Robert Oakley and Oliver North called Amiram Nir asking for Israel's help in finding the *Achille Lauro*. Nir, the prime minister's adviser for counterterrorism, was incredulous that the United States with all its satellites and reconnaissance aircraft could not locate a simple thing like a cruise ship, but he agreed to help.

When an Israeli patrol boat spotted the *Achille Lauro* heading south off the Israeli–Lebanese border, the terrorism analysts in the State Department's intelligence bureau were convinced that their hunch had been correct: the hijackers were Abu Abbas's men and they were headed back to Egypt, most likely to abandon the ill-fated operation. From then on, three American warships shadowed the cruise ship, remaining just over the horizon. Despite the State Department's belief that the hijackers would give up, JSOC planned to use the ships as the launch point for a rescue mission on Wednesday night.

The American hostages had been returned to the relative comfort of the ship's lounge, and Marilyn Klinghoffer was now trying to find her husband. "He was nowhere to be seen and there were conflicting reports," she recalled. "It was suggested that he had been feeling ill and had been taken to the hospital. I pleaded with the terrorists to allow me to see him in the hospital. They refused. Throughout the night I pleaded with them to be allowed to see my husband with no success at all."

It was ten o'clock Tuesday night in Cairo when Egypt's Foreign Minister Abdel Meguid learned that the *Achille Lauro* was returning to Port Said. He immediately called the ambassadors of the countries with citizens aboard for advice about whether to negotiate or follow the Syrian example. All the ambassadors said they would first have to check with their home offices. While the Western democracies pondered their advice to Egypt, Arafat rushed to fill the void, dispatching Abu Abbas to Cairo to negotiate with the hijackers. On Wednesday morning, Arafat sent Craxi a message, claiming the situation was well in hand. "Following our efforts throughout the night we have succeeded in bringing the ship back into the waters off Egypt," the message read. "I can reveal to you that we have a high degree of confidence regarding a positive conclusion to the affair." Arafat seemed determined to end the hijacking before nightfall, so determined that some American officials suspected the Italians had warned him the United States was planning to storm the ship that night.

Over the ship-to-shore radio, Abbas called the leader of the hijackers. "How are you, Majed?" Abbas began.

"Good, thank God," Majed replied.

"Listen to me well," Abbas continued. "First of all, the passengers should be treated very well. In addition, you must apologize to them and the ship's crew and to the captain and tell him our objective was not to take control of the ship. Tell him what your main objective is. . . . Can you hear me well?"

The Israelis heard Abbas extremely well. They recorded the conversation and immediately released the transcript as proof that Abbas, and above him Arafat, had masterminded the entire affair. Abbas had referred to "our objective," implicitly acknowledging that he knew what the hijackers had in mind when they smuggled their weapons aboard the *Achille Lauro* back in Genoa. As a member of the PLO's executive council, the Israelis maintained, Abbas would not permit mayhem aboard an Italian ship without Arafat's approval. The fact that the hijackers had bungled the mission did not absolve Abbas of responsibility for everything that happened after the operation went sour.

In Cairo, Meguid was not interested in attaching blame. He wanted to find a way out of a predicament that threatened to push Egypt off the tightrope it was walking in trying to maintain peace with Israel and at the same time regain leadership of the Arab world. With hundreds of its citizens at risk, Italy, too, cared more about a quick and peaceful resolution to the crisis than about establishing its credentials as an unyielding opponent of terrorism. For Egypt and Italy, international terrorism was a political problem amenable to political solutions, meaning compromise. Israel, on the other hand, and, increasingly, the United States saw terrorism as a form of warfare to be met with military force. In the events that followed, Italy and Egypt would be seen as soft on terrorism in contrast to the hard-line stance of the United States and Israel. The fact was that of all the Western democracies, Italy had probably the most impressive record in dealing with the domestic terrorism of the Red Brigades. If anybody was soft on terrorism, it was the Americans, who had begun secretly trading arms for the hostages in Lebanon.

By late Wednesday afternoon, SEAL Team Six was in position aboard a Navy ship just over the horizon from the *Achille Lauro,* ready to launch a strike with helicopters and small boats. If the SEALs could reach the stern of the ship undetected, the operation would be a cakewalk. The *Achille Lauro* had a sharply tapering stern that could not be seen from the ship's bridge; the SEALs could climb aboard, and the terrorists would never know it. The four terrorists were already spread too thinly, trying to guard hostages in the lounge, the dining room, and on the bridge. Once darkness fell, the terrorists would die.

In Cairo, Meguid was meeting with the ambassadors of the United States, Great Britain, Italy, and Germany, trying to extract a pledge not to seek extradition of the terrorists if they surrendered peacefully. Nicholas Veliotes, the American ambassador, was arguing that regardless of how it ended the crime of hijacking already had been committed and should be punished. Meguid interrupted Veliotes to take a phone call. Turning to the four ambassadors, Meguid announced, "It's all over. They've left the ship without guarantees." The official Egyptian statement said that "at 4:20 P.M. the hijackers, whose number is four, agreed to surrender without preconditions. They surrendered at 5:00 P.M."

In fact, there were preconditions—a promise of safe passage out of Egypt. The deal was based in part on de Rosa's assurances that no harm had been done. "I am the captain," de Rosa reported over the ship-to-shore radio. "I am speaking from my office, and my officers and everybody is in good health." Casualties or no, the Reagan administration, whose Secretary of State had declared just the week before that "terrorism deserves no sanctuary," was not pleased. Casualties or no, terrorists had taken Americans hostages and were walking away free men. It was TWA 847 all over again. "Our position on hostage taking is clear," White House spokesman Larry Speakes said, reading from a hastily prepared statement. "We believe those responsible should be prosecuted to the maximum extent possible." But a satisfied Meguid told reporters, "The four hijackers have left the ship and are heading out of Egypt."

As soon as the four terrorists boarded a tugboat to be taken ashore, Marilyn Klinghoffer went to the ship's hospital to look for her husband, whom she had not seen or heard from for more than twenty-four hours. The hospital staff said he had never been there and sent her to see de

Rosa. "The captain appeared to be waiting for me when I reached the bridge," she recalled. "It was then that I learned of the fate of my husband." The hijackers' dirty little secret was leaking out.

Italy's Prime Minister Craxi found out just thirty minutes before he was scheduled to hold a press conference. He threw out the triumphant statement he had drafted. "Unfortunately, I must give you some bad news," he said instead. "I have learned just now in a radio communication with the ship's captain that a U.S. national was killed aboard the *Achille Lauro.*" Meguid found out when a reporter called him for reaction to Craxi's statement. Veliotes found out when he finally reached the *Achille Lauro* around midnight.

I'm sorry, I'm so very sorry, de Rosa said, as he handed Klinghoffer's passport to Veliotes. I didn't want to lie and say we were all all right, the captain explained, tears welling in his eyes. But they held a gun to my head and said they would kill me and then each of my crew members if I didn't cooperate.

Veliotes radioed the news to one of his aides ashore. "Leon Klinghoffer was murdered by the terrorists off of Tartus when they were trying to get the attention of the Syrians," Veliotes reported. "In my name, I want you to call the foreign minister, tell him what we've learned, tell him the circumstances, tell him that in view of this and the fact that we—and presumably they—didn't have those facts, we insist that they prosecute those sons of bitches."

It was too late, Meguid told Veliotes; the terrorists had already left the country. By noon on Thursday, Egypt's President Hosni Mubarak was confirming the bad news publicly. "They left Egypt already. I don't know where they went, but they possibly went to Tunis," Mubarak said, claiming he had not found out in time about Klinghoffer's murder. "When we accepted the hijackers' surrender, we did not have this information," he said. "This information emerged five hours after the surrender. In the meantime, the hijackers had left the country." As Mubarak himself later admitted, that was a lie.

The National Security Agency knew right away that Mubarak was lying because it was eavesdropping on his phone calls. While the Egyptian president publicly was lamenting that the terrorists had gotten away before their crime was discovered, privately he was screaming at aides to get the hijackers out of the country. They were at that moment at the Al Maza air base northeast of Cairo, still waiting aboard an EgyptAir 737 to be flown to Tunisia. The NSA even had the tail number of the plane.

James Stark, a Navy captain assigned to the NSC staff, had the idea first. If the hijackers were to be transported from Egypt to Tunis, their plane would have to fly through international air space over the Mediterranean where it would be within range of the aircraft carrier *Saratoga*. If the intelligence was good enough to reveal the destination and tail number, the *Saratoga*'s jets might be able to intercept the plane. Stark rushed into Oliver North's office.

Why don't we pull a Yamamoto on these guys? he asked North, referring to the Japanese admiral whose transport plane was intercepted and shot down by American fighters over the Pacific in World War II. The United States could not shoot down an Egyptian airplane, but it could, perhaps, force the plane down. Stark and North discussed where. Turkey would object if they took the hijackers into Cyprus; Greece would object if the plane were forced down in Crete. Israel would be more than willing to accept the hijackers, but American relations with the Arabs could not stand such blatant collusion with the Israelis. Finally, North suggested the NATO base at Sigonella, Sicily. That was Italian territory, and the *Achille Lauro* was, after all, an Italian ship.

North took the notion to John Poindexter, who was in charge at the NSC since McFarlane was accompanying the President on a one-day swing through the Chicago area. Poindexter picked up the phone to Vice Adm. Arthur Moreau, assistant to the chairman of the Joint Chiefs of Staff, to find out if it were physically possible to intercept the Egyptian aircraft. Moreau took the question to the new chairman, Adm. William Crowe, who had been in the job for less than three weeks. "I thought it was a grand idea," Crowe said afterwards.

Crowe, who had graduated in the same Naval Academy class as Jimmy Carter, was an entirely different kind of officer from his predecessor, General John Vessey—much less of a combat veteran, much more of a defense intellectual, with two master's degrees and a Ph.D. His selection as chairman did not reflect any particular change in philosophy; he was simply the most impressive man in uniform. But it did not take a Ph.D. from Princeton to see that for once the terrorists were operating at a disadvantage. Having given up their hostages, they had not disappeared into the slums of Beirut as they usually did; they were about to fly over the Mediterranean where the United States had vast military forces deployed. For once, American technology might be of use in the war against terrorism.

Crowe picked up the secure phone to call General Richard Lawson, the deputy European commander in Stuttgart. At that same moment, Maj. Gen. Edward Heinz, the European Command's chief intelligence officer, was trotting down the hallway toward Lawson's office to show him the NSA intercept revealing that the hijackers were still in Egypt. "Heinz was coming in one door waving it in his hand as I was getting the phone call from Bill Crowe," Lawson related. "Crowe asked me, 'If he comes out of there, is there a chance you can use the carrier?' "

On board the *Saratoga,* Rear Adm. David Jeremiah, the task force commander, had just completed an exhausting three days of participating in a NATO exercise while at the same time keeping track of *Achille Lauro.* The *Saratoga* was steaming northward toward a scheduled port call in Dubrovnik, Yugoslavia, and Jeremiah was sitting in the war room observing the watch team as it lowered the alert status now that the ship had begun its transit through the Adriatic Sea. On the flight deck, the crews were in an "Alert 60" status, meaning they could expect a full sixty minutes warning before they would have to launch any aircraft.

Jeremiah was new to aircraft carriers. It was unusual for anyone but a pilot to be given command of a carrier battle group, but Jeremiah was one of the Navy's front runners, perhaps a future Chief of Naval Operations, which was really saying something since he was not a graduate of the Naval Academy.

Jeremiah didn't think much of it when the watch officer told him he had just received a strange call from Sixth Fleet headquarters in Gaeta, Italy, asking for the exact location of each ship in the task force. Jeremiah and the watch officer joked that all the magnets must have fallen off the Sixth Fleet's plot board. Before the watch team could compile a precise latitude and longitude for each of the ships in the task force, Sixth Fleet headquarters came back with a simpler query asking only for the location of the *Saratoga.* The answer went out, and Jeremiah headed for the ward room and dinner.

★　★　★

It was midday in the United States. The President was in a holding room at the Sara Lee Bakery in the Chicago suburb of Deerfield. While a bagpipe band just outside the door wailed the "Notre Dame Victory March," McFarlane took a phone call from Poindexter at the White House. Ollie thinks we can intercept these guys, and the Joint Staff believes it's feasible, but I'm having trouble with Cap, Poindexter said. I want to know if you think Reagan will approve. Caspar Weinberger was in Ottawa, attending a session of the Canadian parliament. William Taft, the Deputy Secretary of Defense, was trying desperately to reach him.

Hurriedly, McFarlane briefed Reagan on the plan to intercept the aircraft carrying the hijackers. McFarlane explained to the President that the carrier was within fighter range of the airplane's prospective route from Cairo to PLO headquarters in Tunis. The *Saratoga*'s aircraft could get there in time, McFarlane said. The hard part would be sorting out the Egyptian airliner from all the other commercial air traffic—an operation that would be conducted in darkness since it was already night in the Mediterranean. According to McFarlane, Reagan approved the plan in principle, saying, Let's make darn sure we get out there and do it if at all possible.

On board the *Saratoga,* Jeremiah was finishing his dinner when he received a secure phone call from Sixth Fleet headquarters telling him to reverse course and prepare to launch his "alert CAP"—two F-14 Tomcat interceptors and an E-2C Hawkeye radar plane which made up the Combat Air Patrol. "We did not know why we were being turned around," Jeremiah said later. Whatever it was, Jeremiah wasn't taking any chances. He turned to his chief of staff and told him to launch the alert CAP. "I launched them because I could feel the sense of urgency," Jeremiah recalled.

That same sense of urgency flashed through the ship. CAG report to the war room, the public address system boomed. It was the first time Cdr. Robert Brodsky, commander of the Carrier Air Group, had ever been summoned like that. He headed for the war room at a dead run. One of the squadron commanders went dashing through the pilots' ward room, yelling, They're loading real bullets up there! The ward room emptied as pilots dashed for their flight gear, racing to be first in line for launch. Cdr. Ken Burgess, commander of one of the F-14 squadrons, bumped one of his junior officers who had gotten to the cockpit first. This was the real thing, whatever it was, and there was no time for hurt feelings.

The first F-14 took off at 7:10 P.M. local time. The E-2C radar plane, which would direct the intercept, launched six minutes later. One minute after that, said Jeremiah, "we got our mission . . . to intercept and divert to Sigonella, Sicily, a Boeing 737 charter with the *Achille Lauro* hijackers on board en route from Cairo to Tunis." Now that he knew his mission, Jeremiah launched more F-14s, but first he ordered their 20-mm cannons loaded with tracer bullets. Jeremiah's orders permitted his pilots to fire across the plane's nose but not to shoot it down. "We ended up with six F-14s airborne under E-2C control arrayed across the throat of the Mediterranean between Crete and Egypt," he said. The *Saratoga* was still 200 miles from the path the Egyptian airliner was expected to take.

Jeremiah began launching aerial tankers to refuel the F-14s as they flew lazy figure-eights south of Crete, waiting for the plane carrying the hijackers to take off from Al Maza.

From the ship's Combat Information Center, Robert Brodsky tried to explain the mission to the lieutenant on board the E-2C. "He was a young kid, and I didn't think he understood," Brodsky recalled. Brodsky turned to Cdr. Ralph Zia, the commander of the *Saratoga*'s E-2Cs, and told him to take a second plane up and assume control of the operation.

★   ★   ★

In the United States, it was still afternoon, and Oliver North was arguably the busiest man in Washington. On one phone, he was connected to the Israeli Embassy; on another, he was talking to Vice Admiral Moreau at the Pentagon. The Israelis had their own intelligence sources reporting the whereabouts of the EgyptAir plane carrying the hijackers, and those reports were being relayed to North faster than the National Security Agency's intercepts of the Egyptian telephone conversations. North was receiving the reports from Uri Simhoni, the military attaché at the Israeli Embassy, and passing them directly to Moreau. The NSA intercepts were trailing the Israeli reports by about fifteen minutes, but when they arrived they confirmed the accuracy of the information North was getting from Simhoni.

The President had just boarded Air Force One to return to Washington from Chicago. In Washington, North finished drafting a brief National Security Decision Directive ordering the Sixth Fleet to intercept the EgyptAir plane and force it to fly to Sigonella. The document was transmitted to Air Force One for the President's signature.

Weinberger was standing outside the Canadian Parliament, fielding reporters' questions, when an aide handed him a note telling him he had an urgent phone call. It was Deputy Secretary William Taft and Weinberger needed to get to a secure phone as quickly as possible. Returning to his aircraft, Weinberger called the Pentagon. Taft and Admiral Crowe came on the line to explain to the Secretary of Defense what was happening in the Mediterranean and that the President liked the plan to intercept hijackers. A final decision needed to be made within the next thirty minutes, Taft said. Caught by surprise with aircraft already in the air and the decision all but made, Weinberger didn't like the idea. Intercepting a civilian airliner would be a violation of international law and would damage relations with Egypt. Besides, no one had yet figured out what to do with the hijackers once they were on the ground in Sicily. The plan called for transferring them to an American aircraft and bringing them to the United States in chains to stand trial, but no one had asked the Italians about that. Weinberger told Taft and Crowe he would talk to the President and get back to them.

The President's plane was making its final approach into Andrews Air Force Base when Reagan and Weinberger finally made contact. The cryptographic equipment aboard Weinberger's plane was not compatible with the gear in Air Force One. With no time to wait for technicians to rig a secure connection between the two aircraft, the President and Secretary of Defense talked over an open circuit using the code names "Rawhide" and "Finley." Weinberger tried to talk Reagan out of the intercept, warning it would destroy American relations with Egypt. But Reagan was determined to proceed. At 4:37 P.M., Reagan directed Weinberger to intercept the plane and its hijackers. Weinberger called Crowe at the Pentagon and gave him permission to proceed.

South of Crete, Cdr. Ralph Zia's E-2C Hawkeye monitored contacts coming out of the eastern Mediterranean, looking for one that fitted the profile of a commercial airliner following the air traffic corridor from Cairo to Tunis. Three of the radar contacts looked likely enough to merit a visual inspection. With its lights out, an F-14 slipped behind the unsuspecting aircraft long enough for the radar operator in the back seat to shine a flashlight on the tail looking for the number 2843 and the insignia of EgyptAir. All the technological prowess of a carrier task force came down in the end to a hand-held lantern.

Two of the aircraft the F-14s checked out had their running lights extinguished. Creeping up on the blacked-out planes, the Navy pilots recognized the silhouette of an American C-141 transport plane. The pilots didn't know it, but they had intercepted Stiner's JSOC team en route from Cyprus to Sigonella to sieze the EgyptAir plane and its passengers when they landed. Jeremiah told the pilots to leave the C-141s alone.

On the fourth try, the F-14s found their plane. Lt. Cdr. Stephen Weatherspoon pulled behind the airliner and radioed the tail number—2843—to the Saratoga. Weatherspoon and another F-14 then moved in so close to the 737's wingtips that they could see people inside the Egyptian airliner. "Normally, you don't have to get that close," Brodsky explained, "but we wanted to look intimidating when we turned our lights on." As long as the F-14s kept their lights out, the passengers and crew of the EgyptAir plane had no idea they had been intercepted.

One on each wing, the F-14s shadowed the Egyptian plane as it flew westward toward Tunis. "So long as he was going westward, there was no reason to tell him to do anything," Jeremiah said later. From 100 miles away, Zia in his E-2C listened as the Egyptian plane first requested landing rights in Tunis and was denied, then turned to Athens for safe harbor and was denied again. The State Department had already asked them not to allow the Egyptian plane to land. With no place to go, the EgyptAir 737 attempted to contact Cairo for instructions. Ten minutes after the F-14s had joined up with the still-unsuspecting airliner, Egypt-Air 2843 received instructions to return to Cairo. "Okay, thank you, return back to Cairo," EgyptAir 2843 acknowledged.

Before the airliner could reverse course, Zia in his E-2C Hawkeye broke his radio silence. "2843. This is Tigertail 603, over," Zia radioed. No answer. Again. "2843. Tigertail 603, over." Zia tried four times before the Egyptian plane finally answered.

"Tigertail 603. EgyptAir 2843. Go ahead."

"EgyptAir 2843. Tigertail 603. Be advised you're being escorted by two F-14s. You are to land immediately—immediately—Sigonella, Sicily. Over."

The Egyptian pilot sounded dumbfounded. "Say again. Who is calling?"

"Roger. This is Tigertail 603. I advise you [are] directed to land immediately, proceed immediately to Sigonella, Sicily. You are being escorted [by] two interceptor aircraft. Vector 280 for Sigonella, Sicily. Over." The Egyptian plane wanted the message repeated again. "You are to turn immediately to 280," Zia repeated. "Head 280 immediately."

EgyptAir 2843 complied: "Turning right, heading 280." At the same time, the Egyptian pilot asked a passing commercial airliner to relay news of the intercept to Cairo. "I'm telling you, two fighters, two fighters intercepting, demanding me to steer heading for Italy," the still-incredulous pilot reported.

By now, the F-14s had turned on their running lights, and the Egyptian pilot was startled by how close they were. "I'm saying you are too close. I'm following your orders. Don't be too close. Please."

"Okay, we'll move away a little bit," Zia responded, sounding as if he were one of the interceptors when in fact he was 100 miles off. The propellor-driven E-2C was having trouble keeping up with the jetliner, and Zia worried about staying within radio range of the Egyptian pilot. The F-14s had more than enough speed but not enough fuel to stay with the Egyptian plane all the way to Sigonella, so Zia vectored fresh escorts into position while the original interceptors headed back to the *Saratoga*. Cdr. Ken Burgess, the senior pilot aloft, and three other F-14s took over the intercept.

There were now a total of eight aircraft headed toward Sigonella: the

Egyptian 737, four American F-14s, Zia's E-2C, and the two C-141s carrying JSOC. The plan called for JSOC to take the hijackers off the Egyptian plane, transfer them to one of the C-141s, and bring them to the United States to stand trial for the murder of Leon Klinghoffer.

In the Sigonella control tower, Navy Capt. William Spearman, the American base commander, was standing in the gym shorts he'd been wearing when he was yanked off a racquetball court. Brig. Gen. Stiner was on the radio, explaining to him what was about to happen.

Bill, it's coming, Stiner said in his Tennessee drawl. You're the only one that's going to know about it, and you're going to make it happen.

Spearman decided he had no choice but to inform the Italian base commander. It was the Italian's last day on the job; tomorrow was to be his change-of-command ceremony and a lot of Italian brass would be on hand.

It was just past midnight in Rome when the prime minister of Italy got his first clue of what was about to happen. Craxi had retired for the night to his rooms in the Hotel Raphael and the American Embassy was unable to contact him. In Washington, North called NSC consultant Michael Ledeen at home and asked him to try. Ledeen spoke Italian fluently and had known Craxi as a graduate student in Rome twenty years before. Placing his call through the White House switchboard, Ledeen reached Craxi's suite but was told by an aide that the prime minister was unavailable. Knowing Craxi's reputation as a womanizer, Ledeen told the aide that peoples' lives were at stake and that the prime minister would just have to tear himself away. A minute later Craxi came on the line.

As Craxi later recounted it, "I received a telephone call from the White House informing me that U.S. military aircraft had intercepted an Egyptian civil aircraft which the U.S. government believed with a reasonable degree of certainty to be carrying the four Palestinians responsible for the hijacking of the *Achille Lauro*. The U.S. President asked the Italian government for its consent to proceed with the landing of the civil and U.S. military aircraft at Sigonella."

It was not, of course, Reagan who was calling but Ledeen, not from the White House, but from his home. To convince Craxi that the United States had no doubt about who was on the plane, Ledeen identified each of the six suspects by name—the four who had committed the hijacking, along with Abu Abbas and the number two man in the PLO's Cairo office. "He asked, 'Why here?' " Ledeen recalled. "I said, 'Because no other place on earth has such good food, great climate, and historic cultural tradition.' " Ledeen made no mention of JSOC and the plan to apprehend the hijackers. "We could not ask the Italians for those people," Ledeen explained. "They had to say no. We were hoping they might want us to take them. The only way to find out was not to ask them but to try." Not knowing what he was getting into, Craxi, in his words, "decided to consent to a landing at Sigonella base by the aircraft in question."

Craxi's consent was by now academic. EgyptAir 2843 was coming into Sigonella with or without permission. From Washington, Admiral Crowe already had authorized Jeremiah to take the plane into Sigonella no matter what the Italians said. From his F-14 just off the Egyptian airliner's wing, Cdr. Ken Burgess contacted approach control, requesting a vector to Sigonella. Approach control said no and directed Burgess to a nearby civilian airfield. Burgess repeated his request for a vector to Sigonella. Again, approach control said no. Burgess chose his own heading, passed it to the Egyptian pilot, and began his descent into Sigonella. Burgess radioed the tower at Sigonella, requesting permission to land. The Italian air controller refused. Burgess then declared a fuel emergency, turning his transponder to the emergency mode. In fact, he still had more than 2,000 pounds of fuel in reserve. Burgess took the Egyptian plane into its final approach, but he could see the airliner was too low. If this guy goes in the ground, Burgess told his radar officer, you and I have got orders to Adak, Alaska.

The Egyptian plane broke off its approach and circled around for a second try, still without clearance to land. In the Sigonella tower, a Navy lieutenant grabbed the microphone from the Italian controller and granted the EgyptAir plane permission to land. When the 737 touched down, the F-14s broke off and circled overhead taking reconnaissance photos of the scene on the runway to verify that their part of the mission to apprehend the *Achille Lauro* hijackers was successfully completed. The rest was up to Stiner and his commandos.

A handful of SEALs who had remained at Sigonella while the rest of the force had positioned itself for an attack on the *Achille Lauro* now jumped into pickup trucks and raced down to the end of the runway where the EgyptAir plane had rolled to a stop. The two C-141s landed in quick succession, their lights out, and pulled up behind the Egyptian plane. Stiner's men came off the transports and surrounded EgyptAir 2843.

The Italian base commander, flabbergasted by the sight of armed American soldiers, immediately ordered his own troops into action. JSOC had the plane surrounded, but Italian troops had JSOC surrounded, and the Italians had the Americans outnumbered five to one.

Both sides awaited instructions from their governments. Using his satellite communications, Stiner radioed Crowe at the Pentagon. "He started describing the Italian forces coming on the scene," Crowe recalled. "It was clear we weren't going to do it with their permission. The question then was whether we could do it without their permission." With armed Egyptian commandos on board the aircraft, Stiner was facing the prospect of two firefights with supposedly friendly forces—one with the Italians and one with the Egyptians—if he tried to storm the plane and capture the hijackers.

Ledeen, now in the White House Situation Room, called Craxi again. "I assured him nobody was going to do anything crazy, but the President felt strongly about bringing the terrorists to justice," Ledeen recalled. According to Ledeen, Craxi said, If it were up to me, I'd turn them over in a minute, but it's not a political question, it's a legal matter. The Italian courts, not the prime minister, had jurisdiction over crimes committed on Italian territory, or, in this case, aboard an Italian ship in international waters. When Ledeen relayed Craxi's answer, the Reagan administration had no choice but to give in. Ledeen phoned Craxi a third time to tell him he would be receiving a call from the President. When Reagan called, there was nothing he could do except inform Craxi of his intention to file an extradition request for the four hijackers.

At four o'clock in the morning Italian time, Crowe ordered Stiner to back off. Fifteen minutes later, Larry Speakes appeared in the White House briefing room to read a statement claiming that "this episode also reflects our close cooperation with an exemplary ally and close friend, Italy, in battling international terrorism." So far, that "close cooperation" had consisted of the Italians in all probability warning the PLO that JSOC was about to assault the *Achille Lauro,* of Reagan springing one surprise after another on Craxi, of American warplanes violating Italian air space, and of Stiner's troops staring eyeball-to-eyeball at the Italians. Before the *Achille Lauro* affair was over, it would trigger the fall of the Italian government.

The Reagan administration wanted Abu Abbas even more than the four hijackers. They were merely the hit men; he was a kingpin. Abbas's companion, the second in command of the PLO's Cairo office, was nothing more than a political functionary, but he too had been caught up in the administration's dragnet. "To President Reagan's subsequent request that we also arrest the two Palestinians said to be on board the same aircraft, I said that we would carry out checks on them," Craxi later reported. Italy informed Egypt of its intention to arrest the four hijackers and bring the two Palestinians in for questioning. But, said

Craxi, "we received the reply that the two Palestinians . . . refused to leave the aircraft and that, this being so, the Egyptian authorities did not believe they could grant our request." Craxi's legalisms were nothing more than a stall to give the Italian government time to get rid of Abbas. A CIA source within the Italian government was already reporting that the Italians were readying an aircraft to take Abbas out of the country as soon as a safe haven could be found.

By the time the sun came up Friday morning, the four hijackers had been taken off the plane and turned over to the local Italian district attorney, and JSOC had departed for home, leaving Stiner behind to keep an eye on Abbas. Another C-141 landed at Sigonella, this one carrying seventeen of the *Achille Lauro* hostages. Four of them, including Marilyn Klinghoffer, got off the plane long enough to identify the hijackers in a police line-up. All four of the ex-hostages positively identified the Palestinians as the men who had hijacked the *Achille Lauro* and killed Leon Klinghoffer. Marilyn Klinghoffer later told the President she spat in their faces.

EgyptAir 2843 remained on the runway with its crew, the Egyptian commandos, and Abbas and his partner still on board. By 8:00 Italian time Friday evening, the local district attorney had finished processing the four hijackers and announced that as far as he was concerned, the EgyptAir plane was free to go home. However, federal prosecutors in Rome still had some questions they wanted to ask Abbas. At 10:00 P.M. the Boeing 737 took off from Sigonella for the military airfield at Ciampino just outside Rome. Worried that the Egyptian airliner would head for home, Crowe ordered Stiner to make sure the plane went to Rome. Well, let me give it a go, Stiner said.

Stiner ordered a Navy T-39 executive jet to follow the Egyptian aircraft. As the EgyptAir plane took off, the T-39 taxied from its hangar toward the runway. Suddenly, a truck pulled in front of the T-39, blocking it from the runway. The pilot turned his plane around and took off from the taxiway. A group of Italian officers hit the deck as the T-39 zoomed over their heads.

The Italian Air Force put up four fighter planes to escort the 737 to Ciampino. "Do you still have that zombie that's pretending not to hear on your tail," one of the Italian fighter pilots said to another of the escorts. "He's crazy." Over the radio, the Italian cursed the American pilot. "Shithead! You're nothing but an ugly shit! Get out of here before you bang into us. You're dangerous for us and for yourself." The T-39 refused to back off. "Sons of bitches. Goddamn sons of bitches!" an American voice shot back. "That plane is mine, understand. It's mine.

It's you who has to get the hell out of the way." As the 737 touched down at Ciampino, the pilot of the T-39 declared an emergency and landed next to it. The Americans aboard the T-39 had no authority to arrest Abbas, and were badly outgunned by the ten Egyptian commandos aboard the 737. All they could do was sit and watch.

Grabbing Abbas and proving he was guilty of planning the hijacking, much less directing Klinghoffer's murder, were two different things. All the evidence against the Palestinian leader came from the Israelis, and when transcripts of his ship-to-shore conversations arrived in Washington, intelligence officials, wary of any and all Israeli information on the PLO, asked the National Security Agency to confirm the information's accuracy. NSA officials said the transcripts were accurate, but when their colleagues asked them for the U.S. versions of the intercepts, just to be sure, NSA admitted it didn't have any. This time, the NSA had missed. Oliver North spent part of Saturday afternoon on the telephone with Uri Simhoni, the Israeli defense attaché in Washington, arranging for tape recordings of the radio conversations to be shipped from Tel Aviv to Rome and handed over to the CIA station chief.

At 5:30 Sunday morning in Italy, Rabb, the American Ambassador, presented the Italian government with a request for the provisional arrest of Abbas pursuant to his extradition. In Washington, a federal judge issued an arrest warrant for Abbas on charges of piracy, hostage taking, and conspiracy. According to Craxi, "the request for the provisional arrest, though formally correct, did not, in the Justice Minister's opinion, satisfy the factual and substantive requirements laid down by Italian law. . . . This being so, there was no longer any legal basis . . . [for] detaining Abbas, since at the time he was on board an aircraft which enjoyed extraterritorial status."

The Italian argument was a sham. Under the extradition treaty between the United States and Italy, a simple petition for arrest was all that was required to hold a suspect for up to forty-five days while an extradition request was considered. Craxi was more interested in preserving his good relations with the PLO and with Egypt than he was in arresting Abbas, whose apprehension might trigger terrorist attacks against Italy.

Sunday afternoon, October 13, EgyptAir 2843 took off from Ciampino for the short ten-minute hop to Leonardo da Vinci, Rome's main commercial airport. Disguised as Egyptian officers, Abbas and his Palestinian partner transferred to a Yugoslav airliner which had been held nearly two hours past its scheduled departure time. Shortly after the plane took off for Belgrade, Ambassador Rabb arrived at the Chigi Palace to protest the release of Abbas. As he left, Rabb told reporters,

"I'm not happy about what happened here today." The State Department scrambled to prepare another extradition request, this one for Yugoslavia, actually delivering it before Abbas landed in Belgrade. But it was a lost cause. Yugoslavia had diplomatic relations with the PLO, and Abbas, as a member of the PLO's executive council, now enjoyed diplomatic immunity.

As Abbas was taking refuge in the PLO embassy in Belgrade, Leon Klinghoffer's body washed ashore on the coast of Syria.

★　★　★

The dazzling intercept of the hijackers had unraveled badly, but nothing could diminish the President's enthusiasm. At the morning staff meeting on Friday, the commander-in-chief jumped to attention and snapped off a salute to Poindexter. I salute the Navy, Reagan said. At a press conference, he crowed that the intercept had sent a message to terrorists everywhere: "You can run but you can't hide." Abbas, it turned out, could hide, but the four hijackers were now in an Italian jail and would eventually receive sentences ranging from fifteen to thirty years. Four out of five wasn't bad, particularly when measured against the administration's previous record for apprehending terrorists. "GOT 'EM," the headline in the New York Post read. "WE BAG THE BUMS," the New York Daily News reported.

After it was over, McFarlane invited the members of the NSC staff who had supervised the operation to a celebratory dinner at his home in the Maryland suburbs. Poindexter and his wife were there, along with the Fortiers and the Norths. Ollie North was the life of the party and on the way home Alison Fortier remarked to her husband how bright and charming the Marine officer was. Yes, replied Fortier, but you have to watch him every minute.

It did not escape the NSC staff that they, not the bureaucracy, had come up with the idea, even down to figuring out a way to track down Craxi when the State Department could not. Weinberger had been cut out of the operation until it was too late to stop it. Without the bureaucracy and Weinberger to raise objections, the military chain of command—the same chain which had bungled the deployment of the Marines to Beirut, the same chain which had so ineptly delivered the December 1983 bombing raid against Syrian positions in Lebanon—had functioned superbly, had within a matter of hours plucked terrorists from the nighttime sky and delivered them to justice. It was as precise and finely tuned an application of military power as any nation could reasonably expect from its armed services.

However, even at its best, military power is a blunt instrument. Egypt's Mubarak was furious at having been made the dupe and fumed publicly for days, demanding an American apology. Time and $2 billion a year in aid would salve the wound for Mubarak, but Craxi's government, one of the longest running in Italy's postwar history, collapsed under the strain of the incident. The fall of Craxi's government clearly was an unintended consequence of the intercept operation. That was the trouble with military operations—they always had unintended consequences.

★ 10 ★

EL DORADO CANYON

Lt. Col. Fred Allen* was standing Victor alert duty at Lakenheath Royal Air Force Base 75 miles northeast of London. It was a standard NATO alert condition for peacetime; nothing ever happened on Victor alert, but somebody had to be there to man the planes against that least likely of contingencies, nuclear war. Although he was the commander of one of the squadrons of American F-111 bombers based at Lakenheath, Allen pulled alert duty just like all the other pilots—even on New Year's Eve. Allen was the most experienced F-111 pilot at Lakenheath. He had come into the Air Force about the same time as the planes. Fresh out of flight school in the 1960s, his first assignment had consisted of ferrying the F-111s from the factory to Nellis Air Force Base in Nevada, and he had been flying them ever since.

At about four o'clock in the morning on the first day of 1986, Allen received a phone call from Col. Tom Yax, the director of operations for the 48th Tactical Fighter Wing that controlled the F-111 squadrons at Lakenheath. Yax had been home in bed after celebrating the New Year at the officers' club when he was awakened by Col. Sam Westbrook, the wing commander, who said to meet him at the command post right away. There, Westbrook and Yax placed a secure telephone call to the headquarters of U.S. Air Forces Europe (USAFE) in Ramstein, West Germany. They were told to put together a small planning team and have

*This is a pseudonym used at the request of the Air Force to protect the officer from possible retaliation for his role in the events that follow. Four other Air Force officers are also identified by pseudonyms. In each case, an asterisk denotes the use of a pseudonym. All other names are real.

them ready to be picked up by an airplane that would fly them to Ramstein.

Yax called Allen, who was the senior squadron commander at Lakenheath and the only one who had not been out drinking on New Year's Eve. Speaking guardedly, Yax told Allen he was going on a trip and should call a backup crew to stand the rest of his Victor alert duty. Shortly after daybreak, Yax, Allen, and two other officers boarded a C-130 transport plane for the one hour forty-minute flight to Ramstein. They slept most of the way, which was just as well since they were under orders not to discuss their mission, even among themselves.

When they arrived at Ramstein, the officers from Lakenheath were directed to draft strike plans for attacking Libya's two main air bases—Tripoli airfield just south of the capital and Benina 400 miles to the east across the Gulf of Sidra. Nobody mentioned it because nobody had to, but an air raid against Libya's two main airfields would serve as a mirror-image retaliation for the massacres at the Rome and Vienna airports just four days earlier.

★　★　★

Muamar Qaddafi was like a weed: you could cut him down to size, but he would always sprout back unless he was uprooted. The Reagan administration's campaign against him had begun in a blaze of glory in 1981 with the dogfight over the Gulf of Sidra, but it had faltered badly, a casualty of, among other things, the administration's preoccupation with the disastrous events in Lebanon. If the combination of overt military, diplomatic, and economic pressures coupled with the CIA's covert support for anti-Qaddafi exiles had had any effect, it had worn off by the start of Reagan's second term. The State Department reported no Libyan-sponsored terrorist incidents in either 1982 or 1983 but identified fifteen in 1984. Perhaps emboldened by the American defeat in Lebanon, Qaddafi was once again sending out shoots of terror and subversion.

George Shultz claimed to have put Qaddafi "back in his box" in February 1983, when the United States and Egypt headed off what was publicly portrayed as a Libyan plot to overthrow the pro-Western government of the Sudan but what in reality was an entrapment scheme gone awry. Together, the United States, Egypt, and the Sudan had hatched a plot to lure Qaddafi into sending his air force into the Sudan in support of a pro-Libyan coup. Sudanese agents had set up a phony revolutionary cell in Khartoum and had appealed to Qaddafi to assist them. When Qaddafi took the bait, the United States moved AWACS radar planes to Cairo to guide the Egyptian Air Force in intercepting and shooting down Libyan bombers.

The plan, codenamed "Early Call," was closely held within the U.S. government. "This subject is extremely sensitive," one message warned. "Dissemination should be closely controlled and limited to individuals who have an absolute need to know." Classified Top Secret, the planning documents predicted that the "most probable window for an attack by Libyan bombers is 0900Z-1000Z (coincides with Moslem Friday prayer hours) on 18 Feb 83." Four AWACS planes and four KC-10 aerial refueling tankers arrived in Egypt the preceding Monday to begin rehearsing the ambush with the Egyptian Air Force. Despite the extreme secrecy, Early Call involved 600 American servicemen and their equipment, which required a total of 17 transport planes. In addition, the aircraft carrier *Nimitz* was ordered to stand off the Egyptian coast "and be prepared to conduct defensive operations at Cairo West air base in the event of air attack by Libyan Arab air force units."

Early Call started to unravel almost at once. A dust storm at the Cairo West air base forced three of the AWACS planes to land at Egypt's main commercial airport. When Assistant Secretary of Defense Francis "Bing" West arrived in Cairo for a previously scheduled meeting with Egyptian officials, he found the AWACS sitting in full view at the airport, just a few gates down from Aeroflot, the Soviet airline. The operation came completely undone when John McWethy, ABC's Pentagon correspondent, learned of the AWACS deployment. Ignoring last-minute pleas from the White House, ABC broadcast the story on the night of February 16, 1983. "ABC News has learned that the United States has secretly deployed four early warning AWACS planes to Egypt on short notice and has rushed the aircraft carrier *Nimitz* and three escort ships from the coast of Lebanon to Libya," McWethy reported. "Intelligence sources say the movement is a direct result of an apparent military buildup by Libya spotted in the southeastern corner of that country, a buildup which Pentagon sources fear could foreshadow a move to overthrow the pro-American government of Sudan. . . . ABC News has been told if Libya does move militarily, Egyptian fighters, being guided by American AWACS planes, will make the intercept." Alerted to the trap, Qaddafi stood down his air force. Shultz claimed victory when in fact a well-laid plan had gone astray. The entire incident was symptomatic of the Reagan administration's policy toward Qaddafi, which seemed to be composed of equal parts deterrence and provocation.

At a press conference on the night ABC broke the story, Reagan claimed that the AWACS deployment "is not an unusual happening," even though the Joint Chiefs of Staff had sent out a message the night before, once again reminding all concerned "of the unique sensitivity of these operations." When he was asked if he would use force to stop Qaddafi, Reagan replied, "I don't think there's any occasion for that; it's never been contemplated." That was in sharp contrast to the position paper used by the Secretary of Defense and the chairman of the Joint Chiefs of Staff for the meeting at which the President approved Early Call. That paper clearly stated that the "U.S. objective" in sending the AWACS to Egypt was "deterrence of Libyan threat or defeat of Libyan threat by U.S. action." The President's explanation was, to put it mildly, misleading, although with Ronald Reagan there was always the possibility that he simply didn't understand what was happening.

Qaddafi had not remained in his box very long. In March of 1984, he sent a TU-22 bomber on a one-plane air raid against the Sudanese town of Omdurman in a vain attempt to destroy a CIA-backed exile radio station broadcasting anti-Qaddafi propaganda into Libya. In April, he ordered the Libyan People's Bureau in London to open fire on a crowd of anti-Qaddafi demonstrators outside the embassy. Gunfire from the embassy killed a British constable and wounded eleven protestors, prompting Britain to break diplomatic relations with Libya. In May, the official Libyan news agency announced that the "masses have decided to form suicide commandos to chase traitors and stray dogs wherever they are and liquidate them physically." Attacks on Libyan dissidents in Britain, Greece, and Italy killed six exiles that year. The murder campaign reached as far as Philadelphia, where FBI agents arrested two Libyans for trying to buy handguns with silencers, the weapon of choice among Qaddafi's hit squads. In November, one of Qaddafi's hit squads fell into an Egyptian trap. After Tripoli proudly announced that its agents had murdered a former Libyan prime minister living in Cairo, the Egyptians revealed that photographs of the victim had been faked and that the four would-be assassins were in custody. In an attempt to get even, Qaddafi mounted a plot to murder Egyptian President Hosni Mubarak during a visit to Greece. It, too, failed.

Qaddafi's ego seemed to be in one of its expansive phases. He dispatched a ship to scatter mines in the approaches to the Suez Canal. Eighteen merchant ships were damaged before the strategic waterway could be cleared. He sent military advisers to Nicaragua, helped finance the construction of a new military airfield at Punta Huete outside Managua, and tried unsuccessfully to ship warplanes to the Sandinista's fledgling air force. Most worrisome of all were indications he had decided to let the Soviets make use of his military bases. Soviet reconnaissance planes were briefly deployed to an airfield near Tripoli, the Soviet Navy was using Tobruk as an anchorage where it repaired and restocked its ships, and a Soviet-designed airfield was under construction at Jufra in the Libyan desert.

A paper written by the NSC staff summed up the view from Washington: "Qaddafi's adventurism is accelerating and the constraints on his international behavior are fewer. NATO allies, despite Qaddafi's demonstrated capacity for mischief-making, compete with each other for profitable Libyan contracts while pronouncing the convenient rationale that it is better to collaborate with Qaddafi than to isolate him."

The Reagan administration's own track record in isolating Qaddafi wasn't much better, particularly when measured against its rhetoric. Despite the 1981 decree invalidating passports for travel to Libya, more than a thousand Americans continued to live and work there. With its forces concentrated off the coast of Lebanon, the Pentagon was no longer keeping the pressure on Qaddafi with periodic freedom of navigation exercises into the Gulf of Sidra. The CIA's covert efforts to topple Qaddafi consisted of little more than underwriting a feeble exile movement and its propaganda broadcasts. The exiles mounted a coup attempt in May of 1984 but it succeeded only in triggering a purge of the Libyan military in which seventy-five officers were executed. Iraq, not the United States, was the major supporter and trainer of anti-Qaddafi saboteurs, a project the Iraqis launched after Libya began providing arms to Iran.

In June 1984, one month after the failed coup attempt, Graham Fuller, the CIA's National Intelligence Officer for the Near East, produced a twenty-nine-page Interagency Intelligence Memorandum assessing Qaddafi's vulnerabilities. Fuller concluded that despite declining oil revenues, food shortages, and falling public spending, "no course of action short of stimulating Qaddafi's fall will bring any significant and enduring change in Libyan policies." To that end, Fuller recommended increased support for the Libyan exiles plus "a broad program in cooperation with key countries combining political, economic and paramilitary action." As usual, the State Department's Bureau of Intelligence and Research dissented, questioning the reliability and thoroughness of American intelligence on Qaddafi and pointing out that he remained a popular figure in Libya despite his erratic behavior and questionable policies. At the CIA, deputy director John McMahon saw nothing but trouble in providing more covert aid to the Libyan exiles, arguing that they were still too weak, too scattered, and too divided to put any real pressure on Qaddafi.

Faced with this by now familiar bureaucratic gridlock, Donald Fortier, the NSC's director of politico-military affairs, launched another effort to push the administration's policy toward Libya off dead center. On the last day of 1984, the Policy Review Group, an innocuously named body which helped plan covert operations, directed the CIA to draft a new presidential finding authorizing the agency to supply "lethal aid" to armed opposition groups. The proposed directive would be submitted to the top-level National Security Planning Group, chaired by the President himself.

To lay the groundwork, Fortier turned to Vincent Cannistraro, a veteran CIA officer who had served in Libya and headed the agency's Libya task force and who now was assigned to the NSC staff. Fortier asked him to draw up a list of suggestions for turning the screws on Qaddafi. Completed on January 17, 1985, Cannistraro's paper reported that "a consensus within the intelligence community has developed concerning Qaddafi's increasing adventurism and his ability and determination to undermine U.S. interests around the world. A number of new terrorist incidents sponsored by Qaddafi can be forecast as well as new efforts to subvert allies and governments friendly to the West. Soviet exploitation of Libya will increase and represents a major threat to the U.S. Sixth Fleet." The paper recounted the recent increase in Libyan adventurism and attacked the argument that Qaddafi was an irritant but not a threat to American strategic interests. "There is surface plausibility to this argument, but it does not measure the Soviet willingness to exploit the situation to their own benefit, and it does not give full weight to Qaddafi's ultimate objectives, purposes and willingness to support his goals despite heavier political and economic costs. In the absence of any real penalties resulting from his imprudent involvement in other nations, the constraints on Qaddafi's adventurism are diminishing. . . . Continued American vacillation on Libyan policy conceivably may result in a Libya even more hostile and more dangerous to U.S. interests."

Fortier and Cannistraro believed Qaddafi was vulnerable. They pointed out that Libyan foreign currency reserves had declined from $14 billion in June 1981 to $3.1 billion in January 1985, while Qaddafi's quixotic engineering projects like the "great manmade river" to irrigate the desert were estimated to cost $20 billion during the next ten years. If Qaddafi kept buying weapons and building manmade rivers at the same rate, Libya would exhaust its cash reserves within two years. However, Fortier and Cannistraro went on to point out that the administration's ability to take advantage of these vulnerabilities was severely constricted by the existing ban on lethal aid to anti-Qaddafi forces, particularly since that ban sent "the wrong signal to regional friends and western allies and to the moderate Libyan opposition."

They warned that stepping up pressure on Qaddafi was not without risk. "Active American participation in anti-Qaddafi activity by the Libyan opposition may result in the removal of the last restraints against Libyan-sponsored terrorism directed at American citizens and officials," Cannistraro wrote. Provocative American military maneuvers off the Libyan coast could prompt Qaddafi to make good on his repeated threats to sign a friendship treaty with the Soviet Union. Finally, there was the more fundamental problem that American intelligence "has significant gaps which must be covered in order to support better U.S. policy formulation on Libya."

Fortier and Cannistraro then proposed two approaches, one "broad" and the other "bold." The "broad" approach called for increased pressure on the remaining American citizens and businesses to leave Libya and for Reagan to reassure Egypt's President Mubarak that the administration was taking a more activist approach to the Libyan problem. "Followup discussions with the Egyptians on contingency military planning should be initiated, with the emphasis on U.S. possible support to Egyptian contingency plans in the event of armed conflict with Libya," they suggested. At the same time, they proposed that the Pentagon revive and expand the freedom of navigation exercises off Libya, "coupling these exercises with provocative ship movements into the Gulf of Sidra."

The "bold" approach envisioned "a number of visible and covert actions designed to bring significant pressure to bear upon Qaddafi and possibly to cause his removal from power." Specifically, the Reagan administration should: encourage Egypt and Algeria "to seek a *casus belli* for military action against Tripoli and plan with these countries U.S. military support to their possible joint action"; and provide weapons, ammunition, and intelligence to armed opposition groups conducting sabotage campaigns against economic, military, and communications installations. "Actions carried out by the Libyan armed opposition, if successful in augmenting significant pressure on Qaddafi and diminishing the stability of his regime, may lead to action by moderate Libyan army officers who are discontented with Qaddafi's policies," Fortier and Cannistraro suggested. There was, they noted, a down side to the "bold" approach. It might alarm the European allies, who still wanted to practice detente with Libya, and it could drive Qaddafi into the arms of the Soviets.

Fortier's effort might well have gone nowhere had it not been for the hijacking of TWA 847. Qaddafi was not linked in any way to the hijacking, but the seventeen days of helplessness, the murder of another innocent American, and the ease with which the culprits slipped away, all fed an urge to lash out against terrorism. Iran and Hezbollah were the obvious targets, just as they had been in the aftermath of the Marine bombing in Lebanon, but Hezbollah still held Americans hostage and Iran increasingly appeared to be the key to their release. Almost by elimination, Libya became the focus of the Reagan administration's pent-up rage and frustration.

In mid-July, two weeks after the TWA hostages were finally released, Robert Gates, the CIA's deputy director for intelligence, wrote a paper suggesting that American cooperation with Egypt could present an opportunity "to redraw the map of North Africa." With that as ammunition, Vice Adm. John Poindexter, the deputy national security adviser, began pressing an ambitious scheme, codenamed "Flower/Rose," to mount a joint U.S.-Egyptian attack on Libya. Going beyond anything Gates had suggested in his memo, Flower/Rose called for American logistical support of an Egyptian invasion of Libya. But, as always with military operations, there were complications. What if, for instance, the Egyptian Army bogged down in the Libyan desert? Would the United States just sit on its hands and watch the invasion fail? The Joint Chiefs of Staff warned that as many as six divisions might be required if the U.S. Army were forced to come to Egypt's rescue. To the activists on the National Security Council staff, that kind of alarmist warning was typical of the military's unremitting opposition to the use of force. The chiefs were so leery of being sucked in that they didn't want American fighter planes to escort Egyptian resupply flights into Libyan territory. The Americans could go as far as the border and no farther—a prohibition the NSC staff quickly eliminated from the plan. The Joint Chiefs had at least one ally in Nicholas Veliotes, the American Ambassador to Egypt, who was summoned back to Washington and briefed on Flower/Rose. "Talking to this crowd, and especially John Poindexter, was really something," Veliotes said afterwards. "He didn't understand. He didn't want to understand. He wanted action."

By the time Poindexter, along with Fortier and a senior CIA officer, arrived in Cairo over the Labor Day weekend for a face-to-face meeting with Mubarak, Flower/Rose had wilted. Mubarak simply did not trust the United States to keep such a sensitive undertaking secret. The year before, Mubarak had secretly agreed to allow the nuclear-powered cruiser *Arkansas* to pass through the Suez Canal—a violation of Egypt's own prohibition of allowing nuclear ships to use the canal. The transit had barely been completed before it was reported in the American press. With that kind of track record for secrecy, Mubarak was not about to commit himself to a joint operation with the United States against another Arab nation, even Qaddafi's. In the end, nothing came of Flower/ Rose except Poindexter's own conviction that the bureaucracy and the press could be counted on to strangle or expose any and all proposals for bold, imaginative action.

One month later, President Reagan finally signed a new intelligence finding authorizing the CIA to support existing Egyptian, Iraqi, and Algerian efforts to organize, train, and equip Libyan opposition groups. That got past the bureaucracy but ran into opposition on Capitol Hill. Senators David Durenberger and Patrick Leahy, the chairman and vice chairman of the Senate Intelligence Committee, wrote Reagan and CIA director Casey opposing the operation and threatening to close it down. Within weeks, news of the operation leaked to *The Washington Post,* and it had to be scuttled. The leak, which the FBI believed had come from Capitol Hill, infuriated Poindexter. If the bureaucracy and the press didn't kill a good idea, Congress would.

As 1985 drew to a close, the administration's policy toward Libya was right back where it had started. It might have stayed there had not Qaddafi joined forces with the notorious Abu Nidal, once again proving that the mercurial colonel was his own worst enemy.

★　★　★

The State Department described Abu Nidal's band as "probably the best organized and most effective of the radical Palestinian terrorist groups, carefully planning its operations and keeping its information tightly compartmented." That was another way of saying the U.S. government knew very little about Abu Nidal. It knew that his real name was Sabri al-Banna and that he had broken away from the mainstream PLO in 1974 after Arafat claimed to have banned terrorist attacks outside Israel and the occupied territories. Since then, he and his followers had dedicated themselves to wiping out all diplomatic efforts to reconcile Israel and the moderate Arab states, relying on the radical states of Iraq, Syria, and Libya to provide safe haven, financing, and logistics. But Iraq eventually threw him out, Syria tightened its rein on his activities, and by the middle of 1985 Abu Nidal seemed to be finding common cause with Libya, taking up part-time residence in Tripoli and working with Qaddafi to foment revolution in Egypt.

In November of 1985, three of Abu Nidal's men hijacked an EgyptAir plane minutes after it took off from Athens bound for Cairo. An Egyptian sky marshal pulled his gun and killed one of the hijackers, setting off a fusillade of bullets which depressurized the cabin and forced the pilot to make an emergency landing on the island of Malta. The hijackers' only demand was for fuel, and when they didn't get it, they began executing passengers, shooting two Americans and three Israelis at point-blank range. Miraculously, three of the victims survived.

The United States offered to send a team from the Joint Special Operations Command, but the Maltese said no—which was perhaps just as well, given the troubles JSOC had getting airborne. According to a letter written by the Pentagon's Noel Koch, "the team was to assemble at 2200 [10:00 P.M.] for wheels up. They were there. The plane broke. It took four hours to bring another plane in. It broke too. Three planes broke that night." The team finally got to Sigonella, Sicily, but no farther. With the Maltese firmly opposed to any American presence, the most the United States could do was provide air cover for a transport plane carrying a team of Egyptian commandos to Malta. To convince the Egyptians that they were safe from interception by Libyan jets, two American military officers assigned to the U.S. Embassy in Cairo accompanied the commandos on their flight to Malta. The hijacking ended in particularly gruesome fashion when the Egyptian commandos stormed the plane, blowing their way in with a grossly overpowered explosive device. Those passengers who were not killed in the blast and ensuing fire were gunned down by the commandos as they tried to flee the plane. A total of sixty people died, the bloodiest skyjacking on record.

Even before the hijacking had ended, U.S. intelligence was gathering evidence that Libya had played a major role in the bloodbath. The CIA picked up one intelligence report that Qaddafi had paid as much as $5 million for the hijacking. Intercepts of communications between Tripoli and the Libyan People's Bureau in Malta convinced members of the National Security Council staff that the Libyan government was a partner in the hijacking, that it probably had known it was going to happen and certainly had passed instructions to the hijackers once they were on the ground in Malta. The government of Malta was one of Qaddafi's few real allies. The two countries had signed a treaty of friendship complete with secret codicils allowing Libya to operate a radar station on Malta and to refuel its military aircraft at Maltese bases.

Little more than a month passed before Qaddafi was at it again, this time at the Rome and Vienna airports. Twenty people, five of them Americans, died at Rome and Vienna in simultaneous attacks which the State Department said had "the hallmarks of Abu Nidal," Qaddafi's favorite terrorist. In fact, the surviving terrorists in both the Rome and Vienna attacks admitted to being members of the Abu Nidal organization. They had planned to commandeer a fully loaded El Al plane and blow it up over Israel. When they were spotted by security agents before they could board the plane, they turned their guns on the ticket counter. One of those killed in the murderous barrage was an eleven-year-old American schoolgirl named Natasha Simpson who was going home to see relatives over the Christmas holidays. As Oliver North later described it, one of the terrorists "blasted . . . Natasha Simpson to her knees, deliberately zeroed in and fired an extra burst at her head, just in case." She died in her father's arms. It was a typical Abu Nidal operation—no demands, no theater, just murder most foul.

The terrorists who killed Natasha Simpson were carrying Tunisian passports that the Tunisian government identified as having been confiscated or stolen from Tunisian citizens working in Libya—a classic case of state-supported terrorism. It was not so simple as that, however. The one terrorist to survive the Rome attack later told Italian authorities he had been trained at a camp in the Bekaa Valley by Syrian agents who then accompanied him on the journey from Damascus to Rome. Assad, at least, had the good sense to remain silent. Qaddafi hailed the airport massacres as "heroic actions." Qaddafi was not the only head of state who supported terrorism, but he was certainly the most galling.

★ ★ ★

Lt. Col. Fred Allen knew nothing of the investigative details of the airport massacres when he walked into a briefing room at Patch Army Barracks in Stuttgart on Saturday morning, January 4, to present his strike plan to Gen. Bernard Rogers, the commander of U.S. forces in Europe, and his deputy, Gen. Richard Lawson. Allen felt uncomfortable standing before these two four-star generals in a borrowed set of Air Force blues. He had practiced his briefing before lower-ranking officers and had it down cold, but there was always the chance of a surprise question he wasn't prepared to answer.

Allen's plan called for sending six F-111s on a middle-of-the-night, low-level run that would cross the Libyan coast east of Tripoli, circle around behind the airport, turn north and hit the planes parked on the ramp with dozens of 500-pound bombs. Rogers, still smarting from criticism that his command had not done enough to support the Marines in Beirut in 1983, asked what other aircraft Allen would need to back him up—to jam Libyan radars, to knock out Libyan antiaircraft sites, to shoot down Libyan interceptors. Don't be afraid to ask for something just because you think you won't get it, Rogers told Allen.

Allen said he didn't need any help. The element of surprise would be enough. Libyan defenses looked impressive on paper—more antiaircraft guns and missile batteries in the Tripoli area than in any comparable area of Central Europe—but they were almost nonexistent in practice. The Libyans didn't even bother to man much of their air defense network at night. "I was absolutely convinced that given the competence of Libyan armed forces and the state of affairs in Libya . . . we could sneak in there and sneak out," Allen recalled. "I felt a bigger package was much more likely to tip them off."

Allen was not the only briefer to outline a strike plan for Rogers and Lawson. Cdr. Byron Duff, the air wing commander on the carrier *Coral Sea,* explained how the Navy would go after the same two targets. Duff sensed that no decisions were going to be made as a result of this first briefing; Rogers and Lawson were just trying to get a feel for the preparedness of the forces and the confidence of the pilots. Rogers asked Duff the same question he had asked Allen: Do you have everything you need to do the job? Duff's assessment was essentially the same as Allen's—a small force operating with the element of surprise would be more effective than an overwhelming force that telegraphed its punch. Duff shared Allen's low opinion of the Libyan defenses. "Outside of Syria and the Soviet Union, Libya had the best equipment in the world," Duff said later. "Whether they can operate it is another question."

Even before Allen and Duff had briefed their no-frills strike plans to Rogers and Lawson, the Navy had begun to move additional forces into the Mediterranean—and the press had picked it up. On New Year's Day, a squadron of EA-6B "Prowler" electronic warfare planes had left their home base on Whidbey Island, Washington, bound for Sigonella, Sicily. From there, the Prowlers would join the *Coral Sea,* where they could be used to jam Libyan air defense radars. By the time Allen and Duff stood before Rogers and Lawson, the newspapers and airwaves were brimming with talk of retaliation against Libya—most of it way ahead of what the military was ready to do.

On New Year's Day, 1986, just as Allen was beginning to lay out the plan for an F-111 strike against Libya, the Associated Press reported that "the Joint Chiefs of Staff sent President Reagan a list of possible military options to use against terrorists in the Middle East." On January 3, as Allen was rehearsing the briefing he would deliver the following day, *The Washington Post* reported that "the military contingency planning has looked at the use of F/A-18 bombers on the carrier USS *Coral Sea* . . . B-52 bombers based in the United States and F-111 fighter bombers based in England." By January 5, the day after Allen had briefed the plan for an F-111 strike, network camera crews were camped outside the gate at Lakenheath.

It was the beginning of an onslaught of news reports which over the coming months would detail not only the types of aircraft that might be used but the kinds of targets—military, terrorist, or economic—that might be hit. "It really torqued me off," said Rear Adm. Jerry Breast, the commander of the *Coral Sea* battle group. "Some of the info I was holding above the top-secret level would repeatedly come out in the press a day or two after I received it." "We would get a target list and read about it in *Time* magazine," Cdr. Byron Duff complained. "We saw the Libyans responding to some of that information in the way they moved their missile systems around." The drumbeat of news stories about military options was so relentless that Col. Sam Westbrook, the commander of the F-111 wing at Lakenheath, began to think it must be a deliberate campaign of psychological warfare designed to wear the Libyans to a frazzle.

★   ★   ★

Surprise—true bolt-out-of-the-blue surprise—was not something American military forces could realistically expect to achieve in the 1980s. The United States might be at war with terrorists, but it was at peace with the world, and in peacetime, unusual movements of military forces had no background noise in which to hide. In peacetime, the movements of military forces were not accorded the same "loose lips sink ships" sanctity of wartime.

It was true that ever since Vietnam an element of distrust had pervaded American news coverage of its military. But it was not true that reporters were disloyal to their country or cavalier about the lives of American servicemen. Reporters found out about the movements of American military units not from Russian spies but from officials in the Pentagon, State Department, and White House—the ubiquitous "administration sources." If a responsible government official told a reporter about the movement of a military unit, was it not at least reasonable to assume that that information would not be damaging to the nation's security if published or broadcast? Unfortunately, it was seldom so tidy as that. To begin with, certain government officials were not responsible. Some liked to impress reporters with how much they knew; others wanted to show the world the United States really was doing something about the problem at hand; still others didn't like what was happening and tried to kill it by exposure. Add to that mixture of motives the intense competition among news organizations for "scoops," and almost no secret was safe.

Reporters could keep secrets. They had kept the military identities of the TWA passengers secret for seventeen days—secret from the American public, that is; the hijackers knew all along. But in peacetime, when military forces exist as a deterrent, as an advertisement of the consequences of attacking the United States, the presumption was that information about the disposition of American forces was meant to be published. More often than not—the marshalling of forces off Lebanon during the TWA crisis, for instance—that was the case. Sometimes— preparations for the invasion of Grenada, for instance—it was not, and the consequences of exposing them were potentially disastrous. Merit and hypocrisy could be found on both sides of the military versus press argument. The basic fact was that neither side had yet figured out how to operate in the gray zone between war and peace.

★   ★   ★

As time passed, as more and more stories about options for a strike against Libya appeared, the element of surprise vanished, and the planning became increasingly difficult and complex. "It became obvious that strategic surprise was no longer an option," Col. Sam Westbrook the Lakenheath commander, recalled. "The chances of our getting down there undetected—the chances of catching the Libyans sitting on their front porches smoking their pipes—were very, very slim."

In the Mediterranean, the Soviets were now watching the American fleet's every move. When twenty-one U.S. warships surged through the Strait of Sicily at the start of a long-scheduled antisubmarine exercise, the Soviet Navy turned out in force. The waters between Sicily and North Africa became so crowded that an American and a Soviet submarine collided.

No longer able to count on surprise, Westbrook had to plan a SEAD campaign, Suppression of Enemy Air Defenses. Along with the F-111 bombers, other waves of aircraft would have to jam and destroy the Libyan air defenses. In addition to EF-111 electronic combat planes, Westbrook would need Navy F-14s to protect his F-111s from Libyan interceptors as well as carrier-based F-18s and A-7s to fire Shrike and HARM missiles that would home in on the Libyan radar. "That presented us at Lakenheath with significant problems," Westbrook recalled. "We didn't do much with the U.S. Navy. Our focus was on Central Europe." Navy and Air Force pilots began shuttling back and forth between Lakenheath and the carriers in the Mediterranean, trying to learn each other's ways of going to war.

The amount of work to be done was overwhelming. Over the following months, the Joint Chiefs of Staff would forward 36 different targets to Lakenheath and 152 targets to the carriers in the Mediterranean. A special courier run had to be set up in order to keep the planners supplied with up-to-date satellite photographs of the targets. For each potential target, the satellite photographs had to be studied, the coverage of Libyan air defenses plotted, a route in and out of the target area selected, weapons chosen—all while maintaining the normal tempo of NATO training and operations which was, after all, the primary mission. Westbrook deliberately kept the number of officers working on the Libyan contingency small, both to minimize the chances of a leak and to keep the bulk of his men focused on the NATO mission. When one of his Libyan planners fell asleep waiting for him to read a message, Westbrook decided he had kept the circle of knowledge too small and had heaped too much work on too few officers.

Westbrook was away from Lakenheath much of the time as he went about the routine duties of a wing commander. During his absences his deputy, Col. Robert Vencus, was in command. Vencus was new to the F-111 but a veteran fighter pilot who had been through these contingency drills before. Never once in his twenty-four years of active duty had a contingency plan been executed, and this one seemed less and less likely as the horrors of Rome and Vienna began to fade from memory. "The possibility of going decreased," Vencus recalled, "but the workload didn't." Demands for new strike plans kept coming in, usually arriving late in the afternoon with the requirement that they be completed by the next morning. Sometimes the planners at Lakenheath simply could not meet the deadline for a response. "We had to cry uncle a few times," Vencus said.

In Washington, a special targeting committee had been set up under Assistant Secretary of Defense Richard Armitage with representatives from State, CIA, the Joint Chiefs of Staff, and the National Security Council staff. Almost immediately, the chiefs and the NSC staff were at odds. The chiefs proposed targets which could be connected directly to Qaddafi's support of terrorism and subversion but which the NSC staff regarded as virtually meaningless. One target high on the chiefs' list was the underwater swimmers' school at Sidi Bilal near Tripoli, which had been the homeport for the ship that laid mines in the Red Sea in 1984. The NSC staff didn't see the point in using F-111 bombers to empty a swimming pool, but the chiefs refused to countenance outside meddling in what they regarded as strictly a military question. Military officers could still remember what had happened in Vietnam when the White House had picked the bombing targets.

The NSC staff wanted, among other things, to go after economic targets—oil facilities—but the chiefs didn't like the idea of hitting civilian targets. When James Stark, a Navy captain temporarily assigned to the NSC staff, insisted on being briefed by the Defense Intelligence Agency on potential economic targets in Libya, the intelligence officer who reluctantly gave the briefing began by saying, Well, hello, this must be Admiral Stark.

The NSC staff also was interested in exploring different ways of attacking the targets proposed by the chiefs, using some of the Pentagon's newest weapons—the cruise missile and the "Stealth" fighter plane, in particular—to dazzle Qaddafi with American technology. Again, the military bridled at what it regarded as outside interference. Poindexter dispatched Stark to the Navy targeting center in Norfolk, Virginia, to see the work being done on developing the computerized maps needed for the guidance system of the cruise missile—a tiny, pilotless aircraft that could be launched from a submarine. Stark was distressed to find the Navy developing maps to attack antiaircraft sites, which he considered to be a waste of a high-priced weapon. The cruise missile should be saved for attacks against high-value targets like Qaddafi's headquarters, Stark argued. The chiefs said it was none of Stark's business. Besides, they were not about to risk weapons developed to deal with the Soviet threat against a third-rate military power like Libya. The twenty-year-old F-111 was the right weapon for the likes of Qaddafi.

It was purely coincidence, but the F-111s at Lakenheath were commanded by the hottest young colonel in the Air Force. Sam Westbrook had been headed straight for the top ever since he had graduated first in his class from the Air Force Academy and had been handed his diploma by President Kennedy. Rhodes Scholar and combat pilot, Westbrook seemed charmed, a natural for commanding what was potentially the most important Air Force operation since the end of the Vietnam War.

The bombing tactics Westbrook's pilots would use against targets in Libya were the same ones they practiced for targets in Central Europe—low-level, nighttime runs that used the F-111's terrain-following radar to pilot the plane automatically at altitudes and speeds no human could master. What made the Libyan contingency so different was the extreme range involved: thousands of miles from Lakenheath to Libya and back, as opposed to hundreds of miles for targets in Central Europe. Theoretically, the F-111 had unlimited range because it was equipped for air-to-air refueling. But nighttime refueling was a tricky maneuver that threatened to throw off the split-second timing needed to hit targets at the same instant as the Navy.

F-111s based at Upper Heyford Royal Air Force Base set out to test the mechanics of a long-range nighttime run with an exercise called "Ghost Rider," a practice attack against Goose Bay, Canada. "Ghost Rider almost got canceled right off the bat because of the tremendous number of aircraft flogging around in the dark," Westbrook said. "The most important lesson was that when you start talking about going those kinds of distances at night, you need a very simple join-up and refueling plan."

A standard refueling plan called for tankers to rendezvous with bombers at pre-selected points along the way. A bomber crossing the Atlantic, for example, might be refueled by a tanker flying out of the Azores. But at night, in radio silence, with large numbers of aircraft, the rendezvous was too intricate a maneuver for an operation that was to be run, literally, by the clock. The only alternative was to do away with the rendezvous by having the tankers accompany the bombers from takeoff to landing, serving in effect as mother ships. That increased the fuel requirements for the mission enormously, but no one was going to ask how much a raid on Libya cost—unless, of course, it failed.

Westbrook began sending his squadrons on nonstop runs to Incirlik, Turkey, picking up their mother tankers as soon as they took off from Lakenheath and staying with them until they broke off to drop their weapons on a Turkish bombing range. That was about as close to the real thing as he could get. In fact, Westbrook worried that it might be too close, that the Russians might notice the striking similarity between the run to Incirlik and the run to Tripoli and pass a warning to Qaddafi.

★　★　★

For all the intensity of the planning and training, the Reagan administration still was not ready to order a retaliatory raid against Libya. Secretary of State Shultz pressed for a strike at Qaddafi, but again, Defense Secretary Weinberger and the Joint Chiefs resisted. Was the evidence of Libyan involvement in the airport massacres overwhelming? Would a retaliatory strike decrease the likelihood of further attacks against Americans, or would it put Americans in greater danger? Had all other responses been exhausted, leaving military action the last and only option? The answer to all of the above was no. The available evidence of Libyan involvement in the airport massacres was persuasive but not overwhelming. There were still some 1,500 Americans living and working in Libya, all of them potential hostages or even victims of a bombing raid. The United States had not exhausted economic and diplomatic sanctions against Libya.

Despite the sanctions enacted in 1981 and 1982, five oil companies and thirteen other American firms, most of them construction, engineering, or oil service companies, were still doing business in Libya, lifting some 700,000 barrels of Libyan crude a day and helping Qaddafi build his "great manmade river" to irrigate the desert. According to Commerce Department figures, the United States had exported nearly $260 million worth of goods to Libya during the first ten months of 1985—59 percent more than it had during the same period in 1984. The campaign against Libya, which had enjoyed such a high profile during Reagan's first year in office, had run out of steam in the face of entrenched opposition from vested economic and diplomatic interests both in and out of government.

During the fall of 1985, the State Department had looked for ways to tighten the screws on Libya, but the usual bureaucratic deadlock had resulted. "It really was shaping up to be a nice little bureaucratic battle," said Michael Ussery of State's Near East bureau. But now, in the wake of the airport massacres at Rome and Vienna, the bureaucratic resistance to economic sanctions was swallowed up in the rush for retaliation. Donald Fortier, now the deputy national security adviser, directed Elaine Morton, the former State Department North Africa officer now assigned to the NSC staff, to draft a proposal for severing all economic ties with Libya. Morton, who had spent five years laboring in the boiler room of Libya policy, wrote the paper from memory and watched in amazement as it sailed through the bureaucracy. "All those bureaucratic battles and brute labor, and then you write half a page and the people in the State Department, who are utterly opposed to economic sanctions, had to stay up all night drafting the executive order," she marveled.

Morton's memo relied on the International Emergency Economic Powers Act, which empowered the President to impose tougher sanctions if he declared Qaddafi a threat to America's national security. "It wasn't a very good vehicle, but it was the only one available," said David Long of the State Department's Office for Combatting Terrorism. "We had to invoke a threat to national security coming from this pipsqueak. We knew there wasn't, but that's all that was available to us."

Duly declaring Libya "a threat to the national security and foreign policy of the United States," the President on January 7, 1986, severed virtually all remaining economic ties with Libya and ordered all Americans still living there "to leave immediately." In a nationally televised news conference, he also threatened that "if these steps do not end Qaddafi's terrorism, I promise you that further steps will be taken."

Even the first steps, however, were difficult, and they were unlikely to succeed if America's European allies didn't join in taking them—or at least promise not to undo them by filling the vacuum created by the pullout of American firms and technicians. Just getting American citizens out of Libya was hard enough. Qaddafi allowed them to come and go without having their passports stamped, making it impossible to enforce the ban on travel to Libya. When American oil companies complained that they would lose all their assets in Libya if they complied with the President's order to leave within thirty days, they were given six months to withdraw.

Deputy Secretary of State John Whitehead was dispatched to Europe to implore the allies to reduce their purchases of Libyan oil, to cut off sales of military hardware to Qaddafi, to stop extending official credits to Libya, to condemn Libya by name for supporting terrorism, and to shut down Libya's People's Bureaus, which continued to function as recruiting offices and command posts for terrorist activities. The allies agreed not to allow their companies to take up the slack left by the retreating Americans and to cut off official credit to Tripoli, but those were relatively easy decisions because the Europeans were growing tired of waiting for Libya to pay its bills. When it came to the tougher decisions, the allies declined to stop buying Libyan oil, and Greece even refused to join in an arms embargo. Whitehead prepared a report card on the allies for Shultz. Canada and Italy got the highest marks; Britain and Greece both received "Ds." Professor Whitehead also reported that the Europeans unanimously opposed military action against Libya.

The sanctions were a study in frustration. The administration froze $1 billion in Libyan assets in the United States, then watched helplessly as Bankers Trust returned $320 million in deposits and interest and another $2.2 million in damages after the Libyans sued and a British court ruled that Reagan's order did not apply to the bank's London branch. What limited effect the freeze had was more than offset by Qaddafi's decision to sell Libya's share of Fiat, a transaction which raised $3.2 billion. Qaddafi managed to evade a ban on acquiring U.S. technology by using a dummy corporation in Hong Kong to import two Airbus jets with American-made engines through Jordan. At least, the sanction-busting did not come as a surprise. "Everybody went into it with their eyes open," said State's Michael Ussery. "None of us thought: 'Oh boy, this is really going to hurt Qaddafi.' "

It really didn't matter. The sanctions were only a first step. Having got them out of the way, Donald Fortier said, people will step up to more forceful actions. As Fortier outlined it, the plan called for "disproportionate" responses to Libyan provocations. Every time Qaddafi made a move, the United States would up the ante. It was clear to everyone where that would lead. It was only a matter of weeks before Michael

Ussery and David Long wrote a memo to Secretary of State Shultz warning that the shock value of the economic sanctions and the tough talk about military action already were beginning to wear off and that the new Libya policy was likely to fail unless the President was prepared to up the ante again. He was.

★   ★   ★

At the time of the Rome and Vienna massacres there had been only one carrier, the *Coral Sea,* in the Mediterranean, a fact Weinberger used to argue against those who wanted to retaliate immediately. Although Weinberger was reluctant to use military power, he also believed that if and when it finally came to that, there was no excuse for using anything less than overwhelming force. When the Joint Chiefs of Staff had recommended the number of troops needed to invade Grenada, he had arbitrarily ordered them to double the size of the force. The military had used two carriers when it conducted the 1981 exercise in the Gulf of Sidra, and given everything that had happened since, there was even more reason to insist on at least two carriers now. Weinberger wanted three.

An aircraft carrier is an accident waiting to happen—90,000 tons of steel filled with explosives and flammable liquids manned by a crew whose average age is nineteen, two thirds of them on their first overseas deployment. Normal flight operations are risky enough; pilots are lost on virtually every overseas deployment, no matter how routine. Why increase the risks by forcing one carrier to do the work of two or three? A single carrier could not keep its planes up for twenty-four hours a day without risking pilot and flight line fatigue, which could very quickly lead to accidents.

Besides, the Libyans might get lucky against one carrier. They were poor pilots by American standards, but it would only take one missile fired in that split second when everyone was looking the other way. On January 13, an EA-3 electronic surveillance plane was intercepted by two Libyan MiG 25s 140 miles off the coast of Libya—the farthest from land Qaddafi's air force had ever operated. The *Coral Sea* immediately scrambled a pair of fighters, but if the Libyan pilots had wanted to shoot down the EA-3, they could have done it with ease.

The chances the Libyans might get off that one lucky shot were increasing now that a battery of Soviet-supplied, long-range SA-5 surface-to-air missiles located at Sirte, an air base at the foot of the Gulf of Sidra, was about to become operational. The Soviets also had moved the flagship of their Mediterranean fleet, a submarine tender bristling with antennas, into the harbor at Tripoli to provide the Libyans with intelligence gleaned from eavesdropping on the communications of the American fleet.

A second carrier, the *Saratoga* of *Achille Lauro* fame, moved into the Mediterranean on January 17, after steaming at flank speed in electronic silence from its anchorage at Diego Garcia in the southern reaches of the Indian Ocean. With two carriers in place, the Sixth Fleet began a series of exercises, officially titled "Operations in the Vicinity of Libya." Bureaucratically, the exercises were a grand compromise between hawks and doves. They could be whatever you wanted them to be—an innocent freedom of navigation exercise or a deliberate provocation, slicing deeper and deeper into the Gulf of Sidra until Qaddafi was spooked into doing something stupid that would give the fleet a chance to clobber him.

"Each Sidra exercise went a little deeper," the European Command's General Lawson acknowledged, but "we never made the stairstep plan with the idea that we were trying to suck anybody into anything." Sending the fleet in slowly, one step at a time, Qaddafi would give ample opportunity to consider his next move. Not incidentally, it would also give the Pentagon time to move a third carrier into the Mediterranean. The plan had been developed by Vice Adm. Frank Kelso, the commander of the Sixth Fleet, who said its sole purpose was "to show we could operate in international waters and not be blackmailed by Qaddafi into thinking the Gulf of Sidra is his lake." The fact that these exercises were being planned in the wake of the Rome and Vienna massacres was, to Kelso, irrelevant. "Our directions were to operate U.S. Navy forces in the Gulf of Sidra," he said. "You can put any context you want on it, but those were the directions."

Kelso was not a pilot but a nuclear submariner, a product of the harsh, perfectionist culture fostered by Hyman Rickover, the father of the nuclear Navy. Carrier pilots were the glory boys of the Navy, but if there were ever another world war, its outcome probably would be decided by the submariners. Theirs was a secretive society which shunned contact with the outside world, which believed that the less known about their operations the better. Now, after spending most of his adult life in that environment, Kelso suddenly found himself commanding the highest-profile military operation in the world.

The first phase of "Operations in the Vicinity of Libya" was scheduled to begin on January 26. The day before, Qaddafi, looking silly in an admiral's cap and white designer jump suit, boarded a patrol boat and headed out into the Gulf of Sidra, declaring that the invisible line which ran across the top of the Gulf at 32 degrees 30 minutes north latitude would become a "line of death" for anyone who dared to cross it. The sight of Qaddafi in his patrol boat, which quickly returned to shore because of rough seas, only dramatized the mismatch of forces.

Whether or not Qaddafi knew it when he made his threat, the fleet had no plans to cross the "line of death" during either the first or second phase of "Operations in the Vicinity of Libya." For the four days of the first phase, the carriers and their escort ships conducted air and surface operations in the Libyan Flight Identification Region, an area stretching hundreds of miles out into the Mediterranean where all aircraft had to identify themselves to Libyan air controllers but which not even Qaddafi claimed was Libyan territory. A total of fourteen Libyan jets flew toward the fleet and were routinely intercepted by the carrier aircraft—"nothing approaching what might be considered air combat," one of the *Coral Sea* pilots, Lt. Cdr. Robert Stumpf, reported.

During the second phase, from February 12 to 15, the Libyan Air Force was more active. "They came out with anything and everything," said Cdr. Byron Duff, the commander of the air wing aboard *Coral Sea.* According to Lt. Cdr. Stumpf, "during this four-day period, approximately 160 encounters were recorded." Stumpf reported that the Navy pilots "could often maneuver at will to arrive at a firing position behind the MiGs." The MiG 25, one of the Soviet Union's premier combat aircraft, turned out to be a sitting duck. Its engines put out so much heat that the infrared sensor on a Sidewinder missile could track it from 10 miles away. Its air intakes stuck out so far that the pilot could not see anything over his shoulder, which was the direction an enemy was most likely to come from. Sometimes, Stumpf reported, the Libyan pilots "appeared to slide down in the cockpit, as though they could keep from being shot by not exposing their upper torso through the canopy."

The Libyans literally didn't know what was happening. When they were intercepted by F-18s, the Navy's newest fighter, they reported back to their base that they had just encountered a single-seat model of the F-14.

"These guys were grapes," said Cdr. Robert Brodsky, the air group commander on the *Saratoga.* "It was incredible how poor they were at what they were trying to do." Patrolling at 20,000 feet, the F-14 crews could pick up the Libyan jets on radar up to 100 miles away. The F-14 would descend to 10,000 feet and come up behind the Libyan pilot without ever being detected. While the Libyan was scanning the skies with his naked eye, the American pilots were watching him through a television camera that could spot him up to 15 miles away. Brodsky became so confident of his ability to outmaneuver the Libyans that once when his wingman had to return to the ship because of a cracked canopy, he ran an intercept on two approaching MiGs without bothering to wait for a new wingman.

On occasion, Lt. Cdr. Stumpf said, "the Libyans would attempt to lure U.S. fighters below the 'line of death' by flying lazy, predictable patterns, gradually working southward." The Navy pilots always broke off before crossing the line. For that, they would have to wait until a third aircraft carrier arrived.

The *America* steamed into the Mediterranean in mid-March. The United States now had roughly $60 billion worth of planes, ships, and men amassed against a fourth-rate military power. If it looked like overkill, it was. Neither Vice Admiral Kelso, the fleet commander, nor Rear Admiral Jeremiah, the task force commander, had asked for the third carrier, but Weinberger was taking no chances. He convened a secret meeting of his top military commanders—Admiral Crowe, General Rogers, and General Lawson—in Würzburg, West Germany, to review the plan for going into the Gulf of Sidra and, most importantly, to hammer out the Rules of Engagement. No other military operation of the Reagan era had occasioned a similar gathering of operational commanders.

"ROE," said Crowe, referring to the Rules of Engagement, "that's always the problem." Rules of Engagement—the conditions under which American forces can open fire—are a standard part of every operations plan. Until Lebanon, the standard ROE for peacetime had been to fire if fired upon. In Lebanon, the suicide bombings of the American Embassy and the Marine barracks and the continuing threat of kamikaze trucks, planes and boats had prompted a change in the ROE to permit a commander to open fire if he determined the approaching vehicle, aircraft, or vessel to have hostile intent. "That was the first time in my career in peacetime I had seen dramatic changes in ROE," Crowe said. The ROE would be changed for the Gulf of Sidra as well. But, said Crowe, "you just don't put it in a message and say that takes care of it."

The commanders on the scene had to be convinced that the message meant what it said. "It's hard to persuade guys that for fifteen years now have been told Don't get us in a war, that you're serious that if the guy challenges us, we're going to shoot him," Crowe reflected. "That's hard to get across. You have to persuade people the mood has changed, that the situation is now different." Kelso, the Sixth Fleet commander, did not attend the meeting in Würzburg, so he flew to London to discuss the Rules of Engagement face to face with Weinberger. Later, Crowe flew to Naples for another meeting with Kelso. Given all these secret high-level meetings, Weinberger's public nonchalance seemed disengenuous.

"We've crossed that line seven times since 1981," he said, "so it wouldn't be particularly significant one way or the other" if the Sixth Fleet crossed it again.

"There was a big difference in the ROE this time," said Robert Brodsky, the *Saratoga* air group commander. In the previous exercises, "you could retaliate only against the particular party which committed the hostile act. For the March exercise, the rules changed. If one [Libyan] fires, then anybody else who has hostile intent is to be fired upon. Hostile intent is defined as being in a position to fire." In other words, the Libyans still got the first shot, but after that Libyan forces—any ship, plane, or missile battery—in a position to attack any unit of the Sixth Fleet was fair game. "We went at it with the idea that if one American was shot at, we weren't going to wait around for number two to be shot at," Kelso said. If the Libyans actually hit anybody, Kelso had plans to launch an all-out attack against a whole range of targets in Libya. Sam Westbrook's F-111s at Lakenheath were on alert, just in case. We're not going down there to get in a war, Kelso told his pilots, but we'll be ready if something happens.

The third phase of "Operations in the Vicinity of Libya," codenamed "Prairie Fire," began on March 23. The three carriers—*America, Coral Sea,* and *Saratoga*—were spread out east to west more than 150 miles north of the "line of death." On the morning of the 24th, three ships led by the guided-missile cruiser *Ticonderoga* crossed Qaddafi's "line of death." Above them F-14s, A-6s, and A-7s moved deeper into the Gulf. The fire-control radar of the Libyan SA-5 missile battery at Sirte locked on any aircraft that came within range. All the fleet's electronic sensors were focused on the battery, waiting for the first sign that a missile had been launched.

Just before two o'clock in the afternoon local time a pair of F-14s made a run at the Libyan coast, coming to within about 60 miles of Sirte. The battery launched a pair of SA-5 surface-to-air missiles [SAMs]. "That amazed the hell out of me," said Rear Adm. Jerry Breast, commander of the *Coral Sea* battle group. "I was in the war room, looking at a radar. You could see the missiles coming." The F-14s dove toward the surface while the telephone pole–sized SA-5s climbed to 90,000 feet. Unable to lock on a target, the missiles splashed harmlessly into the sea. "When he actually fired," Byron Duff, the air group commander on the *Coral Sea,* recalled, "We said, 'Holy shit! The dumb son-of-a-bitch!' "

Of all Libya's weapons, the SA-5 battery at Sirte was considered to be the one most directly under Qaddafi's control. "This was a very deliberate decision to react," said Rear Adm. Jeremiah. "The decision to engage us was a national command decision as opposed to a pilot who might accidentally have reacted." As Robert Brodsky put it, "the SA-5 site fired for the entire nation of Libya."

Qaddafi had made the mistake the hard-liners in Washington were waiting for. Incredibly to those in the White House Situation Room who were monitoring the action, the fleet did nothing. In Stuttgart, Gen. Lawson's secure phone lit up with calls from Washington. "Everybody is raising Cain with me because the pilots didn't shoot at the SAMs," Lawson recounted. How much longer are you going to wait? Washington wanted to know. What's the commander looking at? Does he need more resources?

"I knew the questions," Kelso said afterwards. "The pressure to fire was clearly there, but I didn't want to do it until we could do it safely." Kelso and Jeremiah plotted their next move. They didn't like the odds of a daylight strike on Sirte. "That place is deep inside the Gulf," Jeremiah explained. "Our aircraft were potentially flanked if the Libyans decided to launch their aircraft." Besides, Jeremiah added, the Libyans "would expect some form of immediate reaction and would be ready for us." Kelso and Jeremiah decided to wait. They could use the time to hand pick the flight crews and brief them eye-to-eye. "It was getting dark," Kelso remembered. "I liked the game plan at night. We operate very well at night. They don't." Kelso and Jeremiah could afford to wait—Libya wasn't going anywhere. "If we learned nothing else from the December 4th thing, it was to take your time and do it right," Brodsky said, referring to the disastrous 1983 raid on Syrian positions in Lebanon in which the insistence on launching at first light had cost one flyer his life and another his freedom.

On the *Coral Sea,* Breast, the only pilot among the three admirals, didn't give a damn about the SA-5 site. "My concern was the friggin' PT boats which we knew to be at sea." The Libyans had five PT boats armed with antiship missiles. "My focus was, let's get those bastards before it gets dark," Breast said. At worst, an SA-5 missile could shoot down an airplane. A PT boat could sink a ship.

In Washington, where it was still morning, Weinberger and Crowe were called to the White House to explain why the fleet had not retaliated. Was Weinberger up to his old tricks again? Weinberger and Crowe entered the Oval Office for what promised to be an extremely unpleasant meeting. "Just before the big conversation started," Crowe recalled, "I was handed a note that we'd sunk a patrol boat."

One of the Libyan patrol boats had begun a high-speed run toward the *Ticonderoga,* which was still operating below the "line of death." By now, Kelso had declared any approaching Libyan aircraft or ship hostile. "The patrol boat was carrying missiles with a forty- to forty-five-mile range," Kelso said. "He was moving to within range. It was clear to everybody that constituted hostile intent." The pilot of an A-6 attack plane armed with Harpoon antiship missiles saw the patrol boat coming but was not sure he had authority to fire. He radioed the *Saratoga,* requesting permission from Jeremiah to fire. The admiral says, Smoke 'em, the voice on the radio responded. The A-6 fired its Harpoon, and the patrol boat went down with all hands.

It was dark now in the Gulf, time to go after the SA-5 battery at Sirte. "It was basically a trap," explained Byron Duff. "I was one of the decoys," said Robert Brodsky, who was flying one of two A-7s high over the Gulf in full view of the SA-5 radar. Far below, less than 500 feet off the water, two more A-7s armed with HARM missiles crept to within 20 miles of the Libyan coast. The radar operators at Sirte took the bait, locking onto the high-flying A-7s. Brodsky and his wingman stayed right where they were. "They were just tweaking on us," Brodsky recalled. "It was a beautiful night. I was about fifty miles away from the SA-5, and I was sure I could have seen a launch." If the SA-5 fired, Brodsky and his wingman would dive for the water, confident that once they got below 1,000 feet, the missile no longer could track them. Before the SA-5 could fire, the low-flying A-7s sprung the trap, launching their HARM missiles, which rode the Libyan radar beam 30 miles back to Sirte. The first missile scored a direct hit on the radar dish; the second was rated a near miss.

The Libyans had the radar operating again in less than four hours. As soon as the radar locked onto another American plane, another A-7 launched two more HARMs. One of the missiles scored a direct hit, but the other was a dud.

The only remaining Libyan threat was the four PT boats still at sea. "We went through a pretty blackass night not knowing where those guys were," Breast recalled. "There were a lot of shadows out there in the dark that night." The cruiser *Yorktown* picked up a contact at 25 miles approaching the fleet at a speed of 37 knots. At a range of eight miles, the *Yorktown* fired a Harpoon missile and reported hitting a French-made La Combattante patrol boat. The destroyer *Richmond K. Turner* fired on another contact which was reported to be shooting at aircraft overhead. Like the *Yorktown,* the *Turner* reported hitting a La Combattante. The next morning, however, reconnaissance photographs showed both of the Libyan La Combattantes sitting safely in port. The *Yorktown* had fired at what turned out to be a flock of birds; the *Turner* at a patrol boat which already had been hit by an A-6 and was sending off streamers of exploding ammunition. "Had there been a well-coordinated enemy and had he aggressively moved against the fleet, they could have done some damage," Breast said afterward. As it was, two of the Libyan PT boats had approached the fleet, and each time they were put out of action by A-6s. After that, the Libyan military gave up.

Qaddafi had sent his forces into a battle they couldn't win. He seemed to relish the role of the Arab David against the American Goliath, but he could only play it for so long. If he kept it up, his armed forces would either be destroyed or turn against him. The first SA-5 had been launched at 1:52 in the afternoon, the last patrol boat was sunk at 7:07 the following morning. Byron Duff said, "We never heard another peep."

In fact, later that same day, March 25, there was a very significant peep—one that revealed Qaddafi had not given up, merely changed tactics. In a terse three-line cable intercepted by the National Security Agency, the Libyan intelligence service directed People's Bureaus in East Berlin, Paris, Rome, Madrid, and three other European capitals to develop plans for terrorist attacks against U.S. military installations and civilian targets frequented by Americans.

It was the first time Qaddafi had ever issued a general order to his People's Bureaus to attack Americans. There was no mention in the cable of the defeat which the Libyan Armed Forces had just suffered. But, given the timing, it was difficult not to conclude, as Gen. Lawson did, that "it's very possible that the March 25th message was a result of the shooting in the Gulf of Sidra on March 24th." Qaddafi himself drew the link. "It is a time for confrontation—for war," he said on the morning after. "If they [the United States] want to expand the struggle, we will carry it all over the world."

The United States, Qaddafi charged, had provoked Libya. Whatever followed would be the consequence of the Sixth Fleet crossing his "line of death." The onus, however, rested on Qaddafi. His support of terrorism, of Abu Nidal in particular, had led directly to the EgyptAir atrocity on Malta and to the airport massacres in Rome and Vienna, to the senseless murder of an eleven-year-old American girl. Qaddafi had brought the exercises in the Gulf of Sidra upon himself, had brought the Sixth Fleet's retaliation upon himself by ordering his forces to fire on planes operating in air space which all the world recognized as international. The United States was unquestionably within its rights and Qaddafi was the outlaw. Still, a more moderate administration, one less eager to make good on the President's pledge to stand tall, might not have pressed its rights so vigorously with so much military force, might not have set the United States and Libya on the collision course they were now on.

★   ★   ★

The first bomb went off on April 2, as TWA Flight 840 from Rome was beginning its descent into Athens. Four people, all of them Americans, one of them a nine-month infant in her mother's arms, were sucked through a gaping hole torn in the plane's fuselage. They fell 15,000 feet to earth, and their bodies were found by a shepherd. Autopsies later showed that three of the four were alive when they hit the ground.

An obscure group called the Arab Revolutionary Cells claimed responsibility, saying the bombing was in retaliation for America's actions in the Gulf of Sidra. There was, however, no evidence linking the atrocity to Qaddafi. The bomb, a 1-pound charge of plastic explosive placed under the seat cushion and triggered by a change in cabin pressure, was a trademark of the Palestinian splinter group May 15 and its master bomb builder Abu Ibrahim. The prime suspect, a Lebanese woman who on an earlier flight had occupied the seat where the bomb was planted, belonged to a left-wing pro-Syrian party with no discernible links to Qaddafi or to Abu Nidal. Later, intelligence officials concluded the bombing probably was the work of a close associate of Yasir Arafat who called himself Col. Hawari and who had recruited two expert bomb makers trained by Abu Ibrahim.

Three days later, at 1:49 A.M. Saturday April 5, a second bomb went off in the washroom of La Belle disco in West Berlin. The disco was packed with American soldiers. Sgt. Kenneth Ford was killed instantly; Sgt. James Goins was mortally wounded; a young Turkish woman also was killed. Earlier that same night, the General Communications Headquarters (GCHQ), Britain's counterpart to the National Security Agency, had intercepted a message to Tripoli from the People's Bureau in East Berlin predicting "a joyous event." The intercepted message had been routed to the operations center for the U.S. Army brigade stationed in West Berlin. It did not identify a specific target but sounded ominous enough to warrant pulling Brig. Gen. Thomas Griffin, the brigade's commanding officer, out of a German-American dinner party. By coincidence, his wife had been complaining of feeling ill, providing the general with a ready-made excuse for a rapid exit.

Griffin and his operations officer thought the American PX and one of the local bars that had been a target of previous terrorist plots were the most likely scenes for this "joyous event." There were, of course, lots of other bars frequented by American soldiers in West Berlin, but Griffin did not have enough MPs to clear them all out on a Friday night. He sent squads of MPs to begin checking the bars, looking for suspicious characters or activity, but it was a long shot at best. The MPs did not even have bomb-sniffing dogs. One team of MPs was only 300 yards from La Belle disco when the bomb went off, but even if they had gotten there in time, there is no guarantee they would have found it.

At almost that moment, GCHQ intercepted another message from East Berlin, this one reporting that the operation was a success and that it could not be traced to the People's Bureau. The Reagan administration had its smoking gun. The package of translated intercepts reached the White House Situation Room shortly after ten o'clock Saturday morning and was immediately relayed to the Western White House in Santa Barbara, California, where the President was vacationing. There was no doubt in anyone's mind what the President would decide to do.

Admiral Crowe called General Lawson in Stuttgart on the secure line. "He asked me, 'Have you looked at all the targets?' " Lawson recalled. "I said, 'Yes, here are the targets we think make the most sense.' " Lawson recommended five targets: three in Tripoli—Qaddafi's compound, the military side of the airport, and the frogman school—and two in Benghazi—the military airfield and Qaddafi's alternate command post. The targets all could be linked to Qaddafi's export of terror and subversion. The Il-76 transport planes parked on the apron at the Tripoli airport, for instance, were used to resupply Qaddafi's troops in Chad. "Anything else would have been too damn difficult to explain to the international community," Lawson reasoned.

Lawson had chosen the targets as much for their location as for their connection to terrorism. "We could minimize the risk to Americans because these targets were all near the coast," he explained. The longer American planes were over Libya, the greater the chance they would be shot down by antiaircraft fire. As far as the men who would execute the strike were concerned, that was the number one priority—no losses. Vice Adm. Kelso had stuck his finger in the middle of Rear Adm. Breast's chest and said, I don't want any of our aviators walking down the streets with a noose around his neck.

The no-loss policy also dictated the timing of the raid—at night when the Libyan antiaircraft network was at its lowest state of alert. As in all military operations, there were tradeoffs. A nighttime raid would not be as accurate as a daytime strike and would almost certainly result in missed targets and civilian casualties. Three of Lawson's five targets were located well away from civilian neighborhoods and were easy to identify on a radar screen, greatly reducing the chances that a nighttime mistake would kill or maim civilians. The other two targets presented real problems, both for the men in the cockpits and the civilians on the ground.

Qaddafi's alternate command post in Benghazi—the Jamahariyah Barracks—was a poor radar target easily lost in the downtown clutter of buildings. "Personally, I didn't agree with the assignment of that target," Jerry Breast said. "Jamahariyah was not a good target, not a good radar target. It was a bunch of flat barracks."

Qaddafi's compound in downtown Tripoli was even worse. Azziziyah Barracks—"the downtown target," as it was called—"was very difficult in terms of trying to find it and in terms of collateral damage since it was right in the middle of a populated area and in the middle of all their defenses," Air Force Col. Sam Westbrook said. There were apartment buildings across the street from the compound, well within range of potential error on a low-level night run at 600 miles per hour. Of all the targets Westbrook's pilots had studied, Azziziyah Barracks looked to be the most difficult and dangerous, so tough that the planners at Lakenheath had not bothered to develop a detailed plan for attacking it. Lakenheath had drawn up strike plans for thirty-six different targets, everything from oil refineries to military bases. Azziziyah Barracks was to be the thirty-seventh. "We had done so much planning against so many different targets," said Lt. Col. Fred Allen, one of the F-111 squadron commanders, "but it was not until the week before the raid that we did any detailed planning against Qaddafi's headquarters." No matter, said the European Command's Gen. Lawson. "I wanted Qaddafi's compound."

Lawson forwarded his recommended targets to the chairman of the Joint Chiefs of Staff in Washington within thirty-six hours of the La Belle disco bombing, and Crowe took them to the President on Tuesday evening, April 8. Crowe also gave the President a list of alternate targets, including one called Al Arafiq, the headquarters of the Libyan intelligence service. But Crowe himself recommended against hitting Al Arafiq on the grounds that the probability of civilian casualties was too high. It was located in the middle of a residential neighborhood, virtually across the street from the French Embassy. Crowe was also lukewarm about attacking Qaddafi's compound because of all the military difficulties involved in hitting what was essentially a political target. But, said Crowe, "there was strong sentiment for psychological purposes that we should do something in his personal compound and get his communications center and his headquarters."

Azziziyah—"Splendid Gate" in English—was the nerve center of the Qaddafi regime. Surrounded by a 15-foot wall, guarded by Soviet-made tanks, honeycombed with underground bunkers, Azziziyah contained within its 200 acres communications facilities, barracks for Qaddafi's personal security detachment, military staff headquarters, the house where his wife and seven children lived, and the Bedouin-style tent where he received visitors. If Qaddafi had to be convinced that he would pay a price for his support of terrorism, Azziziyah was the place to start.

Now it was up to the commander-in-chief to decide, and Reagan personally ordered that Azziziyah be made a target. Crowe said the Air Force would need more time to prepare for Azziziyah, so the raid, originally scheduled for Saturday, was postponed until 2:00 A.M. Tuesday, April 15—still the night of April 14 in Washington.

The President reached his decision just as Lt. Col. Jack Fletcher* and his squadron of F-111s were returning to Lakenheath from another long-distance run to Turkey. Along with Fred Allen and Drew Phillips,* the other two squadron commanders, Fletcher had been working seven-day weeks for the past three months organizing and training for a mission he thought would never happen. There were no orders awaiting Fletcher when he landed at Lakenheath; Allen was on leave in Paris. It would be three more days before any of them found out that they were being sent against Azziziyah Barracks, the target they least wanted to hit. Both Azziziyah in Tripoli and the Jamahariyah Barracks in Benghazi had been put on the target list for symbolic, not military, reasons. Jerry Breast, himself a former combat pilot, looked at the target list and concluded that "at least two of the five targets—I would not have chosen to go against those targets at night."

Aware that the military was not happy with the target selection, the NSC staff tried to find out more about the strike plan—the number of planes against each target, the specific aim points for the bombs. As usual, the Pentagon was reluctant to provide that kind of military detail to civilians—or even to military officers temporarily assigned to the NSC staff. Suspicious that the Joint Chiefs would somehow tamper with the plan the President had approved, the NSC staff secretly ordered the National Security Agency to monitor Sixth Fleet communications in an effort to detect any last-minute change in orders.

★ ★ ★

There were major hurdles still to be cleared, not the least of them was whether Prime Minister Margaret Thatcher would permit the strike to be launched from British bases, but after five years of public talk and internal debate, the Reagan administration was finally going to the source—or one of the sources—of terrorism. Measured by the number of Americans killed, Qaddafi was hardly the world's most dangerous supporter of terrorism. Iran and Syria were much deadlier. Iran and its surrogates in Lebanon had killed hundreds of Americans; Syria had permitted the territory it controlled in Lebanon to serve as a terrorist base camp. The gunmen who killed Natasha Simpson at the airport in Rome had trained in the Bekaa Valley and staged out of Damascus. What set Qaddafi apart was his blatant support for terrorism and his vulnerability to reprisal.

Iran, with its 42 million people, was virtually immune from attack, particularly now that it was involved in secret negotiations to free the Americans held hostage by Hezbollah in Lebanon. Syria was protected by its treaty of friendship with the Soviet Union. An American attack against Syria might not lead to war with the Soviet Union, but it would certainly damage relations between the two superpowers. Besides, the United States did not have a smoking gun tying Syria to any terrorist attacks against Americans.

Libya had only 3 million people, no secret negotiations with the United States, no treaty with the Soviet Union, and almost no friends. Since the earliest days of the Reagan administration, Soviet officials like Anatoly Dobrynin had consistently maintained in private conversations that Libya was an American problem, sometimes going so far as to call Qaddafi a madman. Now, Georgi Arbatov, the ubiquitous mouthpiece of Soviet foreign policy, was cutting Qaddafi loose in public. "What Mr. Qaddafi says is not always true," Arbatov declared.

If Libya was the weak sister of state-supported terrorism, it also represented the most clear and present danger to Americans. Qaddafi had sent his agents on a rampage in the aftermath of Operation Prairie Fire. The People's Bureau in East Berlin had been only one recipient of the March 25 message directing attacks against Americans. On April 5, the same day as the bombing of La Belle disco, the French government expelled two Libyan diplomats for plotting an attack with hand grenades and machine guns on the American visa office in Paris. The next day, in Beirut, Libyan agents attempted to fire a rocket-propelled grenade at the American Embassy. In Africa, three Libyan agents were caught in a plot to kidnap the American Ambassador to Rwanda. There were even reports that Qaddafi was trying to buy the American hostages in Beirut from Hezbollah. Not all the reports could be verified, but there was no doubt Qaddafi and his agents were out to get Americans. The argument that retaliation would only beget more terrorism was moot. It was hard to see how military action could make things any worse than they already were.

The evidence of a continuing Libyan campaign against Americans moved the issue beyond retribution to pre-emption, beyond retaliation to self-defense. A strike against targets linked to Qaddafi's support of terrorism not only would avenge past outrages but also might prevent future ones. The distinction was an important one to Margaret Thatcher, who already was on record as saying that "retaliatory strikes" against Libya would be "against international law." Reagan telephoned Thatcher on the "drop," a secure communications link between the White House and 10 Downing Street, to ask that she permit the United States to launch the raid from British bases. According to Thatcher, Reagan said that the F-111s, "because of their special characteristics," offered "the lowest possible risk of civilian casualties and casualties among United States personnel." Put that way, permitting the use of the F-111s sounded almost like a humanitarian gesture. The fact was that without them, without the ability to deliver 2,000-pound, laser-guided bombs at night, the strike would not be nearly so punishing. By itself, the Navy could not cover all five targets.

Thatcher wanted to know the exact connection between each target and Qaddafi's support of terrorism. Reagan left the details to Charles Price, the American Ambassador in London, who relied on a legal analysis prepared by the State Department to come up with a rationale Thatcher could accept. A strike against terrorist facilities would be, in Thatcher's words, "fully consistent with the right of the United States to defend itself under the inherent right of self-defense recognized in Article 51 of the United Nations Charter." It didn't hurt that Thatcher owed Reagan one for his support of Great Britain during the 1982 war with Argentina over the Falkland Islands or that Qaddafi supported the Irish Republican Army, which in 1984 had nearly killed Thatcher with a bomb planted in her hotel, or that Libyan diplomats had killed a British constable trying to control a crowd of demonstrators outside the People's Bureau in London. Call it "self-defense" or call it "swift and effective retribution," the United States was, for the first time, about to strike with purpose against terrorism.

★   ★   ★

The chairman of the Joint Chiefs of Staff was angry at the Supreme Allied Commander Europe. Admiral Crowe could not believe General Rogers could be so indiscreet. Speaking to a group of high school students in Atlanta on Wednesday, April 9, Rogers had said the evidence linking Libya to the bombing of La Belle disco was "indisputable." Coming from the officer who had overall command of the forces that would conduct the strike, the remark had set off a new frenzy of speculation that the United States was about to retaliate. Rogers knew what was in the works; on the flight to Atlanta from Washington, he had told his military assistant he would not be going on leave as planned. He had gone through with the speech as part of a determined effort by everyone to continue with business as usual, part of an elaborate deception operation designed to conceal the preparations for the strike. Then, he had stood up and all but announced—with television cameras rolling—that the United States had the justification it needed for attacking Libya. If anyone in Libya was listening, the signal could hardly have been clearer.

Rogers returned to Washington that night, checking into Wainwright Hall, the VIP quarters at Fort Myer, just up the road from the Pentagon. At about ten-thirty, Crowe and Lt. Gen. Richard Burpee, the director of operations for the joint staff, drove over to Fort Myer to hand-deliver the strike order to Rogers. The order had been signed by Deputy Secretary of Defense William Taft, acting in place of Weinberger, who was on a tour of Asia. The rooms at Wainwright Hall had not been swept for electronic eavesdropping devices, so Crowe and Rogers could not discuss the execute order. Crowe simply handed it to Rogers, who said he would be returning to Europe first thing the following morning.

The next day, with the execute order in his briefcase, Rogers returned to his headquarters in Mons, Belgium. He stopped long enough to change planes, switching from his commander's aircraft, which was routinely kept under surveillance by the Soviets, to a less conspicuous executive jet. Rogers then flew to Stuttgart, the headquarters of the European Command, and delivered the execute order to his deputy, General Lawson; to Gen. Charles Donnelly, the commander of U.S. Air Forces Europe (USAFE); and to Vice Admiral Kelso, the commander of the Sixth Fleet. Kelso took his copy of the execute order and departed for the carrier *America*. Donnelly took his copy and returned to USAFE headquarters at Ramstein. Meanwhile, the Joint Chiefs of Staff sent out a second strike order falsely stating that the attack would take place on Wednesday, a piece of disinformation designed to foil any would-be leakers. It had gone out unsigned because William Taft had refused to put his signature on a deliberate falsehood.

★   ★   ★

The phone was ringing when Fred Allen walked in the door of his house on Friday night, April 11, returning to Lakenheath from a week's leave in Paris. It was Drew Phillips, who lived just a few doors away and commanded one of the other F-111 squadrons at Lakenheath. Phillips had been watching from his window, waiting for Allen to drive up. "He said, 'I've got to talk to you. Meet me out back,' " Allen recounted. Allen and Phillips walked out into a field behind their homes. "Whispering, he says, 'You know this operation we've been working on? I think we're going,' " Allen recalled. Phillips also told him the operation had grown significantly from the single-target raid Allen had briefed to Rogers and Lawson back in January. Phillips didn't have the details. Those would have to wait until tomorrow when Col. Tom Yax, the wing's director of operations, got back from Ramstein.

Yax picked up the execute order at the USAFE headquarters on Saturday morning. "By direction of the Secretary of Defense," it began, then went on to list three targets for the F-111s—Azziziyah Barracks, Tripoli airfield, and Sidi Bilal—but it did not, even at this late date, specify how many of the targets were to be hit. "The numbers were still kind of up in the air," Yax recalled. According to the execute order, the number of targets depended on whether or not France would grant the F-111s overflight rights. With overflight rights, the F-111s could fly a straight line from Lakenheath to Tripoli. Without them, they would have to fly a giant dog leg around Europe and through the Strait of Gibraltar, roughly doubling the length of the mission and, more importantly, the fuel requirements. Eighteen F-111s would hit all three targets if France allowed them to take the short route; if France did not, the strike would consist of only six planes against a single target.

The United States had first broached the subject of overflight rights with France back in January. James Stark of the NSC staff, Lieutenant General Burpee of the Joint Chiefs of Staff, and a representative of the European Command had visited the Elysée Palace to discuss ways the two countries might cooperate in dealing with Qaddafi's troublemaking in North Africa. The Americans had not spoken specifically of a strike against Libya, but they had raised the question of what France would do if the United States moved against Qaddafi from bases in England. The French had given a non-answer, saying they wouldn't rule out overflights but cautioning that, if it ever came to that, Washington should give the French government plenty of time to consider the request. Now, on Saturday, two days before the raid, an American defense attaché submitted the request in Paris, and an answer was expected by four o'clock that afternoon.

At the same time that Tom Yax was picking up the execute order in Ramstein, Fred Allen, Jack Fletcher, and Drew Phillips were in the intelligence vault at Lakenheath, looking at the target list. "This is the first time I'm told about Azziziyah Barracks," Allen recalled. "I remember thinking, I can't believe they targeted that." As the senior squadron commander, Allen would be the first to hit the target. He would be carrying laser-guided, 2,000-pound bombs and would attack in the direction of the prevailing wind, aiming for a building at the far southeastern edge of the 20-acre compound so that the smoke and debris from his bombs would not obscure the targets for the planes behind him. The building, a two-story rectangular structure, was Qaddafi's residence.

That afternoon, the French said no, adding a piece of advice directly from French President François Mitterand: Don't do a pinprick. The gratuitous advice was particularly infuriating since the denial of overflight rights so directly affected the number of planes that would be launched from Lakenheath. The White House was so annoyed that it sent a backchannel message straight to the Elysée Palace saying, in effect, What the hell do you guys want?

Knowing the F-111s now would have to fly the long way around Europe, "I headed back to Lakenheath thinking six ships against one target," Tom Yax recalled. Shortly after he arrived at Lakenheath, however, Yax received a phone call from Maj. Gen. David Forgan, the director of operations for U.S. Air Forces Europe (USAFE) at Ramstein. We're going the long way, and we're going with the big package, Forgan said.

It was a planner's nightmare. "When you go from six aircraft to eighteen aircraft, and you don't go across France, it's like throwing a bag of live snakes in the room," Jack Fletcher said. Among other things, the crews to fly a mission that size had not even been selected. All the training of the past three months had been designed to prepare a handful of the wing's most experienced pilots and weapons officers for the mission. Now, some of the younger, less experienced, less talented crews would have to be used. The crews, at least, were on hand. The aerial tankers needed for the 5,800-mile round trip were still in the United States.

★ ★ ★

It was noon in Shreveport, Louisiana, when Capt. Scott Wvesthoff got a call at his home just outside Barksdale Air Force Base. Wvesthoff, who flew the giant KC-10 airborne tankers, the military variant of the DC-10 jumbo jet, was told to pack a week's worth of clothes and be at the base by 2:00 P.M. Then, Wvesthoff recalled, "we were simply told we were being positioned at Mildenhall," a Royal Air Force base just six miles from Lakenheath. Wvesthoff took off for England at seven o'clock that night, flying the standard great circle route over the north Atlantic, one of thirty tankers commandeered from bases in Louisiana, South Carolina, and California. His plane was loaded with so much fuel that when he landed at Mildenhall after a ten-hour flight, it was still close to its maximum gross weight.

★ ★ ★

At ten o'clock Saturday night, Col. Sam Westbrook, his deputy, Robert Vencus, and his director of operations, Tom Yax, were attending a local social function at the officers' club, keeping up the appearance of business as usual. The squadron commanders were still in the intelligence vault, drafting the strike plan on yellow legal pads, deciding which crews to send against which targets. They had just finished dividing the crews into three groups, six planes for each target, when Lt. Col. Robert Pastusek, the wing's chief of offensive operations, called Allen and said he needed to see him right away in the command post.

If you could change the number of airplanes against the three targets, would you? Pastusek asked. Yes, replied Allen. There's not enough to hit at Sidi Bilal. The only thing that's worth a shit is the swimming pool. Allen wanted to take three planes off Sidi Bilal and add them to the six going against the wide open spaces of the Tripoli airfield. Plan on it, Pastusek said. Pastusek rushed to the officers' club to check with Westbrook before passing Allen's recommendation to USAFE headquarters. Westbrook slipped away from the party long enough to endorse Allen's change in the mix of planes and targets.

Allen, Fletcher, and Phillips had just finished reassigning the crews to their targets—six against Azziziyah compound, three against Sidi Bilal, and nine against Tripoli airfield—when Pastusek called again. Speaking guardedly over the open phone line, Pastusek told Allen, They won't buy it. They want nine, three, and six. The order in which Pastusek rattled off the numbers told Allen that USAFE wanted nine planes against Azziziyah, three against Sidi Bilal, and six against Tripoli airfield. You're kidding, Allen said. They want nine planes?

"I was already goosey about sending six" against Azziziyah, Allen explained. "Now they wanted three more." Of the three targets, the Azziziyah compound was the most heavily defended. Increasing the number of F-111s against it would increase the chances that one of them would be shot down, particularly since the added aircraft would no longer have the element of surprise.

Maj. Gen. David Forgan, USAFE's director of operations, also had doubts about sending nine planes against Azziziyah. "My concern was that interference from smoke and dust could be a big problem," Forgan recalled. The F-111's weapons officer had to be able to see the target in order to illuminate it with the laser beam that guided the bombs. If smoke and dust kicked up by earlier explosions obscured the target, then the bombs would be falling blind. "We finally concluded that although it was not the optimum, it was do-able," Forgan said.

Changing the mix of planes and targets also "changed the tanker plan totally," Tom Yax said afterwards. The F-111s going after the airport had the farthest to fly, which made their fuel requirement different from that of the planes targeted against Azziziyah and Sidi Bilal. Shifting three planes from the airfield to Azziziyah Barracks set off a chain reaction in the refueling sequence. Forty-four hours before launch time, the mission planners had to prepare a new refueling plan.

The decision to increase the number of planes targeted against Qaddafi's compound was made by Gen. Charles Donnelly, the commander of U.S. Air Forces Europe. According to Donnelly, it was a simple exercise in mathematics. For each structure in the compound, Donnelly's staff calculated a "probability of damage." With one plane, the chances of knocking a building out were less than 50 percent. Laser-guided bombs were more accurate than "iron bombs," but they still had a probable error of 70 feet. That's how much they might miss by if everything went right. The bomb homed in on a laser beam which the F-111's weapons officer aimed at the target, but even with the laser to guide it, the bomb was still a slave to gravity. Add to the forces of nature the possibility of a bent fin or a shaky hand and the bomb could miss the target completely. There was also the "probability of arrival" to consider—the chances that the plane would reach its target without being shot down. So, said Donnelly, "you keep adding aircraft until you arrive at a desirable PD [probable damage]."

While the tanker crews rewrote the refueling plan, the squadron commanders sat down with Lt. Col. Pastusek, the offensive operations chief, to go over the "desired mean points of impact"—exactly where on each target the bombs were supposed to fall. Taking his orders from Maj. Gen. Forgan in Ramstein, Pastusek inked in the nine aim points, one for each plane, on a reconnaissance photograph of the Azziziyah compound spread before him. Two planes—the first and last—would go after Qaddafi's residence with four 2,000-pound bombs each. Allen planned to aim his bombs at the air-conditioning unit on the roof of Qaddafi's house. Two more planes would go after a large administration building in the middle of the compound. The other five would each take one building apiece—barracks and storage sheds.

Sending two planes against Qaddafi's residence obviously increased the chances not only of destroying the residence but of killing Qaddafi, although everyone involved insisted that was not their intent. "The purpose was not to kill Qaddafi," USAFE's Gen. Donnelly maintained. "It was to make a point to Qaddafi." Col. Tom Yax recalled that "at my level and [Fred Allen's] we talked about did we need to kill him, but that was never an objective. We weren't concerned about structuring a strike to actually catch him." As USAFE's Maj. Gen. Forgan put it: "If we caught Qaddafi in bed, that would be a bonus, but that was not the goal."

A raid designed to kill Qaddafi would also have to hit the tent where he frequently held court at all hours of the day or night. "The big round tent was where we thought he was going to be if he was anywhere above ground," Yax continued. "We talked about dropping bombs on it, but decided that that wouldn't show much. Besides, there were underground bunkers, and we figured he would be under two hundred feet of concrete." If he was in the compound at all. The colonel was notorious for never spending two nights under the same roof, playing a perpetual shell game to stay one step ahead of assassins both real and imagined. When Maj. Gen. Forgan in Ramstein called Lt. Col. Pastusek in Lakenheath on Saturday night with the nine aim points for Azziziyah compound, they had no way of knowing where Qaddafi would be at 2:00 Tuesday morning.

In fact, the ever-inventive Oliver North had come up with a plan to lure Qaddafi to his compound that night. As North explained it at a meeting of the administration's Crisis Pre-Planning Group (CPPG), he would ask Terry Waite, the hostage negotiator from the Church of England who earlier had extricated four British citizens from a Libyan jail, to go to Tripoli on Monday to meet with Qaddafi, presumably in the tent where he received visitors. According to North's plan, Waite would importune Qaddafi to use his good offices in freeing the hostages in Lebanon and then depart, leaving Qaddafi to spend the night at his compound. Waite, of course, would not be told that he was being used to set Qaddafi up for a killing. North's plan had a rather large hole in it since it assumed that Waite, not Qaddafi, would set the schedule for his visit, but the real problem was that it was an assassination plot—a clear and simple violation of American law. Reagan administration officials had absolutely no qualms about killing Qaddafi, but they couldn't plan to do it.

North's scheme was discussed and quickly rejected by the CPPG. He had to content himself with drafting a statement to be released by the White House in the event Qaddafi was killed. It called Qaddafi's death "fortuitous."

Working into Sunday morning, the planners at Lakenheath decided to launch a total of twenty-four F-111s to be sure of putting eighteen over the targets. Five EF-111 electronic planes to jam the Libyan radars would launch from the RAF base at Upper Heyford; four would go the distance, and one reserve plane would turn back. Nineteen KC-10 aerial tankers and ten smaller KC-135 tankers would carry the 7 million pounds of fuel needed for the mission; the KC-10s would refuel the F-111s, and the KC-135s would replenish the KC-10s. In all, fifty-eight aircraft would take off from four British bases on Monday evening. There was no way to hide that many aircraft taking off in close sequence. Fortunately, a long-scheduled USAFE exercise called "Salty Nation" was to begin Monday morning. That would be the cover for the real mission, which was codenamed "El Dorado Canyon."

On Sunday, "we did everything just like we normally do," Westbrook said. The maintenance and munitions crews came in at noon to prepare the aircraft for the start of the exercise Monday morning. Only this time the crews loaded live ordnance under the wings and left it there with live fuses. "The crews knew this was unusual," Westbrook said. "We told them what was going on, that this was a real go."

The mission was a go, but nobody at Lakenheath liked the way it was going. For nearly four months, Westbrook and the small circle of officers privy to the planning had been designing a strike to minimize the risk of losing any aircraft. That was a natural act of self-preservation as well as a recognition that the loss of a single aircraft, the capture of a single pilot, would give Qaddafi an excuse to claim victory. Now, with less than forty-eight hours to go, they had suddenly been ordered to alter the strike plan in a way that markedly increased the chances of losing an aircraft. Nine F-111s against Azziziyah "was too many airplanes across the target," Robert Vencus, the deputy wing commander, said.

On Sunday, the wing's senior officers took their concerns to their immediate superior, Maj. Gen. Thomas McInerney, commander of the Third Air Force. McInerney agreed. They discussed altering the plan so that at least the nine planes would be coming at Azziziyah from different directions rather than in a single stream, but they decided it was too late to change tactics. Vencus volunteered to lead the final three planes against Azziziyah, arguing that the presence of a combat veteran might boost the confidence of the greener pilots, but Westbrook declined the offer. Allen, the leader of the strike against Azziziyah, took the other pilots aside and told them that if the antiaircraft fire became too intense, they should not hesitate to break off.

★   ★   ★

As the crews were arming the F-111s at Lakenheath, an exhausted Caspar Weinberger was landing at Andrews Air Force Base outside Washington at the end of a two-week trip to Asia. He had been working virtually around the clock, going through the normal VIP visits, meetings, and dinners, then staying up all night to review the strike plans. At the start of the trip, Weinberger had taken Richard Armitage, his Assistant Secretary for International Security Affairs, aside and asked him if he thought the intercepted messages tying Libya to the disco bombing were convincing. Armitage replied that he thought the case was overwhelming. This time, Armitage could detect none of the reluctance Weinberger usually displayed when it came to satisfying White House or State Department demands for military action. For the first time, the Reagan administration was debating not whether to retaliate against terrorism but how to do it. Weinberger staggered off the plane and went home for a few hours' sleep before going to the Pentagon for a final briefing by the chairman of the Joint Chiefs of Staff.

★　★　★

Thirty F-111 crews were briefed on the mission at three o'clock Sunday afternoon. Allen, Fletcher, and Phillips had deliberately chosen thirty crews for twenty-four planes in the event that somebody showed up sick or got cold feet. The squadron commanders were all old enough to have flown in Vietnam, but most of the crews had never seen combat. They studied their mission folders until well past midnight, then were given a sleeping pill and sent home with orders to be back at the base by two o'clock Monday afternoon. The three squadron commanders stayed to work on the refueling plan, which still had not been restructured to support nine planes against Azziziyah Barracks. "I thought of all the ways this could get cocked up," Fred Allen said, "and my worst fear was not being able to find the tanker." Finally, the squadron commanders went home to sleep.

Going to war in the middle of peace was a strange sensation. "In Vietnam," Allen reflected, "you didn't go home and lay down next to your wife and say goodbye to the kids the next morning." Fletcher's wife was asleep when he got home. She rolled over and asked drowsily how the exercise was going; he kissed her and she went back to sleep. She taught school and would be gone by the time he woke up.

★　★　★

Cdr. Byron Duff did not sleep that night. Aboard the carrier *Coral Sea* steaming in circles north of Sicily, the air group commander was still drafting the strike plan for the Navy's attack on the two targets in Benghazi: Benina airfield and the Jamahariyah Barracks. By now, Duff had seen more combat than any Navy pilot since the end of the Vietnam

War. As a wing commander aboard the *Independence,* he had flown air strikes during the invasion of Grenada, and he had been one of the leaders of the December bombing raid against Syrian positions in Lebanon. As a wing commander aboard the *Coral Sea,* he had flown in the Gulf of Sidra exercises below Qaddafi's "line of death," and now he was just eighteen hours from another combat mission.

For the past few days, the *Coral Sea* and *America* had been making as much electronic noise as possible "to let everybody know where we were," according to Rear Adm. Jerry Breast. Now, they began shutting down their radios, radars, aids to navigation—any electronic signal that might give away their location. At ten o'clock Monday morning, the commanders of the escort ships were brought aboard the carriers and told for the first time what was about to happen.

The Navy and the Air Force were splitting Libya in half, with the Navy on the eastern side of the Gulf of Sidra and the Air Force on the west. The *Coral Sea* would use A-6s to attack Benina airfield just outside Benghazi, while planes from the *America* would hit the Jamahariyah Barracks. The *Coral Sea*'s planes would also go after the Libyan air defenses on the Benghazi side of the Gulf, while fighters from the *America* flew air defense suppression for the Air Force on the Tripoli side.

Vice Adm. Kelso, the Sixth Fleet Commander, had hand-carried the strike order to the carrier, but despite the extraordinary secrecy, the pilots believed the plan had leaked. One pilot, who had taken his plane into the Italian base at Sigonella, Sicily, first heard about the coming strike against Libya by watching CNN in the bar at the officers' club. According to Lt. Cdr. Robert Stumpf on the *Coral Sea,* some of the news reports coming out of Washington "listed target areas and proposed target times which coincided almost exactly with the actual missions. Many [of the pilots] believed chances for success without significant losses had been seriously jeopardized, since a major tactical feature of the strikes was the element of surprise. There was talk of postponing everything until whoever was compromising this vital information could be throttled."

★   ★   ★

At Lakenheath, wing commander Sam Westbrook came in Monday morning at seven-thirty to start the "Salty Nation" exercise. He began by declaring the squadron building where the mission crews would soon be gathering out of action, destroyed by an imaginary direct hit from an imaginary enemy. From now on, the only people allowed to enter or leave that building were those on a special access list kept by an armed guard at the door. Westbrook planned to continue launching and recovering planes for the exercise right up until three o'clock in the afternoon. The first plane that took off after that would be bound for Libya.

The mission crews arrived at 2:00 P.M. for the final briefing—weather, disposition of Libyan forces, refueling schedules, radio frequencies, call signs, altitudes, air speeds, ground speeds, aim points, turn points, radar offsets, escape and evasion plans, and all the hundreds of other details that might prove crucial. By the time Westbrook stood up to speak, there were no more details left to cover.

The first ground rule, he began, the eighteen best airplanes will go out of the twenty-four that launch. It doesn't matter if you're top gun or squadron commander, you will have to turn back if you have a problem with your aircraft.

To minimize the chances of casualties both to the pilots and to the citizens of Tripoli, the Rules of Engagement required that all systems be operating before a plane could drop its bombs. After all the training and that long flight down there, you're going to want to drop those bombs regardless, Westbrook warned. But that's not the way we're going to play the game. Westbrook wasn't worried about the trip down; adrenaline would take care of that. The tough thing is going to be coming off the target and have the adrenaline stop and still have to find the tanker and fly back, he said. That's the scariest to me because it could result in unnecessary losses. Westbrook ended by telling his men there was one other person who wanted to speak to them.

The door at the back of the briefing room opened, and the Air Force chief of staff, Gen. Charles Gabriel, strode down the aisle. When he saw Gabriel, Fred Allen said to himself, Jesus Christ, we really are going. Gabriel gave more of a pep talk than a briefing, pointing out that for many of them this would be the first and last time they ever saw combat. They would be operating under stress and afterwards their actions would be put under a microscope by the news media. Gabriel told the pilots they were not being asked to do anything they had not been trained to do. If everybody followed the plan and no one tried to be a hero, the mission would succeed. We don't need any heroes, Gabriel reiterated. They're a liability.

When Gabriel finished, he asked if there were any questions. One of the pilots, Capt. Fernando Ribas, raised his hand. When are we going back? he asked, meaning would there be a second mission after tonight's. Gabriel said he didn't know. That would depend on Libya's reaction. Ribas would never find out.

Westbrook and Maj. Gen. David Forgan, the USAFE operations

officer who had flown up from Ramstein, left Lakenheath at about four o'clock for the short drive over to Mildenhall, where the KC-10 tankers that would serve as their airborne command posts were waiting. On board their aircraft, they began checking out the radio equipment that would keep them in contact with the other planes, with the command posts at Lakenheath, Ramstein, Stuttgart, and on the carrier. Predictably, there was a last-minute flap.

"I was about to go into orbit," Forgan recalled. The technician who was supposed to insert the cipher key into the radio "wasn't there, and we're right up to engine start time." When at last the technician showed up, he couldn't find the proper cipher key. Finally, somebody spotted the key lying underneath a seat. The command KC-10 was now ready to take off, the lead ship in the stream of aircraft flowing down the Atlantic coast of Europe.

★   ★   ★

As the F-111s taxied onto the runway for takeoff, the *Coral Sea* broke out of its holding pattern north of Sicily and began a high-speed run south at 26 knots through the Strait of Messina between Sicily and Italy. The *America* took off on a similar run down the west coast of Sicily. A Soviet intelligence trawler patrolling the Strait of Messina spotted the *Coral Sea* and radioed a warning to a Soviet cruiser south of Sicily. The cruiser headed north in search of the battle group. After several fruitless hours, the cruiser headed west, hoping to find the *America,* again with no luck. Two Soviet surveillance planes took off from an air base near Tripoli to join the hunt. Eighteen American warships could not simply disappear. But they had. Without any electronic signals to give their position away, the two carrier battle groups successfully evaded the Soviets—only to be spotted by an American news organization.

A plane chartered by NBC News in Rome had spent the past two days searching for the carriers, spending $3,000 a day trying to get a picture of the fleet. At dusk Monday, just as the pilot was about to give up and go home, he spotted the *Coral Sea* coming through the Strait. The NBC bureau in Rome relayed the news to its foreign desk in New York, which immediately passed the word to Pentagon correspondent, Fred Francis. Francis took his information to Robert Sims, the spokesman for the Pentagon. I'm not authorized to tell you anything, Sims responded. You'll just have to let your conscience be your guide. Certain now that a strike was in the works, Francis called the foreign desk in New York and told them to open up a phone line to Steve Delaney, an NBC correspondent in Tripoli. Delaney sat in his hotel room and waited by the phone for the planes to strike.

★   ★   ★

Jack Fletcher and his weapons officer, Neal Ralston,* sat side by side in the cockpit of their F-111 at the end of Lakenheath's Runway 24. Since their target, the Tripoli airfield, was the farthest away, they would be the first to launch. An open phone line connected the Mildenhall and Lakenheath control towers. As soon as the command tanker started to roll at Mildenhall, the Lakenheath tower flashed a green light to Fletcher. He set his cockpit clock for a four-minute countdown.

Fletcher had seen combat before, flying a tiny prop plane over Laos, calling in strikes on the Ho Chi Minh Trail. But this was different. Then, he had been just a tiny cog in the American war machine, one pilot out of hundreds who went up over Laos and North Vietnam night after night. Now he was the lead pilot in America's war against terrorism, and the whole world would be watching. That was what scared him most. "Fear of failure was the biggest problem you had," he said afterwards, "because you knew the American people were looking for some sorts of results."

When the clock showed zero, Fletcher released his brakes and sped down the runway with twelve 500-pound bombs under his wings. Three more F-111s followed at twenty-second intervals. It was 5:36 P.M. in England—exactly six hours and thirty minutes from the moment Fletcher was scheduled to drop his bombs on a row of Soviet-made Il-76 transport planes parked on the northeast ramp at Tripoli airfield. Behind him was another set of four F-111s, each carrying the same load of bombs, designed to cut a swath 300 feet wide and 700 feet long through the aircraft parked at the Tripoli airfield.

From Lakenheath, Mildenhall, Fairford, and Upper Heyford, the F-111s, EF-111s, KC-10s, and KC-135s took off—the first bombing raid launched from these fields in East Anglia since the end of World War II. "I break out of the clouds and darn if there's not my tanker," Allen recalled. They joined up in cells of five—four F-111s taking station on one tanker. They would stay with that same tanker all the way to Sicily, the dropoff point for the final, low-level run to the target.

Col. Robert Vencus watched from the control tower at Lakenheath as the planes took off, then went home to catch the evening news on the BBC to see if the raid was being broadcast to the world. "For the first time in days," Vencus recalled, "the BBC gave no indication of what was going on." Vencus assumed the British government had invoked the Official Secrets Act, making it a crime to reveal what was going on at Lakenheath. There had to be some explanation for why "the flavor and accuracy of the reporting changed so markedly that night," Vencus said.

The U.S. government did not have anything like an Official Secrets Act, but on Friday evening Oliver North had taken it upon himself to leak to ABC News a false report that the raid had been postponed. North used as his disinformation agent an unwitting member of the National Security Council staff named Johnathan Miller. Acting at North's direction, Miller returned a phone call to ABC's John McWethy and confided that a combination of factors had forced the raid's postponement. Miller did not realize he was putting out false information until North complimented him on a job well done. When Miller complained at the way he had been used, North turned on him, cursed him, and told him to get out of his office.

The armada passed north of London and headed southwest toward Land's End. Once over water, the pilots began turning on their electronic systems and testing their refueling rigs, searching for a malfunction that would force them to turn back. Talking over a "Have Quick" radio that constantly shifted frequencies so that his voice could not be intercepted or jammed, each squadron commander polled his aircraft, selecting the ones that would have to drop off. As planned, six F-111s and one EF-111 turned around, peeling off just at the point where they could still make it back to England without having to take any precious fuel from the tankers. That left three F-111s on each tanker—one on each wing and one under the belly.

Marshaled at 26,000 feet, the strike force flew down the French coast at 450 knots. The cells were about one mile apart, but within each cell the planes were so close together that the four would look like one to any radar stations below. "That's a long way to fly formation," Allen said. "My arm got tired. My neck got tired. . . . From time to time I would turn on the autopilot just to give myself a rest, but it couldn't hold formation for very long." Months later, a senior Portuguese Air Force officer would tell Westbrook that a coastal radar had tracked the American planes but figured it was none of their business. Later, over the Mediterranean, an Italian voice came on the radio asking for an identification, but Westbrook said nothing and heard no more.

As they turned the corner around Spain and headed through the Strait of Gibraltar into the Mediterranean, Allen could see the entire armada spread out before him in the pink glow of the setting sun, which at that altitude had not yet disappeared below the horizon. Tankers were refueling other tankers which were refueling bombers—fifty aircraft, carrying 66 tons of explosives.

Up front in the command tanker, David Forgan had a major problem: he was twelve minutes behind schedule. The lead KC-10 was having trouble taking fuel from one of the KC-135s. The refueling had taken longer than planned, and now they had to make up the twelve minutes or the bombers would be late over their target. The command tanker and its three F-111s left their planned route and flew a straight line across the north coast of Africa, violating the air space of Algeria and Tunisia. By the time they reached their fourth and final refueling point west of Sicily, they were back on schedule.

On this final refueling, each F-111 had to be topped off so it would have enough fuel to make it back to the tanker after dropping its bombs. Even with a full load going into the target, each bomber would only have about fifteen minutes to find a tanker or else divert to Signorella, Sicily, with all the political problems that would cause. This time, instead of one long drink, each F-111 took several little sips from the tanker, cycling through the refueling position again and again so that no one burned up too much fuel while the others were filling their tanks. The F-111 nestled in beneath the tail of the KC-10 while a boom operator flashed colored lights on the belly of the tanker, telling the bomber to move forward or backward until it was in position to receive the refueling probe. After all of them had taken a final sip, the F-111s left the tankers at 26,000 feet and began a long, slow descent toward their attack altitude.

Fletcher, who was to be the first pilot over the beach, dropped off the tanker at 1:14 A.M. Libyan time. Until then, he thought the entire operation might be nothing more than a show of force. "But as soon as we dropped off the tanker and started down the chute toward the water, there was no turning back," he said.

With five F-111s behind him at four-mile intervals, Fletcher screamed toward Libya, 350 miles away. Overhead, he could see the silhouettes of A-7s from the *America* moving into position.

The *America* and the *Coral Sea* had begun launching their planes at 1:00 A.M. from a point 180 miles off the coast of Libya. Still operating in radio silence, the carriers had launched their aircraft at twenty-second intervals—F-14s, F-18s, A-6s, A-7s, E-2Cs, EA-6Bs—more than seventy planes in all, flying at 500 feet with lights out.

Flying 200 feet off the water, Fletcher crossed the "line of death" into the Gulf of Sidra. He was heading for a point just west of the SA-5 site at Sirte that the Navy had attacked three weeks earlier. At 50 miles Fletcher turned off his lights, armed his bombs, and ran through a final check of his systems. Once he reached land, he would have to depend on the plane's terrain-following radar to guide him over hills and ridges he couldn't see. One of the planes behind him had to turn back when its terrain-following radar failed to function properly. Fletcher crossed the beach at 1:52 A.M. He was far to the southeast of Tripoli, sneaking in the back door.

★ ★ ★

At five minutes to seven in the evening in Washington, Caspar Weinberger, Adm. William Crowe, and Richard Armitage walked into a small room off the Pentagon's National Military Command Center to monitor the strike. The general on watch in the command center was taken completely by surprise. He had not been told what was happening and had seen only the message with the false strike date. Across the Potomac, members of the NSC staff crowded into the White House Situation Room. The atmosphere was electric. Karna Small, a press secretary on the NSC staff, sidled up to Navy Capt. James Stark, who had done much of the work of selecting the targets, and asked, Does this turn you on, babe?

★ ★ ★

Fred Allen dropped down to 200 feet and accelerated to 600 miles per hour, flying straight at the Libyan coast. He took his hands off the controls and his feet off the pedals and let the terrain-following radar fly the plane. In the right seat, his weapons officer, Brian Peters,* peered at his radar scope, looking for a set of docks along the waterfront that would serve as his "off set" point. Since Azziziyah Barracks would not show up well on the radar in the middle of the downtown clutter, Peters was using the docks as his "off set." He had programmed into the plane's computer exactly how far the barracks were from the docks and in what direction. He could keep his radar on the docks, and the plane would automatically steer itself to the barracks. But at the speed the F-111 was traveling, Peters had only about twenty seconds to find the right set of docks on his scope.

Cdr. Jay Johnson, flying an F-14 from the carrier *America,* moved into position 25 miles off Tripoli, ready to shoot down any Libyan jets that rose to intercept the F-111s. "I came in at low altitude and popped up on the clock and said, 'Holy Cow, this is a city that's asleep!'" Johnson recalled. "They didn't have a clue." The electronic warfare planes switched on their equipment, deliberately triggering the radars of the Libyan antiaircraft network. The A-7s and F-18s began firing HARM and Shrike missiles that rode the Libyan radar beams back to the sites.

Things were happening very rapidly now, faster than it takes to tell. "I'm coming in at the speed of heat," Allen remembered. "I looked up and an A-7 came right over the top of me firing at an SA-3 site." Allen's instruments showed he was 71,000 feet from Qaddafi's residence, traveling 1,000 feet per second. Beneath him, boats in the harbor were firing off flares as he roared overhead. In his headset, Allen could hear a beeping sound, telling him he was being tracked by a Libyan radar. Briefly, he took control of the plane and dived still closer to the water, trying to slip under the radar. The lower altitude made it harder for Peters to find the docks on his scope. "Peters said, 'Get it up. I can't see,'" Allen recalled. Then "he looked out the window and said, 'Holy shit!'" At this altitude, Allen had to worry about running into a building once he crossed the beach. A second tone sounded in his headset, this one telling him he was too low.

"Ready to go?" he asked Peters.

"Yeah, we're looking good," Peters said. He had located his "off set" point and was confident they were zeroing in on the right target.

"Okay. Here we go." The F-111 crossed the waterfront and headed for downtown Tripoli. "All the lights were on," Allen remembered. "I see cars going up and down the street."

The plane was so low that Steve Delaney with his open phone line to New York could stick the receiver out the window of his hotel and the roar of Fred Allen blasting past was heard by 14 million people tuned to the NBC Nightly News.

"Range," Allen said. Peters was supposed to count down the closing distance to the target.

"I'm not on the target," Peters said.

"Range," Allen demanded again.

"Target direct," Peters replied. For the first time, he could see the target through the infrared camera mounted on the belly of the plane. There, in the middle of his screen, was Qaddafi's tent. Just to the left was Qaddafi's house, the air-conditioning unit clearly visible on the roof.

Still 23,000 feet from the target, Peters said, "Ready. Pull."

Allen pulled the nose up sharply and released his bombs, literally tossing them at the target. He could feel the shudder as the four 2,000-pound bombs dropped from the wings and arced toward the building at the far end of the compound. Immediately, he pulled the plane hard left in a 4G turn that drained the blood from his head. Below, a ZSU-23 antiaircraft gun opened up. Allen pulled the plane into an even tighter turn.

"Laser on?" he asked Peters.

"Laser on," Peters replied, as he aimed the laser beam at Qaddafi's house, trying to guide the falling bombs to their target.

"Five-four-three-two-one," Allen counted.

"Come on. Come on," Peters urged the bombs.

"Impact," Allen snapped.

"You pulled too hard," Peters said.

Trying to evade the antiaircraft fire, Allen had turned the plane so sharply that the laser could not stay focused on the target. Just before impact, the laser quit. For the final second of their fall, the bombs were no longer guided. It was the difference between a hit and a miss. Allen didn't have time to worry about it now.

"I'm going down," he told Peters, as he pushed the plane down to 300 feet.

"We hit 'em big time," Peters reported, as his screen filled with the black smoke of the bombs' explosion.

Allen was back over the Mediterranean in less than a minute. He reported "Feet wet" to the Navy command plane, followed by a two-word code, "Tranquil Tiger," for a successful drop. He was out of harm's way, but behind him something had gone terribly wrong. "I could see in my rear-view mirror something had exploded," Allen recounted. "Reminded me of napalm in Vietnam. I turned to Brian [Peters] and said, 'Looks like somebody just hit the water.'"

In his command KC-10, Westbrook listened to the call signs of the planes as they reported "Feet wet"—first Allen with his call sign Remit 31, followed almost immediately by Remit 32 and Remit 33.

"Feet wet. Frosty Freezer," Remit 32 reported, using the code for an unsuccessful bomb run. Remit 32's weapons officer had not been sure of his "off set" point, so the pilot had not dropped his bombs.

Remit 33 reported "Feet wet. Tranquil Tiger." His bombs had landed right next to the large administration building.

Two minutes later Karma 51 reported in, but there was no word from Karma 52. That was Fernando Ribas's plane, the next to last F-111 in the stream of nine going against Azziziyah Barracks.

The last plane over Azziziyah was followed by the first over the naval base at Sidi Bilal. The weapons officer counted off the range to the large building that housed the swimming pool where Libyan frogmen trained.

"25,000 feet. Twenty-three. Pull."

The pilot pulled the nose up in the same toss maneuver Allen had used. "Bomb release," he reported.

"Okay. Tracking . . . tracking . . . tracking," the weapons officer said, as the bombs arced toward the building. To the right he could see three men running for their lives. Another man was trying to hide behind a corner of the building. "This one's for you, Colonel," the weapons officer said. Then, in disgust, "Ah, clouds, clouds, clouds." The smoke from someone else's bombs had obscured the target, blotting out the laser guidance. The bombs "went dumb," and crashed into the mess hall at the base.

At 2:06 P.M. there was a final burst of bombs at Sidi Bilal, and the city fell silent. Twenty miles to the south, Jack Fletcher's F-111 popped up over a ridgeline and began its run on Tripoli airfield. The lights of the international terminal were burning brightly.

"I can see what we're supposed to be going after," Fletcher said. "Can you see the ramp?" he asked his weapons officer.

Neal Ralston could see five Il-76 transports parked on the ramp. "Got it," he told Fletcher. Ralston pointed his laser at the middle Il-76, feeding the computer the data that would tell Fletcher exactly what course to steer and when to release the bombs. Even without the computer, Ralston could see that Fletcher did not have the plane centered on the target. "Come right. Come right," Ralston barked.

"Coming right," Fletcher replied. He still was not lined up on the target. The computer showed they were just five seconds from the bomb-release point.

"Center that steering, quick. Center it up," Ralston ordered.

"Centered now," Fletcher responded.

"Oh baby," Ralston exclaimed at the sight of the Il-76 in the middle of his screen.

"I'm on the pickle button," Fletcher said, as he pressed the bomb-release button. "Here come the bombs."

Ralston could see the falling bombs in his infrared camera. A small parachute popped out to slow each bomb's fall, giving the plane time to clear the blast area. One parachute failed to deploy; the bomb did not explode. If it had, it probably would have blown Fletcher and Ralston out of the sky. Ralston watched as the other eleven bombs descended toward the Il-76s.

"Oh baby!" he exclaimed again as the bombs went off.

"There's our own frag," Fletcher said as the F-111 felt the concussion.

"Turn left," Ralston ordered. Straight ahead lay a now wide-awake Tripoli.

Fletcher snapped the plane hard left, looking at the detonations over his shoulder. Behind him, the other F-111s dropped their bombs at thirty-second intervals. They headed west, skirting the SAMs and antiaircraft guns around the city, then turned north toward the Mediterranean and their tankers.

Fletcher joined on a tanker off the tip of Sicily and began taking on fuel. Suddenly, a second F-111 appeared right next to him, desperate for fuel, virtually pushing him away from the tanker. Fletcher broke away to let him in. Another F-111 was having trouble finding his assigned tanker, so Allen showed the way by dumping some of his fuel into the atmosphere and lighting his afterburner, setting off an explosion that lit up the night sky. Capt. Scott Wvesthoff in his KC-10 thought for a moment there had been a midair collision.

Fernando Ribas and Paul Lorence in Karma 52 were still missing. Westbrook broke radio silence and began quizzing the pilots about what they had seen. Some of the Navy pilots circling offshore reported seeing an inbound F-111 burning fiercely, crashing into the water, and separating into two giant fireballs. Ribas and Lorence, eighth in the stream of nine planes targeted against Azziziyah Barracks, never made it to the target. They were either hit by a Libyan antiaircraft missile or flew too low and crashed into water.

Of the nine planes targeted against Azziziyah only two had dropped their bombs. Neither had scored a direct hit. Fred Allen in Remit 31 lost his laser designator at the last moment, and Remit 33 was unable to use his laser at all because his infrared camera had failed. According to the Rules of Engagement, which required each plane to have all systems operating, Remit 33 should never have dropped its bombs. "We didn't hit it as well as we wanted," USAFE's General Donnelly said. One plane had not dropped because the crew were not sure of the target; another plane had fallen by the wayside with an overheated engine; another had been late coming off the tanker and missed the run to the target; and still another had lost its generator momentarily, scrambling all the electronics. Drew Phillips had not dropped because he couldn't get his infrared camera to work. One F-111 had picked out the wrong set of docks for its "off set" point and had dropped its bombs on a residential neighborhood near the French Embassy. The weapons officer had realized his error and reported it immediately, but Defense Secretary Weinberger would maintain for days that the damage could have been caused by spent antiaircraft missiles falling to earth.

The F-111s orbited for an hour, refueling and hoping for some sign of Karma 52. A Navy patrol plane scanned the water where the fireball had been spotted, listening for the beep of an emergency beacon. One of the warships reported a short set of beeps, then nothing. Finally, David Forgan in the command KC-10 gave the order to return to England, while Sam Westbrook radioed ahead to Lakenheath to notify next of kin that Ribas and Lorence were missing and presumed dead. On the long flight home in their F-111, Allen and Peters tuned in the press conference Shultz and Weinberger were holding in the White House briefing room. The sun was coming up, and Jack Fletcher could see SR-71 reconnaissance planes overhead en route from Mildenhall to Libya to record the damage.

Qaddafi's residence still stood. The front porch had been destroyed, the windows and doors had all been blown in, and the walls were pockmarked with shrapnel, but the nearest bomb craters were 30 yards away. Aides to Qaddafi variously reported he had been in his tent, in the underground bunker, or in a downstairs study at the time of the attack and that he had suffered a bruised shoulder from flying debris. The Libyans said two of his sons, aged three and four, were reported injured, and his fifteen-month-old adopted daughter was killed. American officials contended there was no record of Qaddafi ever having adopted a child, which somehow missed the point that somebody's baby girl was dead.

The carnage in the Bin Ghashir neighborhood where four 2,000-pound bombs had fallen on residential streets was as ghastly as the scene of any terrorist attack—severed hands lying in the rubble, a father grieving over the body of his three-year-old child, exposed electrical wires crackling in pools of blood, water, and sewage. The inhabitants of Bin Ghashir knew nothing of the events leading up to this slaughter, nothing of the Rome and Vienna massacres, nothing of disco bombing. They only knew what Qaddafi told them through the controlled Libyan press. To them, the United States had simply come in the middle of the night and for no good reason blown their lives away. They shook their fists and cried "Terrorists!" at American reporters viewing the scene.

The Defense Department later acknowledged that in addition to the bombs which had fallen on Bin Ghashir, two others dropped by the Navy had missed the Jamahariyah Barracks and damaged two houses 700 yards from the target. In all, nearly 5 tons of explosives had landed in residential neighborhoods. Libya reported that thirty-seven people had been killed and ninety-three injured. By that count, Reagan had killed more Libyans than Qaddafi had murdered Americans. There was no denying that the United States had killed women and children in their sleep, but there was a moral distinction between killing innocent Libyans by mistake and murdering innocent Americans on purpose.

Measured by the bomb-damage assessment, the raid was less than impressive. "We had our head down a little bit in terms of the number of bombs hitting the target that night," Fletcher said. At Tripoli airfield, Fletcher's squadron had destroyed at least three and perhaps five of the Il-76 transports. They had hoped to catch Qaddafi's entire fleet of thirteen Il-76s in the open, but someone in the Libyan Air Force had taken the precaution of dispersing the transport aircraft. The Navy had done a little better at Benina. The *Coral Sea* had sent nine A-6 bombers against the airfield, but two of them had turned back with equipment problems. The remaining seven attacked six hangars and a row of MiGs. Only two of the hangars received any significant damage, but as many as fourteen MiGs were destroyed, setting off towering explosions that forced some of the follow-on planes to break away from their target run. The A-6s also destroyed two helicopters and a small transport plane, but that was collateral damage caused by stray bombs. At Jamahariyah Barracks, the planes from the *America* "only got ten percent of their weapons into the target area," according to Rear Admiral Breast. They hit a warehouse, destroying four MiGs still in their shipping crates, but that was a lucky hit. The warehouse was not on the target list—the pilots missed their assigned aim point and hit the warehouse by accident. All that military equipment could be easily replaced. Qaddafi already had more than he could use.

When the Joint Chiefs of Staff viewed the first reconnaissance photos, they were disappointed. Clouds covered much of the target area, but what they could see showed very little damage. There were some scorch marks on the runway where it appeared some planes had gone up in flames, but the Libyans had quickly removed the wreckage so there was nothing to show the world. There was a host of reasons why the damage had been so meager. Crowe said that "any time you plan a raid when you're over the target fifteen seconds, and you have such a high political content to the raid—to reduce your casualties, to reduce peripheral damage, to reduce all these things that are not military but political—you're not going to have a lot of damage." The denial of overflight rights by France had stretched the F-111s beyond their limits. The wing at Lakenheath knew from long experience that even under the best of circumstances the F-111 was not a dependable airplane. On an average sortie of two and a half hours, 40 percent of the aircraft would suffer a "hard break," a malfunction that had to be repaired before the plane could fly again. Factor that failure rate into the extreme distances the planes had to fly, and the wonder was that any of them had dropped their bombs. Beyond that, said USAFE's David Forgan, "there's no way to estimate the effect of hostile fire on pilots." At night, Admiral Kelso pointed out, "every SAM looks like it's coming at you. . . . Most of these kids had never seen a SAM fired in anger."

The Joint Chiefs had just finished looking at the reconnaissance photographs when General Gabriel, the Air Force chief of staff, arrived from England, carrying the videotapes taken by the infrared cameras on the F-111s. "We saw Gabriel's tapes, and it was much more descriptive, much more definitive," Crowe recalled. The tapes revealed very little about the extent of damage, since in each case the target was lost in a giant cloud of smoke. But they were dramatic evidence that the pilots had had the targets in their sights. The chiefs immediately called Weinberger to come look at them, and Weinberger, knowing his man, immediately took the tapes to the President, who delighted in the instant replay. The tapes were a public relations coup, turning a mediocre damage assessment into a dramatic strike against terrorism.

Public relations was what it was all about. The raid was intended as a signal, a message, a warning, and its success would be measured not in materiel destroyed but by its effect on Qaddafi. In another time, the United States had bombed Hanoi in an effort to persuade the North Vietnamese to give up their guerrilla war in the South. If that had not worked, what reason was there to believe Qaddafi could be coerced into giving up his support of terrorism? Israel, on the other hand, had all but eliminated cross border commando raids by its policy of immediate retaliation. But Israel's policy of retaliation was a sustained and consistent one. For the United States, the raid on Libya was an extraordinary, one-time event. George Shultz could vow privately that the United States would go back again and again until Qaddafi relented, but the fact was Americans had neither the stomach nor the attention span for waging a military campaign against terrorism. Indeed, even Shultz, the foremost advocate of the use of force against terrorism, seemed to recognize the public mood by offering assurances that "we're not going to get into a kind of automatic pilot on this." Margaret Thatcher emphasized that in allowing British bases to be used for this attack, "we were not giving a blank check." Not only had she not given a blank check, she had quietly told the Reagan administration not to ask again.

There were precious few precedents for a single air raid changing the course of history. The surest way to achieve success would be to remove Qaddafi from power. Within minutes after the bombs had fallen, the

Voice of America broadcast a message to the Libyan people. "The people of the United States bear Libya and its people no enmity or hatred," the message said. "However, Colonel Qaddafi is your head of state. So long as Libyans obey his orders, then they must accept the consequences. Colonel Qaddafi is your tragic burden. The Libyan people are responsible for Colonel Qaddafi and his actions. If you permit Colonel Qaddafi to continue with the present conflict, then you must also share some collective responsibility for his actions." It was nothing less than an invitation to rise up and overthrow Qaddafi—orchestrating a coup from the air. "If a coup takes place, it's all to the good," Shultz said, acknowledging that in choosing the targets, "we had in mind the considerable dissidence in the Libyan army." By blowing up Il-76s and MiG-23s, the American planes were supposed to demonstrate to Libya's military the cost of standing by Qaddafi. By attacking Qaddafi's home and his Praetorian guard in its lair, the United States hoped to convince Libya's military that the forces which protected Qaddafi from assassination or overthrow were not invincible.

Such fine-tuning of military force for political purposes was probably worth thinking about but certainly not worth counting on. The purpose of the raid was much more basic than that. "There comes a time in these events and affairs," said Crowe, "when you've got to retaliate just because people are doing things to you they don't have a right to do, and you've got to stand up." The question now was, would Qaddafi sit down?

For nearly twenty-four hours following the raid, Qaddafi disappeared from sight, setting off a brief flurry of hope in Washington that he had indeed been killed or had fled the country. Qaddafi did not tolerate failure well. After Libya's duel with the Sixth Fleet in March, Saudi Arabia's King Fahd had found Qaddafi disoriented and incomprehensible. Perhaps this time he had collapsed entirely. But late Tuesday night, Qaddafi appeared on Libyan television, accusing Reagan of issuing orders "to murder children and attack houses" and vowing to continue "inciting revolution and establishing popular revolution everywhere in the world."

Qaddafi's forces already had attempted to strike back by launching two missiles at the U.S. Coast Guard station on the Italian island of Lampedusa, 160 miles off the coast of Libya. The missiles had splashed harmlessly in the water and stood more as a testament to the incompetence of Qaddafi's forces than to his powers of revenge. That same night, however, William Calkins, a thirty-three-year-old communications officer assigned to the American Embassy in Khartoum, was shot in the head from a passing car—an attempted assassination which was assumed to be the work of a Libyan hit squad. Another American official was shot and wounded in South Yemen. In Lebanon, the bodies of an American hostage, Peter Kilburn, and two British hostages were found in the hills east of Beirut, shot at close range. A third British hostage in Lebanon was hanged. The groups claiming responsibility for these acts of revenge identified themselves by names that Abu Nidal's organization had used in the past. The CIA reported that a Libyan intelligence officer had bought Kilburn from his captors and had him shot. On April 18, officials in Turkey foiled an attempt to launch grenades at a U.S. Air Force officers' club in Ankara, a plot that was traced directly to Libya. Then for three months there was nothing—at least nothing that bore Libyan fingerprints. It was as if Qaddafi had turned off his terror machine.

Whatever effect the attack had on Qaddafi, it clearly had terrified the Europeans. Just the prospect of American military action seemed to have galvanized the members of the European Economic Community. Literally on the eve of the attack, the twelve foreign ministers of the Common Market, who until then had balked at any punitive measure, had imposed the first real sanctions against Libya, reducing the number of Libyan diplomats in their countries and tightening surveillance on those remaining. According to Vernon Walters, the United Nations Ambassador who had toured the European capitals days before the raid, "it wasn't until they felt an American operation was imminent that they began to get together in great haste . . . and draw up that document."

Now, in the aftermath of the raid, the European foreign ministers enacted further diplomatic sanctions, restricting the movements of Libyan diplomats to the cities in which they were stationed and agreeing that any Libyan expelled from a Common Market nation on suspicion of involvement in terrorism would not be admitted to another member nation. The next day, Britain deported twenty-one Libyan students. West Germany said it would reduce the size of the People's Bureau in Bonn by more than half, from forty to fifteen. In all, the Europeans would expel more than 100 Libyan diplomats.

After his television speech, Qaddafi disappeared into the desert where, presumably, he felt safer from American bombs. The CIA reported that he had to call on Syrian pilots to put down a mutiny at a military base in Tarhuna. That wasn't enough for Oliver North, who wanted to keep the pressure on by stationing a ship off the coast of Libya to broadcast propaganda to fuel whatever flames of discontent were flickering. However, both the CIA and the Sixth Fleet refused to provide a floating radio station, in part because it would be a sitting duck for Libyan retaliation. North twice offered the *Erria,* a Danish freighter he had bought to run arms for the Nicaraguan contras, but the CIA was not interested. "Although it only cost $200,000, I got to rent it for a million and a half a month, so it was not the best deal I ever worked for the taxpayers," the CIA's operations director Clair George said, recalling why he spurned North's offer.

Undeterred, North planted a story in two major European newspapers that Qaddafi was about to fall and that his second-in-command, Abdul Halim Jalloud, was plotting to take over. The only basis for the story was a few unconfirmed intelligence reports of short-lived mutinies by Libyan military units.

Almost at once, the administration began planning a second raid to be launched if Qaddafi were caught red-handed again. Peter Rodman of the NSC staff wrote a memo saying that public opinion would only stand for one more strike so it had better be a good one. The NSC staff wanted to use conventionally armed cruise missiles, which theoretically could deliver their payloads without risking the lives or freedom of pilots or inviting the complications of air-to-air refueling and permission to use foreign bases. The Joint Chiefs of Staff had not shown much enthusiasm for the idea when it was first raised back in January and their opinion had not changed. The NSC staff wanted to send the nuclear-powered submarine *Atlanta*—which carried three conventionally armed cruise missiles and was then conducting exercises off the coast of Ireland—into the Mediterranean. The operation ran aground, literally, when the *Atlanta* hit a sandbar going through the Strait of Gibraltar.

Oliver North, the most vocal of hawks, who had even suggested that the Air Force use its supersecret "Stealth" fighter planes to attack Libya so Qaddafi would never know what hit him, believed that one more blow might be enough to topple "Colonel Q." Poindexter directed North and fellow NSC staffers Vincent Cannistraro, James Stark, and Howard Teicher to write a memo for the President outlining the administration's options if Qaddafi launched a new wave of terrorism. Cannistraro and Stark prepared first drafts of the memo, Cannistraro summarizing the intelligence available on Libya and Stark outlining the military options for a second raid. When North rewrote the two drafts into an "action memo" for Reagan to sign, he altered the intelligence section to suggest that the CIA had a better handle on Qaddafi's whereabouts than it really did—and to encourage the President to think that a follow-up attack would be more successful than either the CIA, DIA, or the Joint Chiefs of Staff believed. Poindexter and North took the doctored memo to the President, but no action was taken because Qaddafi failed to produce another *casus belli.* Afterward, Stark and Cannistraro compared notes and agreed that North intentionally had slanted the memo to encourage Reagan to act. The two men complained to NSC executive secretary Rod McDaniel about what North had done.

To North, the truth was raw material to be shaped in the service of a good cause. When he could, he avoided telling outright lies and relied instead on distortion. "I never knew Colonel North to be an outright liar, but I never took anything he said at face value, because I knew that he was bombastic and embellished the record, and threw curves, speedballs, and spitballs to get what he wanted," said Alan Fiers, the chief of the CIA's Central American Task Force. "I have seen Colonel North play fast and loose with the facts."

North was nothing if not resourceful, and he soon had another idea. At an interagency meeting to discuss follow-up action against Libya, North suggested that the United States could get a friendly foreign leader to place a call to Qaddafi that the Libyan leader would have to take, then the NSA could use the call to pinpoint his location and the Air Force or the Navy could pounce on him. The notion was instantly shouted down by North's colleagues, who pointed out to him that such an operation would almost certainly violate President Reagan's Executive Order 12333, which prohibited the assassination of foreign leaders.

After his former mentor Robert McFarlane publicly expressed doubts about the wisdom of another attack, North began arguing that the United States could mine Libya's harbors, a proposal that presented at least as many complications as dropping more bombs. What would the Soviets do—or the Italians for that matter—if one of their ships hit an American mine off the coast of Libya? What would the United States do if the Soviets started clearing the mines?

Qaddafi reemerged on June 11 with a long, rambling televised speech which gave the CIA's psychiatrists their first chance to observe their subject close up. Until then, there had been only scraps of intelligence, such as a report from a Yemeni official who had met with Qaddafi, that the colonel was disoriented and depressed, barely coherent. One CIA analyst, Paul Draper, complained privately of pressure from on high to build those scraps into an assessment that the April raid had had its intended effect. But the videotape of Qaddafi's speech told a different story. Draper and two other CIA analysts brought the tape to the White House Situation Room and played it for members of the NSC staff. Qaddafi prattled on forever and self-consciously imitated the body language of one of his heroes, the late Egyptian leader Gamal Abdel Nasser, but for all his idiosyncrasies he appeared to be in control of himself. The bombing had knocked him down but not out.

On July 30, Rod McDaniel, the executive secretary of the National Security Council, called a meeting of the Crisis Pre-Planning Group to discuss the next steps that would be taken against Qaddafi. McDaniel began by saying that the "family group"—the term used for the President's private get-togethers with Weinberger, Shultz, and Casey—had been talking about Qaddafi, and Shultz liked the idea of rattling his windows with sonic booms created by SR-71 reconnaissance planes, just to remind him that Uncle Sam was watching. The Crisis Pre-Planning Group was not a body which made decisions like that. Instead, McDaniel commissioned a "Libya: Next Steps" paper, to be drafted by the State Department's Intelligence and Near East bureaus. It was classified Top Secret/Vector, the State Department's code name for covert action. A week later, the State Department paper was forwarded to the NSC. "The goal of our near term strategy should be to continue Qaddafi's paranoia so that he remains preoccupied, off-balance, and not in an offensive posture in which he would initiate terrorist strikes and foreign adventurism," the paper read. "Therefore, we will have to convince him that further U.S. actions against him are being planned in response to further terrorism."

The paper concluded that the bombing had left Qaddafi isolated within the Arab world and vulnerable to rising discontent at home, which included unconfirmed reports of attempts on his life. The Libyan standard of living was dropping, and the military was restless. Its commanders were angry at being kept on short rations of ammunition and gasoline and forced to relocate their headquarters to Jufra in the southern desert, out of range of Libyan air conditioning as well as American bombs.

Debates about who might succeed Qaddafi and whether a follow-on regime would be pro-Soviet, pro-Western, or neither were beside the point. The bottom line, the State Department paper concluded, was that "anybody else would be an improvement—it is hard to imagine another leader who would externalize radical policies." Therefore, the paper said, "we must increasingly take direct covert action. In addition, overt Department of Defense actions will be required to contribute credibility to rumors that the U.S. is planning further actions against Libya." The combination "could induce Libyans to action against Qaddafi. Our strategy should take advantage of Qaddafi's paranoia and flaws in his security network and send strong signals to the security forces, the military, and the Libyan people. To the extent possible, these should be seen as coming from other than the U.S."

The paper proposed a mixture of real and psychological pressure on Qaddafi, and sometimes it was almost impossible to separate the two.

The paper noted that Gen. Richard Lawson, the deputy European commander, was scheduled to visit Chad in late August as part of an effort to strengthen French and American support for the Chadian campaign to drive Qaddafi's invaders out of the country. While Lawson's mission was real, the State Department paper suggested that his trip to Chad "provides an opportunity for disinformation to reach Qaddafi that the U.S. and France are developing contingency plans for a Chad option in response to further Libyan terrorism." Bogus reports of a Franco-American attack on Libyan troops in Chad might be a useful "step to undermine Qaddafi within his military," the paper suggested.

Another scheduled trip, this one by Assistant Defense Secretary Richard Armitage to Morocco, Algeria, and Tunisia, "provides a similar opportunity for disinformation," the paper continued. Again, the trip was real, but the paper suggested the CIA should peddle the false notion "that the U.S. has a plan for the introduction of forces into those countries in a multilateral operation against Libya if there is further terrorism."

In the same vein, the paper proposed sending U.N. Ambassador Vernon Walters, who had briefed the allies just prior to the April raid, back to Europe to urge stepping up economic and diplomatic pressure against Qaddafi. Walters's mission was a genuine effort to win more European cooperation in the campaign against Qaddafi, but the drafters of the State Department paper hoped the trip also would make Qaddafi think the United States was getting ready to bomb Libya again.

A section of the paper entitled "Foreign Media Placement" called for the CIA to intensify the low-budget disinformation campaign it had been running against Qaddafi in the Arab world since 1981. Phony stories broadcast on the exile radio station and circulated in exile newsletters and the Arab press would cover all manner of plotting by Americans, Soviets, exiles, and Libyan military officers against Qaddafi. The paper also suggested that the power and frequency of exile radio broadcasts be increased and that they should include bogus coded messages to imaginary revolutionary cells within Libya. Several Zodiac rubber boats had recently been spotted on the Libyan coast, and although no one knew where they had come from, the State Department paper suggested using American submarines to deliver similar boats loaded with weapons, radios, and anti-Qaddafi propaganda. Two specially equipped submarines based in Sardinia could be employed for the job.

The paper also included the proposal for sending supersonic SR-71 reconnaissance planes over Tripoli, the new military headquarters at Jufra, and Qaddafi's new desert home. The sonic booms "would convey the impression that Libyan air defenses continue to be impotent, that the U.S. is preparing for new operations, and nowhere in Libya is safe." Pilotless drones could be used to spook Libyan air defenses and drop anti-Qaddafi leaflets. The Sixth Fleet could continue to use electronic warfare to trick the Libyans into thinking American ships and planes were once again moving south of the "line of death." When the Libyan military reported that it could not locate the intruders, Qaddafi would trust his soldiers even less—or so the reasoning went.

All this plotting and maneuvering would be backed up by what the paper called "public diplomacy," a program of factual background sessions for American reporters to stimulate stories on "the three ring circus" in Libya and "the plight of Libyans under Qaddafi." The public diplomacy was intended to keep attention focused on Qaddafi's retreat into the desert and to highlight the unrest in Libya as one of the benefits of the April bombing.

It amounted to a massive psychological warfare campaign, and, as the paper pointed out, it had obvious risks. "A perceived U.S. hand could forestall Libyan plotting against Qaddafi, rally other Libyans around Qaddafi, and further complicate our working with a successor," it predicted. "Qaddafi may be stronger if he survives this strategy."

When the seven-page document, which had been cleared by officials at the Pentagon and the CIA, reached the NSC, it was boiled down twice—once by Howard Teicher for the cabinet members who would meet on August 14, and a second time by Elaine Morton for the President. The two papers read as if they had been written on different planets. In his condensation, Teicher carelessly merged the bona fide "public diplomacy" and "foreign media placement," writing that "a centrally coordinated public diplomacy and foreign media placement plan should focus media attention on in-fighting among Libyan groups jockeying for the post-Qaddafi era, the threat of resurgent terrorism and threats to Qaddafi's neighbors, the need to continue to deter Qaddafi, speculation about likely Qaddafi successors, and the plight of Libyans under Qaddafi." In other words, administration officials were to tell American reporters the same phony stories about Qaddafi's imminent demise that the CIA was supposed to be spreading in the Arab world. In fact, the whole campaign was an attempt to reverse what Teicher's paper called "recent signs . . . that [Qaddafi] may be coming out of his depression and reasserting control."

Elaine Morton was appalled by the entire project. Morton had labored on the administration's Libya policy since 1981 and increasingly she had found herself fighting a rearguard action against what she thought were hare-brained proposals for political, military, and covert action against Qaddafi. Writing on the NSC's office computer network, she had compared most of the schemes for fomenting a coup in Libya to *The Wizard of Oz*—making the wicked witch disappear merely by sprinkling water on her.

In July, she had had a sharp disagreement with Vincent Cannistraro, another NSC staff member, over the proposal for using SR-71s to create sonic booms over Libya. "Elaine," Cannistraro wrote back,

> I have profound disagreements with the substance of your position. . . . We have established, I think, that pressure against Qaddafi does indeed work and can serve to condition/moderate his behavior. . . . There is a psychological momentum among those opposed to Qaddafi which needs to be sustained. Sonic booms are indications that Qaddafi is not out of the woods, thus encouraging his opposition, and affecting his equilibrium. Not to say this is effective in and of itself, but as part of, albeit [an] important part, of a broader campaign, it is necessary. We should sustain pressure, not release it, and not blindly hope his economy will collapse and save our strategy.

Assigned to write the paper for the President, Morton now had perhaps her last chance to torpedo the policy, not by arguing her case—it was too late for that—but by writing a memo that would make clear to the President exactly what she thought he was being asked to approve. She believed Teicher had removed all the red flags from the paper he wrote for the cabinet. Nowhere, for instance, did Teicher use the word "disinformation," which the State Department paper had used to describe how the CIA could make use of Lawson's and Armitage's trips to Africa. Morton's memo to the President, signed by national security adviser John Poindexter, called for a combination of "real and imaginary events—through a disinformation program—with the basic goal of making Qaddafi think that there is a high degree of internal opposition to him within Libya, that his key trusted aides are disloyal, that the U.S. is about to move against him militarily."

Her three-page memo also said the campaign was not intended to deter terrorism, since, Morton asserted, "the current intelligence community assessment is that Qaddafi is currently quiescent in his support of terrorism." But the same sentence warned that the Libyan leader "may soon move to a more active role," and in fact there already was mounting evidence that Qaddafi's terror apparatus was starting up again. The British believed he had sponsored an attack on their base at Akrotiri in

Cyprus on August 3. U.S. diplomats in the Sudan had reported that they were under surveillance again. In Togo, nine Africans had been arrested for trying to attack the U.S. Embassy with a bomb they got from the Libyan People's Bureau in neighboring Benin. Libyan money had begun moving again to airline and trade offices, which seemed to have taken over the terrorist business from Qaddafi's People's Bureaus in Western Europe. At the time, the bureaucracy could not agree on how seriously to take the reports.

Typically, when the National Security Planning Group met on August 14 to discuss the proposed campaign against Libya, it skirted most of the tough issues. According to notes of the meeting, the word "disinformation" was never used, nor did it appear in the National Security Decision Directive the President signed. As usual, the NSDD was so vague as to be virtually meaningless. It called for more pressure on Qaddafi, continued covert action with Libyan exiles, and the use of military deception against Libyan air defenses, and it said the United States was prepared to attack Libya again if Qaddafi's terrorist allies were caught striking at Americans.

The entire plan blew up in the administration's face when Morton's version, red flags and all, leaked to *The Washington Post*. The administration was caught pursuing a policy which, at least as Morton had presented it, the public would not support. "One of our mistakes was that we couldn't leave well enough alone," said Michael Ussery, a deputy assistant secretary of state and one of the architects of the policy. "He was down, but we had to have him out."

Within months, someone did give Qaddafi a healthy shove, but it was dusty, impoverished Chad, and it did so using Toyota pickup trucks with machine guns mounted on the back, not F-111 bombers or psychological warfare. By driving Libyan troops out of its territory, Chad probably did more to humiliate Qaddafi than the Reagan administration ever did, although there were some who argued that Chad might never have tried if the United States had not gone first. "The day Qaddafi steps down or is driven out or shot or whatever it is, he can mark the beginning of his decline and fall from the raid," said Adm. William Crowe.

★　★　★

Military operations were only the most visible part of America's war against terrorism. Late in 1985, the President signed an intelligence "finding" authorizing the CIA to hunt down and apprehend—to kidnap—terrorists. To carry out its orders, the CIA created a new Counterterrorism Center (CTC).

But the dispute over who should be in charge of counterterrorist operations raged unabated. The staff of Vice President Bush's terrorism task force had proposed a small cell within the NSC staff. But when Reagan's top aides met to ratify the report, George Bush had been no better able to reconcile the warring factions than the President. Weinberger once again argued that the White House should be in command. Attorney General Edwin Meese, always eager to protect the President, insisted that would give terrorism attention it did not deserve. Shultz said terrorism was an international problem, which made it the State Department's job.

Bush left the matter unresolved. But Oliver North quickly convened a small group to discuss the lone new recommendation in Bush's report—that counterterrorist forces be pre-positioned in Europe to cut down the time it took them to respond to terrorist incidents. The group kept meeting, and eventually it was dubbed the Operations Sub-Group (OSG).

In January 1986, the President signed NSDD 207, which made the OSG official and said the State Department was in charge of counterterrorist policy overseas. But this, Reagan's third NSDD on the subject, didn't settle the issue either. None of it, not the F-111s nor the F-14s, not the CTC nor the OSG, could accomplish what Ronald Reagan wanted most—the return of the hostages from Lebanon.

★ 11 ★

INNOCENTS ABROAD

In September of 1985, a few days after Rev. Benjamin Weir was freed from the hostages' cramped prison in Beirut's squalid southern suburbs, his roommates—journalist Terry Anderson, hospital administrator David Jacobsen, Servite priest Lawrence Martin Jenco, and agriculture professor Thomas Sutherland—were moved again. "We were brought into one apartment, then taken up to the top floor of the building," Jenco recalled. "Then we climbed over a wall and jumped down into the adjacent building."

One hundred twenty-five miles to the east, in Cyprus, Brig. Gen. Carl Stiner, head of the Joint Special Operations Command, was standing by with the Delta force for a rescue mission, this time with help from Israeli intelligence agents who were trying to pinpoint the hostages' location. Once again, American military might was powerless. Even if Weir or the Israelis' agents had been able to identify the building where he and the others had been held, Stiner's rescue force would have found it empty.

With Weir's release, the hostages lost their Arabic interpreter and much of their contact with the outside world. Jenco recalled that they had a stack of *International Herald Tribunes* and other old newspapers that contained stories about the TWA hijacking and snippets of news about their relatives. But the newspaper articles were "discouraging" and there was nothing from their comrade Ben Weir. Occasionally, the hostages had access to a radio, and sometimes, when the guards failed to turn down the sound on their television set, the captives could overhear a stray phrase or a comment. For a couple of weeks, the hostages

were given a television set so they could watch "Three's Company."
"The frustration then was we couldn't turn it off," recalled Jacobsen.

"We heard very little about ourselves, and we knew that we'd been
forgotten," Jacobsen remembered. "It wasn't like the hijacking of TWA
Flight 847 in June. . . . There weren't any television cameras zooming
in on our hell, with everybody watching the high drama." One night,
they heard former Secretary of State Henry Kissinger on the radio,
saying that in the last resort the hostages would have to use their own
resources to get out. Jacobsen was sitting in his underwear on a thin
mattress in a windowless room with a double lock on the door, an armed
guard outside, and another one down the hall. He said, "My God, Henry,
what resources do you think I have?" The others had the same reaction.
"Other than the day I was kidnapped," Jacobsen recalled, "that was the
low point."

★　　★　　★

The hostages, however, had not been forgotten. On the contrary, their
fate had become an obsession with the President. According to White
House chief of staff Donald Regan, the President brought up the hostages at about 90 percent of his briefings and asked if there was anything
new about them every morning when he met with his national security
adviser. After one meeting on the subject, Oliver North told Noel Koch,
the Pentagon's chief counterterrorism expert, about the President's concern for the hostages.

This thing is really eating him, and he's driving me nuts about it,
North said. And, he wants them out by Christmas.

Can we do it? asked Koch.

I hope so, North replied.

The CIA, however, was relentlessly downbeat, constantly warning
that the Hezbollah thug Imad Mugniyah and his Iranian backers would
never let all the hostages go. Doing so would cost them their leverage
over the United States and their insurance against American or Israeli
attacks on their bases in the Bekaa Valley. "It was our judgment, which
we passed regularly when asked, that under no conditions would the
government of Iran ever allow all the hostages to be released, because
the only leverage that those who hold the hostages have is the hostages,
so why would they give them up?" said Clair George, the CIA's Deputy
Director for Operations.

The CIA's own hostage would never come home. On October 4, 1985,
Islamic Jihad announced the "execution" of former Beirut station chief
William Buckley, four months after his fellow hostages were sure they

had heard him die. The terrorists claimed they had killed Buckley in retaliation for Israel's October 1 air raid on the PLO's headquarters in Tunisia. The CIA believed that he had long since died, either from mistreatment or neglect or both. North, as usual, preferred to believe the most melodramatic version of events. "Mr. Buckley probably died of pulmonary edema," North said. "He had been kicked so brutally in his kidneys that his lungs filled up with fluid, and he basically suffocated." Before he died, North said, Buckley was believed to have made a videotaped "confession," the transcript of which was said to be 400 pages long.

The capture of the *Achille Lauro* terrorists in October provided a brief respite from the bad news, but the administration continued, almost frantically, to try to free the "forgotten hostages," following a tangle of sometimes conflicting paths in an all-out effort to bring them home by Christmas. "Because there were so many dry holes, you had to take that risk of occasional interference between a couple of your initiatives," explained Lt. Col. Robert Earl, a member of the NSC staff. "You had to simultaneously proceed on a wide variety of fronts in the hopes that eventually one would pan out and lead to results." So many secret schemes were going forward simultaneously that the Pentagon's Noel Koch had trouble keeping them straight. The whole thing reminded him of a Pirandello play. With the possible exception of North, who stood at the eye of the hurricane, it was almost impossible for anyone to tell which plans were real, which were shots in the dark, and which were merely cover stories designed to conceal something else.

★   ★   ★

As if to dramatize America's helplessness, the Soviets quickly retrieved three of four Russian diplomats kidnapped in Tripoli, north of Beirut. With help from the Syrians, the Soviets enlisted Druze militiamen who snatched some relatives of the kidnappers. The Druze forwarded a piece of one of their prisoners to the kidnappers. Although one Soviet already had been murdered, the other three were released immediately. Comparisons with the Reagan administration's efforts to free its hostages were unfair. Moscow, with its ties to the Syrians and through them to the Druze, had more leverage in Beirut than Washington and did not hesitate to act with utter viciousness. But that was the point. The United States had neither the resources nor the ruthlessness required to beat the terrorists at their own game.

After the Soviets retrieved their three diplomats, North proposed kidnapping relatives of Imad Mugniyah, Sheik Fadlallah, and other Hezbollah leaders and exchanging them for the American hostages. The idea was immediately shouted down in the Operations Sub-Group, but North later tried to resurrect it by using money from the secret sale of arms to Iran to recruit a small force of Lebanese Druze, who apparently never got around to kidnapping anybody for North. Nevertheless, North would later tell David Major, a counterintelligence expert on the NSC staff, that he had people in cages all over Europe. He told James Stark, another NSC staff member that he had people in boxes in Tehran. But putting terrorists in cages was harder than North thought.

When the CIA reported that Imad Mugniyah was planning to visit Paris in mid-November 1985, William Casey convinced the President to authorize the agency to kidnap him. North and Duane "Dewey" Clarridge, the swash-buckling head of the CIA's European division, were all for the idea, even though it was never clear what they would do with Mugniyah once they snatched him—turn him over to the French? bring him to the United States to stand trial for the murder of Robert Stethem? trade him for the remaining hostages in Beirut? Secretary of State Shultz and FBI director William Webster balked. Webster was appalled by the idea, in part because it seemed a violation of international law and in part because he doubted it would work. Shultz argued that Casey's scheme would wreck relations with the French and that on balance he would rather lose Mugniyah than France. After ten days of debate, Casey's plan was scotched in favor of telling the French where to find Mugniyah. Reagan sent a message to President François Mitterand, but the idea was quashed by the French Interior Ministry. If Mugniyah was in France as the CIA believed, he returned, untouched, to Lebanon. A picture of Mugniyah's handsome face was posted on the wall in the offices of Lebanese military intelligence, but that was about as close as anyone got. As long as Mugniyah remained in the Shiite neighborhoods of south Beirut, he was untouchable. If anyone got too close, he would find out about it through his own spies inside Lebanese intelligence.

Discouraged by what little news they heard, the hostages enlisted the help of the Church of England by writing an open letter to President Reagan and the Archbishop of Canterbury. Within a week, the towering Anglican Church envoy Terry Waite arrived in Beirut to meet with representatives of Hezbollah. He took with him a copy of *The Times* of London he had signed, and each of the hostages posed for a Polaroid picture holding the newspaper. So, although he never saw the hostages himself, Waite was able to verify that all four of the Americans were alive and relatively well. But the condition for their freedom remained the same—release of the seventeen Dawa prisoners in Kuwait. Waite briefed North on his mission, and North came away more convinced than ever that something had to be done quickly. The NSC staffer wrote a memo saying Waite had reported "that those who hold the hostages are under immense political and military pressure from the Syrians, Druze, Phalange and Amal and that there is the distinct possibility that our hostages as well as the French and British could be killed in the near future."

So far, the only thing that had succeeded in freeing a hostage was selling arms to Iran. Israel's secret shipment of antitank missiles to Tehran in September had not produced all the hostages as promised, but it had produced Benjamin Weir. National security adviser Robert McFarlane would later say that first deal—504 TOW missiles for one hostage—had left him with a bad feeling. But McFarlane by the fall of 1985 was a man nearing the end of his tether. He was physically and emotionally exhausted and mentally preoccupied with preparations for the President's upcoming summit meeting with Soviet leader Mikhail Gorbachev in Geneva. Embroiled in an increasingly nasty personal feud with White House chief of staff Donald Regan, he already had decided to leave the administration right after the summit. On November 8, when David Kimche, his old friend in the Israeli Foreign Ministry, indicated that Israel wanted to keep pursuing the so-called moderates in Iran, McFarlane did not balk. And on November 15, when Israeli Defense Minister Yitzhak Rabin asked him whether the administration would still permit Israel to buy replacements for American arms sold to Iran, McFarlane confirmed that it would.

White House chief of staff Donald Regan recalled that before leaving for Geneva and the summit meeting with Gorbachev, McFarlane mentioned to the President that "there is something up between Israel and Iran [that] might lead to getting some of our hostages out." As usual, Reagan exhibited little curiosity about the details. His reaction, McFarlane remembered, was "cross your fingers or hope for the best, and keep me informed."

With the usual assortment of yellow lights, winks, and nods from Washington, the Israelis dispatched another shipment of American-made arms to Iran—eighty Hawk anti-aircraft missiles labeled oil-drilling equipment. Manucher Ghorbanifar, the Iranian middleman who brokered the deal, claimed Iran wanted the missiles to shoot down Soviet reconnaissance planes. The claim was preposterous, but it was what the Americans wanted to hear.

As if to confirm McFarlane's uneasiness about the deal, the shipment immediately went awry. On November 17, Israeli Defense Minister Rabin called McFarlane in Geneva and said the shipment was stuck en route to Portugal. McFarlane in turn called North, who the next day recruited retired Air Force Maj. Gen. Richard Secord, his partner in arming the Nicaraguan contras, and Dewey Clarridge, the CIA's European operations chief, to deliver the missiles.

Not only were the missiles stuck, the price of the hostages was rising, a fact North tried to conceal from his superiors. In a computer message, he told Poindexter that five Americans and perhaps one French hostage would be freed after three planes carrying a total of eighty Hawk missiles took off for Iran. In his notebook, however, North recorded a very different deal, one in which twenty-seven Hawks would buy two hostages but the last American would not be freed until the Iranians had received a total of one hundred twenty Hawks, 200 Sidewinder air-to-air missiles, and 1,900 TOW anti-tank missiles. In the future, the Iranians would always insist on this kind of sequential trade of arms for hostages, and North would always try to accommodate them.

When the CIA's by-the-book deputy director John McMahon discovered his agency had been dragged into the deal, he went "through the overhead," as he put it, and ordered the CIA to halt its involvement in any further shipments to Iran until the President signed a directive authorizing the action. That same afternoon, CIA general counsel Stanley Sporkin drafted a "finding" which forthrightly explained that the purpose of the endeavor was "to obtain the release of Americans held hostage in the Middle East." The President signed it on December 5, and John Poindexter, in his second day as McFarlane's replacement as national security adviser, put the only copy of the top-secret document in his safe. Later, when the details of what had happened began to seep out, he would tear it up.

The Iranians were as angry as McMahon about the Hawk missile shipment, but for different reasons. They had expected at least eighty state-of-the-art antiaircraft missiles; they had received eighteen older Hawk missiles, half of which still bore Israeli markings. The shipment, a fiasco from beginning to end, did not produce a single hostage.

★　★　★

Throughout this autumn of failure and frustration, the relatives of the hostages were struggling to be heard and discovering strength in unity. Peggy Say, Terry Anderson's sister, quit her job and went to work full time for the release of her brother and the other hostages. The families hounded the State Department's Lebanon desk officer and the Bureau of Consular Affairs until the State Department finally realized it had to do a better job of keeping them abreast of the pitiful scraps of information that were available. As the "forgotten hostages" began attracting more attention, Vice President Bush's task force on terrorism briefly considered transferring the responsibility for meeting with hostages' relatives to the White House. That idea was rejected after it was pointed out that bringing the families into the White House would only increase their visibility and add to the pressure on the President to do whatever it took to free the hostages.

The families, however, were not to be denied. Slowly, persistently, they worked their way through the bureaucracy from the Lebanon desk and the Consular Affairs Bureau, to Assistant Secretary of State Richard Murphy, to George Shultz, to Robert McFarlane, to Vice President Bush. By the end of 1985, there was no one left to hear their pleas but Ronald Reagan.

The meeting with Bush had been a disaster. He had tried to reassure the families that the government was doing everything it could to free their loved ones, but the relatives had heard that line too many times before. Peggy Say called the Vice President a cold fish. Bush replied angrily that he was a good Christian man.

Don't tell me you're a Christian! Peggy Say shouted. Show me!

Administration officials who watched the hostage families climb the ladder of authority to the President knew that putting the problem in his lap, as if it were on a par with the budget deficit or relations with the Soviet Union, was both unfair and unwise. Meeting with the families would only increase the psychological and political pressures on him to end the crisis at any cost. "It was like watching a Greek tragedy," said David Long of the State Department's Office for Combatting Terrorism.

This President was particularly vulnerable to the pressures of the hostage families because terrorism undercut his image as a strong and decisive leader. Some members of the Bush task force on terrorism recommended that Reagan announce publicly he would not meet with hostage families, but that was a non-starter. "Even though our people would acknowledge the merit of that argumentation rationally, objectively, still there was a political constraint against appearing to be insensitive by announcing that you weren't going to meet with hostage families," explained Lt. Col. Robert Earl, a member of the task force staff later assigned to the NSC.

In October 1985, the usually detached President came face to face with the hostage problem, reflected in the anguished faces of Peggy Say and all of the other relatives. These were real people, the kind Ronald Reagan liked to talk about in his speeches, and he could not turn his back on them. But neither could he offer them much hope. Everything his administration investigated that fall—from kidnapping Mugniyah to the

Israeli arms sale to Iran—was coming up empty. The President, of course, couldn't tell the families any of that. He could only express sympathy for their plight and assure them he was making a determined effort to bring their loved ones home, but he said he would not ask Kuwait to free the seventeen Dawa prisoners.

The President was shaken by the encounter, and North, who met regularly with the hostage families, was close to tears. "It is a devastating experience to meet with the wife or the daughter or the mother or the son of a hostage repeatedly and see the anguish in their face and know in your heart that your government can't, try as it would, do anything about it," North said. "The President felt deeply about it, as I did, and I am willing to admit that may have colored my decisions or my recommendations or even his." It was, said the CIA's Clair George, "just too much for the President."

That same month, at a videotaped workshop at the State Department's Foreign Service Institute, North conceded that the administration's policy of making no concessions to terrorists "appears to many as a cruel and heartless and insensitive policy. It is based on the greater good, but for the private American citizens, particularly those who have been long resident in Beirut, it is an approach that they find to be unacceptable." He conceded that the administration was under heavy pressure from the press and the hostage families to "meet the demands of the terrorists who hold their loved ones in Lebanon," and he left himself a little room to try to do just that. "Our policy is not one of no negotiations or no meetings or no dialogue with terrorists, but rather one of no concessions," North said. In time, he and the President would give themselves more room simply by denying that what they were doing was making concessions.

Even as the President's emotions were dragging him deeper into the hostage morass, some of his advisers were urging him to stop the arms sales to Iran. Cut your losses, Donald Regan, the White House chief of staff, told him. Robert McFarlane, who had launched the program, suggested to the President that the negotiations with Iran "seemed to be getting skewed toward arms going that way and hostages coming this way." The Vice President's task force on terrorism submitted a top-secret report reaffirming the policy of not making concessions to terrorists. The State Department demanded a high-level meeting at which it hoped to kill the arms sales for good. The opponents never had a chance. Ronald Reagan's anguish, Oliver North's energy and determination, and the iron will of the President's new national security adviser, John Poindexter, swept all doubts, all reason, aside.

The President had not chosen Poindexter as his national security adviser so much as approved his selection by McFarlane and Regan. Both had agreed that Poindexter was the man for the job—McFarlane because he thought his deputy had mastered the system and its players; Regan because he was confident the taciturn, pipe-smoking admiral would pose no threat to his own dominance. When he sent the President a memo asking him to approve the choice, McFarlane pointed out that Poindexter would be giving up a chance to take command of the Sixth Fleet, an important rung on the ladder to becoming Chief of Naval Operations. When Reagan checked the box naming Poindexter his national security adviser, he wrote a note beside it saying, I hope this doesn't hurt his future career.

The day after he was named to succeed McFarlane, Poindexter gave Secretary of State Shultz a lengthy briefing on the Iran initiative—but he never mentioned that on that very morning the President had signed an intelligence finding authorizing the CIA to help the Israelis ship arms to Iran in return for hostages. Poindexter kept the only copy of the top-secret directive locked in his safe.

John Poindexter seemed a contradiction in terms. His was a life dedicated to God and country. He had graduated first in his class at the Naval Academy and had gone on to a distinguished career. He married a woman who now was studying for the Episcopal priesthood. He routinely worked seven-day weeks, taking time out only for church on Sundays. Yet he seemed to exhibit little faith in the Constitution he had sworn to defend. He considered Congress and much of the executive branch enemy territory, and he divided the press into two categories: those reporters who were incompetent and those who willfully distorted the news. Poindexter seemed obsessed with secrecy and kept a thick binder filled with clippings of newspaper stories that had been generated by leaks. He seemed to believe not in democracy but in a meritocracy in which the ablest people—and he had no doubt that he was one of them—gave the orders and everyone else carried them out, no questions asked. He was the ultimate systems analyst who believed that if he were left alone he could solve any problem. He was not the man to impose order on the national security bureaucracy. He would just as soon do without it.

Oliver North was as zealous as John Poindexter was secretive. Robert McFarlane observed that while he had left Vietnam convinced the United States should never again enter a war it wasn't determined to win, North had come home vowing that America must never again turn its back on its friends. He was dedicated to the Nicaraguan contras and to "bringing Americans home from faraway places," as he put it. In the face of a wounded contra who called himself "Tigrillo," the little tiger, North saw the reflections of the Meo, the Hmong, the Montagnards, and all those who struggled to climb onto the roof of the American Embassy in Saigon as the last helicopter lifted into the sky.

North's passion, his heroism in battle, and his considerable charm made him a master manipulator, especially of other men. Even those who had seen more combat than North felt like wimps when they said no to his schemes. He was the Boy Scout who would dare you to run across the railroad trestle as the train was coming—and make it impossible to say no by leading the way himself. People always seemed to think he was 6 feet tall, which was 2 inches taller than he really was. He cultivated like-minded men of action—William Casey and Dewey Clarridge at the CIA, and Vice Adm. Arthur Moreau, the special assistant to the chairman of the Joint Chiefs of Staff. The relationship with Casey was almost a father-son one. North saw in Casey a man who had grown older and wiser without losing any of his willingness to take risks or his romantic fondness for covert derring-do.

North, like Casey, was not above using guile, intimidation, or deception to get his way. He frequently threatened to resign from the NSC staff and return to the Marine Corps. He would burst into a room saying, I'm getting out of this god-damned place. I'm putting in my papers. I'm calling the Commandant. I'm out of here in a week.

The threats were always short-lived, the product of the frustration felt by the ultimate in can-do military officers attempting to throw off the coils of bureaucracy. North would soon be back to the grind of eighteen-hour days and seven-day weeks. That was the real source of his power—the ability to work man-killing hours with an intensity that only a true believer could sustain. There were, of course, other true believers in government, but none of them projected so strongly that special aura that whatever he was doing was what Ronald Reagan wanted done.

Over time, more and more of North's colleagues grew wary of his *modus operandi,* but the uneasiness was always tempered by the fact that he got the job done. In late 1985, when an outside consultant named James Roche reviewed the organization of the NSC staff, he privately recommended to Donald Fortier, the deputy national security adviser, that North be transferred to a less intense environment, preferably the Naval War College. That would advance his Marine career and get him out of the trenches before his free-wheeling caught up with him. The recommendation went nowhere, and Poindexter kept handing North assignments. "They treated him like the Marines treat their mules,"

Richard Secord said. "They kept piling the work on his back until he broke down."

North wasted no time in pressing John Poindexter not to abandon the arms-for-hostages gambit. In a computer memo written at two o'clock in the morning of the day Poindexter was named to succeed McFarlane as national security adviser, the indefatigable North brought Poindexter up to speed on the botched delivery of Hawk missiles and argued for another try. "Like you and Bud [McFarlane], I find the idea of bartering over the lives of these poor men repugnant," North wrote. "Nonetheless, I believe that we are, at this point, barring unforseen [sic] developments . . . , too far along with the Iranians to risk turning back now. If we do not at least make one more try at this point, we stand a good chance of condemning some or all to death and a renewed wave of Islamic Jihad terrorism. While the risks of proceeding are significant, the risks of not trying one last time are even greater."

His memo did not reflect it, but North had another reason for trying to revive the arms sales to Iran. The Nicaraguan contras were increasingly desperate for money, and North knew the Iranians were willing to pay top dollar for American weapons. At a meeting with Israeli officials in New York on December 6, North said he wanted to continue selling arms to the Iranians at inflated prices in order to generate some profit for the Nicaraguan rebels. The idea violated a cardinal rule of intelligence—never mix two covert operations—but North played by his own rules, not the CIA's. To North, overcharging the Ayatollah and giving the windfall profit to the contras was "a neat idea," which enabled him to circumvent a congressional ban on official American aid to the Nicaraguan rebels.

In his memo to Poindexter, North detailed an elaborate package deal for the hostages which included 50 up-to-date Hawk missiles and 3,300 TOW missiles. The memo set forth the deal in unmistakably clear terms. "H + 16 hours: 1 747 w/ 50 Hawks & 400 TOWs = 2 AMCITS [American citizens] . . . H + 24 hours: 1 747 w/2000 TOWs = French hostage." North recognized that "this does not meet one of the basic criteria established at the opening of this venture: a single transaction which would be preceded by the release of the hostages. However . . . we all believe it is about the only way we can get the overall process moving." North claimed he had reviewed the plan with Dewey Clarridge at the CIA, but he said that "the only parties fully aware of the dimensions of what we are about are you and RCM [Robert C. McFarlane]."

At ten o'clock on Saturday morning, December 7, five days before North's "H Hour," President Reagan sat down with his senior foreign policy advisers in a meeting the State Department hoped would kill the arms sales. George Shultz and Caspar Weinberger again objected to trading arms for hostages. As Weinberger later recalled it, he warned the President that "there are legal problems here . . . in addition to all of the policy problems." According to Weinberger, Reagan responded, "Well, the American people will never forgive me if I fail to get these hostages out over this legal question." Afterwards, Shultz said the President had seemed "rather annoyed" at him and Weinberger for opposing the arms sales to Iran. "You could feel his sense of frustration," Shultz recalled.

The ever-cautious John McMahon, sitting in for Casey, was troubled by the President's questions about strengthening "moderates" in Iran. McMahon later testified that he pointed out to the President that the CIA "had no knowledge of any moderates in Iran, that most of the moderates had been slaughtered when Khomeini took over." In Iran, a moderate was a mullah who was running low on ammunition. "Are there any pragmatists in Iran?" the CIA's Clair George once asked rhetorically. "Does anybody play the piano in the Fiji Islands? Yes, somewhere."

In fact, U.S. officials had already concluded that Manucher Ghorbanifar's principal—if not his only—contact in the upper reaches of the Iranian government was Ahmad Kangarlu, an aide to Prime Minister Mir Hussein Musavi, whose main function was trying to buy arms for the war against Iraq. U.S. intelligence believed Musavi was behind the December 1983 bombings in Kuwait which had touched off the Lebanese hostage drama in the first place. His inner circle also included the new Interior Minister, Mohammed Mohtashami-pur, who as Iran's Ambassador to Syria had set up the Iranian terror network in Lebanon. Even by Iranian standards, it was hard to consider Kangarlu and his associates moderates.

McMahon also told the President that any weapons sold to Iran would be fired at the Iraqis, not at Soviet reconnaissance planes, as Ghorbanifar claimed. From Reagan's questions, it appeared that his old friend Bill Casey had been telling the President something other than what the professional intelligence officers were saying.

As usual, Reagan did not make a decision. McFarlane, who had given up his job as national security adviser but not his role in the Iran arms sales, left that night for London and a meeting with Ghorbanifar carrying no written instructions. McFarlane wanted to talk about opening a strategic dialogue between Washington and Tehran. Ghorbanifar wanted to talk about trading arms for hostages. McFarlane disliked the

Iranian intensely and returned to Washington determined to shut down the initiative and put Ghorbanifar out of business.

North had other ideas. He had accompanied McFarlane to London, and as soon as he got back to Washington he wrote a memo warning it would be "very dangerous" to back out now. "U.S. reversal now could ignite Iranian fire—hostages would be our minimum losses," he warned. North proposed instead that the United States begin delivering arms directly to Iran. That way, he argued, the administration could sell the Iranians modern Hawk missiles the Israelis didn't have. North wasn't sure if Ghorbanifar could be trusted, but he considered him "irrefutably the deepest penetration we have yet achieved into the current Iranian government," which was a revealing comment on the quality of American intelligence about the Islamic republic.

The next morning, December 10, McFarlane reported to the President and his senior foreign policy advisers. North's memo seemed to have caused him second thoughts. Instead of recommending a halt to the undertaking, McFarlane waffled. The United States, McFarlane suggested, could let the Israelis go ahead with what they probably would do anyway and hope to get some benefit from it. The President was in a pensive mood, McFarlane remembered, which was "not uncommon when he was uncomfortable with the situation, when in this case everybody else in the room seemed to be of one view and he didn't want to oppose that view." According to Donald Regan, the President complained that it would be another Christmas with the hostages still in Beirut and that he was looking powerless and inept because he could not free them. Again, the President made no decision, leaving those present to draw their own conclusions.

Shultz was away on a trip, but his staff cabled him an account of what had happened based on a debriefing from Poindexter. "White House meeting this morning," the cable said. "The turn-off is complete (we think). McFarlane turned down in London. Ollie did paper saying this means hostages will die." Casey gave McMahon an entirely different account. "As the meeting broke up, I had the idea that the President had not entirely given up on encouraging the Israelis to carry on with the Iranians," Casey reported. "I suspect he would be willing to run the risk and take the heat in the future if this will lead to springing the hostages."

★　　★　　★

For the hostages, Christmas of 1985 was every bit as dreary as their families, Ronald Reagan, Oliver North and everyone else feared it was.

The hostages got only fleeting glimpses of the world outside. Father Jenco once heard his nephew on the Voice of America, and the guards produced a videotape of Terry Anderson's family celebrating a birthday. Those were the highlights; most of their days were empty.

Some of the hostages thought Thomas Sutherland spent an inordinate amount of time trying to retrieve his shoes, which he said had cost him $75 and which were slowly collecting mildew in the hallway outside the room where the hostages were chained. Father Jenco often dreamed of food. Terry Anderson, true to his profession, was always trying to wheedle a scrap of news out of the guards and inevitably, it seemed, just when he was making progress David Jacobsen would interrupt to ask if the hostages could have some ice cream. "It was so frustrating," remembered Father Jenco, softly drawing out the word "so."

On Christmas Eve, Jenco recalled, a heavy blow fell: the BBC reported that Anglican envoy Terry Waite's negotiations had faltered. The young Shiite guards tried to brighten their captives' holiday season by bringing a cake with "Happy Birthday Jesus" written on it, but even the guards were appalled by the conditions. Once, recalled Jenco, the guard nicknamed Haj took a whiff of the hostages' quarters and declared: The air in this room is not good.

★   ★   ★

With the future of the initiative in the balance, the Israelis, their timing perfect as usual, weighed in with a pitch to continue the arms sales and to use some of the profits to underwrite other secret operations. On the second day of the new year, Amiram Nir, the counterterrorism adviser to Israel's prime minister, visited Poindexter, North, and Donald Fortier, Poindexter's deputy, and proposed reviving the arms sales minus the two Israeli arms dealers he blamed for botching the November Hawk missile sale. According to Poindexter's notes of the meeting, Nir proposed that Israel would ship 4,000 TOW missiles to Iran and that after the first 500 had arrived, the Iranians would release all five American hostages while the Israeli-backed South Lebanon Army simultaneously would free "20–30 Hezbollah prisoners who don't have blood on their hands." After the prisoners had been swapped, Nir said, the rest of the missiles would be delivered to Iran and the Iranians would promise an end to hostage taking and terrorism.

The following day, January 3, North drafted a new presidential "finding" authorizing arms sales to "moderate elements within and outside the government of Iran." The draft, which was prepared without consulting the Pentagon, the State Department, the CIA's operations directorate, or the intelligence officers on the NSC staff, but which adopted much of the Israeli proposal, suggested that under a loophole in the National Security Act of 1947, Congress should not be notified of the operation. It made no mention of the hostages until CIA general counsel Stanley Sporkin insisted on inserting one. In an accompanying background paper, North wrote, "this approach through the government of Iran may well be our only way to achieve the release of the Americans held in Beirut."

Poindexter gave a draft of the finding to Reagan on Monday morning, January 6, at their regular nine-thirty meeting, and the President signed it, apparently by mistake. A day later, he met with his top aides in the Oval Office, ostensibly to solicit their advice. Once again, Shultz and Weinberger argued against selling arms to cultivate so-called moderates in Iran and to free the hostages, but Poindexter, Casey, and the President all wanted to press ahead. Donald Regan, who a month earlier had favored halting the transactions, changed his mind after Poindexter claimed there were "new contacts" to be exploited. The President did not mention that he had already signed the finding, and he made no decision at the meeting, although by now Shultz and Weinberger could sense that they had lost.

North wasted no time telling his Israeli partner, Amiram Nir, what Poindexter didn't tell the Secretaries of State and Defense. Secret operations brought out the small boy in North, who immediately telephoned Nir with a message in a crude code that spoke volumes about the slapdash operation. "Joshua [Reagan] has approved proceeding as we had hoped," North said, according to his notebook. ". . . If these conditions are acceptable to the Banana [Israel] then Oranges [the U.S.] are ready to proceed."

Four days later, Manucher Ghorbanifar, the man the administration was counting on to open doors in Iran, reported to the CIA for a five-hour polygraph examination. Michael Ledeen, the NSC consultant who had started it all, had been urging the CIA not to give up on Ghorbanifar as the intermediary in the dealings with Iran. According to one memo, Ledeen described Ghorbanifar as "a good fellow who is a lot of fun."

This "good fellow" whom North believed to be the Reagan administration's "deepest penetration" of the Iranian government was, as far as the CIA was concerned, worse than worthless. In July 1984, the CIA operations directorate had issued a rare "burn notice," warning all its operatives that Ghorbanifar was a liar. According to one CIA memo, "He had a history of predicting events after they happened and was perceived to be a rumormonger of occasional usefulness. His information consistently lacked sourcing and detail notwithstanding his exclusive interest in getting money for his questionable pursuits." Ghorbanifar had volunteered information about William Buckley's kidnapping and about an alleged Iranian hit team plotting to assassinate American presidential candidates, but lie detector tests and an investigation had "determined that he deliberately provided false information about both incidents." Ledeen, however, kept pushing Ghorbanifar, taking his case directly to Casey, who arranged for the Iranian to take another lie detector test.

Ghorbanifar took his test on January 11 and, to put it kindly, he flunked. "He showed deception on thirteen out of fifteen questions," said the CIA's Clair George. "The only questions he passed were his name and his nationality." In fact, the polygraph indicated Ghorbanifar was an Iranian agent, and the CIA's operations directorate concluded he also had been recruited by the Israelis. The polygraph examiner reported: "Ghorbanifar clearly is a fabricator and wheeler-dealer who has undertaken activities prejudicial to U.S. interests." A report on the exam by the Near East operations division said, "It is not at all clear which side he is working for. . . . Unfortunately, the U.S. government has enhanced this fabricator's credibility with the Iranians by using him as an intermediary in the negotiations for the hostages."

Clair George called Oliver North at the White House and told him the results of Ghorbanifar's lie detector test. George also told William Casey he would not work with Ghorbanifar. "I said, 'Bill, I am not going to run this guy anymore,' which means in our language, 'I will not handle him. He is a bum.' " Casey asked if George would object to turning Ghorbanifar over to Charles Allen, the CIA's National Intelligence Officer for Counterterrorism. Casey was always willing to take a chance. Besides, there was nowhere else to turn. As North's assistant Robert Earl later explained it, "Everyone recognized that Ghorbanifar was untrustworthy, that he was making up stuff and looking out for his own interests, which were probably to make an enormous profit, but [he] was the only channel available."

Once again, Clair George was philosophical. "This is not the first administration and will not be the last that becomes totally frustrated with its spy service," he said afterwards. "You want a spy service that produces regularly and we don't. Life is tough. And so at what point [does] a director [say], 'I am going to set up an operation, and I am going to run it around these bureaucrats'?"

On January 17, George's operations directorate issued a notice that it would no longer do business with Ghorbanifar, its second "burn notice" on him in eighteen months. That same day, President Reagan signed the final version of the intelligence "finding" authorizing direct U.S. arms sales to Iran, sales which were to be brokered by Manucher Ghorbanifar. That afternoon, Casey and Poindexter discussed Iran at one of their periodic "family group" lunches at the White House with Shultz and Weinberger. Neither Casey nor Poindexter mentioned that the President had just signed an intelligence "finding" authorizing U.S. arms sales to Iran.

The President had authorized an operation which not only contradicted his publicly avowed policies of making no concessions to terrorists and selling no arms to Iran but also entrusted that explosive secret to a man the CIA believed was a foreign agent. It was a measure of the administration's breakdown that Casey and Poindexter could trust Manucher Ghorbanifar to look out for America's interests and the lives of the hostages but could not tell the Secretary of State, the Secretary of Defense, or the appropriate committees of Congress.

★   ★   ★

Armed with the presidential "finding," Poindexter and North went to work arranging a new arms sale to Iran. The day after the finding was signed, Poindexter summoned the CIA's Clair George and Thomas Twetten, deputy chief of the Agency's Near East division, to the White House to discuss the operation with North and his partner, Richard Secord. For openers, North needed 4,508 TOW missiles from the Defense Department, a secret Swiss bank account from the CIA, intelligence on the disposition of Iraqi troops to be passed to the Iranians, and recording and videotape equipment to bug an upcoming meeting with Ghorbanifar in Europe.

Clair George was almost as unhappy to find Secord in the middle of the operation as he was to discover that Ghorbanifar was still its linchpin. "The good General Secord's reputation inside the CIA was not of the highest," George said later. George knew of nothing illegal Secord had ever done, but a report by the agency's inspector general had linked Secord too closely for comfort with Edwin Wilson, a notorious renegade CIA agent who had been sent to prison for, among other things, peddling explosives to Qaddafi. The day after the meeting at the White House, both George and the CIA's general counsel, Stanley Sporkin, went to Casey and told him that if the administration insisted on shipping arms to Iran for hostages, at least it should not employ Secord in the enterprise. "He was just not a guy I wanted to do business with," George explained later. I hear you, Casey replied.

Casey heard, but he didn't listen, perhaps because he believed that operators like Secord and Ghorbanifar could do things better and faster than his own clandestine service, people Secord called "shoe clerks." Saddled now with both Ghorbanifar and Secord, George saluted his superiors and followed his orders. "I suffer from the bureaucrat's disease," he explained later. "When people call me and say, 'I am calling from the White House for the National Security Council on behalf of the national security adviser,' I am inclined to snap to."

Robert McFarlane shared George's misgivings. "For what it's worth," McFarlane told Poindexter in a January 21 computer message, "I think it is likely that the Israelis are sucking us in on the arms transactions and consequently it might be worthwhile to just go back and turn off this latest ploy, which started as if it would involve them taking all the risks but has become more complicated."

Poindexter responded to McFarlane from his computer terminal, which was how he preferred to talk to people: "We have the Israelis under control. . . . I wanted to get the hostage deal out of the way first. I now have everybody here agreed on the logistics arrangements, but Cap [Weinberger] and George [Shultz] still are against it on policy grounds. The President has overruled them." In a subsequent computer message, Poindexter informed McFarlane that he, Casey, White House chief of staff Donald Regan, and Attorney General Edwin Meese were "fully on board this risky operation, but most importantly, President and VP [Bush] are solid in taking the position that we have to try." Bush apparently was untroubled by the glaring contradiction between the no-concessions plank in his own task forces report and the policy of trading arms for hostages.

On January 22, North, Secord, and Amiram Nir flew to London to meet Ghorbanifar. The CIA secretly recorded the Iranian's sales pitch. "I think this is now, Ollie, the best chance because we never would have found such a good time, we never get such good money out of this," the Iranian said laughingly. "We do everything. We do hostages free of charge; we do all terrorists free of charge; Central America for you free of charge; American business free of charge; [Ahmad] Kangarlu visit. Everything free."

North, who knew the meeting was bugged, was uncharacteristically at a loss for words. "I would like to see . . . some point this, uh, idea, and maybe, y'know, if there is some future opportunity for Central America. You know that there is a lot of Libyan, a lot of Libyan and Iranian activity with the Nicaraguans."

The surreptitious tapes also revealed something of Ghorbanifar's business ethics. He demanded that in addition to arms, a hundred Lebanese Shiites held by the pro-Israeli South Lebanon Army be released in exchange for the American hostages. Even after he was told that the South Lebanon Army held fewer than fifty Shiite prisoners, Ghorbanifar demanded that fifty be freed, even if that required picking up a few new ones.

North returned from the meeting with Ghorbanifar and wrote a detailed operational plan for the release of the hostages. Titled "Notional Timeline for Operation Recovery," the document was a testament to Ghorbanifar's salesmanship and North's boundless optimism. It called for the United States to provide 4,000 TOW missiles and intelligence on Iraqi defenses to Iran in exchange for the hostages and William Buckley's remains. Among other things, North's timetable predicted the Ayatollah Khomeini would step down on February 11, the seventh anniversary of Iran's Islamic revolution.

The CIA immediately got cold feet at the prospect of handing satellite photographs of the Iran-Iraq border over to the Iranians. Giving them TOW missiles is one thing, CIA deputy director John McMahon told Poindexter. Giving them intelligence gives them a definite offensive edge, and that can have cataclysmic results.

Poindexter didn't contest the point, but he insisted it was a small price to pay to see whether the Iranians were serious. If the kidnappers did not release all the hostages after the first thousand TOWs and the first intelligence sample had been delivered, the United States would simply halt the deal, Poindexter said. McMahon appealed to Casey but got nowhere. Once again, the intelligence professionals were ignored, so they saluted, and carried out their orders.

On February 5, North flew to Europe to meet with Ghorbanifar, Nir, and some low-ranking Iranian officials. The group agreed that after Ghorbanifar deposited payment for 1,000 TOWs in an Israeli account and the Israelis transferred it to a CIA account in Switzerland, the missiles would be delivered from the United States to Iran via Israel. The next day, Ghorbanifar borrowed $10 million from Saudi Arabian highroller Adnan Khashoggi to pay for the TOWs. Khashoggi, his eye on the bottom line, not the fate of the hostages, demanded a 15 to 20 percent return on his investment.

On February 13, the Army transferred 1,000 TOW missiles to the CIA for shipment to Israel, having mistakenly shaved $4,866 off the price of each missile. "Operation RESCUE is now under way," North wrote Poindexter. "This would keep our schedule for releasing the Americans on Sunday, Feb. 23. Something to pray for at church that day." Four days later, on February 1, 500 TOW missiles were delivered to the Iranian port of Bandar Abbas aboard a plane chartered by Richard Secord. Ghorbanifar told Secord that Kangarlu, his contact in the Iranian prime minister's office, would meet with the Americans in Europe, and following that all the hostages would be released—if Iran liked the intelligence the United States provided. The irrepressible North could not contain his optimism. "We appear to be much closer to a solution than earlier believed," he wrote Poindexter. The plan for meeting with Kangarlu "tends to support our hope that this whole endeavor can succeed this week if we appear to be forthcoming." Somehow Ghorbanifar had conned North into thinking it was the United States that had to be forthcoming.

When Kangarlu finally appeared in Frankfurt on February 25, six days late, it quickly became apparent that Ghorbanifar had lied to both sides. According to a report filed by the CIA's Tom Twetten, Ghorbanifar had promised Kangarlu hundreds of Phoenix air-to-air missiles, howitzers, and just about anything else he wanted. "And we are promised that all the hostages will come out after the first two transactions and that we are going to have a meeting with [speaker of the Iranian parliament Hashemi] Rafsanjani and President [Ali] Khamenei within the first two months of this procedure, and one of the things in the scenario was that sometime in April there was a precise date given that Khomeini was going to step down and he was going to resign all his powers. This is extraordinary nonsense. Essentially Ghorbanifar, as a negotiating technique, lied to both sides to get them to the table, and then sat back and watched us fight it out. It was a real slugging match. It was awful."

North, incredibly enough, was still looking on the bright side. "The Govt. of Iran is terrified of a new Soviet threat," he wrote. "They are seeking a new rapprochement but are filled w/fear & mistrust. . . . While all of this could be so much smoke, I believe that we may well be on the verge of a major breakthrough—not only on the hostages/terrorism, but on the relationship as a whole."

North would later boast that he had lied to the Iranians every time he met them. "I said a lot of things that weren't true," he recalled. "I'd have told them they could have free tickets to Disneyworld or a trip on the space shuttle if it would have gotten Americans home." But North's lies were no match for the Iranians' fairy tales. Time and again, they told him exactly what they knew he wanted to hear about the hostages, about the Soviet threat to Iran, and about a thaw in U.S.-Iranian relations. All of it was exactly what Tom Twetten said it was: "extraordinary nonsense."

Two days later, Secord's pilots delivered another 500 TOW missiles to Iran. North reported to McFarlane, whose home computer was still linked to the White House, that the Iranians "may be preparing to release one of the hostages early," and that Rafsanjani would be McFarlane's counterpart in the next meeting between Iranians and Americans. "With the grace of the good Lord and a little more hard work we will very soon have five AMCITS home and be on our way to a much more positive relationship than one which barters TOWs for lives," wrote North. He added a revealing insight into the mind set of Poindexter and some of the NSC staff: "My part in this was easy compared to his. I only had to deal with our enemies. He has to deal with the cabinet." The next day, Poindexter told Shultz that the hostages would be released in a week, but he didn't say a word about U.S. arms sales to Iran.

By the end of February, the Iranians had received 1,000 antitank missiles and some intelligence, parts of it doctored, on the strength and disposition of Iraqi forces. The United States had gotten nothing except a shouting match with a minor Iranian official described by Tom Twetten as being "on the low end of the scale for intelligence." White House chief of staff Donald Regan told the President, "I think we ought to break it off. . . . We've been snookered again, and how many times do we have to put up with this rug merchant type of stuff?"

Poindexter had assured the CIA's John McMahon the arms sales would end after the first 1,000 TOWs if the hostages were not released, but the administration continued to pursue the Iranians through Ghorbanifar for another two months, making still another arms sale in the process. After another frustrating meeting with Ghorbanifar, this one in Paris on March 8, Tom Twetten of the CIA summarized the negotiations. "We had delivered our missiles and the shoe was on their foot, but they were acting like the shoe was still on our foot," he said.

By now, even Poindexter was fed up and wanted to cut off the program, but it continued. Twetten explained why. "North, who you must have sensed by now is a man of a lot of energy and a lot of determination, essentially kept it alive because of the President's personal and emotional interest in getting the hostages out—in my view," he testified. There was always the strategic rationale of improving relations with Iran, but, said Twetten, "the real thing that was driving this was that there was in early '86, late '85, a lot of pressure from the hostage families to meet with the President and there were articles in the magazines about the forgotten hostages, and there was a lot of things being said about the U.S. government isn't doing anything. . . . And there is a lot of fear about the yellow ribbons going back up and that this President would have the same problems that the last President had with Iranian hostages."

While North was charging ahead, the intelligence community was changing its mind about whether Khomeini's Iran really was about to collapse, and thus invite the Soviets to rush in and fill the vacuum. As Secord was preparing to deliver the first TOW missiles, the intelligence community was putting the final touches on a new Special National Intelligence Estimate on post-Khomeini Iran which reversed the controversial one completed less than a year before. The new estimate, twenty-five pages long, noted that Iran had held successful parliamentary elections in the fall of 1985 and had elected a successor to Khomeini, the Ayatollah Hussein Ali Montazeri. The Islamic republic was not in jeopardy, it said, and there was little reason to believe the Soviets could make significant inroads there any time soon.

The intelligence community's reversal had absolutely no impact on the administration's secret Iran policy. CIA director William Casey published the revised estimate, then ignored it and continued to rely on his own analysis of the situation. In a perverse way, the new analysis even strengthened Casey's conviction that the secret policy was on the right track. If the current leaders in Iran were firmly in control, as the new estimate said, then the Reagan administration was dealing with the right people. Casey had become both advocate and analyst, and the combination was disastrous. "One [lesson of the Iran arms affair] is . . . separating the function of gathering and analyzing intelligence from the function of developing and carrying out policy," George Shultz reflected afterwards. "If the two things are mixed in together, it is too tempting to have your analysis and your selection of information that's presented favor the policy that you're advocating." The CIA's Clair George agreed. "You cannot have the operators doing the analysis," he said. "We become emotionally involved. A man becomes involved when he is in a project."

★   ★   ★

In the field of terrorism, the CIA had deliberately decided to unite analysis and operations. Late in 1985 the CIA had created a Counterterrorism Center (CTC) in which the CIA's analysts and covert operators worked side by side. The idea had originated in response to the almost insurmountable problem of gathering intelligence and running operations against tiny, family-based terrorist cells like the one Imad Mugniyah commanded. Like organized crime families, the terror families usually recruited only blood relatives, and CIA agents on several occasions had run afoul of demands that new members participate in bombings or assassinations to prove their loyalty. To head the CTC, Casey turned to Dewey Clarridge, a veteran of the agency's contra operations as well as the ill-fated November shipment of Hawk missiles to Iran.

Operating under a presidential intelligence "finding," Clarridge had a mandate to harass terrorists—intercept and sabotage their supplies, disrupt their finances and recruiting, foment dissension among rival groups, and mount both pre-emptive and retaliatory strikes.

The most controversial aspect of the finding was one which authorized the CIA to kidnap suspected terrorists overseas and return them to the United States to stand trial. FBI director William Webster and his top aide on terrorism, Oliver "Buck" Revell, vehemently objected to the strategy for the same reasons they had objected to Casey's earlier, aborted plan to kidnap Mugniyah in France: grabbing terrorists overseas probably violated international law and, in any event, was unlikely to work. At the CIA, both deputy director John McMahon and operations director Clair George questioned the wisdom of "snatch, grab, and deliver operations." The provision's proponents found legal precedent for kidnapping terrorists in an 1886 ruling by the Supreme Court upholding the conviction of an Illinois man who had been kidnapped in Peru and returned to the United States for trial. "You might call it abduction, you might even call it a kidnapping," said Senator Arlen Specter, a Pennsylvania Republican and a former prosecutor, "but given the problems of international terrorism, this is a minimal type of force."

Legal or not, snatching terrorists was no easy task. Early in 1986, the CIA tracked down Imad Mugniyah in Paris for a second time. American officials again notified the French, who this time sent police to the hotel room where Mugniyah allegedly was staying. Inside, they found an innocent fifty-year-old Spaniard.

Another attempt to use law enforcement tactics against terrorists failed in April. It had begun in the summer of 1985, when among the hundreds of offers to free the hostages, always for a fee, came one which to everyone's surprise checked out. A Canadian of Armenian descent who claimed he represented the group which had kidnapped Peter Kilburn, the librarian at the American University of Beirut, said Kilburn's freedom could be purchased for $500,000. Not a word had been heard from or about Kilburn since his kidnapping in December of 1984. David Long of the State Department's Office for Combatting Terrorism consigned the offer to his "scumbag file," but when the Canadian produced Kilburn's university identification card with his picture on it, the FBI and CIA entered the case.

The price for Kilburn's release ballooned to $3 million, payable in small bills, but the CIA and FBI played along, and by March of 1986 the trail was warm. They planned an elaborate "sting" operation in which the kidnappers would be paid with chemically treated bills that would dissolve a few days after the swap for Kilburn had been made. North told Kilburn's only relatives, his nephew and niece, that their uncle would soon be free, but he added, "If I told you what we were doing, you'd probably never speak to us again."

Ross Perot supplied $100,000, all of which was paid to the Canadian intermediary, and the ransom money, frozen solid to keep it from dissolving prematurely, was delivered to Europe. But the CIA did not move fast enough. On April 17, three days after the United States bombed Libya, a Libyan intelligence agent in Lebanon paid to have Kilburn and two British hostages murdered. The episode confirmed North's low opinion of the bureaucracy. "The CIA took too long and then botched the Kilburn effort," he complained. Increasingly, North looked elsewhere for help, and increasingly, elsewhere meant Israel.

Israel's cooperation in the hunt for the *Achille Lauro* hijackers the previous October had cemented the relationship between North and Amiram Nir, the Israeli terrorism adviser. After the seajacking, North and Nir had established a secure phone link so they no longer had to talk in code over open lines. In January 1986, when Nir had come to Washington with Israel's new proposal for arms sales to Iran, he had suggested that some of the profits from the sales be applied to joint efforts to rescue the hostages and fight terrorism. "Mr. Nir very clearly wanted to support other activities, as he put it, through these transactions," North recalled.

Using some of the money from the February TOW missile sale, Nir and North enlisted help in locating the hostages from the Druze militia which had shelled the Marines at the airport in Beirut; from the PLO, which had hijacked the *Achille Lauro;* from the Phalange militia which had massacred hundreds of innocent people in the Palestinian refugee camps at Sabra and Shatila; and from the Lebanese intelligence service, which had been implicated in the 1985 car bomb attack on the residence of Sheik Fadlallah. None of the baksheesh produced a worthwhile lead, but as William Casey put it in a memo, "Of course, we will do almost anything to get our hostages back."

Almost anything included paying ransom. During the spring of 1986, while the CIA and FBI were trying to mount their sting operation, the two Drug Enforcement Administration officers North had recruited the previous year, William Dwyer and Frank Tarallo, supported by proceeds from the Iran arms sales, assembled what North called "a 40-man Druze force working 'for' us." By mid-May, the agents thought they had worked out a deal to ransom the hostages for a million dollars each, and Texas billionaire H. Ross Perot had agreed to provide $2 million. The operation was not deterred in the slightest by a State Department statement, issued May 6, which said: "The U.S. government will make no concessions to terrorists. It will not pay ransoms, release prisoners, change its policies or agree to other acts that might encourage additional terrorism. . . . The policy of the U.S. government is, therefore, to reject categorically demands for ransom, prisoner exchanges, and deals with terrorists in exchange for hostage release."

The transfer was to be made off the coast of Cyprus, but when North's aide, Lt. Col. Robert Earl, went to the Pentagon, he was told no naval vessels were available in the eastern Mediterranean to receive the hostages. Earl called the ever-available Richard Secord, who once again produced when the Pentagon could not. Secord dispatched a Danish freighter named the *Erria,* the same vessel North had offered to the CIA to broadcast propaganda to Libya, to the Cypriot port of Larnaca. Secord assigned one of his aides from the contra arms operation, retired CIA agent Thomas Clines, to go to Cyprus at the end of May to assess the ransom operation. Clines initially estimated the chances for success at 40 percent, then cut his estimate in half. But before Clines's judgment could be tested, more important business intervened.

★   ★   ★

After the February TOW missile sale had failed to produce any hostages, North had worked overtime with Ghorbanifar and the Israelis to arrange a high-level, face-to-face meeting between Iranian officials and an American delegation which would be headed by former national security adviser Robert McFarlane. The delegation was scheduled to fly to Tehran on April 20 to meet Hashemi Rafsanjani, the speaker of the Iranian parliament, and to deliver the first of several shipments of Hawk missile parts that were to be made in exchange for all of the hostages. Howard Teicher and Peter Rodman of the NSC staff drafted extensive "terms of reference" for the mission, which emphasized the Soviet threat to Iran and sought an end to Iranian support for terrorism. North drafted a fifteen-page background paper for the mission which would later become famous because it said $12 million of the profit on the sale "will be used to purchase critically needed supplies for the Nicaraguan Democratic Resistance Forces."

Just two weeks before the delegation was scheduled to leave Washington, La Belle disco in West Berlin was bombed and the mission to Tehran was postponed while Poindexter and North turned their attention to Muamar Qaddafi. Two days after the United States bombed Libya, Ghorbanifar reported that the Iranians were prepared to release only one hostage if they did not get all the Hawk missile parts they wanted on the plane that brought the American delegation to Iran. Poindexter finally balked. "You may go ahead and go," he wrote North in a computer memo, "but I want several points made clear to them. There are not to be any parts delivered until all the hostages are free in accordance with the plan that you layed [sic] out for me before. None of this half shipment before all are released crap. It is either all or nothing. Also you may tell them that the President is getting very annoyed at their continual stalling. He will not agree to any more changes in the plan."

Poindexter's hard line disappeared almost immediately as a new bout of hostage fever set in after Kilburn's murder and amid intelligence reports that both Qaddafi and PLO leader Yasir Arafat were trying to buy the remaining hostages. On April 24, Maj. Julius Christensen, a member of the CIA's Hostage Locating Task Force, wrote North a memo analyzing the options for freeing the hostages and concluding that the "back channel initiative" with Iran was the only one with a chance of succeeding. Christensen warned that selling arms to Iran could tip the balance in the Persian Gulf war and that the longer the operation lasted, the greater the chances it would be revealed, but he found little promise in any of the alternatives.

By now, Poindexter was going to extremes to keep the secret from leaking out. When Charles Price, the American Ambassador to Britain, got wind that something was afoot, Poindexter blithely told him there was "only a shred of truth" in his information. Poindexter lied to Secretary of State Shultz, telling him everybody involved in the operation had been ordered "to stand down." Later, Poindexter would claim that because "stand down" means to suspend temporarily, he had not deceived Shultz. "I agree that we cannot trust anyone in this game," North seconded in a memo to Poindexter.

Nevertheless, North urged his boss to schedule a meeting with the President, Shultz, and Weinberger to discuss the pending McFarlane mission to Tehran. "I don't want a meeting with RR, Shultz and Weinberger," Poindexter shot back. In a later message, the national security adviser added, "From now on, I don't want you to talk to anybody else, including Casey, except me about your operational roles. In fact, you need to quietly generate a cover story that I have insisted that you stop." North went overboard, planting a story that made its way through Republican conservatives in Congress into two prominent newspaper columns that Poindexter was trying to fire him.

On May 23, McFarlane's delegation, which included North, NSC staffer Howard Teicher, retired CIA officer George Cave, and two CIA communications technicians, left Washington for Tehran, stopping in

Israel to pick up Amiram Nir, a pallet of Hawk missile parts, and a chocolate cake in the shape of a key. The delegation arrived in Tehran on May 25 and left three days later with the Iranians still demanding the release of the seventeen Dawa prisoners in Kuwait. The Iranians unloaded the Hawk missile parts, but Rafsanjani never appeared for the promised meeting. The Iranians had expected all the missile parts; the Americans all the hostages. "When we exchanged letters face to face with the Iranians in Tehran," North recalled, "it was very obvious that [Ghorbanifar] had lied to both sides. And we knew that he did this, but we didn't know that the lie was quite so blatant."

There was much North and his colleagues didn't know, including the cost of their trip to Tehran. The Iranians adamantly had demanded a critical part of the Hawk missile's radar, one on which the entire antiaircraft battery depended. Because the Army's supply of the parts was limited, it had been reluctant to part with the few it had and had relented only after the CIA demanded all the parts the Iranians had requested. Congressional investigators later concluded that the U.S. Army's readiness was "adversely affected" by the sale of the critical Hawk parts to Iran. The U.S. Navy and its pilots would later discover that the delivery of the crucial Hawk parts had had an even more adverse effect.

Meanwhile, off the coast of Cyprus, the Danish freighter *Erria* and the two DEA agents Dwyer and Tarallo waited for the hostages with a million dollars of Ross Perot's money. But the ransom plan collapsed when their contacts demanded the money up front. Wisely, the two DEA agents refused and after forty-eight hours the *Erria* returned to port.

★　★　★

Back in Washington, Poindexter turned his attention to the possibility of mounting a hostage rescue operation. "I am beginning to think that we need to seriously think about a rescue effort for the hostages," Poindexter wrote North on May 31. For once, North was skeptical. "You will recall that we have not had much success with this type of endeavor in the past. . . . In regard to U.S. military rescue ops, JCS [the Joint Chiefs of Staff] has steadfastly refused to go beyond their initial thinking stage unless we can develop some hard intelligence on their whereabouts," he wrote, scarcely concealing his contempt for bureaucratic do-nothings. "We already have . . . one ISA [the Pentagon's Intelligence Support Activity] officer in Beirut, but no effort has been made to insert personnel since we withdrew the military mission to the LAF [Lebanese Armed Forces]."

At his morning national security briefing on June 6, the President directed the Pentagon to prepare a plan for rescuing the hostages. On June 19, Poindexter directed Casey to intensify the CIA's efforts to find them. Within a week, the Hostage Locating Task Force reported a major breakthrough in locating at least two of the hostages in the basement of the old Basta Prison in Shiite south Beirut. "There hasn't been this much enthusiasm on the issue in a long time," North reported to Poindexter.

Both the Defense Intelligence Agency and the State Department's Bureau of Intelligence and Research, however, questioned the CIA's conclusion, noting that the intelligence came from a single Lebanese source. Hezbollah was known to be running a disinformation campaign, deliberately using its sympathizers to plant false reports of the hostages' whereabouts in the Beirut rumor mill. Even if this source's report was accurate, it was already dated, and would be even more dated by the time a rescue mission could be organized. Although intelligence analysts had prepared detailed maps and numbered every building in West Beirut, military officers warned that a rescue operation in the alleys of Beirut would be a high-risk venture and might get all the hostages killed, just as the Reverend Weir had feared when he had refused to tell the CIA what little he knew about where he had been held. Nevertheless, Delta began planning for a rescue attempt. The CIA, which already had constructed a model of the Sheik Abdullah Barracks in Baalbek, spent $30,000 to erect a small-scale replica of Basta Prison. The agency asked the Syrians if they could confirm that the hostages were in the prison. The Syrians promised to help, "but we had intelligence they weren't doing anything," said Tom Twetten. "Nice words, but no action." Like all the other rescue schemes, this one died for lack of hard intelligence. The Reagan administration had run out of options.

★　★　★

The hostages—David Jacobsen, Terry Anderson, Father Martin Jenco, and Tom Sutherland—remained in chains, blindfolded and cut off from the outside world, sitting on mattresses in their underwear, subsisting on a diet of cheese and water for breakfast, rice and beans for lunch, and bread and jam for supper. In February, the guards, poor Lebanese Shiite youths who earned $25 to $50 a month for watching over the Americans, had taken their radio away and had stopped letting them see newspapers and magazines.

When Jacobsen asked why, he was told, You're just asking too many questions, and you know more than we do. We don't have time to do our work if you are always asking questions.

Jacobsen later concluded that the real reason for the blackout was that

Terry Anderson's father had died in February and his captors did not want him to hear the bad news. When Anderson's brother Glenn died of cancer a week after videotaping a haunting plea for Terry's release, that news, too, was withheld by the guards.

Their captivity was cruel, but some of the guards occasionally were kind. Sutherland suffered from hemorrhoids and the guards got some Preparation H for him and even kept it in a freezer. Sutherland and Jenco both received dyazide pills for high blood pressure, but the supply was so uncertain that they broke the tablets in half and kept half the dosage in reserve. The guards taught Jenco to suck on lemons to relieve a sour stomach and although it seemed illogical, he found that it worked. "I received two gifts from the guard we called Haj," remembered Jenco. "My glasses and a visit from a dentist." When he was pulled out into the hallway, told to open his mouth, and found a needle in his face, Jenco first thought his captors were searching for hidden radio transmitters in his teeth. He fainted. When he came to, he found that a dentist had extracted a cavity-riddled tooth.

Jenco's fear was not entirely unfounded. The guard once asked him for his fillings, saying they were radio transmitters. When one of them accused him of working for the CIA, Jenco replied: If anything, I'm VIA. That stood, he later explained, for the nonexistent "Vatican Intelligence Agency." The young Shiite guards seemed certain that at least one of their prisoners was a spy, as William Buckley had been. They forced Jenco to make a list of all the Americans in Lebanon, but he could do little more than name the nuns who worked at Catholic Relief Services.

The hostage the guards most suspected was Thomas Sutherland, and when he would not confess to being a spy they ordered him to copy a statement that William Buckley had given them. Sitting on the floor, with his back against a column, Sutherland transcribed in his own handwriting a lengthy "confession" that Buckley had written. In contrast to the devastating document, extracted under torture, that Oliver North later described, the confession that Father Jenco heard Sutherland read was almost boring. "There was nothing in it," Jenco said. "It said: 'First I lived here, then I lived there.'"

During the first week of July, the guards once again began permitting the hostages limited access to television and magazines. About three weeks later, an American-educated Shiite named Ali came into the room where the four hostages were chained, bringing each of them shoes, a shirt, and trousers.

You have to be quiet, Ali said. Get ready. You'll be going out one at a time into the bus.

The hostages assumed they were being taken to a Red Cross exchange. Jacobsen was led out first, but not to a bus. He was marched into another room. When Sutherland and Anderson joined him at five-minute intervals, Jacobsen recalled, he knew that Father Jenco was going home.

Jenco, however, wasn't so sure. Are you going to kill me? he asked Ali. No, you're going home, Ali replied.

Nearby, Jenco could hear the other hostages making videotapes again. The guard named Haj said to him: Father Jenco, we should build on what is common to us. We believe in the same God.

In his soft voice, the priest recited from the Psalms.

"I love the Lord because he hears my prayers and answers them," he began. ". . . Death stared me in the face—I was frightened and sad. Then I cried: 'Lord, save me!' . . . Now I can relax. For the Lord has done this wonderful miracle for me. He has saved me from death, my eyes from tears, my feet from stumbling. I shall live! . . ."

Then, quoting the Apostle Luke's account of Christ's words from the Cross, Jenco said: "Father forgive them, for they know not what they do."

The guard called Said translated, then he told Jenco to take two dyazide pills for his high blood pressure. When Jenco said that would make him urinate, Said replied: Who cares? Pee in your pants.

It was July 26. As they were putting Jenco into the trunk of a car, the guards gave him back a cross his kidnappers had taken on the day they seized him almost nineteen months before. He clutched the cross in the palm of his hand and as he bounced along in the darkness, he used it to cut the tape that bound his wrists. He was transferred to another car and driven across the mountains to the Bekaa Valley. The car stopped and someone opened the trunk. When Jenco climbed out, Haj handed him some money and said: Here, *Abuna* [Father]. Here's two pounds, catch your taxi to go home.

Haj handed Jenco the videotapes the other hostages had just recorded and warned him not to give them to the Syrians. If you do, said Haj, we will kill the other hostages. If the Syrians take them from you, just say so at a press conference. Here are the tapes and tell the Syrians we hate them. Haj got back into the car, and it turned and drove away.

Local authorities found Jenco and turned him over to Syrian military intelligence officers, who delivered him to Damascus, where he was handed over to American Ambassador William Eagleton. Jenco was joined in Damascus the following day by Terry Waite, the representative of the Church of England who had been working tirelessly for the hostages' release. Later that same day, Jenco and Waite flew to Wiesbaden, West Germany, where he was debriefed by CIA and FBI agents along with Oliver North. Jenco told the awful story of hearing William Buckley die, all alone, hallucinating and coughing.

★　★　★

Jenco's release marked the beginning of David Jacobsen's darkest days in captivity. In the videotape he had made on the day Jenco was freed, Jacobsen had expressed his condolences to the widow and children of William Buckley, whom he erroneously believed had been married. A few days later, he was shown the videotape as it had appeared on Lebanese television, complete with the commentary that Buckley had been a lifelong bachelor. The Lebanese television report speculated that Jacobsen's condolences were in fact a coded message. "The guards were very unhappy," Jacobsen later recalled. "They yelled and screamed and threatened."

A month later, Jacobsen got into worse trouble. His captors demanded he write a letter attacking the Reagan administration for ignoring the plight of the hostages while trying to negotiate the release of *U.S. News and World Report* correspondent Nicholas Daniloff—who had just been jailed in the Soviet Union on a trumped-up spying charge. Within an hour, one of the guards returned to Jacobsen's cell and said, It's no good. We don't trust you. We are going to rewrite it. You are going to write it down exactly as dictated. You are going to spell it like we tell you. You are going to punctuate it like we tell you.

Jacobsen did as he was told, and his captors proofread his letter carefully. When the letter appeared, the news media quickly pounced on all its grammatical errors, and his captors accused him of making them deliberately. The guard who had dictated the letter did not speak up, and Jacobsen was taken into another room where the soles of his feet were beaten with a rubber hose. He was put into isolation in a room 6 feet square. The only light filtered in over the transom, and there was little to do there but exercise.

★　★　★

Father Jenco's release was Manucher Ghorbanifar's last gasp. After McFarlane's abortive mission to Tehran, Ghorbanifar kept pressing for more weapons and another meeting in order to produce a hostage in time for the Fourth of July. But Israel's Amiram Nir told the Iranians that the arms deal would end if they did not deliver hostages in return for the Hawk missile parts McFarlane had taken with him to Tehran in May. Within a matter of days, Iran's prime minister sent word to Nir that Iran was arranging the release of one of the hostages, whom he referred to as "the priest." On July 26, Father Jenco was driven into the Bekaa Valley, and two days later the Iranians paid Ghorbanifar $4 million for the Hawk missile parts they had received.

Poindexter attributed Jenco's sudden and unexpected appearance to another con job by Ghorbanifar. "Ghorba [nifar] has cooked up a story that if Iran could make a humanitarian gesture then the U.S. would deliver the rest of the parts and then Iran would release the rest of the hostages," Poindexter explained in a memo to his predecessor Robert McFarlane. "Of course we have not agreed to any such plan." Poindexter could see Ghorbanifar's next con job coming. "The problem is that if parts aren't delivered, Gorba will convince [the Iranians] that we welched on the deal."

North, as usual, was upbeat. "The release of Father Lawrence Jenco is a second positive step in our protracted and difficult dialogue with Iran," he wrote in a paper for Poindexter to use in briefing Reagan about Jenco's release. At the CIA, William Casey was equally optimistic. "In summary, based on the intelligence at my disposal, I believe we should continue to maintain the Ghorbanifar . . . contact and consider what we may be prepared to do to meet [Iran's] minimum requirements that would lead to the release of the hostages," Casey wrote Poindexter. "Although I am not pleased by segmented releases of the American hostages, I am convinced this may be the only way to proceed, given the delicate factional balance in Iran." Three days later, on July 29, North wrote a memo recommending that the President approve the immediate shipment of the 240 remaining Hawk missile parts. Reagan did so the next day, and twelve pallets of parts were delivered to Iran on August 3.

At the beginning of September, after returning from his first vacation in five years on the NSC staff, North wrote Poindexter a memo on "Next Steps with Iran" in which he pressed the national security adviser to approve a seven-step process for the delivery of another 2,000 TOW missiles along with Hawk missile radars and spare parts in return for the sequential release of the hostages. "CIA concurs that the . . . Ghorbanifar connection is the only proven means by which we have been able to effect the release of any of the hostages," North wrote. That same evening, he complained to his former boss McFarlane that Poindexter had not yet responded. "The things one must do to get action," North lamented. He already had asked Casey to press the matter with Poindexter, and if that didn't work, he predicted, Amiram Nir, who was due in town the following week, "will raise enough hell to move it if it hasn't all fallen apart by then."

The pressure was building again. The families of the three remaining hostages began calling North to ask why their government was willing to trade an accused Soviet spy for the magazine correspondent Nicholas Daniloff but not to negotiate for the freedom of Anderson, Jacobsen, and Sutherland. "Some, like Jacobsen's son Paul, accused us of being callous to the LebNap victims—and unwilling to pressure the Kuwaitis because the issue has 'slipped from the public eye and that we are more willing to make deals for Daniloff because it was more important to the President because of the visibility.' " North reported to Poindexter. "All indicated they are planning to hold a press conference later this week to 'turn the heat on' the administration."

That same day, Charles Allen, the CIA's top terrorism analyst, reported a new threat to kill the hostages, apparently because Imad Mugniyah and his clan realized they were no closer to freeing the Dawa prisoners in Kuwait than they had been when they started kidnapping Americans two and a half years earlier. "No threat from Mugniyah should be considered idle," Allen wrote Poindexter. "He is a violent extremist capable of impetuously killing the hostages."

Mugniyah did not kill the hostages. Instead, Hezbollah seized new ones. On September 9, 1986, Frank Reed, the director of the Lebanese International School in West Beirut, was kidnapped, followed three days later by Joseph James Cicippio, the controller at the American University of Beirut. Six weeks later, Edward Tracy, an American author, was seized by a group calling itself the Revolutionary Justice Organization, bringing the number of American hostages in Lebanon back to six, exactly what it had been when Israel shipped the first ninety-six TOW missiles to Iran thirteen months before.

Oliver North, however, never gave up. Albert Hakim, the Iranian-born business partner of Richard Secord, had found a "second channel" into Iran in the person of a nephew of Hashemi Rafsanjani. Although the intelligence directive the President had signed in January said the objective of the secret arms sales was to strengthen moderates in Iran, this new intermediary had distinguished himself as a member of the fanatical Revolutionary Guards in the war against Iraq. North, at least, appreciated the irony of dealing with one of the most radical elements in Iran. "If I told you who we've been dealing with you wouldn't believe me," he said after the secret arms sales had been revealed. He did not mention that at least two shipments of TOW missiles, one from Israel in September 1985 and the February 1986 shipment from the United States, had gone directly to the Revolutionary Guards. Ronald Reagan didn't know that either. No one told him the "moderates" he thought he was selling arms to were in fact the same Revolutionary Guards who had helped organize the attacks on the American Embassy and the Marines in Beirut.

After a meeting with the young Revolutionary guardsman in Brussels, Secord had reported to North, "My judgement is that we have opened up a new and probably much better channel into Iran. This connection has been effectively recruited and he wants to start dealing." On September 19, Rafsanjani's nephew visited Washington. "Talks . . . going extremely well," North reported to Poindexter. "They and we want to move quickly beyond the 'obstacle' of the hostages. Sincerely believe that RR can be instrumental in bringing about an end to Iran/Iraq war—a la Roosevelt w/Russo/Japanese War in 1904. Anybody for RR getting the same prize?" North asked, referring to the Nobel Peace Prize awarded Theodore Roosevelt. Having already played on the Reagan administration's obsession with the hostages and the Soviet Union, the Iranians had found still another soft spot.

Two days later, North wrote Poindexter, "You can brief RR that we seem to be headed in a vy [very] positive direction on this matter and have hopes that the hostage resolution will lead to a significant role in ending the Iran/Iraq war." North gave Rafsanjani's nephew a nighttime tour of the White House, and according to Secord, the CIA paid for forty-four telephone calls to escort services to arrange for night visitors to the young Persian's hotel. One of North's assistants loaned the Iranian a gym towel on which to pray.

On September 24, North wrote a full report on the meetings for Poindexter, concluding: "We appear to be in contact with the highest levels of the Iranian government. . . . It is possible that the Iranian government may well be amenable to a U.S. role in ending the Iran-Iraq war. This, in and of itself, would be a major foreign policy success for the President." North requested instructions on how to proceed, asking, among other things, "who, if anybody, at the State Department should be brought into this activity."

Another meeting with Rafsanjani's nephew was set for October 6 in Frankfurt. The Iranian sent word that he would bring "good news" about the hostages and a Koran for the President. North asked Poindexter to have the President inscribe a Bible to be given to the Iranian in return. North also pointed out that Rafsanjani's nephew was more interested in obtaining American intelligence than in buying more weapons.

North did not consider that a problem. "We all recognized the information need not be accurate and that it was highly perishable given the dynamic nature of the conflict," he wrote to Poindexter. "In short, we believe that a mix of factual and bogus information can be provided at this meeting which will satisfy their concern about 'good faith.'" But the CIA officer who prepared the intelligence package warned that "such information, if it were to come into Iranian possession, would likely help Iran plan and execute military operations against Iraq." North had long since stopped listening to the CIA when it said things he didn't want to hear.

Once again, Poindexter was optimistic. "They are playing our lines back to us," he wrote McFarlane. "They are worried about the Soviets, Afghanistan and their economy. They realize the hostages are obstacle to any productive relationship with us. They want to remove the obstacle." Poindexter was right about one thing, at least. The Iranians were playing the Reagan administration's lines back to Washington. The trouble was that Poindexter, Casey, and North were buying them.

At his meeting with Rafsanjani's nephew in Frankfurt, North tried out a new line, making up a story about private conversations he had never had with the President and claiming the United States agreed with Iran that Iraqi President Saddam Hussein "must go" and that Washington believed the Persian Gulf war must end in "an honorable victory" for Iran. He then presented a seven-point proposal to trade 1,500 TOWs, the remainder of the Hawk missile parts, medical supplies, updated intelligence, and technical support for the Iranian military in exchange for the American hostages then in captivity, William Buckley's body, a copy of the transcript of Buckley's "confession," and the release of an American whom the Iranians had arrested in Tehran.

On October 6, North had to break away from the talks and rush back to Washington when a plane carrying supplies to the contras was shot down over Nicaragua. Richard Secord departed shortly thereafter, leaving his business partner, Albert Hakim, to continue the discussions. Hakim immediately transformed North's seven-point deal into a nine-point proposal which for the first time incorporated what Imad Mugniyah had wanted from the start—a plan to obtain the release of the seventeen Shiite terrorists imprisoned in Kuwait.

The plan violated every public statement the Reagan administration had ever made about the Kuwaiti prisoners, but that did not bother North. "It is a simple fact of reality that there will come a time when those seventeen will be released," he later testified. "It is not unusual in that part of the world to see those kinds of transactions work."

When North, Secord, Hakim, and CIA representative George Cave met with the Iranians again in Mainz, West Germany, on October 29, North told the Iranians he had "already started" on a plan to free the Dawa prisoners and had "already met with the Kuwaiti foreign minister, secretly. In my spare time, between blowing up Nicaragua." In an aside to the other Americans at the meeting, he said he had spent seven days working out a plan for the Dawa prisoners.

Poindexter and North did meet the Kuwaiti Foreign Minister on October 3, but they did not try to pressure him to release the Dawa prisoners. Instead, Poindexter reassured the Foreign Minister that the United States was not seeking the early release of the seventeen convicted terrorists and asked only that Kuwait give Washington advance notice if it planned to execute any of them. North's remark to the Iranians about meeting the Foreign Minister was, in typical fashion, not an outright lie but cleverly and completely misleading.

North wrote Poindexter that his act with Rafsanjani's nephew "had quite an effect" and reported a new arms-for-hostages deal—500 TOWs for "two hostages (if possible, but no less than one) released w/in 4 days of TOW delivery." George Shultz, for one, was not impressed with North's negotiating skills. "It galls me," he said later. "Our guys . . . they got taken to the cleaners. You look at the structure of this deal. It's pathetic that anybody would agree to anything like that. It's so lopsided. It's crazy."

Nevertheless, the 500 TOW missiles were shipped to Iran three days later with President Reagan's approval. North wrote to Poindexter: "This is the damndest operation I have ever seen. Pls let me go on to other things. Wd very much like to give RR two hostages that he can take credit for and stop worrying about these other things."

★   ★   ★

When he went to bed on Saturday night, November 1, David Jacobsen had an overpowering feeling he was going to be released. It was so powerful, he later wrote, that he knew he was going home within a few hours. He had just fallen asleep when a stranger entered his cell.

Mr. David, we're happy you're going home, the stranger said. You'll be going home in a couple of hours, but first we have to move everyone.

Jacobsen was set free near the old American Embassy on Beirut's seafront, where, in 1983, a suicide bomber had struck the first fatal blow in the Shiites' war against America. In his excitement, Jacobsen walked 200 yards past the bombed-out embassy, now a symbol of American failure occupied only by a small security force. One of his guards tapped him on the shoulder and said he had gone too far and should turn and walk back. For a dreadful moment, Jacobsen thought he was being kidnapped again.

David Jacobsen was perhaps the luckiest of all the hostages. His release was the last gasp of a dying policy. If it had been delayed only a few days, it might never have happened.

★ ★ ★

By the middle of October, the Reagan administration's secret began leaking out. Leaflets reporting Robert McFarlane's secret trip to Iran began appearing in the streets of Tehran. Less than two weeks later, the news of McFarlane's trip appeared in a small Hezbollah newspaper in Baalbek. Meanwhile, a New York businessman named Roy Furmark warned his old friend Bill Casey that some of the investors in the Iran arms sales wanted their money back. Casey warned North, who began shredding the records of his secret dealings.

The end came quickly. On November 3, the day after David Jacobsen was freed, the Lebanese magazine *Al Shiraa* picked up the story of McFarlane's trip, touching off the inevitable firestorm in Washington. At first, the administration tried to deny it had traded arms for hostages while North struggled feverishly to keep the second channel open and get Terry Anderson and Thomas Sutherland freed. White House spokesman Larry Speakes said the U.S. arms embargo against Iran would continue—another bit of deception crafted by Poindexter—and Reagan said reports of McFarlane's trip to Tehran "have no foundation." In a nationwide radio address on November 13, Reagan declared, "We did not—repeat—we did not trade weapons or anything else for hostages."

The President also sent a telegram to Rev. Benjamin Weir, the first hostage released in exchange for a shipment of TOW missiles. "I was saddened to learn from press reports that you may have accepted at face value speculative stories in the media alleging arms for hostages," Reagan wrote. "Let me assure you that no ransom was paid for your release. The longstanding policy of our government has been to make no concessions to the demands of terrorists. I firmly believe in that policy. To do otherwise is to encourage additional acts of terrorism and place many more Americans at risk. All of the extensive efforts your government has undertaken to obtain your release and the release of all the other American and foreign hostages in Lebanon have been fully consistent with that policy."

William Casey's CIA made one last stab at keeping the secret policy alive. In early December, Charles Allen, the National Intelligence officer for counterterrorism, convened a meeting of the intelligence community's terrorism analysts, inviting one representative each from the DIA and the State Department's intelligence bureau and packing the rest of the room with his colleagues from the CIA. Allen infuriated the DIA and State Department officials by demanding that they sign an Interagency Intelligence Assessment [called an IAIA, pronounced ya-ya] that said Iran had only limited influence over the Lebanese terrorists who were holding Americans hostage. That flew in the face of everything the United States had learned since 1983 about the role of the Iranian Embassy in Damascus and the Revolutionary Guards in Baalbek in supplying and supporting the Lebanese terrorists.

Worst of all, the State and DIA officials concluded, Allen's position wasn't dictated by the evidence; it simply was an attempt to rationalize the secret policy of selling arms to Iran. It was against U.S. policy to make concessions or pay ransom to terrorists, so if the secret arms sales were to continue as Casey wanted, the administration would have to pretend that the Iranians weren't terrorists, or at least weren't responsible for Shiite terrorism in Lebanon. But now that the secret policy was exposed, Casey's power was waning and both State and Defense refused to go along with Allen's assessment. When the top secret IAIA was finally completed, it concluded that Iran substantially controlled most of the radical Shiite groups in Lebanon through the Revolutionary Guard Corps and that hostages probably were neither seized nor released without approval from Tehran.

Another meeting with the Iranians was set for December 13 in Frankfurt. The State Department succeeded in writing new ground rules which limited the discussions to intelligence matters. But on the morning of the day the meeting was held, Casey met alone with White House chief of staff Donald Regan and secretly managed to reverse the ground rules to permit discussions of policy. When George Shultz found out what had happened, he observed: "Nothing ever gets settled in this town." That seemed especially true with Ronald Reagan in the White House.

This time, however, the State Department sent a representative to the meeting with the Iranians and when he reported back that the CIA and the Iranians were talking about freeing the hostages in Lebanon in exchange for more American arms and the liberation of the Dawa prisoners, Shultz was shocked. As he later related it, he went directly to the President and told him the plan "made me sick to my stomach." Reagan gave no indication that he knew about the plan. He "reacted like he had been kicked in the belly. . . . The President was astonished, and I have never seen him so mad," said Shultz. "He is a very genial, pleasant man

... very easygoing. But his jaws set and his eyes flashed and both of us, I think, felt the same way about it, and I think in that meeting I finally felt that the President understands that something is radically wrong here."

★ ★ ★

"By their very nature, covert operations or special activities are a lie," Oliver North said later. "There is great deceit, deception, practiced in the conduct of covert operations. They are at essence a lie. We make every effort to deceive the enemy as to our intent, our conduct, and to deny the association of the United States with those activities."

The trouble was that North, Poindexter, Casey, and the handful of others who knew what was happening had not confined themselves to deceiving the enemy. They also peddled bogus information to one another and to the President, telling him that Iran had stopped sponsoring terrorism and was in danger of losing the war with Iraq. North admitted that virtually no intelligence analysts agreed with either point, but that did not deter him, nor Casey, nor Poindexter, all of whom preferred to rely on their own nonexistent Middle East expertise rather than listen to timid, do-nothing bureaucrats. After the policy collapsed, Secretary of State Shultz told the President bluntly: We have been deceived and lied to.

The architects of the policy had indeed lied to the President, to the Secretary of State, to Congress, and to the public. But first, they had lied to themselves.

EPILOGUE

"Strike U.," as the Navy calls it, is located in Fallon, Nevada, where the air is clear and the distances are vast. It was created by Navy Secretary John Lehman in response to the Navy's dismal performance in attacking Syrian antiaircraft sites in Lebanon in December of 1983—the first American air raid since the end of the Vietnam War. One reason the raid had gone so poorly, Lehman felt, was that it had failed to take advantage of the new technologies developed in the intervening decade. "The Navy air wings produced what had been trained into them, and what had been trained into them was a twenty-year-old Vietnam, daytime 'Alpha' strike, and it was totally inappropriate," Lehman said.

At Fallon, the Navy has recreated a modern battlefield complete with all the radars and antiaircraft missiles its pilots might have to fly against. Before going overseas, each of the Navy's thirteen air wings rotates through Strike U. for three weeks "to see what works and what doesn't work," Lehman explained. Most of the radars and missiles the Navy pilots train against are of Soviet manufacture. But beginning in the fall of 1987, Navy pilots encountered a new missile on the training ranges at Fallon—the American-made Hawk.

The Iranians used the spare parts the Reagan administration sold them to activate Hawk missile batteries at the entrance to the Persian Gulf, where the U.S. Navy in 1987 began escorting ships flying the American flag. If the Iranians ever made good on their threats to attack those ships, and if the Navy were ordered to retaliate, American pilots would fly into the teeth of those American-made Hawk missiles. Learn-

362

ing to fly against the Hawk is not cheap; it costs about $1 million a session. The secret arms sales to Iran cost far more than that, however.

Each month, the Department of Defense spent between $15 and $20 million escorting Kuwaiti oil tankers through the Persian Gulf—an operation that probably never would have come about were the United States not so eager to reverse the impression that it had tilted toward Iran, the archenemy of the moderate Arab states. Where once a sleepy task force of four or five ships sufficed to protect American interests, the United States amassed the largest peacetime armada ever, one that included everything from the newest F-18 jet fighter to dolphins trained to hunt for mines.

The display of American muscle failed to make the Gulf safe for shipping or to deter the Iranians from exporting their holy war beyond the Gulf. There were more attacks on ships in the Persian Gulf in 1987 than in 1986, and more signs that Shiite terrorists were planning terrorist attacks in the United States. On October 23, 1987, three Lebanese-born Canadian citizens were picked up at a border crossing in Vermont, trying to smuggle a bomb into the United States. U.S. intelligence officials say they were the first Middle Eastern terrorists ever to be apprehended smuggling explosives into the United States.

During the Reagan years, Hosein Sheikholislam, Mohsen Rafiq-Doust, Mohammed Mohtashami-pur, and their colleagues in Tehran created the world's most ambitious terror network, one that is not merely state-sponsored but state-run. In Lebanon, Iran continued not only to inspire but to direct the operation Mohtashami-pur first created, and Americans continued to be its victims. In June 1987, Hezbollah discovered that Charles Glass of *ABC News* had ventured into Beirut. Unable to believe that any American could be so foolhardy after all that had happened, the Lebanese terrorists asked Iranian officials what they should do. Grab him, the Iranians replied.

Glass was lucky; he got out. At the end of 1987 there were more American hostages in Lebanon than there had been when the administration had begun selling arms to Iran, and President Reagan had stopped threatening terrorists and started warning Americans. When four teachers at the American University of Beirut were kidnapped by Hezbollah, Reagan issued a statement cautioning that "there is a limit to what our government can do for Americans in a chaotic situation such as that in Lebanon today." That whimper of resignation measured the distance his administration had traveled since the day six years before when he so blithely had vowed "swift and effective retribution."

Although a hostage crisis had helped the Reagan administration to power, it learned nothing from Jimmy Carter's travail. The pressure to do something—anything—to end the cruel drama of Americans held hostage overwhelmed the defiant, never-again policy of the Reagan administration as surely as it had the sweet reason of the Carter administration. "With the pressures that were everywhere, you tended to be more willing to take a risk," Marine Commandant Robert Barrow had said, looking back at the scorched hulks of American helicopters at Desert One. "I think the emotionalism of the hostage issue throughout the entire affair with Bill Casey, with the President and with me . . . led them to do and run operations that are now after the fact foolish," the CIA's Clair George had said, surveying the wreckage of the Reagan administration's secret policy toward Iran.

The Reagan administration was, if anything, even more vulnerable than its predecessor to the violence and theater of terrorism. Reagan played to emotion, not intellect, and the terrorists beat him at his own game. He could use videotapes of the raid on Libya to make it look better than it was, but they could mesmerize the nation with the image of John Testrake leaning out of the cockpit of TWA 847 with Castro's gun at his head. Magnified by television, the drama of lives in the balance made people—President Reagan, in particular—feel more strongly about terrorism than they did about other pressing issues. It was easy to confuse the emotional intensity of terrorism with its significance.

Emotions came more easily than answers. What was the Soviet role in terrorism? Who blew up the Marines? Where were the hostages? The intelligence was never good enough to settle the arguments. No issue was more contentious than terrorism, and Ronald Reagan seemed incapable of resolving contentious issues. "Nothing ever gets settled in this town," George Shultz had complained in frustration. The President could never decide whose advice to take, so his CIA director and the members of his National Security Council staff tried to do his job for him. The President wasn't badly served by William Casey, John Poindexter and Oliver North; he got exactly what he deserved.

It was more than just emotion and frustration, however. From the very first dispute over the Soviet role in terrorism, the Reagan administration confused the war against terrorism and the war against Communism. Alexander Haig worried about Soviet bases in Libya, and William Casey was afraid the Kremlin would take over Iran. The confusion, compounded by emotion and frustration, made terrorism into something it wasn't.

The suffering of its victims is all too real, but the damage terrorism does is by almost any measure slight. Drunk drivers kill more Americans than terrorists do. There are more missing children in the United States than hostages in Lebanon. As the word implies, the power of terrorism lies almost exclusively in the fear it creates. The inability of a superpower to protect its citizens in the 1980s gnawed at the nation's self-confidence and tempted it to take actions not in its best interest, such as sell arms to Iran. "Most of the damage to U.S. interests done by terrorism has been self-inflicted," concluded Noel Koch in a speech given after he had left the Pentagon in disgust. Terrorism, Koch said, "depends for its power on our reaction to it."

★   ★   ★

How *should* the United States react to terrorism?

Fadlo Massabni, who was the American defense attaché in Beirut in 1983, remembered having lunch one day at the apartment of a leading Shiite cleric. After a pleasant meal, they adjourned to the seventh floor balcony and looked out over the slums and refugee camps of south Beirut. "He said, 'If I were to take 100 men and tell them to jump from this balcony, all 100 would jump,'" Massabni recalled. "I asked him, 'Would you jump?' He wouldn't answer. I asked him again, but he still wouldn't answer. So I said, 'Too many people in Lebanon are willing to have other people make sacrifices.' And I thought to myself, there's the key to fighting terrorism. We should not be trying to kill the young kids but the people who don't want to die."

Should the United States mount an assassination campaign against terrorist leaders? It is tempting to turn the terrorists' own tactics against them. One well-placed bullet might save a hundred lives. What moral distinction is there between Delta shooting up a roomful of terrorists and the Air Force dropping bombs on downtown Tripoli? Air raids inevitably kill innocent bystanders; assassination can be more precise. The argument is moot: whether it is morally defensible or not, assassination is not palatable to the American people.

Americans prefer to do their killing antiseptically and at as great a remove as possible. But even in an era of high-tech weapons, military power remains a blunt instrument. So far as is known, the raid on Libya did not kill a single terrorist, and who knows where the *New Jersey*'s shells fell? Israel's attempt to eliminate the PLO with its 1982 invasion of Lebanon only created more terrorists.

The military is not likely to get much better at fighting terrorism. High priced equipment frequently fails. In 1980, three of eight Sea Stallion helicopters dropped out of the Iran rescue mission. Six years later, after record increases in the Pentagon budget, seven out of nine F-111s failed to drop their bombs on Muamar Qaddafi's headquarters. Malfunctions and snafus are endemic to military operations. Best laid plans often go astray. All the training and equipment in the world cannot adequately prepare a young man for the first time he is shot at. The raid on Libya might have gone better if more of the pilots had seen combat before, but their lack of experience is one of the by-products of peace. If America is lucky, the next pilots ordered into action will not have any combat experience either.

Nor is intelligence likely to get much better. The CIA can do better than the likes of Manucher Ghorbanifar, but it is unrealistic to expect any intelligence service to penetrate tiny terrorist cells and come up with the date, time, and target of their next attack. As William Corbett, the European Command's special assistant for security matters, said: "Any security professional who is waiting for intelligence to warn him is going to fail."

Railing against military incompetence and intelligence failures is no substitute for constructing a policy that recognizes the limitations of armed force and espionage. Though they lack the dramatic appeal of air raids and secret agents, diplomacy and law enforcement must be the cornerstones of any successful attempt to contain international terrorism.

Without diplomatic action, the raid on Libya would have achieved nothing. After the attack, America's European allies finally began to apply real pressure against Qaddafi, shutting down the People's Bureaus that had been the bases for his terrorist operations. Depriving Libya of the use of its diplomats, its official communications, and its diplomatic pouches vastly complicated Qaddafi's life and forced him to transfer his terrorist apparatus into commercial fronts, including Libyan Arab Airlines, trading companies, and banks—none of which enjoyed diplomatic immunity.

After the Syrian intelligence service was implicated in an attempt to blow up an Israeli airliner, Western diplomatic and economic pressure prompted Hafez Assad to boot the notorious Abu Nidal out of his country and to close his training camps in Syria. After a defector exposed the elaborate commercial network Abu Nidal had created in Eastern Europe, the United States was able to embarrass Poland and East Germany into closing down his business fronts in Warsaw and East Berlin.

Whether Oliver North was an American hero or a loose cannon, the fact that he was more likely to stand trial than Imad Mugniyah was grotesque. As North himself observed when he was charged with illegally diverting profits from the Iran arms sales to the Nicaraguan rebels:

"It is a sad irony that the decision to indict me should occur today
. . . a day which is the fourth anniversary of the abduction of William
Buckley and the third anniversary of the kidnapping of Terry Anderson—two of the American hostages we tried so hard to rescue." It is said
that ours is a nation of laws, and indeed, most of our great controver-
sies—the Iran arms sales, for instance—sooner or later end up in court.
That is where terrorists belong, too.

Despite its imperfections, the law is an indispensable—perhaps *the*
indispensable—weapon in the war against terrorism. The law treats
terrorists as criminals and helps strip the veneer of martyrdom and
heroism from their crimes. The law doesn't consider the existence of
Israel justification for machine-gunning a schoolbus, or the corrosive
effects of Western culture on Islam just cause for kidnapping an American missionary.

For all the noise they made about terrorism, the Reagan administration and Congress were slow bringing the law to bear on the problem.
It was not until 1984 that taking an American hostage overseas became
a crime punishable under U.S. law. It was not until 1986 that President
Reagan signed a bill declaring it a violation of American law to assault,
maim, or murder a U.S. citizen anywhere in the world. It was not until
1987 that the FBI arrested a terrorist overseas and returned him to the
United States to stand trial.

On September 13, 1987, FBI agents lured a young Lebanese man
aboard a yacht in the Mediterranean with promises of women and drugs,
arrested him and brought him back to the United States to stand trial
for hijacking a Jordanian airliner with two American citizens aboard.
Although it attracted a fraction of the attention, the arrest of Fawaz
Younis was as much a watershed event as the bombing of Libya. It may
not have been what Ronald Reagan had in mind when he declared war
against terrorism, but it was about as swift and effective as retribution
is likely to get.

Terrorism is a threat to law and order, not to national security. Fighting it is mostly a job for law enforcement agencies; arrests and convic-
tions are the best measure of success. According to figures compiled by
William Corbett, in 1986 and 1987 European law enforcement agencies
arrested sixty terrorist suspects and expelled forty-eight suspected supporters of terrorist organizations. On January 15, 1986, Mohammed Ali
Hamadi was arrested while trying to smuggle liquid explosives in wine
bottles through customs at the Frankfurt airport. Hamadi was better
known to the passengers of TWA 847 as "Castro," the alleged killer of
Robert Stethem.

Arresting terrorists can be a risky business, as the Kuwaitis can testify. Some of the grisliest terrorist attacks have been committed in the name of freeing the seventeen Dawa prisoners serving sentences for the December 1983, wave of bombings. Hezbollah retaliated for the arrest of Hamadi, a.k.a. Castro, in West Germany by kidnapping three German businessmen in Lebanon.

The temptation to trade away or go easy on accused or even convicted terrorists instead of risking retaliation sometimes has proved irresistible. In order to get their citizens back from Hezbollah, the West Germans agreed not to extradite Hamadi to the United States where he would have been tried for the hijacking of TWA 847.

★   ★   ★

Any victories in the war against terrorism will be partial ones. Although Abu Nidal's camps in Syria were closed in 1987, his camps in Lebanon were busier than ever. Forcing Qaddafi's terror and subversion apparatus underground did not bring it to a halt. Pakistan's President Zia privately told American officials he believed Libya assisted in the September 1986, hijacking of a Pan Am jetliner in Karachi in which twenty-one people died and more than a hundred were wounded. Almost certainly the Pan Am hijacking was the work of Qaddafi's new-found ally, Abu Nidal.

Just keeping pace with the terrorists is not easy. Abu Ibrahim invented new bombs faster than security men came up with ways to find them, and shoulder-fired SA-7 missiles brought down two Navy jets over Lebanon. In an age when the world's superpowers have lost their monopoly on the technology of war, and when terrorists have the same access to the media as the President of the United States, the battle between terrorism and civilization is fought on remarkably even terms.

As L. Paul Bremer, the head of the Office for Combatting Terrorism, put it, "This is a game of drag bunts and stolen bases, not home runs." It is a game of constant pressure, not dramatic breakthroughs. It is a struggle that must be borne as a price of doing business in the world today. There will be no treaties of unconditional surrender and probably no treaties at all. The best laid diplomatic, economic, legal, and even military plans will only contain terrorism, not defeat it. Forcing Abu Nidal to find a new home may not seem like a victory, particularly when measured against the record of his crimes, but in the war against terrorism, it will have to do.

SOURCE NOTES

A discussion of the origins and evolution of terrorism is beyond the scope of this book. Readers interested in learning more about the history of terror as a political instrument might consult a number of recent works on the subject, including: *Terrorism and International Order* by Lawrence Freedman, et al.; *The Age of Terrorism* by Walter Laqueur; *The Terrorism Reader,* edited by Walter Laqueur and Yonah Alexander; *Terrorism, Ideology and Revolution* by Noel O'Sullivan; and *Hydra of Carnage* by Uri Ra'anan, et al.

PROLOGUE

The account of the reconnaissance mission to Desert One is based on an interview with John Carney. The name of the CIA pilot has been omitted because he still undertakes intelligence missions. The meeting in the White House Situation Room was described in interviews with James Vaught. It is also described in Gary Sick's *All Fall Down* and in Beckwith's *Delta Force,* both of which served as valuable sources of information.

1: DESERT ONE

The account of Dick Meadow's mission to Tehran is based on an after-action report he wrote immediately after completing the mission. Meadows's account was supplemented by interviews with James Vaught, Charlie Beckwith, Logan Fitch, Wade Ishimoto, Burr Smith, and a retired CIA officer who requested anonymity.

Several of the agents who entered Tehran are identified only by a first name or nickname in order to allow them to remain anonymous. At least one of them has relatives living in Iran who might be subject to reprisals. Others at last report were still on active duty in the U.S. military, performing undercover missions.

Meadows was not the last American agent out of Tehran. Fred, the young Air Force sergeant of Iranian descent, hid out with his relatives in Iran for about ten days before slipping out of the country. Being of Iranian birth, Fred needed to obtain an exit permit before he could leave. While the Pentagon was making preparations to extract him by helicopter, Fred suddenly showed up in Europe. He had qualified for an exit permit by answering a classified ad for an overseas job.

The account of the mission itself is based on interviews with those who participated in its planning and execution. In alphabetical order, they were: Robert Barrow, Charlie Beckwith, Bob Brenci, Donald Buchanan, Lewis Burruss, John Carney, Logan Fitch, Philip Gast, Wade Ishimoto, James Kyle, Dick Meadows, Edward Meyer, Cecil Morgan, Charles Pitman, John Pustay, James Schaefer, Ed Seiffert, and James Vaught. Vaught in particular spent many hours answering questions. In addition to those interviews, the "Rescue Mission Report" of the commission headed by Adm. James Holloway provided a wealth of information, as did Beckwith's *Delta Force*, Gary Sick's *All Fall Down*, Zbigniew Brzezinski's *Power and Principle*, and an article by Fitch in the March 1984 issue of *Penthouse*. The most detailed and extensive study of the mission is contained in an unpublished manuscript by James Kyle entitled "Having the Guts to Try."

The description of events leading up to the creation of Delta is derived from interviews with Logan Fitch, Wade Ishimoto, Robert Kingston, Noel Koch, Robert Kupperman, Edward Meyer, Cecil Morgan, Steve Pieczenik, Sam Wilson, and a retired CIA officer who requested anonymity. Beckwith's *Delta Force* again proved valuable.

The plans for a second rescue mission were described by James Vaught, Richard Secord, and one U.S. Army officer who cannot be identified by name. Secord's sworn testimony during the Iran-contra hearings also provided information about the second rescue mission.

2: "SWIFT AND EFFECTIVE RETRIBUTION"

Much of the background material on Iran's plans and efforts to spread revolution is drawn from Robin Wright's *Sacred Rage*, R. K. Ramazani's *Revolutionary Iran*, and *Shi'ism and Social Protest*, edited by Juan R. I. Cole and Nikki R. Keddie. The terrorist apparatus organized by Sheikholislam and Mohtashami-pur was described in interviews with U.S. and Israeli intelligence officers who declined to be identified by name and with a former Lebanese intelligence officer, Gassan Chamas. "Iran's Ayatollahs of Terror," by Nathan M. Adams in the January 1985 *Readers Digest* was also useful. The details of Hosein Sheikholislam's life in California, including his proximity to the Patricia Hearst kidnapping, were first revealed by Fred Garretson in *The Oakland Tribune/ Today* on April 26, 1981.

Background material on terrorism was found in a number of published sources, including Claire Sterling's *The Terror Network,* Henry Kissinger's *Years of Survival,* and *Hydra of Carnage,* edited by Ra'anan, et al. The following unclassified reports published by the CIA and State Department were a valuable source of official information: "Terrorist Bombings: A Statistical Overview of International Terrorist Bombing Incidents from January 1977 Through May 1983," Department of State, September 1983; "Combatting Terrorism," Department of State, September 1982; "Lethal Terrorist Actions Against Americans, 1973–1985," Department of State, Bureau of Diplomatic Security; "International and Transnational Terrorism: Diagnosis and Prognosis," CIA, April 1976; "International Terrorism in 1978," CIA, National Foreign Assessment Center; "International Terrorism in 1979," CIA, National Foreign Assessment Center; and "Patterns of International Terrorism 1980," CIA, National Foreign Assessment Center. Walter Laqueur's writings, particularly in *The New Republic,* July 29, 1985; *Foreign Affairs;* and *A World of Secrets,* were especially valuable. Interviews were conducted with Kenneth Adelman, Jeremy Azrael, Herman Cohen, Lincoln Gordon, Alexander Haig, Bob Inman, Richard Mansbach, Frank Perez, Anthony Quainton, Ronald Spiers, Philip Stoddard, and several U.S. intelligence officers who declined to be identified.

3: THE KNOCK ON THE DOOR

The account of the Dozier kidnapping and its aftermath is based on interviews conducted with Stanton Burnett, Mrs. Wilson Cooney, James Dozier, Philip Gast, Noel Koch, Robert Kvederas, Richard Lawson, H. Ross Perot, Robert Sayre, and Richard Shultes. Details were also provided by an interview with Dozier in the November–December 1986 issue of *Counterterrorism.* The role played by Perot was first reported by Bob Woodward in *The Washington Post,* Dec. 2, 1986.

4: THE SHORES OF TRIPOLI

The dogfight over the Gulf of Sidra was described by Larry Muczynski and David Venlet. Their accounts were supplemented by the transcript of a press conference immediately following the incident, which is the source of remarks attributed to Hank Kleeman. Kleeman was killed in 1985 when he lost control of his F-18 while landing on a slick runway at Miramar, California.

The description of the debate over U.S. policy toward Libya is based on interviews with Herman Cohen, Frank Fukuyama, Richard Haass, Alexander Haig, Lillian Harris, Bob Inman, Arnold Kanter, Elaine Morton, James Roche, Dennis Ross, Henry Schuler, Philip Stoddard, Paul Wolfowitz, and a former CIA officer who did not want to be identified. Alexander Haig's *Caveat* and the testimony he gave at his confirmation hearings as Secretary of State before the Senate Foreign Relations Committee also served as sources of information. The July 8, 1981, testimony of Assistant Secretary of State Chester Crocker before the Senate Foreign Relations Committee was the first public formulation of the administration's case against and policy toward Qaddafi. Additional details concerning the formulation of the administration's Libya policy were drawn from a still-classified NSC planning document.

Background information on Qaddafi was found in *Libyan Sandstorm,* by John K. Cooley; *Qaddafi and the United States Since 1969,* by Edward P. Haley; *Libya a Source of International Terrorism,* by Kenneth Adelman, Department of State Bulletin, January 1983; "A Global Perspective on Transnational Terrorism: A Case Study of Libya," Raymond H. Cleveland, et al., Air War College, 1977; "Qaddafi's Nervous Neighbors," John K. Cooley, *Middle East International,* September 4, 1981; and "Libyan Activities: Libya's Role in Sub-Saharan Africa and the Near East, Hearings," Senate Foreign Relations Committee, 1981.

The first report of the Reagan administration's determination to cut out the Qaddafi cancer was written by Lars Erik Nelson in the *New York Daily News.* The memos describing plans for military action against Libya were first revealed by Bob Woodward in *The Washington Post.* Michael Getler of *The Washington Post* first pointed out to the administration the inconsistency of confronting Qaddafi while continuing to buy his oil.

The details of Qaddafi's alleged plot to assassinate the President were provided by anonymous sources who were directly involved in the "hit squad" flap. Shadowy hit squads were not Qaddafi's only weapons. In Nairobi, Kenya, two loudspeakers, each packed with twenty kilograms of plastic explosive, were intercepted as they were being loaded aboard a plane for delivery to the American Recreation Club in Khartoum, the capital of the Sudan. According to one intelligence report, "bombs of this size could have completely destroyed the club and killed or maimed several hundred innocent people." The report said the speakers "were prepared by Libyan intelligence officers assigned to a Libyan People's Bureau [in Nairobi]. A Libyan intelligence officer personally assured that the bombs were boarded on a flight to Khartoum."

5: THE SKY IS FALLING

The account of the Sea Spray mission is based on interviews with U.S. military and foreign service officers who asked not to be identified.

The description of Lebanon's political landscape and the spreading Islamic revolution is drawn in part from Robin Wright's *Sacred Rage;* Fouad Ajami's *The Vanished Iman; Shi'ism and Social Protest,* edited by Cole and Keddie; and *The Shia'a Community and the Future of Lebanon,* by Helena Cobban. "Lebanon's Continuing Crisis," by Charles Waterman in *Current History,* January 1978; "How to Rebuild Lebanon," by David Ignatius in *Foreign Affairs,* Summer 1983; "Lebanon: A New Republic?" by Ghassan Tueni in *Foreign Affairs,* Fall 1982; "After the Lebanese-Israeli Agreement," by Ghassan Tueni in *Middle East Insight,* Vol. III, no. I, 1983; "Lebanon: The Hour of Truth," by David Kimche in *Middle East Insight,* Vol. III, no. 1, 1983; "Prospects for Peace in Lebanon," *Middle East Insight,* Vol. II, no. 4; and numerous articles by Richard Augustus Norton all proved valuable, as did articles by Frederick Kempe in the Dec. 13, 1983, *Wall Street Journal* and by David Ottaway in the Jan. 9, 1984, *Washington Post. Militant Islamic Movements in Lebanon: Origins, Social Basis, and Ideology,* by Marius Deeb of Georgetown University's Center for Contemporary Arab Studies, also was useful.

The account of Israel's invasion of Lebanon and its aftermath relies heavily on Ze'ev Schiff's and Ehud Ya'ari's *Israel's Lebanon War. Begin,* by Ned Temko; "The Beirut Massacre: The Complete Kahan Commission Report,"; "The War for Lebanon: 1970–1985," by Itamar Rabinovitch; and Ze'ev Schiff's "The Green Light" in *Foreign Policy,* Spring 1983, also provided information. A more complete account of the attempted assassination of Shlomo Argov is contained in *Abu Nidal: Portrait of a Terrorist,* by Yossi Melman.

The most complete account of PLO tactics during the invasion is *Under Siege,* by Rashid Khalidi. *The PLO: The Rise and Fall of the Palestine Liberation Organization,* by Jillian Becker; *The Palestine Liberation Organization: People, Power and Politics,* by Helena Cobban; "The Future of the PLO," by Eric Rouleau in *Foreign Affairs,* Fall 1983; and "Whither the PLO?" by Aaron D. Miller in *Middle East Review,* Vol. XVI, no. 3, 1984, all provided information.

The Iranians' first attempt to intervene in Lebanon occurred in the summer of 1980. Mohammed Montazeri, a son of Iran's powerful Ayatollah Montazeri, had appeared at Tehran's Mehrabad Airport with a group of armed followers and commandeered an Iran Air plane to take them to Damascus, the first leg of the journey into Lebanon. When Montazeri and his men arrived in Damascus without passports, the Syrians greeted them warmly, saluted their courage, and marched them off to a Palestinian camp for "training." After three weeks of push-ups and obstacle courses, the young Montazeri returned to Iran, where he was later killed by a terrorist bomb.

The story of the Marine presence in Lebanon relies on some material which first appeared in the official Marine Corps history *U.S. Marines in Lebanon: 1982–1984,* by Benis M. Frank; in *The Root,* by Eric Hammel; and in an unpublished outline by Dennis Ross. "The Lebanon Experience," by James M. Mead in the February 1983 *Marine Corps Gazette;* "Lebanon Revisited," by Mead in the September 1983 *Marine Corps Gazette;* and "Keeping the Peace in Lebanon," by Capt. Dale A. Dye in the August 1983 *Marine Corps Gazette,* all provided firsthand accounts of the Marines in Lebanon. "U.S. in Lebanon: Anatomy of a Foreign Policy Failure," by Patrick Sloyan and Roy Gutman in *Newsday* April 8, 1984; "U.S. Knew of Syria Link to '83 Embassy Blast," by Jim McGee in the *Miami Herald* Aug. 3, 1986; a case study of Lebanon done at the John Fitzgerald Kennedy School of Government under the direction of Robert Murray; "Lebanon Revisited," by David K. Hall of the Naval War College, and a paper delivered by W. Hays Parks to the National War College on Jan. 14, 1988 all contained valuable information and insights. The quotation from the McFarlane cable was provided by Mark Gatanas, who took contemporaneous notes of the meeting.

Interviews for this chapter included: Richard Armitage, Randy Beers, Lincoln Bloomfield, Rayford Byers, Herman Cohen, William Corbett, Morris Draper, Lawrence Eagleburger, Joseph Englehardt, Richard Fairbanks, Arthur Fintel, Mark Gatanas, April Glaspie, Richard Haass, Philip Habib, Alexander Haig, Fred Hof, Arnold Kanter, Geoffrey Kemp, Noel Koch, Richard Lawson, Fadlo Massabni, Robert McFarlane, Robert Murray, Robin Raphel, Dennis Ross, Willie Y. Smith, Philip Stoddard, Howard Teicher, H. O. Thompson, Nicholas Veliotes, John Vessey, James Watkins, Francis West, Caspar Weinberger, and several U.S. intelligence and foreign service officers who did not want to be identified.

The military chain of command was only one of the many confusing aspects of the American involvement in Lebanon. On paper, the Marines in Beirut were under the command of Gen. Bernard Rogers, the Supreme Allied Commander, Europe, who was based at NATO headquarters in Mons, Belgium. In practice, Rogers delegated day-to-day authority for U.S. forces in Europe to his deputy, an Air Force general who had a headquarters of his own in Stuttgart, West Germany. Most of the U.S. military operations described in this book, including the Marine presence in Beirut, were run out of Stuttgart, first by Gen. Willie Y. Smith, then by Gen. Richard Lawson.

6: DEAD. ALL DEAD

The account of the Marine bombing and its aftermath came from interviews with Richard Armitage, Michael Burch, John Butts, Morris Draper, Lawrence Eagleburger, Joseph Englehardt, Arthur Fintel, Howard Gerlach, Fred Hof, Richard Lawson, Fadlo Massabni, Robert McFarlane, Robert Murray, Robin Raphel, Peter Rodman, Dennis Ross, Donald Rumsfeld, Ray Seitz, Robert Sims, Howard Teicher, John Vessey, James Watkins, Caspar Weinberger, and several unnamed U.S. military, foreign service, and intelligence officers.

The report of the commission headed by retired Adm. Robert Long, officially titled "Report of the DoD Commission on Beirut International Airport Terrorist Act, October 23, 1983," was a major source of information, as were three reports by the House Armed Services Committee—"Adequacy of U.S. Marine

Corps Security in Beirut," "Full Committee Consideration on Investigations Subcommittee Report on Terrorist Bombing at Beirut International Airport," and "The Situation in Lebanon: Hearings, October 25, 31, 1983"—and Gen. P. X. Kelley's October 31, 1983, testimony before the Senate Armed Services Committee. Benis Frank's *U.S. Marines in Lebanon: 1982–1984,* Eric Hammel's *The Root,* Michael Petit's *Peacekeepers at War,* "America's Failure in Lebanon," by Thomas L. Friedman in the April 8, 1984, *New York Times;* "The Marine Tragedy: An Inquiry into Causes and Responsibility," by Philip Taubman and Joel Brinkley in the Dec. 11, 1983, *New York Times,* and "U.S. in Lebanon: Anatomy of a Foreign Policy Failure," in the April 8, 1984, *Newsday,* all provided information that was not available elsewhere. James Watkins provided a summary of a "Workshop on Ethics and Terrorism at the Naval War College."

The report that Sheik Fadlallah blessed the suicide bomber was passed to U.S. intelligence by the Lebanese Christians through a Syrian informant. A number of American analysts now have concluded it probably is not true. These analysts believe that while Fadlallah serves as Hezbollah's spiritual adviser, terrorist operations are directed by Iranian officials working through Lebanese Shiites like Imad Mugniyah and Hussein Musawi.

The account of the Dec. 4, 1983, raid on Lebanon was drawn from George Wilson's *Supercarrier* and an investigation conducted by the General Accounting Office. Those were supplemented by interviews with Jay Coupe, Byron Duff, Robert Goodman, Richard Lawson, Jerry Tuttle, and John Vessey.

Information about William Buckley came from Noel Koch, Fadlo Massabni, Dick Meadows, and U.S. intelligence and law enforcement officers who requested anonymity. Buckley's kidnapping is also discussed in the report of the Tower Commission and in the hearings and final report of the House and Senate Iran-Contra Committee. Several members and staff members of both the committee and the commission were interviewed.

The administration's attempts to produce a counterterrorism policy were first described in detail by David Ignatius in "U.S. Readies Anti-Terrorism Policy," in the March 12, 1984, *Wall Street Journal,* and in "A Clear Plan to Handle Terrorism Still Eludes Divided Reagan Camp," in the June 20, 1985, *Wall Street Journal,* and in "Administration Debating Antiterrorist Measures" by Leslie H. Gelb in *The New York Times,* June 6, 1984. Interviews with Terrell Arnold, Lawrence Eagleburger, Noel Koch, Robert McFarlane, Robert Oakley, and Robert Sayre, and two intelligence officers detailed the battle over counterterrorism policy.

The account of the bombing of the embassy annex is based on interviews with William Corbett and Noel Koch, and on "The Security of American Personnel in Lebanon: A Staff Report," by the Senate Foreign Relations Committee, 1984. General information on the security of American embassies is contained in the "Report of the Secretary of State's Advisory Panel on Overseas Security."

7: "A BLOODY CIRCUS"

The reconstruction of the hijacking of TWA flight 847 relies heavily on daily newspaper and television accounts, and on Kurt Carlson's *One American Must Die,* John Testrake's *Triumph Over Terror on Flight 847,* Thomas Ashwood's *Terror in the Skies,* and Peter Hill's interview in the April 1986 issue of *Life.* Steve Twomey's "How U.S. Faced Crisis in Algiers," in the June 23, 1985, *Philadelphia Inquirer* provided information unavailable elsewhere. A chronology prepared by the White House and the transcript of a background briefing by Robert McFarlane were also used.

The Federal Aviation Administration's "Aircraft Hijackings and Other Criminal Acts Against Civil Aviation Statistical and Narrative Reports" was the source of the figures cited in this chapter.

Fixing responsibility for terrorist acts is difficult and often impossible. Some officials continue to blame the bombing of TWA Flight 840 on Abu Ibrahim's May 15 Organization, and at least one U.S. analyst suspects it may have been the work of Abu Nidal.

However, Col. Hawari, whose real name is Mohammed Abdel-Ali Labib, remains the prime suspect. Hawari is believed to have operated from both Iraq and Tunisia, Yasir Arafat's capital-in-exile, and after being expelled from both countries, from Yugoslavia. His whereabouts in early 1988 were unknown.

In addition to the TWA bombing, Hawari operatives are believed to have tried to smuggle Abu Ibrahim–type suitcase bombs from Baghdad to Rome in November 1985 as part of a plot to attack the U.S. Embassy in Italy. Swiss officials caught another alleged member of Hawari's group trying to smuggle grenades hidden in Chianti bottles onto a Swissair flight, apparently as part of a scheme to attack Syrian and Libyan dissidents living in Switzerland.

U.S. intelligence officials believe that in April 1986 Hawari sought help from Hezbollah leader Imad Mugniyah in freeing one of his operatives who had been arrested in Cyprus. Two Cypriot students in Lebanon were kidnapped, probably by Mugniyah's men, and released on June 21. The Cypriot government publicly thanked Yasir Arafat for his mediation.

During the fall of 1986, Duane "Dewey" Clarridge, the head of the CIA's Counterterrorism Center, suggested recruiting a team of foreign nationals, perhaps Moroccans, to set off a bomb in front of Hawari's residence in Tunisia. The explosion was not supposed to injure anyone, merely to convince Hawari to flee for his life, and the operation was to be carried out without the knowledge of the Tunisian government. Although the President's January 1986 counter-terrorism intelligence "finding" authorized the CIA to conduct preemptive attacks on terrorists, the suggestion was quickly rejected because it was judged perilously close to an assassination attempt and because, if exposed, the operation might have destabilized the government of Tunisia.

The distinction between Col. Hawari, the May 15 Organization, Force 17, and Fatah (Western Sector) is in many ways an artificial one. Western analysts believe Arafat created the various terror groups much as he created the notorious Black September after the PLO was expelled from Jordan in 1970: to conduct terrorist operations that could not be blamed on the main Fatah leadership.

The leaders of all the groups have close ties to Arafat and their organizations all routinely use the PLO's network of diplomatic missions and pouches, communications, and finances. Col. Hawari is considered an Arafat protegé and spent seven years as a member of the PLO leader's personal security force and as intermediary with other radical PLO leaders. The leader of Force 17, Mahmoud Ahmed Mahmoud Natour (Abu Tayib), and the head of the Fatah western command, Khalil Wazir (Abu Jihad), are also close associates of Arafat.

With the exceptions of the hijacking of the *Achille Lauro,* which went awry, and the bombing of TWA 840, PLO terrorist attacks have mostly been directed against Israeli targets and anti-Arafat Arabs like Ali Naji al-Adham, a journalist who had satirized the high living of the PLO's top leaders and who was murdered in London in the summer of 1987. Force 17 is believed to have murdered three Israelis on a yacht in Cyprus on September 25, 1985 (the crime that triggered the Israeli air raid on PLO headquarters in Tripoli), and the group claimed responsibility for killing two Israeli seamen in Barcelona on October 9, 1985. Force 17 and Abu Jihad's Fatah (Western Sector) are believed responsible for a series of abortive attempts to infiltrate terrorists into Israel by sea between April and August 1985.

Interviews were conducted with Thomas Ashwood, Donald Engen, Noel Koch, Richard Lawson, David Long, Philip Maresca, Robert McFarlane, Michael Newlin, Howard Teicher, John Vessey, Billy Vincent, and a half dozen U.S. Navy and intelligence officers who asked not to be identified.

Robert Sims provided a copy of an off-the-record speech he gave to the Council on Foreign Relations discussing the role the press played in the hijacking. Terrell Arnold provided an advance copy of *The Violence Formula,* which contains a valuable discussion of the role played by the media in terrorist incidents. Other sources of information dealing with the media and terrorism were: "Terrorism and the Media in the 1980s," The Media Institute, 1984; "Beirut Hostage: ABC and CBS Seize an Opportunity," *Public Opinion,* August–September 1985; and "Closer Look at Network Coverage of TWA Flight 847," *Broadcasting,* Aug. 5, 1985.

The account of President Reagan's phone call to Hafez Assad was provided by a U.S. official who read from a transcript of the conversation.

8: PRISONERS OF GOD

The most complete account to date of the hostages' ordeal and of their relatives' efforts to free them is Benjamin and Carol Weir's *Hostage Bound, Hostage Free.*

David Jacobsen has provided two excellent accounts of his captivity—one on the NBC News broadcast "1986" on Dec. 2, 1986; the other published in the *Los Angeles Times Sunday Magazine* on March 1, 1987. Father Lawrence Jenco was interviewed by one of the authors. Because the hostages were kept blind-folded and isolated, their accounts understandably conflict on some points, including the approximate dates on which certain events took place.

The evidence about William Buckley's captivity and death remains inconclusive. Senior members of the Hostage Locating Task Force and a number of U.S. intelligence officers all agreed that there is no hard evidence to substantiate the claim by Oliver North that Buckley died as a result of torture. Father Jenco's recollections suggest Buckley suffered from neglect but not torture and was, in fact, treated marginally better than the other hostages. It seems likely, however, that given who he was, Buckley was beaten and brutally interrogated in the weeks immediately following his abduction, and that his condition may have improved some by the time he and Father Jenco first crossed paths in February 1985. In any event, those who took from him his liberty are responsible for his death.

Many of the details of the Reagan administration's efforts to free the hostages were unearthed by the Senate Select Committee on Intelligence and reported either in its published report on the Iran-contra affair or in an unpublished draft; by the President's Special Review Board chaired by former Senator John Tower; and by the House and Senate Select Committee on the Iran-contra affair. The thousands of pages of exhibits which were declassified and then released by the House and Senate committees are an invaluable resource and supplied the direct quotations from memoranda, notes, and CIA officials that appear in this chapter.

The National Security Archive's "Chronology" of the Iran-contra affair, edited by Malcolm Byrne, supplied a useful history of the affair and an exhaustive guide to contemporary news accounts. In that category, Stephen Engleberg's report on the DEA affair, published in *The New York Times* on May 31, 1987, provided new information, as did numerous articles by David Rogers, Andy Pasztor and Edward Pound of *The Wall Street Journal* and Doyle McManus, William Rempel, and Michael Wines of *The Los Angeles Times*.

Robin Wright's *Sacred Rage* provided a detailed account of the Kuwaiti bombings and of the trial of the Dawa prisoners. R. K. Ramazani's *Revolutionary Iran,* and *Fighting Back* by Neil C. Livingstone and Terrell E. Arnold, supplied additional details on the Dawa bombings and the seizure of the first hostages. The description of the brutal hijacking of a Kuwaiti airliner to Tehran is drawn from "Destination Tehran: Anatomy of a Hijacking," by Nathan Adams, in the October 1985 *Readers Digest.*

One of the best accounts of the Reagan administration's early flirtations with Israeli arms sales to Iran is Benjamin Weiser's "Behind Israel-Iran Sales, 'Amber' Light from U.S.," in the Aug. 16, 1987, *Washington Post.* Former Secretary of State Alexander Haig still insists that he firmly opposed such sales and said so to Israeli Defense Minister Sharon on several occasions. Nevertheless, between Haig and then national security adviser Richard Allen, the Israelis perceived enough flexibility in the Reagan administration's position to proceed with the sales until the spring of 1982 without fear that Washington would punish them. A copy of the July 1981 contract between the Israeli Ministry of Defense and Israeli arms dealer Yaacov Nimrodi was provided by an anonymous source.

On the subject of the administration's early efforts to unseat the Khomeini regime, a number of U.S. officials confirmed and expanded upon Leslie H. Gelb's "U.S. Said to Aid Iranian Exiles in Combat and Political Units," in the March 7, 1982, *The New York Times.*

9: "A MOST RIDICULOUS THING"

Daily television and newspaper reports were used to reconstruct the hijacking of the *Achille Lauro.* Other published sources included Benito Craxi's report to the Italian Parliament and Franco Gerardi's book *Achille Lauro Operazione Salvezza,* which contains transcripts of intercepted ship-to-shore communications. Oliver North testified publicly before the Iran-Contra committee about some of the events surrounding the *Achille Lauro* hijacking. Peter Kohler shared his research on the *Achille Lauro.*

The account of the intercept of the Egyptian airliner is based on interviews with Robert Brodsky, Ken Burgess, William Crowe, David Jeremiah, Noel Koch, Richard Lawson, Michael Ledeen, David Long, Robert McFarlane, James Stark, William H. Taft, Nicholas Veliotes, and a U.S. Navy officer who insisted on anonymity. The transcript of the air-to-air dialogue with the Egyptian airliner was obtained under the Freedom of Information Act. The transcript of the air-to-air dialogue between the American T-39 and the Italian fighter escort was first published in the Italian press. The conversation between President Reagan and Caspar Weinberger was monitored by a ham radio operator who reported the conversation to CBS News.

In November 1987, the Justice Department withdrew a warrant it had issued for the arrest of Abu Abbas; prosecutors admitted they didn't have enough evidence to convict the Palestinian leader in the *Achille Lauro* case.

10: EL DORADO CANYON

The description of both the Gulf of Sidra exercises and the raid on Libya is based on interviews with Richard Armitage, Jerry Breast, Robert Brodsky, William Crowe, Charles Donnelly, Byron Duff, David Forgan, Charles Gabriel, Thomas Griffin (through a spokesman), Steve Hays, David Jeremiah, Jay Johnson, Frank Kelso, Richard Lawson, Bob Vencus, Sam Westbrook, Scott Wvesthoff,

Tom Yax, and a U.S. Navy officer who refused to be identified. The Air Force pilots identified by the pseudonyms Fred Allen and Jack Fletcher were also interviewed. Some material also came from Robert E. Stumpf's "Air War with Libya" in the August 1986 *Naval Institute Proceedings.*

Several months after the raid on Libya, Gen. Charles Gabriel, the Air Force Chief of Staff, met the head of the French Air Force at a convention in Las Vegas. Gabriel, who believes that the refusal of French overflight rights was the primary reason why so many of the F-111s were unable to drop their bombs on target, said to the French general, You notice we didn't hit the British Embassy.

The account of Operation Early Call is based on documents obtained under the Freedom of Information Act. The short-lived attempt to revive covert action against Libya was first revealed by Bob Woodward in *The Washington Post* on Nov. 3, 1985. Woodward and Don Oberdorfer were the first to report the abortive proposal to mount a joint U.S.-Egyptian attack on Libya.

The NSC and State Department planning documents, the computer messages, the memos to the President and members of the NSC, the notes of the NSPG meeting and the NSDD—all of them still classified Top Secret—were provided by a number of officials who for obvious reasons cannot be named. Some of the information on Libyan support for terrorism in 1986 was taken from a January 1988 State Department report: *Patterns of Global Terrorism: 1986.*

In October 1986, Bob Woodward reported in *The Washington Post* that the administration had launched a "disinformation campaign" against Qaddafi and that some of that disinformation had found its way into the American press, most notably in a front-page story in *The Wall Street Journal* written by one of the authors. The *Journal* story was factually accurate but seriously flawed in claiming that the United States and Libya were on a "collision course," suggesting that military action against Libya was imminent while failing to note that psychological warfare had been a major element of the administration's Libya policy since the beginning of 1986. The errors, however, were the author's and not the result of an administration "disinformation campaign," or even of a few officials peddling lies on their own. One administration official did make a number of comments, some of which were quoted anonymously in the *Journal* article, suggesting that the administration was preparing to take new military action against Libya. Past experience with that official dictated that those remarks should have been discounted more heavily than they were. Several publications have identified that source as Howard Teicher; they are wrong. Preparations for military action were made, but such action was always contingent on finding new and indisputable proof of Libyan terrorism, something the *Journal* article failed to make clear. On the other hand, the State Department in January 1988 finally concluded that, contrary to Elaine Morton's claim that Qaddafi was "quiescent" in August of 1986, "Libya resumed terrorist activity in July" of that year, as the *Journal* had reported.

11: INNOCENTS ABROAD

This chapter, like Chapter 8, relies heavily on an interview with Father Lawrence Jenco and on David Jacobsen's accounts of his captivity to NBC News and *The Los Angeles Times.* Other interviews included Abe Azzam, Mark Belnick, Gassan Chamas, Noel Koch, Richard Lawson, David Long, Robert McFarlane, Robert Oakley, H. Ross Perot, Peter Rodman, Howard Teicher, and several U.S. intelligence and law enforcement officials. Some material was drawn from an interview with Richard Secord in the September 1987 *Playboy.* Reports and documents released by the Tower Commission, the Senate Select Committee on Intelligence, and the Senate and House Select Committees on the Iran-Contra Affair all provided reams of raw material. Lance Morgan, the spokesman for the Senate committee was both helpful and always cheerful.

The French newspaper *Le Figaro* published three articles on Imad Mugniyah's alleged trip to Paris: "Négociations avec les terroristes: nouvelle révélations," Feb. 26, 1986; "Responsable chiite en France: d'autres révélations," Feb. 27, 1986; and "Ce terroriste que la France n'a pas voulu arrêter," Mar. 6, 1986.

The account of national security adviser John Poindexter's meeting with the Kuwaiti foreign minister on October 3, 1986, was provided by Dennis Ross of the NSC staff, who was present.

A capsule summary of the administration's stated policy on terrorism is contained in the *Public Report of the Vice President's Task Force on Combatting Terrorism,* February 1986.

In July 1983, terrorist expert Brian Michael Jenkins of the RAND Corporation wrote a brief description of the terrorists' psyche, which helped explain what had gone so wrong. There was no equating North's morality and that of Abu Nidal or Imad Mugniyah, but much of the diagnosis fit Oliver North, trapped and increasingly alone in a White House pressure cooker, to a tee. Wrote Jenkins, in "Some Reflections on Recent Trends in International Terrorism":

> Cut off from most normal contacts with society, having only each other to talk to, terrorists live in a fantasy world. Their organizations are extravagant assertions. They imagine themselves to be armies and brigades. They believe themselves to have legions of supporters or potential supporters on whose behalf they claim to fight, but their constituencies, like their military formations, are largely imaginary.
>
> Terrorists carry out operations they believe are likely to win widespread approval from these perceived constituents. But they do not seem to be able to distinguish between a climate that is favorable to them because of what they do and a climate that just happens to be favorable to them. . . .
>
> Terrorists fall prey to their own propaganda. They overestimate their own strength, their appeal, the weakness of their enemies, the imminence of victory. And they continue to fight, for to quit is not simply to admit defeat. It requires an admission of irrelevancy.

Insights into the effects of hostage crises on American policymakers can be found in "Hostage-Taking, the Presidency, and Stress" by Margaret G. and Charles F. Hermann of Ohio State University and in "Taking Vows: The Domestication of Policymaking in Hostage Incidents" by Gary Sick. Both were presented at a seminar on terrorism at the Woodrow Wilson Center for Scholars in Washington, D.C., on April 30, 1987.

EPILOGUE

The description of the Navy's Strike Warfare Center is based on interviews with John Lehman and Robert Brodsky. The description of the Iranian terror network comes from interviews with U.S. intelligence and law enforcement officials. Interviews with L. Paul Bremer III, Sen. William Cohen, William Corbett, Alison Fortier, David Long, Fadlo Massabni, Sen. Arlen Specter, and Victoria Toensing provided valuable insights, as did a speech by Noel Koch to the American Society for Industrial Security on March 12, 1987.

The material on legal responses to terrorism came from a number of sources, including "Terrorism and the Law," by Abraham Sofaer in *Foreign Affairs,* Summer 1986; "The Political Offense Exception and Terrorism," by Sofaer before the Senate Foreign Relations Committee on Aug. 1, 1985; "Terrorism: A Challenge to the Law," a speech by British Attorney General Sir Michael Havers to the American Bar Association on Aug. 7, 1984; "Protecting our Citizens: When to Use Force Against Terrorists," by Representative James Courter, in *Policy Review,* Spring 1986; Hearings Before the Senate Judiciary Committee, Feb. 4, March 4, 1987; Hearings Before the Senate Judiciary Committee, Subcommittee on Security and Terrorism, July 30, 1985; and Terrorism: Laws Cited Imposing Sanctions on Nations Supporting Terrorism, U.S. General Accounting Office, April 1987.

INDEX